Jeffrey
Schein
216- 464-4070
Ext R3

MAKING THE BIBLE MODERN

MAKING THE BIBLE MODERN

Children's Bibles and Jewish Education in
Twentieth-Century America

Penny Schine Gold

CORNELL UNIVERSITY PRESS

Ithaca and London

First published 2004 by Cornell University Press

Printed in the United States of America

Library of Congress Cataloging-in-Publication Data
Gold, Penny Schine.
    Making the Bible modern : children's Bibles and Jewish education in twentieth-century America / Penny Schine Gold.
        p. cm.
Includes bibliographical references and index.
    ISBN 0-8014-3667-2
    1. Jewish religious education of children—United
States—History—20th century.   2. Bible. O.T.—Children's use—United
States—History—20th century.   3. Bible stories, English—Study and
teaching (Elementary)—United States—History—20th century.   4.
Jews—Cultural assimilation—United States.   5. Jews—United
States—Identity.   I. Title.
    BM103.G65 2003
    296.6'8'0973—dc21   2003013275

For David and Jeremy

Contents

Preface

Reading stories at bedtime was a cherished ritual throughout my child's early years. From Goodnight, Moon *to* The Jolly Postman *and* Box Car Children, *stories provided the occasion for the quiet, intimate communication of love and truth: sitting on the bed, one of my arms around Jeremy and the other on the book, we ended together a busy, active day.*

When my son was about four, I thought it time to include some Bible stories. It seemed the right thing to do for a Jewish child. The first one I picked was a telling of the story of Noah's ark by Peter Speier, an award-winning book found on many lists of recommended books for children. I told the story many times, prompted by the detailed pictures in Speier's wordless book. Then one evening Jeremy stopped me at one picture, which showed crowds of animals gathered at the ark, water lapping at their knees, and only two of each animal walking up the ramp to the ark. "What happened to all the other animals?" my son asked. His question pulled into the foreground disturbing moral implications that my retelling of the story had ignored.

"They died," I said. "Why?" he asked. I had no answer. I never read this book to my son again.

This bedtime confrontation with the disturbing moral implications of a biblical story was one factor contributing to the research project that has become this book.[1] On finishing my first book some years before—on the subject of women in twelfth-century France—my interests shifted from medieval Christian Europe toward the study of Judaism and Jewish history. A few years of intensive reading led me to a focus on modern Jewish history, and in particular, to the examination of the remaking of Jewish life and identity in response to the demands of modernity. I was fascinated with this process of transformation, how each element of Jewish practice and belief was held up to scrutiny. Did it pass the test of modernity? If not, should the dissonance be ignored and the element kept? Should it be dropped entirely (e.g., liturgical references to the renewal of sacrificial worship)? Could it be altered and kept (e.g., moving Sabbath worship to Friday night or Sunday, keeping kosher at home but not outside)? A similar triage was done on texts. The Bible, for example, was a "keeper," seen to be in accord with modern values, while the Talmud—once the heart of Jewish education and learning—was dropped as an embarrassment. This particular choice perplexed me, as in another new role—that of religious school teacher to young children—I found the children's versions of rabbinic material more in keeping with modern ethical sensibilities. And so these questions followed: Why was the Bible elevated over the Talmud as the central text of Jewish education? How were the text and teaching of the Bible adapted to make this archaic text fit with modern life?

Use of the Bible is a crucial part of the story of Judaism, modernity, and identity, exposing fault lines of conflict between harmonization with modern demands and fidelity to a distinctive Jewish tradition, as well as indicating possibilities for resolution. This story is played out in all arenas of Jewish life and in every modernizing country in which Jews have lived. A revolution in Judaism and Jewish life occurred in the modern period, but it has been a staggered revolution, begun in some places in the late eighteenth century and started in others only in the twentieth. The American scene provides a particularly fruitful venue within which to observe this process of change, as here an earlier small population of Jews (of Sephardic and German origin) was numerically and culturally overwhelmed by the rapid influx, from 1880 to 1914, of over two million eastern European Jews. Transplanted to a new American setting, these more observant Jews experienced within a generation a decline in ritual observance, and traditional schooling was immediately challenged by the availability of free public education. In this changed world, the supplementary religious school became the enculturating instrument on which newly American Jews depended to forge a modern, Jewish, and American identity. It was crucial to the success of a modernized Judaism that a new Jewish identity and a new understanding of Jewish values and tradition be available to the Jewish children so openly exposed to modern influence and opportunity.

The subjects "children" and "education" have been marginalized in many scholarly fields, including Jewish studies. But the challenge of transforming and transmitting Jewish life in the modern period can be most fully understood when we take into account the relations between generations. Those relations are experienced in multiple arenas, but the school plays an especially important role in the modern period. Spending their days in public school, the children of Jewish immigrants brought America home; it was up to the adults to fashion a Judaism that their children could take back out into America. The supplementary religious school thus became a key locus of the re-creation and perpetuation of Judaism.

Can Judaism be perpetuated? Will it survive? If so, in what form? Will it be recognizable as Judaism? How are the new forms to be passed on to succeeding generations? These questions are posed with an urgency in modern times matched only in the period of upheaval brought about by the destruction of the Second Temple a thousand years ago. The rabbinic Judaism that then developed was radically different from the priest-centered, sacrificial religion it replaced, yet its claim to be "Judaism" was successful. The challenge to Judaism in the modern world is no less profound, even though it is caused by what can be seen as fortunate circumstances (the dropping of legal boundaries and restrictions imposed by ruling non-Jewish groups) rather than by catastrophe. Jewish leaders in the modern period have been fully aware of this challenge and have developed strategies explicitly intended to address it. We will here examine the strategies proposed and carried out by educators. Will this transformation be as successful as the rabbinic one? We'll probably need another century or two to know.

I relate personally as well as intellectually to the subject of this book. My fascination with the Jewish confrontation with modernity is in part driven by my own pursuit of a religious identity in accord with my life as a highly assimilated college professor, while also connected to the richness of a textured Jewish past. As a child, I was educated first in a Reform and then in a Conservative congregation, going through bat mitzvah and confirmation. I learned as much as these synagogues provided. As I turned to serious learning about Judaism in my late thirties, I was astonished to discover all that I didn't know. Given my own discomfort with the Bible, it was a great reassurance to discover that the Bible had not always been the central text of Jewish education, and that much rabbinic material expressed moral concerns about the Bible not so different from my own. It was thus with a sense of personal loss and bewilderment that I set out to understand why American Jewish educators had made the choices they had. Why had I been deprived of the wealth of Jewish tradition, and why had I been led to believe the Bible was a thoroughly positive, unproblematic text? My first impulse was to expose the "mutilation" of the biblical text that had been made to serve the new purposes of the American milieu. But slowly, with immersion in the world of the educators and with the help of insights from colleagues, I have been able to step back and complete the task of the cultural historian: to discover the social and cultural meanings of texts and institutional structures, and to analyze how changes in cultural artifacts reflect, mediate, and promote fundamental changes in mentality and social life.

But I have to admit that settling into a relationship with this subject has been more difficult for me than when I studied twelfth-century women. In that case, the strangeness of the subject and its distance from my personal experience was clear (even while the study centered on questions about gendered imagery directly related to personal concerns). With this Jewish material from the first half of the twentieth century, the relationship has been more complicated. I could at one moment puzzle at the seeming naiveté or obtuseness of one position and then stop in the next paragraph to jot down notes on something to follow up on in my own religious school teaching. I am, in this project, what Ruth Behar has called a "vulnerable observer" in a way that is new to me.[2] I come to this subject laden with concerns as a third-generation American Jew, a parent raising a Jewish child, a religious school teacher, a college teacher of Jewish studies. These concerns cannot help but influence what I have seen when looking back into the past. But, like others sympathetically inclined to some reflexivity in scholarly work, I'm convinced that all research is in some way or another grounded in the personal issues of the researcher, and one may as well be as honest as possible about it, even while knowing that significant elements may remain unconscious.[3]

While most of this book is written in standard historical discourse, I have inserted from time to time personal stories (my own and some I've heard from others). I hope these stories help us keep in mind that issues of concern to Jewish educators of seventy and eighty years ago are still with us, that the task is not yet done, and that the stakes are high—not just for Jews, but for any religious or ethnic group negotiating the path from a separate life and identity enforced by discriminatory exclusion to something new, forged by the pleasures and pain of interpenetration.

Note: A full bibliography is available at http://faculty.knox.edu/pgold/.

Acknowledgments

This research has taken me into fields in which I had little previous preparation, making me especially reliant on and thankful for the help I have received from other scholars. This project might not have been launched without the encouragement and example of Tony Yu and Jock Weintraub, who convinced me to go ahead and take the risk. A 1990 Midwest Faculty Seminar at the University of Chicago on the theme of "What's the Story?" helped suggest questions about the telling of stories in human life. Two National Endowment for the Humanities summer seminars in 1990 and 1994 led by Mark Krupnick and Benjamin Harshav provided me with occasions for stimulating interchange with colleagues in Jewish Studies. I am grateful to Ayalla Dvoretsky and Ariela Finkelstein for their inspired teaching of Hebrew. A suggestion from Marcia Colish led me to Ruth B. (Sue) Bottigheimer, who was at that time just completing her book on children's Bibles. Sue has been a colleague par excellence, sharing her work in progress and reading mine, helping at every turn.

I am especially grateful to those scholars and Jewish educators who have read and commented on chapters in progress: Tzvi Howard Adelman, Gideon Aran, Michael Fishbane, Manny Gold, Zali Gurevitch, Sam Joseph, Michael Meyer, Deborah Dash Moore, Gary Porton (who also shared work in progress), Jerome Reich, Natania Rosenfeld, Seymour Rossel, and David Sorkin. Others gave guidance in particular areas of the research. Thanks to Lanny Beyer and Sue Books for help with literature on the history of education; Lib Caldwell for Christian religious education; Fred Jaher for democracy and America; Jill May for children's literature; Rev. Norman Myer for Protestant religious education; Tzvi Howard Adelman and Muhammed Abu Samra for the teaching of the Bible in Israel; Alice Nash, for a great conversation on the use of story in scholarly writing and for the example of her own work; Nancy Eberhardt for our ongoing research conversations. For sharing with me reflections on their own Jewish education in the 1920s and 1930s, in Germany and in the United States, I am indebted to Fred Schubach and Mitchell Rudman. Years of conversation with Mitch and Rose Rudman, two of the founders of Temple Sholom in Galesburg, Illinois, helped change me from a hesitant visitor to an active participant in Jewish life and learning. The Temple Sholom community has provided a stimulating and supportive environment while I conducted this research; I'm also thankful for the interest of my religious school students, who unknowingly helped me work out ideas on teaching the Bible to children. Finally, without the collegiality and support of the members of the Midwest Jewish Studies Association, it would have been difficult to initiate and sustain this research.

Thanks also to Peter Bailley for photographs, to Sharon Clayton, librarian at Knox College, who has answered all my obscure reference questions, to Claire Rasmussen for checking quotations, and to Irene Ponce and the dedicated interlibrary loan staff at Knox College. The people at Cornell University Press have been consistently encouraging and helpful. I am especially grateful to Peter Agree, my initial acquisitions editor, who helped me understand the potential scope and promise of the book, and to Sheri Englund for making the book hers when Peter left the press. John LeRoy's superb editing has enhanced the clarity of my prose throughout.

Support from several sources enabled the completion of this project: the American Academy of Religion, which funded an initial research trip to the American Jewish Archives and the Klau Library at Hebrew Union College (with thanks to Kevin Proffitt and the archives staff for their help); the National Endowment for the Humanities, for a year-long fellowship as well as the two summer seminars; the Institute for the Advanced Study of Religion of the Divinity School at the University of Chicago, where I spent a sabbatical year, writing the first chapters. Knox College has been continuously generous in funding ongoing research expenses, most recently with additional funding from the Edgar and Ruth Burkhardt Fund; special thanks to John Strassburger and Larry Breitborde, the two deans who not only have disbursed faculty development funds over the course of this project but have sustained an environment in which research is a valued component of undergraduate teaching.

And to David Amor, who still, after all these years, reads every word—
love and thanks.

The final year of working on this book was also the final year of my parents' lives. I write these words as I try to imagine my life without the sustenance of their love for me and of their pride in my work. May the memory
of Helen Schine Gold and of Joseph Gold be for a blessing.

MAKING THE BIBLE MODERN

Introduction

For centuries, Jewish children—or more precisely, young Jewish boys—began their formal religious study with the Bible, learning directly from the original text, word by word. Christians, on the other hand, had been devising special children's versions of the Bible—abridged, adapted, and in the vernacular—since the sixteenth century.[1] The first Jewish refashioning of the Bible into stories for children took place in nineteenth-century Germany, in the context of the development of a reforming movement there.[2] As reform spread through Europe, so too did efforts to reshape the structure and content of education for Jewish children, including new versions of the Bible for children. The largest-scale, most systematic, and most sustained effort occurred, however, in the United States in the 1920s and 1930s. The stimulus was the desire of newly immigrant eastern European Jews to adjust to American life. Unlike the small number of Jews already here prior to 1880, mostly of central European origin and influenced by the reforming efforts of German Jews, the new masses of Jews came from an area that had been less touched by reform. Antipathy between the relatively modernized German Jews and the "primitives" from Poland and Russia prevented a continuous development building on earlier American/German efforts. Rather, a rupture occurred in American Jewish life, a new beginning, with a new past, new sensibilities, and new authorities. Being welcomed into the surrounding culture was a fresh experience for these immigrants, who had faced continuous exclusions and widespread pogroms in eastern Europe. The first generation improvised a new life here, continuing many of the practices and institutions familiar to them from Jewish life abroad. But the second generation undertook to adapt fully to the new setting: to continue as Jews while they became American. The result was the creation of a panoply of institutions to serve and sustain the Jewish community—religious, philanthropical, social, and educational.[3] While much of the educational innovation took place under the umbrella of the Union of American Hebrew Congregations, an institution dating back to the 1880s and dominated by German Jews, the work of the Commission on Jewish Education of the UAHC was formulated and carried out by second-generation eastern European Jews. They looked for educational models not in their forerunners in the Old World but in contemporary schooling in America—the secular education of the public schools and the religious education of Protestant Sunday Schools—with the goal of creating a specifically *American* Jewish education.

A detailed analysis of the educational theory developed by these men, of the role of the Bible in their educational program, and of the Bible stories created—by both women and men—for use in this setting will form the heart of this book. Yet none of this can be understood before reviewing the place of the Bible in traditional Jewish culture, the challenge of modernity, educational change in Europe, and the specific influences of the American context. Before embarking on analysis of these multiple contexts, we stop for a preview of the new Bible stories, sampled from two popular 1930s collections for children; for contrast, a direct translation taken from the 1917 translation of the Bible published by the Jewish Publication Society precedes each story. First, the story of Cain and Abel.

> And the man knew Eve his wife; and she conceived and bore Cain, and said: "I have gotten a man with the help of the Lord." And again she bore his brother Abel. And Abel was a keeper of sheep, but Cain was a tiller of the ground. And in process of time it came to pass, that Cain brought of the fruit of the ground an offering unto the Lord. And Abel, he also brought of the firstlings of his flock and of the fat thereof. And the Lord had respect unto Abel and to his offering; but unto Cain and to his offering He had not respect. And Cain was very wroth, and his countenance fell. (Gen. 4:1–5)[4]

In contrast, a modern version in Edith Lindeman Calisch's *Bible Tales for the Very Young* (1930):

Cain and Abel

After Adam and Eve went out into the world, God sent them two sons, and as the years passed these boys grew to be strong young men. They helped with the care of the cattle and with the farming, for there was much to be done.

The name of the oldest son was Cain, and he ploughed the earth, planted the seeds, and watched over the growing trees and vines. But Cain did not like to work, and often he forgot to water the corn and it withered, and the weeds grew in his garden until the tiny plants were choked and weak. The apples on his trees were always hard and sour, and the potatoes small and knotty.

The younger son was named Abel, and he was the keeper of the sheep. Abel loved the sheep, and the tiny lambs were like children to him. He found the greenest grass for them to eat, and he led them to the clearest pools of cool water. In summer, he found great trees to shade the little animals, and in winter he built shelters to protect them from the snow and wind. The sheep were fat and fine, and the lambs were frisky and happy, and they, too, soon grew to be strong sheep, so that Abel's flock became larger and larger.

One day Abel looked about him and said to himself: "What a fine flock I have. How good God has been to me to let me have all these sheep. I must share my good fortune with Him. I will give Him the finest of my lambs."

Now it happened that on that same day Cain was very cross and angry, for it was hot in the fields. And Cain said to himself:

"Why do I have to work so hard? It is not my fault that we cannot live in the Garden, where everything grows by itself. I will take some of my best fruit and vegetables and give them to God, and perhaps He will be so pleased that He will let us all go back to the Garden, and then I will not have to do any more work."[5]

Next, the story of Abraham leaving Haran:

Now the Lord said unto Abram: "Get thee out of thy country, and from thy kindred, and from thy father's house, unto the land that I will show thee. And I will make of thee a great nation, and I will bless thee, and make thy name great; and be thou a blessing. And I will bless them that bless thee, and him that curseth thee will I curse; and in thee shall all the families of the earth be blessed." So Abram went, as the Lord had spoken with him; and Lot went with him; and Abram was seventy and five years old when he departed out of Haran. And Abram took Sarai his wife, and Lot his brother's son, and all their substance that they had gathered, and the souls that they had gotten in Haran; and they went forth to go into the land of Canaan; and into the land of Canaan they came. (Gen. 12:1–5)[6]

In contrast, a children's version in Lenore Cohen's *Bible Tales for Very Young Children* (1934):

> *Abraham Goes to the Promised Land*
>
> > "We are the shepherds who tend the sheep,
> > Under the stars we eat and sleep;
> > Ever we wander, ever we roam,
> > The plain and the desert is our home."

Abraham stood in front of his tent. He was a tall man, sunburned and strong. All these hundreds of sheep were his. All the shepherds who were watering the sheep were his servants.

Sarah, his wife, came out of the tent and stood beside him.

"What are you thinking about, Abraham?" she asked.

"I am thinking of a dream I had last night," he replied. "I seemed to stand alone in a field. Suddenly I heard the voice of God saying, 'Abraham, leave your father's house. Go to the west. There is a land of green pastures and silver streams. I will bless you, Abraham. You will be the father of a great nation.'"

"Is there really such a land?" asked Sarah.

"Yes," answered Abraham. "Look! What do you see, far in the distance?"

"Mountain tops, which look like huge, black points against the setting sun."

"There is the land I dreamed about. Tomorrow we shall rise with the dawn and start to travel there."

Abraham blew a shrill whistle. All the shepherds came running. At their head came Lot, Abraham's nephew.

"Herd all the sheep and cattle together. Pack up the tents and all our household goods. We leave this place at dawn."

"Where are we going, Abraham?" asked Lot.

"To the mountains. To a new country! A country where I can worship the one Almighty God in peace."

What a hustle and bustle there was. At dawn everything was ready. Abraham, tall and brave, rode at the head of his household on a camel. Sarah rode beside him, while the shepherds and their wives and children followed behind. They moved slowly, for the sheep and goats had to be kept together. In this manner they traveled for many days.

At last they came to the mountains. How green and inviting they seemed!

"Let us stop here," said Abraham.[7]

If your response to these stories is anything like my own or that of the various audiences to whom I have spoken in the past several years, it would include a sense of dismay and bewilderment at the transformation undergone from biblical narrative to "Bible story." Understanding the forces that contributed to this transformation is the task of this book. The "Bible story" as a genre, while not new within Western culture generally, was an innovation within modernizing Judaism. Why was this genre adopted at this point in Judaism, whose educational program had for so long used the original text? Why was the original text of the Bible now seen as inappropriate for children? How were the messages of these stories particularly shaped for a Jewish—an American Jewish—audience?

These questions also need to be put in the larger context of the cultural life of sacred texts. Religious traditions—whether embodied in rituals, beliefs, or texts—are kept alive over the centuries through a delicate balance of continuity and change. In Judaism, the Bible has been a central force of continuity, and one cannot imagine a Judaism without it. Yet, as happens with all sacred texts—for whom an "afterlife" of selection and adaptation is part of their life[8]—only the external form of the Bible has remained the same. Even when words are transmitted intact, the meaning of words changes, as social, cultural, and religious transformations make new demands on the text. The ways in which the Bible has been used and transmitted have also varied over time, with the most profound shifts coming in two periods of revolutionary change in Judaism and Jewish life.

In the wake of the destruction of the Second Temple, the sacred texts that carried the beliefs and practices of the past were canonized into the Tanakh, or Hebrew Bible, while a new body of texts was also developed—the Talmud and other rabbinic writings—that radically transformed religious practice while it embodied new attitudes. While the Bible—the "old" text—was placed at the center of religious ritual, the newer texts became the backbone of the lived religion that has since been termed "rabbinic Judaism."

In the course of the modern revolution—catalyzed by the Enlightenment and emancipation—the centuries of textual production spawned by the rabbinic revolution were rejected. The Talmud and its corollary texts came to be seen as embarrassing, even revolting. The Bible, however, was seen as consonant with modern sensibilities, both literary and ethical. The rejection of the Talmud was thus paralleled by a commitment to the study of the Bible, and Jews of the modern revolution put at the heart of Judaism the text that the first revolution had subsumed within a medieval discourse.

The task of re-forming text was repeated. Just as the rabbis had plucked at, added to, and layered over the biblical heritage in order to shape new texts consonant with the social, religious, and psychological experience of the Diaspora, so too modern rabbis, intellectuals, and educators had to confront the ways in which the Bible was discordant with modern discourse and modern ethical inclinations—to translate biblical culture into a new setting.

The concept of cultural translation is useful to clarify the complex cultural dynamics at work here.[9] Acts of cultural translation can be found at the interface of any two cultures, where products of one are simultaneously appealing and off-putting to the second. The translation can be *intra*cultural, between two stages or geographical variations of one culture; for example, between two strands of Judaism (traditional and modern, German and eastern European). Or it can be *cross*-cultural, between two cultures not related to each other but in close contact, often because of shared geographical space; for example, between Judaism and American culture. If cross-cultural, the translation may weigh the two cultures equally, or an assimilating translation may favor the dominant culture. Finally, one can distinguish between vertical and horizontal dimensions in cultural translation, where the vertical dimension consists of a leap back in time (to an earlier stage of a culture) and where the horizontal dimension consists of a transfer between two contemporaneous cultures, either two variations of one's own culture or two separate cultures.[10]

Applying these concepts to the case of American Jewish Bible stories, we can see that second-generation American Jews were carrying out a complex sort of cultural translation. It was both intracultural (vertically: reaching back to biblical culture; to a lesser extent horizontally: considering influences from modernized Jews in Europe) and cross-cultural (with American culture and with "modern" culture more generally). It was also an assimilatory translation, aimed at harmonizing with the dominant culture. The navigational strategies between these various cultural worlds were shaped by particular demands of the moment, the "present exigencies," in the words of Wolfgang Iser: "The past to be revived is not just an available entity waiting to be channeled into the present but is variously invoked according to present exigencies. In other words, current necessities are projected onto the past in order to make it translatable into the present. This mutuality ultimately decides the nature of the past invoked."[11]

The figure below provides a sketch map of the cultural translation taking place between Judaism, modernity, and American culture within the

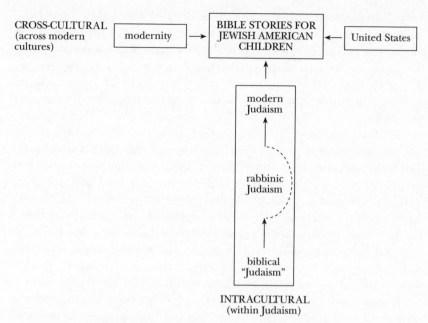

Cultural translation and Bible stories for Jewish American children.

texts of children's Bibles. Within the vertical dimension of intracultural translation, these books aim to bring biblical "Judaism" into harmony with modern Judaism, skipping over the long rabbinic tradition in Judaism. Within the horizontal dimension of cross-cultural translation, the books bring the ancient Jewish text into relationship with contemporary demands of modernity and American life. It will be the task of much of this book to identify the selections and adaptations made in the course of this complicated process of cultural translation and to relate them to the "present exigencies" of the time.

During periods of intense cultural interface, the transformations of sacred texts—through translation and interpretation, in ritual and educational use—are prime markers of concerns and values in conflict. The sacred character of these texts demand that they remain intact, and yet they can survive only if they are porous enough to fill up with each new culture into which they travel. Such texts are prime sources for the cultural historian, as the metamorphosis of the original source as it moves from place to place and time to time can serve as a marker of what each new culture cares about most. Sacred texts reshaped for children provide an especially clear window on contemporary values, as they tend to stress prominent, widely agreed upon values. Attention to the most popular of these children's versions further reinforces this focus on leading values.

A diachronic approach to the life history of a sacred text gives us a panoramic view of change over time, allowing us to see clearly what is continuous as well as what is changed. Ruth Bottigheimer's superb survey of the genre of children's Bibles—*The Bible for Children from the Age of Gutenberg to the Present*—has done exactly this. The present book takes another tack, a synchronic approach, taking one small slice of this variegated development in order to examine a subset of children's Bibles within a detailed, local context. By narrowing my focus, I am able to broaden the context and multiply the relationships between text and contexts. From Bottigheimer's carefully woven fabric, extended in time, I pull one strand—that of Jewish children's Bibles in America. As I pull, I find the thread connected to other layers, other fabrics—to Judaism, the Enlightenment, American religious education, political culture, and more. As a cultural historian, my task is to make sense of the visible artifact by explicating it within the social and cultural web within which it is situated. This can only be done by artificially freezing a culture at a particular point in time. Comparison to other moments is still crucial for discernment of what is special (or not) to the chosen point. Bottigheimer's work provides that check for children's Bibles. The first and third chapters of this book will also provide comparisons with traditional and modernizing Jewish education in places other than America.

Some reference will also be made to the various strands of Jewish education in America, as the Jewish scene here was by no means uniform. But my focus rests on the Reform movement, as it is here that we can see the most complex engagement with the challenge of modernity on the American scene. The inclination of Orthodox Judaism was to retain traditional beliefs and practices, including traditional educational structures, while the inclination of a radically secular approach (such as the Yiddish folk schools) was to abandon them. These responses, while certainly a significant part of the American scene, entailed less struggle, less soul-searching, and so provide less illumination of the conflicts between Jewish tradition and modernity. And while the Conservative movement has grappled with many of the same issues as Reform, it did not begin to publish educational curricula and material until the 1940s, well after the Reform movement, which was the pacesetter for Conservative Judaism not only in educational change but in congregational life generally.[12] In Reform Judaism of the 1920s and 1930s, we can follow an extensive effort to create new forms of and materials for Jewish education, adapted self-consciously to a twentieth-century American environment.

The core of this study is based on two types of sources: curricular material produced for Jewish children and professional literature discussing the education of these children. Foremost in the curricular material are the more than two dozen Bible story collections, designed specifically for Jewish American children, published between 1915 and 1936.[13] The professional debate over Jewish education was tracked primarily through the periodical literature of the newly professionalized Jewish educators (*Jewish Education* and *The Jewish Teacher*) as well as that of the Reform rabbinate (the *Yearbook* of the Central Conference of American Rabbis, the *Proceedings* of the Union of American Hebrew Congregations). From that base, I have reached out to a wide variety of materials for the purpose of comparison and contextualization, both within Jewish religious, educational, and interpretive traditions and within the multiple modern social, political, religious, and educational contexts that influenced the shaping of Jewish education and hence the production of children's Bibles.

And a path not taken: One of the pleasures of presenting this material to audiences, particularly in congregational settings, has been listening afterward to stories of childhood experiences with the Bible. I have used one or two of these stories in the book as illuminating moments. With more time and energy, I would have liked to include an oral history component to my research, interviewing both educators and students. Perhaps another will take up this work.

1

The Bible in Traditional Jewish Culture

As experienced within traditional Jewish culture, the Bible was both a fixed, unchangeable sacred object, subject to elaborate practices regulating its production and restricting access and touch, and at the same time a text open to interpretation and handled with intimacy—read by young and old, at home, school, and synagogue. It was an object held in awe while also treated with familiarity and affection. These paradoxical characteristics of Torah—both closed and open, awesome yet familiar—were for centuries bound in close relationship to each other: the closed canonical nature of the text necessitating interpretation of elements that had become cryptic to later readers; its awesome, sacred character marking it out as a key text with which one was to become intimately familiar. We will examine later the rupture that developed in the modern period between the text's sacred stature and the approaches taken to its study. First we must understand the place of the Bible within traditional Jewish culture. Within this culture, the sacred stature of the text was in consonance with its use in synagogue, home, and school.

In speaking here of "traditional Jewish culture," the key referent is Ashkenazi Jewish culture of the early modern period, as found primarily in central and eastern Europe. By "early modern" I refer to the period from the late Middle Ages to the late eighteenth century (or later, depending on place), a time in which the *Shulhan Arukh* (a sixteenth-century summary of Jewish law) served as a common source of religious and social expectations. This period formed the cultural background of most Jewish immigrants to America in the great wave after 1880. To understand the impact of modernity and America on the Bible in Jewish life, we must first understand the religious, emotional, and social role of the Bible in the world from which these immigrants came.

To speak of the place of the Bible in this culture, we must first adjust our language and speak of "Torah." While the word "Torah" can refer to a wide range of ancient and rabbinic texts, we here invoke the word in its restricted sense as referring to the first five books of the Hebrew Scriptures—the Pentateuch or *Humash*, the Greek and Hebrew names referring to the five books. These books have a special stature as divine revelation, believed to have been God's own words spoken directly to Moses and recorded by him. No matter that the texts that make up this collection were—according to modern views—written at different times, with different purposes. From early on in Jewish life they circulated together and for centuries have been inscribed on one scroll, exclusive even of other texts included in the canon of Scripture. This body of text was preserved and used in special ways that highlight its profoundly sacred stature. "Torah" in this sense refers not only to the text of these five books but to the physical object of the scroll on which the words are preserved. This Torah is potent and holy. More than a book, it has been the central identifying emblem of Jews for many centuries, the "flag" of Judaism.[1]

Ritual Use

As "the Torah" of synagogue ritual, the Bible has been accorded special treatment, even while its contents have also been copied and reproduced in a manner similar to other ancient scrolls or books. The Torah for ritual use is always a parchment scroll, prepared by a specially trained scribe, using carefully prescribed materials and procedures. The scribe prepares for a day's work with purification and prayer; his copying of the Torah is a religious act. Each sheet of parchment is checked and rechecked, as any mistake in the scroll would render it unusable for ritual purposes. It is an utterly fixed text, inscribed with great care to be identical to other copies. In its preparation the text is treated with the utmost respect, as will be the completed scroll when in use. An irreparably damaged or worn out Torah scroll or piece of scroll must be buried, not discarded, treated with the respect given to a human being.[2] The scroll is not simply rolled up but is sewn onto wooden rollers and then "dressed" in a special decorated velvet covering and further adorned with silver ornaments—often a crown, a breastplate and, at the least, a *yad* ("hand"), or pointer.[3] When unrolled, the scroll should not be touched with the bare hands but by means of its rollers or with a *tallit* (prayer shawl). The pointer is used by the reader to avoid touching the scroll as he keeps his place in the text during the public reading. Reverence is also shown through bodily posture—the congregation stands as the Torah is ushered into its presence—and by the reservation of a special place in the synagogue where the scroll is kept—the holy ark. The ark is placed in the wall pointing to Jerusalem, the wall toward which congregants face as they pray, and hence prayer is done facing the Torah as well.[4] The removal of the Torah scroll from the ark and its subsequent reading are the central moment of high drama in the Sabbath liturgy.

But this holy object is not to be kept at a distance. Rather, when taken out of the ark for the weekly and festival readings,[5] it is held close to the body, is carried among the congregation where it is touched and kissed (with the mediation of a tallit or prayer book) by any who wish to reach out to it, and is then lovingly undressed for its reading. When the reading is completed, the opened scroll is lifted high, the holy words displayed to the congregation. The scroll is dressed again and returned to its special place in the ark. An enhanced version of the parade of the scroll through the congregation is the highlight of the most joyous festival of the Jewish year, Simchat Torah (the joy of the Torah), the day on which the yearly cycle of reading the Torah is concluded and begun again, symbolically renewing the year and the community. On this day all the Torah scrolls of a congregation are taken from the ark and carried around the congregation not just once but seven times, with exuberant dancing and singing.

The special way in which the reading of the text within the scroll is ritually performed further emphasizes the sacred stature of this body of words. The text is read not to be learned but to be experienced, to be absorbed. The ear has primacy over the eye.[6] The text is divided into fixed portions, with one (or occasionally two) portions assigned for each week of the year and certain portions assigned for various holidays. The cycle repeats each year. The portion may be read by more than one member of the congregation, each of whom recites special blessings before and after the reading. The text is not read in the usual way but chanted, according to a fixed system of cantillation. The special production of and reverence toward the Torah scroll and the repetition, blessing, and chanting of the text when read—all this marks out the text not as studied but as performed, not learned but experienced, not understood but absorbed. In this way the Torah, the embodiment of Judaism, is passed from one generation to the next, a quasi-procreative act, insuring the ongoing life of the Jewish community.[7]

Home Use

The synagogue was only one of several venues within which encounters with the Torah took place. Other locations included the home, the academy, and the *heder* (school for children). In all of these places, the relationship to the Torah was dominated by men. The synagogue ritual described above was centered on men; women were observers, not participants. Adult religious learning—whether done at an advanced level in the school setting of a *yeshivah* or on a more rudimentary level in the *bet midrash* (communal study hall)—was exclusively a male activity. Children's religious learning was organized for boys; only a small number of girls participated in the lowest level of training. The home, however, was one location in which women played a central and visible role. Here they came close to the biblical text, although they accessed it in an attenuated form because of the general lack of Hebrew training for girls and women.

In the home as in the synagogue, the reading of the Bible (here in book form, not scroll) was connected with the Sabbath. Recollections of the Sabbath in traditional Jewish homes commonly mention three scenes, two involving the father and male children, the other involving the mother. On Friday evening, father and sons would read over carefully the portion of the Torah that was to be chanted the next morning in synagogue. According to some accounts, the portion was read twice in Hebrew and once in the Aramaic of the Targum.[8] In addition to this shared intergenerational activity, another practice stressed the hierarchy in the household: it was common on Friday night or Saturday afternoon for the father to test a young son on the weekly portion, which he would have been learning in heder.

Women read the weekly portion also, but not with the men or in the same way. Rather, from the seventeenth century on they approached the text through the *Ts'enah U-re'enah*, a Yiddish compilation of biblical text, commentary, and *midrash* (rabbinic interpretation) that was widely used in homes throughout Yiddish-speaking Europe.[9] The irony is that in many homes, the mother, reading the text in the (low prestige) current vernacular and with commentary pitched to an unlearned audience, would have a greater chance of understanding what was being read than the father and son, reading the text in Hebrew and Aramaic. Yet it was male study, carried out not just at home but also in a public arena, in the company of peers at the bet midrash, that was regarded as "true study of the Torah," while the women's study—taking place in the home with only the family as an audience, read in Yiddish and so easily understood, studied in private, without recourse to the help of others—was regarded as "merely an act of piety."[10] This picture should be further qualified: the text that the men studied in public was the Talmud, not the Bible. Yes, serious study was certainly in the realm of men, not women. But as we shall see, the Bible, as an object of study, was particularly in the realm of women and children, not men.

Commentary and Interpretation

The Talmud rather than the Bible was the central focus of adult male learning in traditional Jewish culture. Yet rabbinic Judaism of the late ancient and medieval worlds had also produced learned texts of biblical interpretation and commentary, texts that, along with Mishnah and Talmud fall within the category of Oral Torah. The Pentateuch, along with the other canonized books of the Tanakh (Prophets and Writings), are Written Torah, a fixed text, a set canon that is unchanging and to which words can neither be added nor subtracted. But the closure of the canon in turn stimulated the opening of the text to a wide variety of interpretations, as the fixed text was probed and massaged in order to accommodate ever-changing contexts.[11] Beginning in the Second Temple period, interpretive texts developed, many of them the product of oral tradition solidified into writing, which came to be understood as also part of Torah—as Oral Torah. Unlike Written Torah, Oral Torah is comprised of an open-ended and eclectic body of texts, accumulated over successive generations of rabbinic teaching.

We need to distinguish here between two bodies of material within Oral Torah. The Mishnah and Talmud are essentially legal texts, which gather oral traditions regarding practice and interpretation of practice. They are texts oriented toward the regulation of everyday life in all its aspects, from business transactions and sexual relations to the proper observance of religious holidays and temple sacrifice. The texts assume knowledge and acceptance of the Bible, but they refer relatively infrequently to it and have an entirely different format and purpose from the biblical texts.[12] They are, in essence, a separate and separable body of texts. But a second body of material within Oral Torah—that of midrash and commentary— is built on and directly connected to the Bible. The collection and anthologization of midrash was an activity of the ancient and early medieval periods; the writing of biblical commentaries was the interpretive mode of choice in the medieval period, with the eleventh-century commentary of Rashi widely adopted as an integral accompaniment to the biblical text.

While the Bible had been a focus of sustained adult male interpretive attention in the ancient and medieval periods—hence the development of midrash and commentary—it was the Talmud, the nonbiblical part of

Torah—that became the focal point of Jewish education and learning in the medieval period and later. Midrash and commentary were still referred to and passed on, particularly through incorporation into sermons centered on the weekly Torah portion, but serious learning, beginning with the entry of male teenagers into the yeshivah and continuing with adult study, was centered on the Talmud. It was the Talmud that served as the "binding text" for the Jewish community, the common text around which identity was shaped;[13] it was the knowledge of the Talmud that conferred prestige and status within that community. The Bible—as an object of study rather than as a ritual object engaged in liturgy—was a text for children and women.

The Bible and the Education of Children

The education of Jewish children in the ways of Judaism was not a separate activity carried out primarily in school, but was engaged in as well in the home, in the synagogue, and in the streets of the community. Many things that today are central to a Reform Jewish religious school curriculum— Jewish values, practices, beliefs, laws, and holidays—would have been absorbed as a matter of course in the premodern period, simply by living within an environment in which Jews and Jewish culture were a child's basic experience, where interaction with non-Jews was minimal, and where the politically dominant non-Jewish society was not viewed as a model to follow or aspire to. The holidays and Sabbath (along with the accompanying customs and prayers), the giving of *tzedakah* (charity), the caring for the poor and others in distress or need, the recital of blessings concerning multiple events of daily life—all this would have been learned by osmosis within the home and synagogue and by participation in communal activities and institutions. Jacob Katz describes the interconnected web of institutions (in addition to the family) that contributed to the upbringing of a Jewish child:

> Under the cramped conditions of existence, with the activities of the public institutions as intertwined with one another as they were, it was obviously impossible to keep the children from seeing and hearing everything that took place in the community. The life of the community was carried on as in a public arena, before the eyes of young and old, and children absorbed whatever they were intellectually capable of absorbing.[14]

Formal schooling, needed for the learning of holy texts—the one part of Jewish tradition that could not be picked up informally—was a supplement to the pervasive (while more casual) learning in family and community settings. From an early period, Jewish communities took on responsibility for providing for the education of male children. The institutions of heder and yeshivah, which were in place by the sixteenth century if not earlier, not only shaped the nature of Jewish education but were a closely integrated part of a larger system that delivered Judaism and Jewish life to the next generation.

The heder, the institution devoted to the education of the youngest children, is our main concern, as the Bible was central to this lower level of education. The contours and content of heder education were remarkably consistent across time and place until the convulsions of World War I and the Russian Revolution. Communal differences certainly existed, yet there is significant continuity among the many accounts.[15]

The Setting

Elementary schooling took place in two types of school, different in funding and prestige but identical in nature and purpose: the heder and the Talmud Torah. The heder was a private institution, with instruction paid for by the family of the pupil. The Talmud Torah was a charitable institution maintained by the community for the benefit of poor children whose families could not pay for a private *melamed*, or teacher. The Talmud Torah might have larger classes than the heder, and the teacher there had even less prestige than the melamed of the heder (elementary teachers not having much prestige in the traditional Jewish world), but since the curriculum and methods of instruction were the same, we can consider these two institutions together.

Classes were held in the home of the melamed, with the home setting providing a continuity between family life and school life. The melamed might be assisted by one or two helpers (the *belfer* or *behelfer*), responsible for taking the children to and from school and in helping to care for them during the day. Children usually began their heder education at the age of five, though many were sent as young as three or four. Children were at the heder from eight to twelve hours a day, five days a week, with a half day on Friday. It was not uncommon to have forty or more students in one heder, with students of several different ages and levels in the same room. Direct attention from the teacher came in individualized sessions in which the child would be called to the teacher's table, two or three times a day; some of the day would also be taken up in play, outdoors in good weather and indoors in bad.[16]

There were three levels of heder instruction: the elementary heder (*dardeki* heder), in which the fundamentals of reading were obtained, the *Humash* heder, in which the study of the Bible was the focus of the curriculum, and the Talmud heder, in which students moved on to study of the Talmud, a move that could occur as young as age eight.[17] Sometimes, in a large community, there would be separate hadarim for each level, but it was also possible for one teacher to have all three levels in his heder at once. A small number of the most promising students from the Talmud heder would then go on to a yeshivah for advanced study of the Talmud; this move occurred at about age ten.

Heder education was designed to set the young child on the path to learning the central text of premodern Judaism: the Talmud. The study of this text was a male-only affair, and the heder also was a male-dominated institution. But some elementary hadarim were open to girls, where a few would be given basic instruction in reading and also in writing and the handling of figures (with the latter two practical skills seen as more important for girls to learn than for boys); another practice was for a town to have a separate girls' heder, with a female teacher.[18] The higher levels of schooling, from the *Humash* heder on up, were closed to girls. Their learning of the Bible would come elsewhere, in connection with their mother's reading of the Yiddish *Ts'enah U-re'enah* rather than learning the Hebrew text in heder with boys of their own age. We saw above the limitations on female access to Torah in the ritual setting of the synagogue. In school, too, girls were held back from the presence of the holy text. Only in the home did they have access to the text, there in the attenuated form of a vernacular translation/commentary.

Methods of Instruction

Traditional Jewish education can perhaps best be understood as an apprenticeship, in the course of which the skills necessary to the practice of a trade were developed.[19] Unlike a modern educational program, in which—ideally—systematic and comprehensive pedagogical goals are translated into a graded, systematic curriculum, traditional Jewish education proceeded simply by doing. And here the doing, the trade that one practiced, was the reading of holy texts, first the Bible and then, as soon as one was ready, the Talmud, the crown of learning. There was no attempt to teach the fundamentals of Judaism or the principles of Jewish life in a systematic way. Children would have been learning values and customs in the course of daily life. Torah learning in heder was skill learning, and the primary skill of reading was treated not unlike a trade. Certainly the main concerns of Judaism and Jewish life were embedded in the texts being studied, but they were not themselves the focus of the curriculum, which was devoted to a mastery of the texts that was arguably as much physical as mental.

The first step in the apprenticeship was learning the mechanics of reading: the letters (in Hebrew, all consonants), vowel sounds, and the combination of syllables into words. These beginning steps might take half a year. The first textbook for actual reading was commonly the prayer book. The children learned to read the prayers rapidly and mechanically, without translation and without attention to their meaning. The fact that some of the prayers would have been familiar to the child from attendance at synagogue facilitated the learning of fluent reading. The benefit went in the other direction as well: learning rapid reading of the prayers at heder enabled the child to participate in the adult world of synagogue ritual, giving him a ready reward for this first stage of learning.

The child then moved on to the *Humash* (also sometimes used instead of the prayer book as the first reading text), beginning with the book of Leviticus. At this level also, now in the *Humash* heder, the primary emphasis was on mechanical facility, with some additional attention to comprehension of at least the literal meaning of the text. Beginning in about the sixteenth century, this comprehension was facilitated by the translation of the *Humash* into Yiddish, word by word. The text was learned by rote through the word-for-word translation.[20] The teacher would translate a word, repeated by a pupil. Then another word, repeated by a second pupil, proceeding through to the conclusion of a verse, at which point the class would repeat the verse in unison, all done aloud. All accounts comment on constant repetition as basic to the learning of the text.[21] Such repetition was an aide to memorization of the text. Before the era of printing, memorization was a major mode of learning (not only in Jewish culture), but it persisted well past the time in which books became available. As explained by Moshe Halbertal, the repetition embedded in this method of learning is akin to other mnemonic activities in Jewish ritual such as

> placing the text on the doorpost of the house [*mezuzah*], binding the text upon one's arm and between one's eyes [*tefillin*], or carrying the text around. [And, I would add, to the repetition of the cycle of Torah reading in synagogue ritual.] In those contexts learning does not mean reflecting or discovering. The text is not an object of art with many meanings and layers; it has surface rather than depth, and one must listen to it again and again in order to overcome forgetfulness. Used in this manner, the text is not problematized. It has no contradictions to resolve, hints to follow, or allusions to grasp.[22]

It was the incorporation of the text into one's being that was important, not the understanding of the text, and repetition and memorization were prime methods of such incorporation. "Learning was by rote; repetition, repetition, and still more repetition."[23] While the introduction of a translation added the potential for at least a literal understanding, the translation itself was not necessarily understood:

> In the course of time the text of this translation became fixed and in a sense canonized. As the Yiddish language developed, especially in Eastern Europe, the language of the by then traditional translation became less and less comprehensible to children. Ultimately, not only did the child have to master a text written in a foreign language, but also to commit to memory a barely understood translation which was often translated in turn to colloquial Yiddish.[24]

The rote learning of the text, with a translation itself not necessarily understood more fully than the original, could result in a combination of a sense of mastery and mystery, as illustrated in the following story from an American setting.

> *Mitchell Rudman was one of the founders of the Reform congregation I belong to in Galesburg. One afternoon I was chatting with him about his early Jewish education. He had grown up in the early twentieth century in an Orthodox family in Rock Island, Illinois, and had a heder education, not unlike that which he would have experienced in eastern Europe. "Yes," he told me, "we learned the* Humash *by heart. I had a Protestant minister come to me once, some years ago, because he wanted me to explain to him the Hebrew text of a particular passage from the Bible. I took out the Bible, and I read off the Hebrew and gave the Yiddish translation from memory. But I couldn't translate it into English for him." As Mitch told me this story, there was a mixture of pride — that he knew the Hebrew text, and that the minister had come to him for help — and bemusement — that he couldn't get past the Yiddish (which came out automatically from him as the translation) to an English version.*

When learning sections of Torah, some commentary might be taught as well, usually derived from Rashi's eleventh-century commentary. In later years of schooling, Rashi's commentary would be taught more extensively—either through a Yiddish translation or learned word by word in the distinctive typeface used for Rashi—a few verses of commentary at the beginning of each week's biblical portion, mastered through a similar repetitive methodology. The addition of commentary, itself canonized close to equivalence with the originating text, did not alter the basic approach to the biblical text, which was one of "reminding and reciting," rather than "inquiring, investigating, contemplating."[25] This was a kind of learning entirely consonant with the way in which the Torah was experienced in the ritual setting of synagogue use, even while it was being brought closer to and into each individual learner.

Another link to ritual use, and a further way of establishing intimacy with the text, was the practice of chanting the text while learning it (Rashi, as well as the *Humash* itself, and of course the prayers that were learned at the very beginning). Chanting, like repetition, served as an aid to memory, and both practices made the text felt within the body, readily available to the lips. Chanting began at the very earliest stage of learning, with Hebrew letters put into syllables according to a common sequence and chant: "komets, alef, aw; komets beyz, baw; etc."[26] The chanted alphabet lessons were a kind a dialogue between teacher and student, not necessarily with a set meter or melody, but "clearly rhythmic, repetitive and soothing."[27] Chanting was used at each successive stage, with a distinctive chant for each type of text, all of which could have been going on at once in a multilevel heder. As in prayer, the body would sway or rock back and forth, further reinforcing the rhythm of the chant and the incorporation of the text into the body. The sway and chant of studying would be continued into adult years, with the child's observation of his father's studying an early introduction to this style of learning.

Repetition, chanting, rhythmic swaying—this learning through the body effected the union of learner and text; students were able to deliver up passages on demand and to recognize the text in other settings, such as within synagogue ritual. This bodily incorporation of the text was graphically symbolized in food rituals that marked stages of heder life. A child's first entry into the heder and then later his beginning of Torah study were both marked by rituals in which Torah was equated with food, to be ingested by the body.

The first ceremony is a vivid acting out of the bodily incorporation of Torah, and although this medieval ceremony survived into the modern period only in attenuated form, we include it here since the educational methods with which it was in close conjunction did not significantly alter between the Middle Ages and the nineteenth century.[28] The ceremony centers on the young child, brought to heder for the first time on Shavuot, the holiday commemorating the giving of the Torah at Sinai. The child was to eat three foods symbolic of Torah. First, he was handed a slate on which letters of the alphabet and a few verses of Torah were written, and after repeating the names of the letters after the teacher, the slate was smeared with honey, which the child was then to lick off, licking the letters along with the honey and thus tasting the "sweetness" of Torah.[29] Second, the boy was given a cake to eat, on which had been traced several verses from Prophets and Psalms, verses in praise of Torah. And finally he was given an egg to eat, which was also inscribed with verses of Torah. Before the ingestion, the teacher would read the verses on the food, have the boy repeat the verses, and then the foods-with-words would be eaten. This food ingestion ritual is consonant with the methods of learning that themselves emphasize the incorporation of the text into the body. In later centuries, the elaborate ceremony was greatly attenuated, but the association of sweet food and Torah was maintained, with the teacher dropping candies (or sometimes coins) on the open book from which the child learned his first letters; the custom of smearing honey on the first letters continued into the twentieth century. Other accounts tell of children being given alphabet-shaped biscuits or almonds engraved with Hebrew letters. The notion of "education as ingestion"[30] thus continued to be reinforced ritually.

A second initiation ceremony occurred when the child began the study of the Pentateuch, which sometimes also meant a move from the elementary heder to the *Humash* heder. Yekhiel Shtern describes the ceremony as it took place in Tyszowce in the early twentieth century. In this ceremony the food was provided to all in attendance. Honey cake, brandy, nuts, and candies were set out on a table at which sat the teacher, the father of the child, and invited guests; the mother and other women stood off at a distance. The initiate was then put through a dialogue of questions and answers that he would have been preparing for some time, focused on details of the Torah and the book about to be begun (Leviticus). In the middle, the child was blessed by three older children (this, like the dialogue with the teacher, in a set chant), after which the adults would shower candy and nuts on the boys. At the conclusion of the ceremony, refreshments would be shared among the guests.[31]

These food rituals are pleasant ways of reinforcing the association of learning with the body. This association was also reinforced negatively, through corporal punishment for misbehavior. Many accounts detail this practice. As characterized by Shtern, "Discipline in the kheyder was severe, even brutal. Corporal punishment was used in all its forms. The lash was always at work."[32] The body was the vessel engaged in learning; it was the location of punishment when learning was amiss, as well as the location of pleasure and mastery; this duality is captured in a seventeenth-century heder alphabet and prayer chart that shows students both whipped and rewarded with treats.

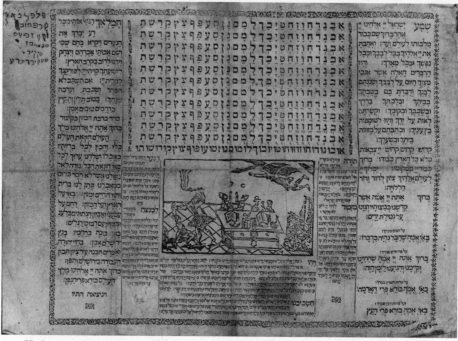

Heder scene in a wall chart, Venice, 1656. Courtesy of the Library of the Jewish Theological Seminary of America.

The Content of Instruction

In relating methods of instruction, we have mentioned briefly the subject matter and the texts being taught. In contrast to modern approaches to curriculum, "subject matter" was not a defining construct, as study was totally centered on the mastery of particular texts. Since the number of texts to be mastered was limited, the curriculum was quite simple. That the texts themselves were exceedingly difficult is another matter.

As we have seen, the child began with learning to read Hebrew, accomplished through use of the prayer book or sometimes the Bible itself. As soon as the students could read, they began with Torah, traditionally with the book of Leviticus, which opens with the laws of sacrifice. Why begin here, rather than with what seems to us the more appealing narrative material of Genesis? Traditional explanations, carried forward into the ritual dialogue repeated by the young child beginning *Humash* study, held that sacrifices are pure, and the child is pure, and thus the pure should engage in study of the pure. There was also a sense that the child's study of Torah, beginning with the law of sacrifice, was a kind of substitute for the performance of sacrifice no longer possible after the destruction of the Temple. Another explanation was that the law of Israel, rather than the history of Israel, should be at the foundation of learning. The practice of beginning with Leviticus was not maintained through the centuries everywhere, but it remained at least symbolically in the entry-into-*Humash* ritual, in which the child would answer questions about the opening chapter of Leviticus.[33]

After Leviticus—or at the start of *Humash* study, if Leviticus was not the entry point—the students went through the Pentateuch on a schedule in synchrony with the weekly portion (*parshah*) that was to be read in the synagogue on the coming Sabbath. Each week, students would begin with the opening verses of the parshah, proceeding with a word-by-word translation into Yiddish, and eventually, once fluent, reading in Hebrew alone, with the teacher providing explanation when necessary and with Rashi used as the source for interpretation. But each portion is long and would not usually be completed in the week. The cycle repeated itself each year, so that students every year read once again the beginning of the portion—through the whole of the Pentateuch—never reaching the end of each portion; stories were perpetually left incomplete, discontinuous.[34]

To a modern audience geared to narrative, this practice of cutting the portion off arbitrarily and moving on to the next to keep up with the synagogue ritual seems a kind of "reading interruptus," incomplete and unsatisfying. But this method makes perfect sense in its educational context. First of all, it should be remembered that much of the Pentateuch is legal material, not narrative. Interruption of such portions would be less problematic, as they are often a compilation of relatively short, discrete units rather than longer comprehensive passages. More importantly, coordinating the school reading with the ritual reading in the synagogue (as well as the weekly Sabbath reading at home) integrated children's education into the life of the Jewish community. Education was not something set apart with a different agenda or methodology; children's study served to connect them directly with adult use of the sacred text. Finally, if the pedagogical goal had been to prepare students for interpreting the text, or to use the stories in the text for moral purposes—goals that we will see take on prominence in the modern period—then the traditional methods would certainly have been inadequate. But in the heder the prime goal with regard to the Bible was to develop an intimate familiarity with the words of the sacred text. The conjunction of the heder lesson with synagogue and home readings and the yearly repetition of the same portions were fully in accord with this goal.[35]

The way children learned the Bible, strange as it may seem to modern eyes, was well suited to the place of the Bible in the traditional Jewish community and to the nature of the community itself, which was permeated by Jewish values, practices, and customs. Through the multiple chanted repetitions of sacred words, the text became a part of the child, who could then recognize these words when sounded in synagogue or home and who could readily offer up pieces of text when called upon do so. Intimate familiarity with the text, not an understanding of it, was the goal and the result. The text was learned by heart and was, thus, in the heart. For those few who went on to higher levels of education, this deep textual intimacy would serve them well as they developed interpretive and analytical skills, but even here, such skills were used primarily on the Talmud. Talmud was the text whose meaning needed to be understood—and on whose knowledge prestige in the community was based—because *it* was text upon which actual community practice was founded. A man learned in Talmud could not only untangle complicated arguments preserved from centuries past in the Talmudic text, he could also (and might well be called upon to) solve problems within his community, on the basis of principles and precedents laid out in this text. Not so the Bible, which was preeminently a text of ritual awe and devotion, not of practical use.

How did it happen that the Talmud came to be supplanted as the "binding text" of Judaism, with the Bible taking its place as the central text of education and of moral guidance? The first context to explore is the dramatic change of intellectual and social environment in eighteenth- and nineteenth-century Europe, as the related movements of the Enlightenment and emancipation wrought their influence on so many aspects of Jewish life.

2

The Challenge of Modernity

The premodern education of Jews was closely circumscribed, focused on the mastery of sacred texts, in service of the interpretation and application of Jewish law in all areas of life. This education served well a population that itself had been circumscribed for centuries, marked out as "other" from the rest of the population by legal restrictions imposed from without on residency, status, and vocation; this separation was reinforced by a distinctive culture developed from within the Jewish community. But when both cultural and legal boundaries were breached in the eighteenth century by the challenges of the Enlightenment and emancipation, Jews throughout Europe were faced with the necessity of response. This encounter between tradition and modernity and the complicated interactions between these conflicting forces within the Jewish communities of Europe is clearly a dominant motif in modern Jewish history.[1] Before the eighteenth century, a European Jewish understanding of self and the world was based on the reading of only Jewish texts and on speaking with Jewish interlocutors. When the conversation partners changed—with new voices from books, correspondence, and face-to-face interchange—new ideas were introduced, and all that had been taken for granted in the past now was reexamined. Jews now responded to ideas and values previously kept outside their experience. This movement of ideas was not uniform in time or space—it was not a flood that overwhelmed Jewish society all at once. But the same currents have appeared again and again in the history of modernizing Judaism and the transformations, while certainly not identical over place and time, yet bear a resemblance one to the other.

The encroachment of these new ideas created "present exigencies" according to which new understandings of Judaism and Jewish life were forged in the eighteenth through twentieth centuries, and it is within this context that the Bible was remade into a core text of Jewish education and adapted for audiences of modern Jewish children and adults.[2] To understand this process, we will look primarily at developments within Germany during the eighteenth and nineteenth centuries, as it was here that the initial conversations between Judaism and modernity began; the issues that were addressed in this time and place reappeared again and again across Europe and in America. Evidence from the American scene will also be included, as the American reshaping of the Bible is the eventual focus of our story. While American developments are generally later, the terms of the discussion are much the same.

The discordances between traditional Judaism and modern ways of thinking traveled through a vast territory within Jewish life: from birth (controversies over circumcision) to death (controversies over timely burial), from belief to law, from ritual and prayer to education and language. We will focus here on attitudes toward the Hebrew Bible, examining the impact of three ideas fundamental to the intellectual history of eighteenth- and nineteenth-century Europe: reason, universalism, and historicism. These ideas produced contradictory impulses with regard to the Bible. On the one hand, all three effected a loss in the special sacred stature of the Bible; on the other hand, they ironically led to a repositioning of the Bible, replacing the Talmud as the central text for reform-minded Jews.

Modernity's Challenge to Traditional Judaism: Reason, Universalism, Historicism

The European Enlightenment has had a fundamental and pervasive impact on Judaism and Jewish thought in the modern period. At the heart of the Enlightenment project was the glorification of reason as the vehicle of truth. In this "rationally saturated atmosphere,"[3] all principles of social, economic, religious, and intellectual order, heretofore received via tradition or revelation, were put to the test of reason. While in revolutionary France this test resulted in an outright denunciation of religion—with Temples of Reason erected to replace the institutions of the Catholic Church—the German *Aufklärung* challenged received religion without being antireligious. The result was extensive discussion of principles of "natural religion"—that is, religion formulated on the basis of reason, that source of understanding considered most natural to human beings. The challenge to Judaism, as a religion based on the authority of a revealed text and on centuries of accumulated law and tradition, was made explicit by such German Enlightenment thinkers as Lessing and Kant; Kant's *Religion within the Limits of Reason Alone* (1793) included a denunciation of Judaism as not even a religion at all, given its emphasis on ritual observance rather than on conscience and belief.[4] Principles of belief and morality were to be sought through the effort of individuals exercising their natural reason, rather than being passively received through the authority of religious institutions, texts, or personages. Given that reason was common to all humans, of whatever nation or time, Kant and others held that a sustained endeavor on such rational grounds would result in a universal religion, whose tenets would be obtainable by and acceptable to all who committed themselves to this approach.

This emphasis on universal religious truth had a profound influence on the development of Reform Judaism. Much was at stake in demonstrating that Judaism was in accord with the principle of universality, since the political project of emancipation rested on this same principle. Citizenship and other legal rights were available to Jews only when and where authorities were convinced (or forced to accept) that Judaism did not mandate a fundamentally separate, distinct existence for its adherents.[5] As Michael Meyer has argued, the tolerance of the Enlightenment was based not on a pluralistic acceptance of multiple truths, but rather on the conviction that all peoples were fundamentally capable of coming to the unifying universal truths newly available through the exercise of reason.[6] Thus, ironically, the Enlightenment can be seen as less tolerant of significant cultural and religious difference than were earlier intellectual and political regimes that, while disdainful of Jews as an inferior people, yet made space for Jewish communities with their own relatively autonomous communal authorities as well as their distinct customs. In the Enlightenment drive for universal truth and conformity, all such separateness was deeply offensive.[7] With regard to Judaism, the primary source of offense was *halakhah*, the complex of Jewish law, based ultimately on the Bible but built up in large part by the rabbis of the post-biblical and medieval periods. Jewish law governed all aspects of life—not just prayer and holiday observance but eating practices, sexual behavior, business relations, and more. Jewish law, for the most part, applied only to Jews. The laws of *kashrut*, for example—which foods were allowable and which not—had no application to non-Jews, nor did the laws governing rest on the Sabbath, two areas of the law that in addition effected a strict separation of and distinction between Jews and non-Jews. Even matters that in modern terms would be considered "civil" law rather than "religious" were, before the eighteenth century, handled within the Jewish community by Jewish authorities.[8] Such a separate, virtually autonomous legal system was inconsistent with the results of emancipation, which presumed that all people within one state would be governed by the same set of laws and judged by the same authorities. Given the various disabilities (of residence, vocation, education, etc.) embedded in the premodern system of separation, most Jews across Europe welcomed the possibility of integration into the dominant legal system.

By the latter part of the eighteenth century, the outside pressure to conform was answered from within Jewish circles with a twofold response: on the one hand, a multifaceted effort to change Judaism in order to put it in accord with the demands of modernity, and on the other hand, an assertion of the already universal nature of Judaism.[9] Moses Mendelssohn (1729–1786) was a key figure in shaping this understanding of Judaism, as was Hermann Cohen (1842–1918) and after him Leo Baeck (1873–1956). These men stressed that the heart of Judaism was its ethical monotheism, which was in accord with reason and was of universal application; that is, all human beings were included within the compass of the universal God of Judaism.[10] Mendelssohn and other *maskilim* (participants in the *Haskalah*, the Jewish Enlightenment movement) stressed that Judaism was a religion, not a nationality, and that particularist customs and practices that had developed over the centuries were incidental to Judaism, not its essential core. Judaism was thus presented as a religion like Christianity, founded on beliefs and on basic ethical principles (all in accord with reason), not on law derived from revelation and tradition. This conviction led to a plethora of books, pamphlets, and essays devoted to identifying and explaining these beliefs and ethical principles, with a culminating text being Leo Baeck's *The Essence of Judaism,* first published in 1905. Just a few years later, the Central Conference of American Rabbis (the organization of Reform rabbis in the United States) began a pamphlet series of "Popular Studies in Judaism," intended for general distribution, with a pamphlet by Rabbi H. G. Enelow on "What Do Jews Believe?" followed not long afterward by one on "Jewish Ethics" by Rabbi Samuel Schulman.[11] The centrality of the Bible to this universalistic program can be seen in an instructional manual on "Bible ethics," published in the United States in 1884. The authors claim that the religion and moral code of the Bible that they present is "pure Judaism," as well as being "that in which Jew and non-Jew agree, because it is religion shorn of that added material in which no two sects entirely coincide."[12] This aim of teaching the "essence" of Judaism was also furthered through the writing of catechisms, a doctrine-

centered genre borrowed from Protestant practice. Numerous Jewish catechisms were published in Germany and elsewhere from the late eighteenth century through the nineteenth.[13]

The third element of modern intellectual life contributing to the transformation of Judaism was historicism. In contrast to the Enlightenment
promise of universal truth and a society constructed in accord with the
principles of reason, the historical approach introduced by nineteenth-
century European Romanticism led to an understanding of each present-
day society and culture as having been shaped by a particular past, and of
each past moment as having to be understood in its own context. Such
historical thinking, rooted in time and in chronology, promotes an understanding of each period as unique and each moment as conditioned by its
development out of the past. Ideas, values, and institutions—all are conditioned by their historical setting. The present, while conditioned by the
past, is also fundamentally discontinuous with it, necessarily distinct from
the past in its existence in a different era, with different circumstances
and necessities.

Such a historicist understanding was a profound challenge to traditional Judaism, which was fundamentally nonhistorical, with God's will as
revealed at Sinai—even while reinterpreted over time—never changing
and ever relevant over the centuries.[14] Historicism was also a radical
change from Enlightenment views, which saw truths—derived from reason rather than revelation—as being as valid and fitting in the modern era
as they were in ancient times. In contrast, historicism opened up the vista
of deep difference rather than universality or eternality, and this divisive
potential was also evident in historicism's close relationship with the bur-
geoning nationalist movements of the nineteenth century, as peoples
began to understand themselves as having a particular destiny, shaped by
their relationship to a past circumscribed by language, territory, and
"race." Yet historicism was also linked to Enlightenment modes of thought
by the common reliance on rationality. That is, the past was to be understood through a reasoned, "scientific" approach—through a careful, systematic sifting of evidence—rather than through a reverent acceptance of
the past as inherited verity.

This common link of reason helps us understand how it could be that
many Jewish thinkers in Europe and America accepted a historicist
approach to understanding Judaism at the same time that they clung persistently to the rational, universalist approach more characteristic of the
Enlightenment. Given the disappointing record of emancipation,[15] and
the heightened anti-Semitism fed by nationalist movements across
Europe, stress on the universal rights of humans—which necessitated a
stress on the similarity between Jews and Gentiles—was crucial to the

emancipatory goal for which many Jews still hoped: the full integration of Jews into the life of the surrounding society.[16]

The historicist approach presented an obvious conflict with religious understanding, given that religion—particularly scriptural religions like Christianity, Judaism, or Islam—tends to emphasize the permanent nature of truths revealed long ago in the past. But religion, like other elements of culture, is adaptable to multiple intellectual approaches, and by the end of the nineteenth century religious thinkers in Europe and America, along with the educated classes generally, had incorporated a historical consciousness, and a wide acceptance by the lay public was well in evidence by the 1920s and 1930s. Within Judaism, the historical approach was so dominant among the modernizing, intellectual elite that it was embodied in a named movement: *Wissenschaft des Judentums*.[17] The usual translation for this term is "the scientific study of Judaism," but in this context *Wissenschaft* can also be understood as "scholarship" or even more narrowly as "historical study." It was the "academic" study of Judaism, a study based on the kind of systematic research methods one learns at university, and as such, a method in fundamental opposition to the enclosed, self-referential text-based study of the yeshivah. Indeed, the purpose of this new study of Judaism was as much to educate non-Jews as Jews. Jewish scholars hoped that the detailing of Jewish history and religion would open a general audience to a more knowledgeable and hence respectful relationship to Jews and Judaism.[18] In the words of Leopold Zunz, a pioneering practitioner of *Wissenschaft des Judentums*: "Will not a spirit of humanity pour out over the land from the font of scholarship, paving the way for understanding and harmony? The extension of equality to Jews in society will follow from the extension of equality to the academic study of Judaism."[19] There was a social consequence to *Wissenschaft des Judentums* within the Jewish community as well, in that a historical approach to Judaism tended to legitimize changes in Jewish practice made in accord with changing times.

Historical thinking was the intellectual arena within which Judaism encountered modern culture, and it became "the dominant universe of discourse" in Jewish life as well as in the surrounding culture.[20] One sphere in this universe profoundly affected by the shifting ground of historicism, as well as by the Enlightenment ideals of reason and universalism, was biblical study.

Implications for the Role of Sacred Texts

One early consequence of the intellectual revolution of the modern period was the development of the "higher criticism" of the Bible, an approach initiated by Protestant biblical scholars. Whereas "lower" criticism was concerned with the establishment of the original text, free of later scribal errors, "higher" criticism applied a historical approach to even this sacred text. The Bible was to be treated just like any other literary text. Early questions centered on issues of authorship: who wrote the various books of the Bible, when were they written, and why? The first works in the field of Old Testament criticism were written as early as the 1820s and 1830s, but the most widely influential one was the synthetic work of Julius Wellhausen, dating from the 1870s. Wellhausen challenged the unity of the biblical text (as had others before him), demonstrating that different parts of the Pentateuch must have been written at different times by different authors with different interests. The traditional view of the Bible as a sacred text, revealed directly by God through Moses, was challenged at its very foundation. It was not just the application of historical criticism to the Bible—radically different as it was from the traditional ahistorical approach—that was unsettling; so too were the results of that criticism, since they challenged the Mosaic authorship of the Pentateuch. The assertion that the Bible was composed by multiple human authors undermined belief in the divine origin of the text, while also obviating its unity and potential universality, paralleling the results of historicism for religious truth in general. As Jon Levenson has written: "When a scripture comes to be seen as a product of culture, one that comes into existence through a long, variegated historical process, then the unity of the scripture—the simultaneity, self-referentiality, and mutual implication of all its parts—is thrown into doubt."[21] In a further result, the authority of the text was replaced by the authority of the individuals now interpreting the text.

Traditionally, the Bible itself had not been the subject of serious study in Ashkenazic Jewish culture, and the fact that the newly introduced method of study was potentially destructive of basic Jewish attitudes toward the text led to serious hesitation on the part of Jewish scholars to accept the findings of this scholarship or to engage in it themselves.[22] Contributing perhaps even more strongly to this Jewish hesitancy was the blatant anti-Semitism of much of the Christian scholarship on the Bible. Even among those Jewish scholars and reformers who were open, in general, to a historicist method, there was a "visceral distrust" of Protestant biblical research.[23] With good reason. The documentary hypothesis not only undermined Mosaic authorship but was used (most influentially by Wellhausen) in support of a historical reconstruction of Judaism that elevated the prophetic writings as the earliest strata in the Bible and denigrated as later impositions all legal elements in the text, which were seen as representative of a degeneration from ancient Israelite religion to "Judaism." The writings of the prophets were considered early texts; the authority of these books of the Bible was further enhanced in Christian eyes by the predictions and foreshadowings of the coming of Christ that Christian interpreters found in these texts. Later developments in Judaism—including all of rabbinic and medieval contributions—were considered as further "inauthentic" accretions to the true core of the text, the teachings of the prophets.[24] This unveiled hostility to Judaism kept Jewish scholars in Germany (the home of higher criticism) from embracing a critical approach to the Bible well into the twentieth century, even while they engaged in historical studies of other aspects of Judaism.[25] Isaac Mayer Wise, the first president of Hebrew Union College (1875–1900), forbade there the teaching of biblical criticism.[26] Solomon Schechter—the prominent British rabbi who came to the United States to head the Jewish Theological Seminary—coined the phrase "the higher anti-Semitism" to describe higher criticism, and he so influenced the Conservative seminary against it that critical approaches to the Bible were not taught there until the mid-twentieth century, fifty years after his death.[27]

American rabbis were more accepting of a historical approach, as can be seen in a comparison of programmatic statements put out by rabbinical conferences in Germany and in the United States. The Leipzig Synod of 1869 was a gathering of rabbis, scholars, and lay leaders, the majority of whom were moderately progressive. But in order to avoid religious disunity and to preserve Judaism, the measures approved tended to be conservative.[28] Relevant here is their explicit rejection of the use of "the critical method" in religious instruction, even while acknowledging that the results of the "scientific point of view" must somehow be acknowledged:

> The assembly declares that religious instruction in the school must avoid the critical method; the idealistic outlook of the young should not be blurred by the suggestion of doubts. For this very reason, however, the assembly expects our teachers to be wisely discreet in not ignoring the results of science, but to anticipate and prevent a conflict, which may arise later in the soul of our growing youth, between religion and the commonly accepted scientific point of view.[29]

Some sixteen years later, American Jewish leaders endorsed a historical perspective on the Bible in a plank of the Pittsburgh Platform:

> We recognize in the Bible the record of the consecration of the Jewish people to its mission as priest of the one God, and value it as the most potent instrument of religious and moral instruction. *We hold that the modern discoveries of scientific researches in the domains of nature and history are not antagonistic to the doctrines of Judaism, the Bible reflecting the primitive ideas of*

its own age, and at times clothing its conception of Divine Providence and justice dealing with man in miraculous narratives.[30]

Evidence of the wide acceptance of higher criticism among American rabbis is also found in a published address and discussion on this subject from 1902. Rabbi S. Sale addressed the Central Conference of American Rabbis on the topic of "The Bible and Modern Thought," asserting the lack of conflict between science and religion ("when these are properly understood"), and promoting higher criticism as a "blessed mediator" between modern thought and the Bible, in that it provides a means of reconciling the Bible with "the modern view of life" and shows us the Bible's "imperishable value as an ideal factor and moral force in the upbuilding of humanity."[31] Of the four discussants, three also supported higher criticism. Even the one discussant who argued against higher criticism, H. Barnstein, insisted that he was not against it in principle. He held that the questions posed by higher criticism were fine, but the results obtained so far had been destructive, shaped as they were by anti-Semitic leanings in Christian authors. "The goal of many of these critical theologians," Barnstein says, "seems to be to glorify Christianity, at the expense of Judaism, and to make disparaging comparisons between the Old and New Testaments."[32] But the other rabbis were apparently willing to view the anti-Semitism as a peripheral aspect of higher criticism, with the more central benefit being the ability to participate in the mainstream of modern thought and to emphasize the contributions this central Jewish text could make to human life generally. In this acceptance of a higher critical approach to the Bible, these American rabbis were fully in step with the general American scene, in which the authority of the Bible declined among the well-educated in the last decades of the nineteenth century, and more generally a generation later.[33] Thus, rabbis had to question the (divine) authority of the Bible in order to maintain the credibility of the text as a possible source of authority in the modern world. A historical/critical approach to the Bible also fit well with the greater openness to change in religious practice in America as compared to Europe, since it was an easy next step, once divine authorship of the Bible was abandoned, to discard the laws embedded in the text—as is clear, indeed, in the plank of the Pittsburgh Platform that immediately follows the declaration of the historicity of the biblical text: "We recognize in the Mosaic legislation a system of training the Jewish people for its mission during its national life in Palestine, and to-day we accept as binding only the moral laws, and maintain only such ceremonies as elevate and sanctify our lives, but reject all such as are not adapted to the views and habits of modern civilization."[34]

Desacralization of the Talmud

Despite support for scientific biblical scholarship, active engagement in such scholarship did not develop in America either, until much later in the twentieth century. Rather, on both sides of the Atlantic the focus of Jewish scholarly endeavor was on the Talmud and other rabbinic literature, not the Bible. A *Wissenschaft* approach to these writings was a major break with the traditional approach, which held the Written Torah (the Bible) and the Oral Torah (Mishnah, Talmud, midrash) to be all of a piece. Why was rabbinic literature a more acceptable object of historical/critical scholarship than the Bible? In part this was a defensive response on the part of Jewish scholars to Christian critiques of Judaism, which focused on post-biblical developments. Jewish scholars felt a mission to explain the part of Judaism most subject to Christian critique: the Talmud and rabbinic Judaism. Rabbinic literature was also little known to Christian scholars,[35] whereas the Bible, well known to Christians and accepted by them as a sacred text, needed no such defense.

But there were also internal developments and concerns within Jewish circles that made rabbinic literature more vulnerable to the critical eye of a scientific approach than the Bible. Just as it was easier for Christians to accept higher criticism of the Old Testament than the New (even while both texts were included in the Christian Bible), Jewish scholars found they could distinguish between rabbinic literature and the Bible, even though they had previously been taken together as "Torah." A fundamental distinction was now drawn between rabbinic literature as a human creation, as opposed to the divine origin of the Bible. Joshua Heschel Schorr, an eastern European *maskil*, provides a clear and early statement of this differentiation:

> The holy Torah, as given to us by Moses, lies before us. Who dares criticize it or doubt its veracity? Who would deny its divinity? Who cannot see that it is imbued with the divine spirit? The purity of its language, the clarity and grandeur of its teachings, the portrayals which leave far behind anything other old nations have to show forth in their myths, must convince even the most ordinary mind that God's spirit is revealed therein! Looking at the sources of the so-called oral teachings which are accessible to us and which are meant to constitute a supplement to the Mosaic law, any expert who examines them without prejudice will have to realize at once that their expression and wording is merely the work of earthborn humans, and therefore subject to error.[36]

Schorr's distinction between the Bible and the "so-called oral teachings" is in fundamental contrast to the traditional *ahistorical* understanding of the unity of written and oral Torah. The texts were understood to be united by their single divine author, with no meaningful chronological distinction to be made within or between the texts of Scripture and of rabbinic literature. The rabbinic mode of exegesis of Scripture worked the biblical text without any regard for historical context or chronological order of authorship, ignoring the individuality of texts, and instead bringing into relation similar motifs and topics across textual boundaries. The Talmud, at one with the Bible, subsumed it, and, as we have seen, thus played the primary role in traditional Jewish education after the beginning years.

A modern, historical approach detached the Talmud from the Bible, identifying it as later and of human origin. This divorce resulted in the possibility of different standings for the two bodies of texts. The Talmud and other rabbinic literature were free to be desacralized, while the Bible was preserved as sacred. Through a prodigious amount of research in the mid-nineteenth century, Jewish scholars put rabbinic literature in the historical context of Persian and Greco-Roman history, effectively breaking up what had been a unified, harmonious, and venerated corpus of sacred literature into its diverse historical components.[37]

This split between the Bible and rabbinic literature greatly facilitated the Reform impulse to question the continuing validity of Jewish law in the changed circumstances of the modern world. Reformers tended to gloss over the legal aspects of the Tanakh, focusing attention on the prophetic books of the Bible. This left the Talmud as the repository of Jewish law, and, with the Talmud dethroned from its sacred position, reformers were more free to criticize multiple elements of Jewish law as outdated. In the words of Ismar Schorsch: "Critical history . . . is ideally suited to soften the *halakhic* incrustation of Judaism. Uncovering the all too human origins of the system tarnishes its infallibility and grants contemporary Jews an equal right to modify its contours."[38] We have already seen the disavowal of laws "not adapted to the views and habits of modern civilization" in the 1885 Pittsburgh Platform. In 1895, rabbis gathered at the annual meeting of the Central Conference of American Rabbis again asserted the nonbinding nature of rabbinic law in a resolution that "our relations in all religious matters are in no way authoritatively and finally determined by any portion of our Post-Biblical and Patristic literatures." This literature is a "treasure-house in which the successive ages deposited their conceptions of the great and fundamental principles of Judaism," but the current age is itself engaged in the task of adding a new "wing" to this house.[39]

Thus, the impulse to question the centrality of rabbinic literature was fueled by a desire to attack the authority of halakhah in Judaism. Halakhah, it will be remembered, was seen as a major affront to the value of universalism so important to the Enlightenment and so readily embraced by Jewish maskilim. Jewish law was the epitome of particularism, both in the sense of Jewish "exclusiveness," which served to separate Jews from others through innumerable practices relevant only to Jews, and also in the sense that it concerned particular details of practice—of external behavior—rather than "spiritual" principles of religious belief.[40] The desire to attain the promise of legal equality held out by emancipation was another pressure brought to bear on the authority of halakhah; in order to gain citizenship rights Jews had to accept the authority of the modern state, overriding the authority of rabbinic law.

The simplest way to undermine halakhah was to undermine the text which was its prime repository: the Talmud. Hostility to the Talmud could go so far that one mid-nineteenth-century German Jewish historian, Isaac Marcus Jost, applauded the intent of the burning of the Talmud by Church authorities in Paris in 1240.[41] Antipathy developed to the style of the text as well as to its legalistic content. Modern Western discourse, as embodied in Enlightenment texts and beyond, developed modes of thinking and writing that were fundamentally different from modes embedded in traditional Jewish texts.[42] Modern discourse favored directional discourse, an argument or narrative that proceeded systematically, by principles of logic or chronology. Traditional Jewish texts, and certainly the Talmud, proceeded in an entirely different manner, through association, dialogue, and questions. One rabbi's opinion elicits a counter-opinion, which leads to an association with the opinion of another rabbi or to a biblical text, and so forth. The text is organized by a series of questions, each of which elicits multiple answers, in dialogue with one another. The traditional study of the text replicated the method within the text: students paired in dialogue with each other and moved forward through the questioning of their teachers. The text of the Talmud was difficult and required years of training to find one's way in it. Jews newly immersed in modern Western discourse came to find the Talmud a distasteful text. Moses Leib Lilienblum, for example, who had himself established a yeshivah, found himself "weary and exhausted from studying the Talmud, its disputations and various absurdities. When I heard of something new that was rational, I was drawn to it, just like an escaped prisoner coming upon a field of flowers. . . . So weary was I of the casuistic books and their sophistries that I looked for spiritual sustenance in other sorts of books."[43] Or Moses Samuel, an Anglo-Jewish reformer, who complained of rabbinic learning as consisting of "farfetched and distorted quotations, arbitrary and preposterous definitions, together with eccentric deductions."[44] One of the "other sorts of books" in which modernizing Jews were able to find "spiritual sustenance" was the Bible, which, in contrast to the Talmud and other rabbinic literature, was seen to be "clear and understandable" and "easily grasped and available to all," as opposed to the Talmud, which required long years of study under the tutelage of experts.[45]

While rejecting the Talmud as authoritative sacred text, reformers did not argue for dropping the Talmud entirely, but rather for seeing it as a historically placed document, reflecting the needs of its time. From this vantage point, the text could even be held up as a model of religious adaptation, and hence a precursor of their own work. It was to be understood historically as a text created in its own particular place and time and out of the need to adapt biblical Judaism to the radically changed circumstances following the destruction of the Second Temple. As a committee of the Central Conference of American Rabbis affirmed in 1895, "Our age is engaged in the same task," that is, the adaptation of Judaism to contemporary circumstance and need.[46]

Thus, the historical approach—the hallmark of a modern approach to religious texts—was readily accepted with regard to the Talmud and contributed to its demotion from sacred, authoritative text to an ordinary text in time. Reformers were much more hesitant, however, to apply such an approach to the Bible—and were certainly reluctant to utilize it to diminish the special stature of the text—even while expressing a general acceptance of a historicist perspective. With the Talmud—once the crown of Jewish education and the central authority of Jewish life—pushed aside, the Bible was free to stand alone, and to represent to modern Jews the "essence" of Judaism.

Repositioning the Bible

The Reform approach to the Bible was fundamentally contradictory. By the late nineteenth century, most Reform rabbis fully supported a historical/critical approach to the Bible—viewing it as a text with various parts, written at various points in time by various authors—yet they just as firmly held that the Bible was universal, timeless, and in some way specially revealed by God. In the words of Rabbi Ettelson, commenting on a 1908 address by Rabbi Julian Morgenstern on "The Significance of the Bible for Reform Judaism in the Light of Modern Scientific Research":

> Our duty . . . is to show from pulpit and in classroom that we can accept the fundamental principles of Biblical science, and, at the same time, find

in our Bible something infinitely more than a mere outgrown stage in the development of Judaism. . . . The question of authorship and origin does not affect what is true in the ethical or religious ideals or inspirational power of Psalmist or Prophet. Tested indeed by all the canons of criticism, the Bible remains *the* Bible still, and is shown to be no less a divine revelation because it is also seen to be so intensely a human revelation.[47]

Ettelson's comment comes from his uneasiness regarding a point in Morgenstern's address concerning the benefits to Reform Judaism of higher criticism in its stress on change and development in religion over time. Morgenstern had said, "I wish to emphasize . . . the positive message of Biblical Science, the actual, historical, incontrovertible fact, that Judaism is the result of a long process of evolution . . . of natural revelation, part and parcel of the development of human life, thought and culture." This finding gives Reform Judaism a "sane and logical basis" as the latest stage in the development of Judaism, rather than basing reform on the expedient, illogical, and dishonest "principle that the laws of the Pentateuch are in the main not applicable, and consequently not binding, today." And yet, despite this clear emphasis on the Bible as a reflection of its own time, Morgenstern concludes his remarks with a paean to the Bible as "the truest means of determining [the] principles [of Judaism], the guide and text-book and source of inspiration of all evolution of Judaism." The origins of particular customs in the biblical past may have been "gross," and yet these customs still in our own day "voice for us . . . the sublimest truths that religion has yet realized."[48] Here again we are faced with a contrast between the readiness with which rabbis and scholars accepted a historical perspective of the Talmud as destructive of its special normative role and their profound hesitancy to do the same with the Bible. How, then, did these men, so eager to demonstrate the irrelevancy of the Talmud for modern life, demonstrate, in contrast, the relevancy of the Bible, a text coming from a period even more removed from the modern world in time and religious/social structure than the body of rabbinic literature?

The basic answer is that the Bible was claimed to be fundamentally in accord with modernity. Underlying this claim were three elements of circumstance or understanding: (1) unlike the Talmud, the Bible was a text shared with Christians; (2) the Bible better fit the category of "classical" text, appealing to modern sensibilities; and (3) the Bible was seen as the primary source of universalist principles that stood as the essence of Judaism.

The first factor was largely unexpressed and yet was certainly a prime motivating force: the Bible was retained as *the* central sacred text in Judaism because it was a text also recognized as "Scripture" and "Bible" by

Christians. The success of the emancipation/enlightenment project was made difficult by the ways in which Jews continued to be perceived as not fitting in the non-Jewish environment into which they sought entry. Emphasizing the shared Scripture of the Bible/Old Testament and abandoning the Talmud, long the object of Christian disdain, was one way for Jews to accommodate to Christian culture even while maintaining something they could claim as continuous with traditional Judaism. It is not surprising, then, that the Bible was a focus of attention in early maskilic circles, even while not approached with the tools of higher criticism. The early Hebrew journal *Ha-Me'asef* included much about the Bible, examining it as a source of "spiritual satisfaction" and "religious exaltation."[49] Also enormously influential was Moses Mendelssohn's translation of the Bible into German, through which he hoped to immerse Jews into the biblical text, from which they were distanced by language, and at the same time introduce them to the reading of literature in German.[50] Yet the commentary that accompanied Mendelssohn's translation was in Hebrew as well as traditionalist in approach, rejecting emendation of the Masoretic text in which Christian scholars were engaging and that was part and parcel of their new critical approach to the Bible.[51] While the commentary was significant as a demonstration of a modern Jewish focus on the Bible, its substance was quite traditional, staying close to rabbinic and medieval interpretations of the text, which were themselves under attack by contemporary Christian scholars.

The Bible had been prominent in American life from the earliest years of the Puritan colonists, and it has continued as a central feature of the cultural landscape to the present day. The dominance of Protestantism in the United States, with its strong preference for the Bible over later commentaries or exegesis, contributed to the dominating presence of the Bible in American life.[52] Enormous numbers of English-language editions of the Bible have been published in America (2,500 different ones between 1777 and 1957), and billions of copies of the Bible have been sold or given away.[53] The prestige of the Bible reached a peak in the middle decades of the nineteenth century, and Jews were then able to read the first English translation of the Bible done by an American Jew, Isaac Leeser (1853–54).[54] This focus on the Bible as the key sacred text of both Protestantism and Judaism continued into the twentieth century, and an emphasis on the shared nature of this text facilitated the interfaith movement that developed in America after World War I.

Related to Protestant understandings of the Bible was a modernist impulse toward classicism—an interest in the earliest, originating elements of a culture, rather than later accretions or emendations, and in texts commonly understood to be relevant to all times.[55] Just as Protes-

tants preferred the Bible to later works by theologians and church authorities, Jews came to prefer the Bible to the accretions of the Talmud.[56] The
positioning of the Bible as a classic text is clearly expressed in the *Bible
Ethics* manual of 1884, where quotations from ancient and modern non-
Jewish greats such as Horace, Livy, Shakespeare, and Dryden are included
in support of biblical values.

The preference for the Bible was reinforced by the prestige of Hebrew
as a classical language within both European and American universities.
Among Jewish intellectuals, this preference could be expressed as an
appreciation of the "beauty" of biblical Hebrew, as opposed to the "deriv-
ative" languages of Aramaic, rabbinic Hebrew, or Yiddish.[57] And even
while suspicious of the Christian, higher-critical preference for "Israelite"
religion over "Judaism," some Jews also began to refer to themselves as
"Israelites" or "Hebrews" rather than "Jews," and to their religion as "the
Mosaic religion" or "Mosaism" rather than "Judaism," a preference still
embodied in the name of the organization of Reform congregations in
America, founded in 1873: the Union of American Hebrew Congregations.[58]

Two other avenues of linking the Bible to modernity are connected to
the preference for classic or originary texts. The style and content of the
Bible were perceived as consonant with modern preference and mentality; the Bible was "clear and understandable" as opposed to Talmudic legal
discourse, perceived as arcane and convoluted. Another stream of late-
nineteenth-century Jewish life, the Zionist movement, also contributed to
this preference for the "classical" Bible over the traditionally emphasized
Talmud. Zionists found in the Bible an ancient, legitimizing source of Jewish claims on the land, making the Bible a key link between original, pre-
exilic Judaism and the modern nationalist aspirations of Zionism.[59]

But the major means of repositioning the Bible as a text in accord with
modernity was the refashioning of the Bible as the expression of universal
values. Given Reform Judaism's drive to defend and explain Judaism as a
"universal" religion, founded on essential, universally applicable truths,
the Bible was put forward as the fountain of this universalism, while the
Talmud was rejected as the time-bound source of Jewish particularism. A
consistent historicist perspective would find *both* the Talmud and the Bible
to be products of the specific historical time periods during which they
were composed, reflective of the particular values and needs of those circumstances. This fundamental inconsistency of a historicist approach to
the development of Judaism over time (which insisted on the outdated-
ness of the Talmud and the appropriateness of change in the modern
world) with an understanding of the Bible as an eternal fixture/base of
Judaism is clearly visible in Leo Baeck's discussion of "the essence of

Judaism." On the one hand, Baeck stresses that the Bible is Judaism's "secure and immovable foundation, the permanent element amid changing phenomena"; it is "the most authoritative element of Judaism."[60] On the other hand, he stresses that Judaism has developed over time, with this development made possible by the "driving and dynamic forces" within the Bible.[61] The Bible was a kind of open text, so that "each generation heard in the Bible's words its own wishes, hopes, and thoughts." But Baeck then lets slip the emotional connection to the Bible that impels its exemption from a historical approach: "The Bible lay so near to the heart that *it could not be viewed from the historical standpoint.* . . . It speaks to all of us about ourselves."[62]

Two hundred years earlier, it would have been the Talmud that lay most "near to the heart," at least of an educated Jew, and if one had wanted to find "universalist" elements in the Talmud, one undoubtedly could do so. But a potent combination of factors produced in the nineteenth century a commonly accepted understanding of the Bible as universal and thus outside of history: the drive to be understood as a universal religion, the need to maintain connection with at least some long-standing elements of Judaism, and the convenient fact of Christian acceptance of the Bible as holy text. Weak as this last factor might be on its own as a logical argument for Biblical universalism, this fact of a shared text made it possible for Jews to claim universalism for the Bible.

Certainly there were impediments in the text to an interpretation of universalism. Much of the Bible is taken up with an account of the laws and rules that God instructed Moses to tell the Israelites, and the "legalism" of the Talmud had its origin in this biblical focus on law and ceremony. Hundreds of passages assert or reflect a special, exclusive relationship between God and the Israelites. Some commentators also expressed awareness of the disjunctions between biblical and modern morality, and between biblical and scientific accounts of the natural world. These disjunctions, indeed, would take on salience in the 1920s and 1930s, as American Jewish educators plotted the adaptation of the Bible to an audience of children, but from the late eighteenth and into the twentieth century, the dominant impulse was to ignore or de-emphasize these problematic parts of the Bible, and to hold up high those elements that fit the universalist form.

Which element of the Bible was the foundation of universalism? Not surprisingly, it was the same element most prominent in Christian use of the Tanakh: the prophetic writings. Reform-minded Jews all agreed that the prophets provided the essential message of the Bible, which was a fundamentally spiritual and ethical (as opposed to legal) message. Baeck, for example, refers to the prophets as the "spiritual kernel of Judaism," with their "religious legacy" being "the determining characteristic of Judaism."[63] This religious legacy consisted of ethical monotheism, with the prophets serving both as ethical exemplars and as the voices that formulated the religiously grounded ethical commitment that was Israel's special contribution to a developing human understanding.[64]

Implementation

This understanding of the Bible—as *the* central text of Judaism, expressing the universal nature of Judaism as well as its essential principles—was not just promoted among the rabbis and intellectuals who formulated principles of Reform Judaism; it was also put into effect among the lay public. A key element in the implementation of an enhanced familiarity and identification with the Bible was the translation of the Bible into vernacular languages, undertaken as part of a reforming agenda as early as Moses Mendelssohn. Other important translations were those of Samuel Cahen (France, 1831–51), Leopold Zunz (Germany, 1838–39), Isaac Leeser (United States, 1853), the Jewish Publication Society of America (1917), and a joint translation by Martin Buber and Franz Rosenzweig (Germany, 1925–29). All these translations were done with a sense of the urgency of creating not just vernacular translations (in an up-to-date style appealing to a modern audience) but *Jewish* translations, untainted by Christian approaches and interpretations.[65] Commentaries in the vernacular were also written, for example: Samuel Cahen (France, 1838–51), Samuel Luzzatto (Italy, 1858), M. M. Kalisch (England, 1867–72), Julian Morgenstern (United States, 1919), Joseph Hertz (England, 1929–36), Julius Greenstone (United States, 1939), and Umberto Cassuto (Italy, 1949), with other commentaries continuing to be produced through the twentieth century.

Another modern approach to the Bible, less controversial than a historical one, was the "Bible as literature" approach, adopted, for example, by the Jewish Chautauqua Society in its adult Bible home-study courses. Such an approach, which claimed no special sacred stature for the Bible, was in accord with modernity. Yet it still satisfied the desire to keep the text "special"—now as a great work of classic literature like Homer or Shakespeare. A further way of promoting the Bible in modern mode for a wide audience was to include selections in anthologies of Jewish wisdom. Such anthologizing allowed the selection of biblical material deemed illustrative of modern values and the suppression of problematic passages and principles.[66] Even when a historical-critical approach came to be accepted by most Reform rabbis, there was concern about its usefulness in preaching to the laity. Rabbi Krass, commenting on a 1908 address to the Central Conference of American Rabbis by Rabbi Julian Morgenstern in support of higher criticism, cautioned against the use of this approach from the pulpit, even while it was the "foundation" for the rabbis themselves:

> Do not preach Higher Criticism from your pulpits. Higher Criticism should be the subterranean foundation, as it were, inverted, the foundation which you carry in your brain, the foundation on which you will erect your superstructure of righteousness, your fortress of religion. But do not preach Biblical Criticism in an *academic* way to your congregations. They are not prepared for it and are shocked and their feelings wounded, their sensibilities hurt, whenever you tell them those things, which to you have philosophic value.[67]

Once again, the confrontation of modernity with the Bible led in two contradictory directions. The modern principles of reason, universalism, and historicism undermined the status of the Bible and Talmud as sacred, eternal texts. Jews eager to accommodate modernity were accepting of such "demotion" of the Talmud—which had for centuries stood at the center of Jewish education and ritual life—but when it came to the Bible, Jews insisted that these same principles actually provided a basis for bringing the Bible front and center as the exemplar of both Judaism and modernity. The pervasive lack of self-consciousness about the internal contradictions of these positions, and of the vast expanses of biblical material that had to be ignored if such a view was to prevail, is a sign of the troubled nature of this solution of the Bible's relationship to modernity and to Judaism. The trouble only deepens when the audience of concern is children rather than adults. For if adults in the laity might be shocked by a critical approach to the Bible, what of children who might learn it as their first approach?

Educational Change

Education was a critical arena to be engaged by those who wanted to make fundamental change in the nature of Judaism and Jewish life in the modern world. Just as the institutions of heder and yeshivah were crucial to the dissemination and perpetuation of the worldviews, values, and practices of traditional Jewish society, so new educational institutions and new curricula were needed to foster the modernization of Jewish society. Education was one of several arenas of reform, with many of the most controversial elements of change centered in the synagogue and the home rather than the school. But the school was an institution that could provide the key bridge between Jewish culture and the surrounding world. As such, schooling was a center of attention not only for Jews looking to change themselves and future generations but also for governments looking to change Jews.

Once again we begin by looking at central Europe, where the task of remodeling Jewish education was first proposed and undertaken in German-speaking lands, and western Europe, where a similar educational pattern developed. In both central and western Europe, new Jewish schools were created that incorporated a significant body of secular learning while retaining Jewish learning, though in new forms. By the mid- to late-nineteenth century, state schooling—with supplementary religious instruction—was also an option, taken advantage of by varying proportions of Jewish families (high in Germany, lower in France). In eastern Europe, the region from which many of the American educational reformers of the early twentieth century were to come, change was much slower and took different forms, with an array of different types of Jewish schools developing in the late nineteenth and early twentieth centuries. This process of change was abruptly cut off in Russia by the Revolution and its insistent secularism and then later in Poland (and in Germany) by the Nazi takeover and the murder of the Jewish population.

Education in Relationship to Emancipation and Enlightenment

Educational change was inextricably connected to the projects of emancipation and Enlightenment, with the goals of these two projects themselves deeply intertwined. The goal of emancipation was civil equality, which was to carry with it integration into the modern state. The marked, restricted status of Jews would be left behind, as well as their separate, segregated communal existence. Fueling these notions of equality and integration were Enlightenment notions of rationalism and universalism. Education was central to Enlightenment thinkers generally, beginning with John Locke and continuing through Rousseau; it was through education that the irrational divisions of traditional hierarchical society were to be unlearned, replaced by the universal truths binding all humans, to be discovered by the reason that we have in common. The transformative power of education was fundamental to the optimism of Enlightenment thought; through education a new society could be shaped, no longer bound by the inherited strictures of the old regime. Central too was a new notion of childhood as a distinct stage of development, and of the child, whose talents were to be nurtured not by an authoritarian educational regime but by an environment of freedom and play geared to a young person's special psychological needs.[68]

But Enlightenment education had another side as well, as its program of emancipation and universalism supported the state's goal of a unified citizenry. Governments of newly modernizing states saw education as a prime means for shaping a dutiful and loyal citizenry, and education was brought into the arena of state regulation. Jews eager for emancipation and its perceived benefits also supported state-sponsored education as the means through which Jews could learn the information about the surrounding culture necessary to a successful adaptation to that culture. Throughout Europe, then, initiatives to transform the institutions and content of Jewish education came both from the state and from within the Jewish community. This conjunction of interest is vividly demonstrated in two documents of the 1780s: The Edicts of Toleration of Emperor Joseph II of Austria, the first of which was promulgated in January 1782, and Naphtali Herz Wessely's *Divrei Shalom Ve'emet* (Words of Peace and Truth), written in the same year and partly in enthusiastic response to Joseph's Edict.[69]

The policies of Joseph II regarding Jews were motivated by an enlightened despotism. They both promoted state power, through the unification of the heterogeneous groups within his domain, and served the humanitarian goal of removing unreasonable restrictions on subordinated groups.[70] Restrictions that had physically and monetarily marked Jews off from others were abolished, such as the obligations of wearing distinguishing badges or clothing and of paying a body tax when entering a city. The abolition of restrictions was paired with permission to Jews to leave their segregated spheres of education and work. Such an opening up was economically useful to the state at the same time that it provided new opportunities to Jews. Various trades and professions were opened to Jews, including agriculture, though restrictions remained on guild membership and land ownership. Educational institutions were opened from the primary level up through university, excluding only the Faculty of Theology. A stress on abandonment of distinctiveness for the sake of promoting homogeneity is particularly clear in the Edict's insistence on German as the language of schooling and business. Jews were given permission to send their children to state schools, where the language of instruction was German, or to set up Jewish schools equivalent to Christian elementary schools, with German included in the curriculum. Jews were also to use German, not Yiddish or Hebrew, in their bookkeeping, business correspondence, and legal documents.[71] The Austrian government's insistence that equality of rights was necessarily linked to assimilation into German culture is also evident in regulations that made secular education a prerequisite for the privilege of marriage, with a later specification of successful examination on a particular religious textbook, written by a disciple of Moses Mendelssohn and expressing a version of Judaism deemed compatible with loyalty to the state.[72]

The issue of language was critical wherever and whenever the relationship between Jews and their surrounding culture was considered for change. Understandably, since language—even more than dress, taxation, occupation, or ritual practice such as keeping kosher or observing the Sabbath—was the fundamental instrument for establishing either distinction or commonality. Without being able to communicate in words, both spoken and written, no intellectual, cultural, political, or economic commonality was possible. Commonality of language was the fundamental link to be established before any other cultural substance could be transmitted.

As we have seen, some Jews were eager to learn the language of the surrounding culture, to adopt it as the main language of cultural life, and to include it even in religious life. Moses Mendelssohn's translation of the Bible into German, the first volume of which had been published in 1780, was both a signpost of this turn and a continuing influence in the direction of language change. Mendelssohn's intellectual and religious project can help us distinguish between the goals of Jews and of state governments, even while they pursued similar programs. The goal of Jewish cultural and religious leaders was acculturation, while that of the state and of many in the surrounding culture was assimilation. If one imagines a segregated minority culture as an island and the surrounding majority culture as an ocean,[73] assimilation would mean that the island is engulfed by the ocean so that no distinction remains—the island is gone. Acculturation is a more judicious process; the island would acquire some of the ocean's aquatic aspects—perhaps ponds and streams—while still maintaining its discrete, distinctive island identity. In the interface between Jewish culture and European, one of the ultimate forms of assimilation was conversion to Christianity, while one of the typical signs of acculturation was the incorporation into Jewish ritual of Christian religious practices, such as the organ and prayer in unison. But once the boundary between island and ocean is breached, how does one prevent the flow of water everywhere? It is emblematic of the difficulty of maintaining acculturation in the face of assimilatory pressures that even while Mendelssohn himself, in the vanguard of modernizing Judaism, maintained traditional religious practice and a firm sense of Jewish identity, four of his six children converted to Christianity.[74]

The state's strong interest in assimilation—in the elimination of boundaries in service of the goal of greater commonality and hence smoother governing of all elements of the population—was confirmed by developments in France, where the conferring of rights of citizenship in 1791 was conditional on the dissolution of autonomous institutions of Jewish self-governance. While many leaders of the Jewish community viewed this loss of autonomy as unfortunate, the gain of citizenship rights was seen to be well worth the price, and Jewish authors and spokesmen put forward vigorous defenses of the primary allegiance of Jews to the French nation and of the compatibility of Jewish law with duties to the French state and society.[75] The acculturative impulse of these Jews—who aimed to preserve Judaism even while they adapted it to new circumstances—resulted in agendas that overlapped significantly with the assimilative goals of the state. The prime example of Jewish advocacy working hand in hand with an Enlightenment state agenda is Wessely's *Words of Peace and Truth*. Much debated and extremely influential in its day, the treatise lays out in full the implications of emancipation and Enlightenment for a Jewish educational program.[76]

Wessely's enthusiasm for Joseph II is proclaimed on the title page of the first letter, which reads: "Words of peace and truth to the congregation of Israel residing in the lands of the domain of the Great Emperor, who loves mankind and gladdens people, His Majesty, Josephus II."[77] Wessely praises Joseph lavishly for his attentiveness to his Jewish subjects and for his granting of many privileges to them. He sees Joseph as an instrument of God and exhorts Jews to pray for Joseph and to carry out the provisions of his edict. Wessely is boundlessly enthusiastic about Jews learning German thoroughly, from a young age. They need to know the dominant vernacular and to use it with fluency for both sociopolitical and intellectual ends. They need it in order to be able to deal effectively with non-Jews in official settings and the courts. And they need it in order to access the vast resources of secular subjects.

Wessely advocated the continuation of the traditional Jewish study of Bible and Talmud, but the hours spent each day were to be reduced to provide time for studying the large realm of knowledge that had for centuries been ignored by Jews. Wessely distinguished between the study of *Torat Elohim*, the law of God, accessible through the revealed knowledge embedded within ancient Jewish texts, and *Torat ha-adam*, human law, accessible through human effort, and spanning a variety of subjects from good manners and diction (a continuing motif in Wessely's treatise) to history, geography, mathematics, the natural sciences, and ethics. Wessely stressed the importance of human knowledge because of its usefulness to society and to human success therein. He referred to the subjects within this human realm as *derech eretz,* "the way of the land," and asserted that knowledge of such subjects "teaches man how to fare in worldly matters and to enjoy everything under the sun. It brings success to a man's undertakings and helps him to be of assistance to his fellow men in all their actions and daily affairs."[78] Human knowledge was important even for the understanding of divine law itself: for example, Hebrew grammar as well as ancient history had to be understood in order to properly understand the Bible.[79]

While study of the texts of Torat Elohim was to be continued, the mode and content of such study was to change. Wessely advocated a method of instruction that would be adapted to children, in keeping with Enlightenment notions of the distinctiveness of childhood and the importance of considering developmental factors as well as individual difference in children's education. Instructors were to teach with gentleness and love, recreation was to be included in the school day, and corporal punishment was to be abandoned. The texts as well as the methods of instruction needed to change. The Bible should be taught in German, with Mendelssohn's translation highly recommended. Prayers, too, should be translated from Hebrew into German. This was yet another means to teach children the German they would need for easy communication with non-Jews about both Jewish and secular knowledge; they would be learning Hebrew at the same time. While knowledge of the Bible was central, Wessely also promoted the writing of textbooks designed especially for Jewish children and taking into account their level of comprehension. He recommended the production of catechism-like books that would summarize the principles of Judaism, based on Scripture but always in harmony with reason.[80]

Wessely lays out elements for a new education for Jewish children that will be found time and again across Europe wherever the reform of education was undertaken: use of the vernacular of the surrounding Christian culture; introduction of extensive study of secular subjects; the teaching of Judaism through textbooks designed especially for children; and a concern to take into account the emotional and intellectual development of the child in the design of educational structures. The subject of educational reform also figured prominently in the Haskalah journals *Ha-Me'asef* and *Sulamith,* and the ideas were soon put into action in both German-speaking lands and in France. The goals of this education were to make Jews useful in society (a goal consonant with the state's interest in the emancipation of Jews) as well as to teach children a Judaism both faithful to old traditions and in accord with Enlightenment principles of reason and universalism.

New Institutions and Curricula: Central and Western Europe

The first direction taken by educators, influenced both by the Enlightenment and by the state's invitation, was the founding of new Jewish schools, established by Jews for Jews, with a modernized curriculum that included substantial training in secular subjects as well as reduced offerings in Jewish learning. Such schools were established in German cultural areas as well as in France and England from the late eighteenth century and into the nineteenth.[81] These schools were often intended especially for poor children, while wealthier families provided private education (both religious and secular) for their children. Vocational training was commonly part of the new school curriculum, too, following up on the interests of both the state and the Jewish community to train Jews in a broader array of employments.[82] Some of the schools were open to Christian students, a sign of the integrative goal that was important to these new institutions.[83] By the mid-nineteenth century, however, these separate Jewish schools lost much of their enrollment to state schools, which grew throughout western and central Europe with the beginnings of compulsory schooling. Instead of a predominantly secular curriculum within a predominantly Jewish school, children instead received a predominantly secular curriculum within a mixed but predominantly Christian school, with supplementary religious education provided for both Christians and Jews, either within the school itself or in special supplementary schools that were developed in the wake of the move to state schools. In German schools the move to state schooling did not mean an abandonment of religious instruction, since the state held religion to be important to the inculcation of civic virtue.[84] One might have expected a strong secular cast to education in France after the Revolution, and yet religious instruction was included in the state school curriculum there as well.[85] In England the Education Act of 1870 established a national system of nondenominational primary schools, which eventually supplanted the separate modernized Jewish schools founded earlier in the century. By the early twentieth century, Jewish education was supplied mainly in the form of supplementary education, provided either during the school day by those government Board Schools that were predominantly Jewish, or after school hours by a Jewish organization.[86] In both western and central Europe traditional heder education was largely abandoned, even prohibited in some places.[87]

Jewish religious education continued in these new institutional settings, but the purposes and content were fundamentally transformed. Traditional Jewish education, carried out completely separately from the educational institutions of Christians, had served to maintain and advance traditional Jewish society, distinct in language, texts, values, and purposes from the surrounding society. In contrast, a central goal of the new Jewish education, even when found in separate Jewish schools, was to promote the integration of Jews into larger society—to support Jews in the process of becoming useful members of that society as citizens and workers. Acculturation was understood to be fundamental to—even a precondition of—this process of emancipation.

Acculturation involves continuation of previous values and cultural patterns at the same time that new values and patterns are imported and superimposed, in a process of adapting the old to conform with the new. Educators, perceiving a widespread decline of a home- and community-based inculcation of Judaism, were concerned about the difficulty of maintaining continuity in Jewish belief and practice. This concern was to become particularly acute in the twentieth century, but it was felt even in the nineteenth. In premodern society one hadn't needed to think self-consciously about "Jewish education," as Judaism was fully integrated into the closely connected realms of home and community; schooling was needed only for competency and expertise in sacred texts. As characterized by Emanuel Gamoran, who was to become a key shaper of American Jewish education, "The daily life to which the child was subject—the home, the synagogue, the ideals of the community—tended to produce an intense Jewish consciousness within the child."[88] With the loss of a separate—and in many ways autonomous—Jewish community, and with the diminution and even abandonment of home-based Jewish practices, a whole new conception of Jewish or religious education had to be developed. Religion was now one of a number of school subjects, seen as important (especially in Germany) as the basis for one's duties as a human being and a citizen. This new form of education was installed in a new institutional setting—modernized Jewish schools—but had as well a new content and new methods, as recommended early on by Wessely and carried forward by educators throughout the nineteenth century. The first and fundamental step toward acculturation had to be adoption of the vernacular of the country as the language of instruction. In the words of a French Cantonal Committee, writing in 1831 to the director of the Jewish school in Haguenau, where French was being neglected: "Only the language of our country can make commerce with our fellow citizens easy and pleasant."[89] Not just the language but also what was taught underwent change. In consonance with new ideas about the fundamental bases of Judaism, the educational sphere stressed principles of morality rooted in the universalism of human reason rather than in Jewish laws or observances. A new genre developed to teach these principles to children: the religious textbook, often in a form borrowed from Christian education—the catechism.[90] This genre was new in form—a simple, brief textbook rather than original sacred texts—and in content—stressing ethical principles and creedal affirmations rather than the details of narrative and law (as encompassed by the Bible and Talmud) within which principles and beliefs were embedded. The new textbooks often distinguished between "the Moral Law" and "the Ceremonial Law" (that is, observance), with the moral law superior to the ceremonial.[91] This stress on moral education encompassed both a substantive shift away from distinctively Jewish halakhah, as well as a shift away from distinctively Jewish texts. These old, sacred texts were now obsolete. One French catechism author explains the need for new educational texts:

> We have long complained in the French Israelite community concerning the poverty of educational works. The ancient *Tsénah-Ourénah*, delight of our mothers, has had its day; the Talmud is in a mummified state; the Bible itself—that is the Chumash—that our ancestors translated from the age of five, is devalued from day to day. A little catechism, well made, very methodical, but perfectly thin and dry, this is the only religious nourishment that we have to offer to our boys and girls today.[92]

In addition to the straightforward method of the catechisms, another way of putting forward clear moral lessons was to adapt traditional texts to the new goal of moral education. The "mummified" Talmud was dropped from the curriculum rather than adapted. In contrast, the Bible, recast in the form of Bible stories—a genre long popular among Christians and in use in school and home—was construed as the proper source for moral education. In Germany, France, and later in England the biblical narrative was broken up into brief stories told in the vernacular. In this form the Bible was not only more easily consumed (because of brevity and language) but also more amenable to moralization. Moralizing was accomplished in a number of ways: reduction of the biblical text to stories (eliminating the abundant legal and chronicle material); deletion of morally problematic stories; addition of explicit moralization. The earliest such collection of Bible stories for a specifically Jewish audience was Moses Mordechai Büdinger's *Derekh Emunah, Der Weg des Glaubens, oder: Die kleine Bibel* (The Way of Faith, or the Little Bible), published in 1823.[93] The book was very successful, going through thirteen editions between 1823 and 1889, making it a greater market success than its now more famous contemporary, Grimm's *Fairy Tales*.[94] It was also translated into English in 1848 by David Asher, and published by a firm that had been publishing family Bibles for Christian readers for a hundred years. Even more successful was Jakob Auerbach's *Kleine Schul- und Haus-Bibel: Geschichten und erbauliche Lesestücke aus den heiligen Schriften der Israeliten* (Little School- and House-Bible: Stories and Devotional Selections from the Holy Writings of the Israelites), published in Leipzig in 1854; subsequent editions were published annually until at least 1934.[95] These very popular story collections were used in both home and school settings and were directed at an audience of girls as well as boys.[96] The stories were selected, retold, and commented on with an eye to clarifying moral issues.[97] A contemporary French collection by J. Ennery makes moralization a focus of the stories by preceding each with a biblical adage (usually from Proverbs or Psalms) that emphasizes a moral appropriate to the story. The chapter that recounts the sending away of Hagar and Ishmael, for example, is headed by "The Lord is close to the brokenhearted; He delivers those who are crushed in spirit" (Ps. 34:19). The story of the binding of Isaac is headed by a quotation from Joshua: "Do not be discouraged or afraid, for the Eternal is with you wherever you go" (Josh. 1:9).[98]

The authors of these collections were conscious of discordant sensibilities between the time in which the Bible was written—an "epoch of patriarchal simplicity"—and their own age. As Ennery expressed it in his preface, the Bible "includes certain passages that the chaste language of our modern civilization commands us to eliminate. I believe, therefore, that I am filling a gap and rendering a real service to Israelite youth, in publishing this abridged Bible, containing the sacred substance of all the Old Testament, while leaving aside those elements contrary to the usages of our epoch, and responding exclusively to the needs of the time."[99] Ennery was particularly concerned to make the Bible appropriate for the new audience of girls, previously deprived of "the pure and salutary milk of religious instruction." He is confident that they will be able to read this book "without hurting the delicacy of taste proper to their sex."[100]

Thus in children's education we see a repeat of the changed attitude toward the Bible among intellectual and rabbinical leaders in the eighteenth and nineteenth centuries. The Bible should be central (here to religious education), and its ethical messages should be stressed; but also the text is problematic and needs to be refashioned for a modern audience. These concerns are laid out in full in a preface to a late-nineteenth-century English Bible story collection, *The Bible for Home Reading*, written by the prominent British scholar and philanthropist Claude G. Montefiore and published in 1896.[101]

Montefiore's collection was aimed at a somewhat different audience from the ones described so far, and different from the American ones we will examine later. As the title indicates, the book was specifically intended for home use. Montefiore envisioned parents using his volumes for read-ing with their children, although he thought the book, both stories and commentary, could be read by children themselves as well.[102] Montefiore was committed to the centrality of the Bible for Judaism, and his aim was to aid in making the Bible "*the* Book of Home Reading."[103] He was con-cerned that parents, faced with difficulties presented by the Bible, were avoiding it. The difficulties he identified fall into two categories, historical and moral. Modern readers questioned the historical accuracy of the bib-lical text and the traditional interpretation of its authorship and age. They also found ethical and religious teachings in the Bible not in accord with present values (i). He considered the moral/religious issue as the most important, as it is worse to imply something as "morally and religiously true, when it is believed to be morally and religiously false" than to include something that is historically false (iii). It matters little if we let children believe that a man called Elisha made "iron swim" (2 Kings, 6:1–7), but it matters a great deal if we allow children to believe "that God deliberately sent two she-bears out of a wood to destroy forty-two children because they had happened to say a rude word to a passing stranger" (2 Kings 2:23–24) (iii). Montefiore handled such morally problematic sto-ries in two ways: he either omitted the story (as he did with the story of the children killed by bears) or he added an explanation that accounted for the discordant practice or belief and provided interpretive help.

Unlike most other Bible story collections, which are meant for children rather than their parents and are generally quite brief, Montefiore's com-mentary is longer than the biblical text it includes, which is set off in larger type. Some of the omissions are large. Chapters 1–11 of Genesis are relegated to the end of the volume, as "these early chapters [are] too full of grave moral and religious difficulties to form a suitable beginning," and the books of Joshua and Judges are omitted entirely (except for the story of Samson) because these "tales of bloodshed and slaughter [are] unre-deemed by moral teaching" (v).

Morally problematic as the Bible may be, its moral and religious truths had to be passed on to children, as these truths "constitute alike the essence of the Bible and the creed of Judaism" (vii). Montefiore's selec-tion of texts and his commentary are designed to highlight and explain these truths, detached "from any dross or alloy by which they may be sur-rounded, or from the temporary or obsolete setting in which at the first they may have been presented to the world" (vii). Montefiore's approach is a vivid amalgam of the contradictory attitudes we have seen toward the Bible among Jewish intellectual and religious leaders. The Bible is, on the one hand, a universal text, presenting the central truths that all humans must know. It is "the best and most important book in the world," speaking of things that are "common to all, . . . in a grand, simple, and truthful way, which has appealed to men of all races and times" (1, 2). Yet while the Bible appeals to all, Montefiore is insistent on its specifically Jewish origin and audience: "It was written *in* Hebrew *by* Hebrews and primarily *for* Hebrews. Hebrew was the name of a people (as English is the name of a people), who were afterwards called Jews. I who write this book and you who read it are Jews" (4; emphasis in original). He writes with pride that "it is the Jews who have been the great world-teachers about goodness and God" (5), a statement that combines the universality of the message (as these lessons are for all the world) with the particularity of its origin in the Jewish people.

Yet in the midst of proclaiming the universality of the biblical message, he cautions that not all that is in the Bible is equally valuable or true: "No other book has told men so well and so truly of goodness and God as the Bible. All that it says about God and all that it says about goodness is not indeed of equal value and of equal truth: there are degrees of excellence and of worth. But, taken as a whole, no other book has spoken and still speaks of God and goodness as this book, the Bible" (4). The problem of the coexistence of good and less-good things in the Bible is explained by an account of how the Bible was written over a long period of time, by a variety of people, who "in all sorts of ways, were very different not only from ourselves to-day but from most of the races and men who have heard and read it" (1). The long stretch of time results in "differences of style and opinion." Yet this explanation of difference is immediately followed by an assertion of the presence of "important things" on which all parts of the Bible "think the same" (2). Thus Montefiore, like so many other Jewish thinkers, maintains a relativistic, historical approach at the same time as a universalistic assumption of unchanging, absolute values.

These last passages come from the first chapter of the book, "What the Bible Is and Who Wrote It," rather than from the preface, where Montefiore explains more bluntly the need to omit some parts of the Bible entirely because of their moral/religious unsuitability. To guard against young people reading the preface, with its frank discussion of the dilemmas of presenting the Bible to children, the book was produced in such a way that the preface could be detached by following the instructions to cut a yellow string between pages iv and v. In this disposable preface, Montefiore also queries whether he has attempted an impossible combination: to apply both intelligence and emotion, "to combine criticism with reverence, truthfulness with affection" (vii). It is a question that not all modern Jewish commentators on the Bible express directly, but it is one they all embody in their editions and commentaries. The source of the problem is that they want the child to love and revere the text, as well as to understand it.

In sum, the developments in central and western Europe—both political developments external to the Jewish community and religious developments internal to it—led to extensive changes in the nature and delivery of Jewish education, from as early as the late eighteenth century. These changes were influenced by and helped reinforce a new permeability in the boundary between Jews and Christians. The virtual disappearance of the traditional heder in these regions is a sign of the effectiveness of this change. The American educator Emanuel Gamoran later referred to the educational accommodation to external structures and values in Germany as "a process of assimilation that brought disastrous results," "not an adjustment, but a self-effacement."[104]

Eastern Europe

Developments in Jewish education in eastern Europe differed from those in central and western Europe in two fundamental ways: in timing and in content. First of all, change was much slower to come to eastern Europe, largely because the legal status of Jews remained unchanged there until the twentieth century. With neither opportunity nor mandate for an end to a segregated community, education continued for the most part in its centuries-old forms. As early as the mid-nineteenth century, the Russian government promoted a plan for the education of Jewish children in state-sponsored schools, a plan that had the support of some of the Haskalah-influenced Jewish elite. But the vast majority of Russian Jews were skeptical of the plan, correctly suspecting the government's main purpose to be the Christianization of the Jews, and very few Jewish children attended Russian schools at this time.[105] The most dramatic and creative period of change in eastern Europe came in the wake of the profound political changes wrought by the First World War. While the emancipation movement further west had little effect on eastern Europe, there was some penetration of Haskalah ideas and attitudes. But their impact was felt later and produced different results, both within the region (Poland and Russia following different paths) and between eastern and western Europe.[106]

The dominant trend in central and western Europe had been the development of new Jewish schools that centered on secular learning while incorporating Jewish subjects, as well as participation in the school institutions of the surrounding society, with supplementary Jewish education given either within those schools or in separate Jewish institutions. These developments made a great deal of sense in societies in which citizenship was being extended to previously excluded groups, with a resulting emphasis on diminution of difference. In eastern Europe, however, the dominant paradigm was one of ethnic, national, and religious minorities maintaining their distinctive languages and cultures. The Minorities Treaty (the Little Treaty of Versailles) between Poland and the Principal Allied and Associated Powers in 1919 addressed this issue by guaranteeing the rights of all citizens of the Polish Republic irrespective of nationality. All minorities were to be treated equally and were free to establish their own educational and religious institutions, conducted in the minority's own language.[107] Even in the internationalist communist state that developed in Russia after the Revolution of 1914, certain accommodations of "national" minorities were seen as necessary. Not surprisingly, then, separate educational institutions had a stronger role in eastern Europe than further west, and they also took quite different forms from the modern Jewish schools of Germany and France.[108]

A striking array of Jewish educational institutions developed in Poland in the early twentieth century. The following analysis centers on Poland, with comparison to Russia. Each type of institution in Poland was connected with a particular social, political, or religious movement. These fell into four major categories: the Cysho schools, which were secular and Yiddish-speaking, taking their name from the Central Yiddish School Organization; the Tarbut schools, which were secular Hebrew schools; the Yavneh schools, Hebrew language schools of the orthodox religious Zionists; and the Chorev schools, sponsored by Agudat Yisrael, the ultra-orthodox religious anti-Zionists. In contrast to the west, traditional heder education continued with a strong presence, in Poland through the destruction of the Second World War, and in Russia until the suppression of the hadarim in 1921.[109]

Secular Yiddish Schools   The creation of schools entirely secular in orientation and focused on Yiddish culture and language is distinctive of schools in eastern Europe. While Jews in western and central Europe turned to the vernacular of the dominant non-Jewish culture, eastern European Jews turned to the Jewish vernacular of Yiddish, rejecting Hebrew, the sacred language of religious tradition.[110] This choice was influenced by the ideological commitment of these schools to socialism. As Miriam Eisenstein explains, Yiddish was "the language of the masses, the symbol of liberation from the chains of the Jewish tradition, the announcer of a new era in economic, social, and cultural life," whereas Hebrew was considered the language of "the Jewish religious tradition, of the intellectual, and of the political conservative."[111] Yiddish schools began to be established at the turn of the century, and by 1921 so many schools existed that a postwar conference of Yiddish teachers in Warsaw drew four hundred delegates; it was at this conference that Cysho was founded.[112]

This same type of school was promoted in Russia in the same period, with the additional ideological element of a commitment to Jewish nationalism as well as socialism. That is, just as other national minorities struggled for recognition in Russia, some Jews maintained that Jews also constituted a nationality, with Yiddish as their national language, and that secular Yiddish schools should thus be instituted.[113] Such institutions developed clandestinely in Russia during the Tsarist regime, and then rapidly once permitted by a 1914 law of the Duma. These schools continued for a couple of decades after the Revolution under state sponsorship, though stripped of most of their Jewish content;[114] other Yiddish cultural institutions, including higher education and professional schools, also flourished in Russia in the 1920s to early 1930s.[115]

Whether in Poland or Russia, these Yiddish schools were deeply opposed to Jewish religious tradition as well as to Zionism, even while maintaining as a central goal the imparting of the Jewish heritage—in a secularized version—to their students. Religious texts were avoided, but Jewish history, from the biblical period to the present, was taught. A stress on secular education resembled that of the new Jewish educational institutions of central and western Europe, but the Yiddish schools were distinctive in their active antagonism to religion as well as in their commitment to Yiddish rather than to the Christian vernacular. In Germany especially, but also in England, modernized education was paralleled by the development of a modernized religion, in the form of Reform or Liberal Judaism. But such religious reform made few inroads in eastern Europe; there, one was either orthodox or secular, with no middle ground.[116]

Tarbut Schools and the Heder Metukan   The second type of secular school that developed in Poland was Zionist in ideology rather than socialist—the Tarbut school. Here the language and culture of study was Hebrew, not the Hebrew of religion but rather a living, spoken Hebrew. Religion was taught only as a historical subject. The Bible was included in the curriculum, but as a literary and cultural document rather than a religious one. A large place was given to modern Hebrew literature, as well as European literature, and a devotion to Palestine and pioneering efforts was central. The Tarbut schools were related to the somewhat earlier and parallel development in Russia of the *heder metukan*, the "improved heder." Central to the heder metukan was a focus on Hebrew as a spoken, living language, with clear Zionist implications in this language switch. But the heder metukan in other ways maintained strong connections in curriculum and approach to the traditional heder, in part because of religious commitment, in part because of the prohibition in Czarist Russia of any schools with other than Russian as the language of instruction. Hadarim—where the language of instruction was Yiddish—were exempted from this prohibition, and hence the practice of calling the Hebrew-speaking heder metukan a "heder," despite its new concerns with spoken Hebrew, Jewish nationalism, secular subjects (taught in Russian), and a reduced place for or abandonment of learning the Talmud. Traditional hadarim still greatly outnumbered the "improved" hadarim, but the heder metukan continued to exist until the Revolution, after which it was superseded by the government-supported schools, in which Yiddish— considered in the Russian context as the "national" language of the Jews— was the language of instruction rather than Hebrew.[117]

Chorev and Yavneh Schools　In addition to these two types of Jewish secular schools, two new types of religious schools developed in Poland. The Chorev schools, sponsored by the Orthodox and anti-Zionist Agudat Yisrael, were the closest to the traditional hadarim and yeshivot, but like all the self-consciously modern schools, they included a large program of secular subjects in addition to the traditional Jewish curriculum. Another hallmark of modernist concerns was the extension of schooling to girls (provided for in all these movements), in the case of the Orthodox through the foundation of a parallel set of Bais Ya'akov schools for girls.[118] Finally, the Yavneh schools were founded by the Mizrachi Zionist religious party, with a stress on modern Hebrew and the goal of reconstructing Jewish life in Palestine, but with a commitment to the past foundations of religious life rather than a fundamental secularism.[119]

The period from the late nineteenth century through the 1930s in eastern Europe thus saw intense and wide-ranging experimentation in the education of Jewish children. Beyond the four main types of new schools described above, there were also in Poland some bilingual schools (Hebrew-Polish or Hebrew-Yiddish) and vocational schools, and in both Poland and Russia a good number of Jewish children attended government or municipal schools rather than separate Jewish institutions.[120] This experimentation did not, however, have a chance to follow a course of natural development. What would the educational landscape across Europe have looked like, had it not been for the Russian Revolution (which eliminated all but the secular Yiddish schools and narrowly channeled even them) and for the massive disruption and destruction of World War II?

While cut off in eastern Europe, Jewish religious education bloomed in the United States, with new institutions created largely by individuals whose roots were in eastern Europe. Emanuel Gamoran, one of the key shapers of American Jewish educational policy and the person who criticized German Jewish education as "not an adjustment, but a self-effacement," was one such emigré. Gamoran came to the United States from Russia in 1907 at the age of twelve; his own childhood education took place in an eastern European setting. Yet the American education that Gamoran so actively shaped, while much influenced by the experience of eastern Europe, was in other ways shaped by a situation in America parallel to that of central and western Europe, most notably with regard to the more equal legal status of Jews and the availability of public schooling.

3

The American Scene

The period between the wars was a period of intense development of Jewish educational institutions in the United States. In some ways this development paralleled those in Europe, and in other ways it responded to conditions unique to the American situation. Unfettered by wartime occupation and war on the home front, the institutions developed in the interwar period continued during and after World War II. This chapter examines the contextual influences on the educational scene and the educational institutions that developed in this setting.

Given the cultural influences common to both sides of the Atlantic—in particular, the modern ideology of reason, universalism, historicism, and science—there were many strong similarities between the European and American contexts in the timing and content of change. Yet the development of Jewish education in the United States was also heavily shaped by the particularities of the American context, the specific circumstances within which Jewish educators acted. Jewish educators in the United States were knowledgeable about previous and contemporaneous developments in Europe, but in shaping American institutions of Jewish education they were most attentive to their immediate surroundings. In the United States, Jewish education intersected with two educational arenas: state-sponsored public education and Christian religious education. American Jewish educators had extensive connections to educators in both arenas. We will focus first on the intersection between public education and Jewish education, taking into account the ways in which demands for Americaniza-tion and moral education, and the formulation of theories of cultural plu-ralism, shaped the educational landscape within which Jewish education developed. Then we will turn more briefly to Protestant religious educa-tion during this period and the ways in which it served as a model for Jew-ish education.

The infrastructure of Jewish education in America was constructed in response to needs arising from Jewish emigration from eastern Europe, a tidal wave of immigrants that lasted from the 1880s into the 1920s.[1] Insti-tutions for the education of Jewish children had been set up earlier, in particular to serve the German Jews who came to the United States from about 1840 to 1870, with fourteen all-day Jewish schools established in six cities by the early 1860s.[2] But given the relatively small numbers of these earlier immigrants, the institutions were limited in scope and number, and they receded in importance with the increasing availability of free public education in the mid- to late nineteenth century. German Jews embraced public schooling, with the result that by the mid-1870s most Jewish day schools had closed and religious education was provided instead in Sabbath, Sunday, or supplementary afternoon schooling. The relationship between Jewish education and public schooling in the United States resembled, then, that found in western and central Europe.[3]

Public Schooling, Americanization, and Character Education

By the time the wave of immigration from eastern Europe began, Ameri-can public education was well established, free, and compulsory.[4] Rather than being excluded from state schooling, or subject to quotas, as was the case in eastern Europe, Jews, like other immigrants, were expected to go to public schools, and they did so in great numbers. What was the nature of the public education into which Jews entered? Given the profound impact of public education on both the structure and content of Jewish education as it later developed, we need to examine the cultural and social expectations of the institutional environment that transformed Jews from immigrants into Americans.

As in Europe, the school was understood to be a socializing agent, with curriculum and methods oriented toward the inculcation of habits and ideology needed to train up citizens of the state, the sponsoring institu-tion of modern education. This purpose was, if anything, intensified in the American context by the challenge of integrating millions of immi-grants into American culture and society—not just Jews, of course, but many others as well. In Europe, the task had been to bring local outsiders into the common fold. In the United States the challenge was even greater—to Americanize complete foreigners to a totally new cultural, social, and political environment. Irish immigrants, who had come en masse in the mid-nineteenth century, had been judged problematic and were scorned for their poverty and their Catholicism. The new immigrants of the late nineteenth century, overwhelmingly from southern and eastern Europe, were seen as distinctly inferior to Americans of northern European origin. In the early twentieth century the general public and educators were agreed that it was the public school's task to remedy the danger presented by these aliens by making them into Americans, inculcating them with Anglo-Saxon values and attributes. Ellwood Cubberley, a major figure in American education, said it clearly in 1909:

> These southern and eastern Europeans are of a very different type from the north European who preceded them. Illiterate, docile, lacking in self-reliance and initiative, and not possessing the Anglo-Teutonic conceptions of law, order, and government, their coming has served to dilute tremendously our national stock, and to corrupt our civic life. . . . Our task is to break up their groups or settlements, to assimilate and amalgamate these people as part of our American race, and to implant in their children, so far as can be done, the Anglo-Saxon conception of righteousness, law and order and popular government, and to awaken in them reverence for our democratic institutions and for those things in our national life which we as a people hold to be of abiding worth.[5]

Cubberley notes that the school has been transformed from a means of imparting the rudiments of learning to "one of the most important institutions of democracy," with its task being to offer "some practicable solution" to the situation created by this new population.[6]

This explicitly assimilative goal of "amalgamating" immigrants into the dominant culture was captured by the notion of America as a "melting pot," an image—popularized by a play by Israel Zangwill with that title—that soon became the dominant motif of popular social ideology. Such amalgamation could not be entrusted to parental upbringing, since the parents came from and were imbued with exactly the values and habits from which the children were to be turned. State intervention was necessary, and schools and curricula were organized to provide the "citizenship education" (also called "Americanization") that would educate the children of immigrants away from their foreign ways and toward "Anglo-Saxon" standards.[7] The task was huge. Between 1891 and 1920, over 11½ million immigrants from eastern and southern Europe entered this country, and by 1909, more than half (57.8 percent) of the students in the schools of thirty-seven of the country's largest cities were immigrants or children of immigrants.[8]

The anti-immigrant, nativist sentiment was given political sustenance in 1907, when Congress created a Federal Immigration Commission (the Dillingham Commission) to investigate the problems of the recent immigration. The commission report, published in 1911, documented the "inferiority" of these immigrants, fueling the educational campaign of Americanization and contributing to the eventual restrictions on immigration put into effect in the Immigration Acts of 1921 and 1924.[9] Such nativist fervor intensified during World War I, leading to an "Americanization Crusade." Even before the United States entered the war, anti-German fervor led to a new, intense hostility toward a group of immigrants— German Americans—who had long been assimilated and widely accepted. This hostility, joined with the general xenophobia and intense patriotism of wartime, lessened what tolerance there may have been for different values and cultures and fed into growing antipathy toward those who became referred to as "hyphenated Americans." Citizenship for this "large body of citizens and permanent residents who wear a hyphen" was, in the words of Gregory Mason, a commentator on the public schools of Rochester, "as dangerous to a republic as a cancer to the human body." The cure was education, "the knife to use in cutting out the hyphen."[10] Theodore Roosevelt coined the wartime motto of "America for Americans," and the war years also produced the expression "100 percent Americans," to contrast with the fractionalized identity of "hyphenate" Americans.

Socialization of new Americans had been a goal of nineteenth-century educators as well, but the means used in the previous century had been the rather simple ones of learning English and civics. For the larger, more daunting challenge of the recent immigrants, more thoroughgoing efforts were needed, aimed at encouraging disdain for the immigrant heritage while inculcating middle-class American values. The educational programs that developed to carry out this purpose were programs in "character education," also called character building, ethical instruction, or moral education, the last being the oldest of the terms. Moral education had been a central part of the educational mission from the early years of American education, aiming toward a general social conformity of values and behavior. But the challenges of the early twentieth century brought consideration of such education to a feverish pitch, and discussion of character education became pervasive in educational literature through the first decades of the century.[11]

At the same time, the extent to which "moral education" overlapped with sectarian religious education became a contested issue. From the early common schools of the 1830s, public education had been permeated by Protestant religious practices, including Bible reading, prayers, and other devotional exercises.[12] Such religious practice was considered inseparable from the essentially moral goals of education, but there now developed disagreement as to whether such practices might inappropriately favor a particular religious sect.[13] In the mid- to late nineteenth century the Protestant character of school activities was challenged by Catholic, and then Jewish, immigrants. Despite this challenge to sectarianism in the classroom, the overall Protestant character of the schools remained clear. Bible reading and Protestant prayers were fixed parts of the school day, even while a Bible-based curriculum was left to Sunday schools. Protestant groups worked to insure that at a minimum the Bible would be read daily in all classrooms, insisting on the King James Bible as the "obvious" choice. But Catholics and Jews objected to the dominant mode of Bible reading in the schools. Both groups opposed the sole use of Protestant translations, knowing the differences in interpretations embedded in Protestant, Catholic, and Jewish versions. Catholics wanted to be able to read the Catholic (Douay) version rather than the King James, and they objected to reading the Bible on its own, without the accompaniment of authorized (Catholic) interpretation. Jews, on the other hand, found the exclusion of commentary preferable to Christian commentary, and did not have a strong objection to the King James version, but they wanted readings to be selected from the Old Testament only, not the New.[14] These critiques were rejected vehemently and consistently. Protestants insisted that Bible reading was a nonsectarian means of ethical instruction, and they saw stories from the Bible as preeminent vehicles for needed ethical instruction.[15] Ella Lyman Cabot, the author of a popular guide to moral education, referred to Bible stories as "the great inheritance of our race" and insisted that they are "never sectarian," but rather "pervaded by a perennial humanity, a direct simplicity that makes them appeal to the young of every century."[16] Catholics, of course, understood the Bible differently, and the Catholic challenge to religious sectarianism in public schools, joined later by concerns of Jews and educational reformers, eventually led to the displacement of the Bible as the most commonly read school text, and also, further down the road, to the diminution of any explicitly religious presence in the schools. But the severely hostile response to the Catholic challenge—even to the extent of riots—and the commitment of Catholics to religious education integrated with secular education, led to the widespread founding of parochial schools, which served a large percentage of the Catholic population through the nineteenth and twentieth centuries.[17]

American Jews took a different path, largely accommodating themselves to the public educational system rather than abandoning it for parochial schooling. But while Jewish children continued to stream into the public school system, Jewish leaders kept up a persistent critique of the presence of religion in the public schools. In 1906, the Central Conference of American Rabbis (CCAR) established a standing committee on church and state, with one of its foci of activity being the issue of religion in public schools.[18]

Jews, like Catholics, readily saw through the claim of biblical similitude, which held that the Bible was common to Protestants, Catholics, and Jews (other religions and possible atheist objections were not even in the picture). If the Bible was not to be the vehicle of moral education in the schools, what would? Some Jews argued that ethical instruction should be excluded from the public schools entirely and reserved instead for institutions of explicitly religious education. A CCAR committee, mandated to study ethical instruction in the public schools, argued that since ethical instruction should be religious in nature, it did not belong in public schools, whose secular character "should be maintained sacred and inviolable."[19] While logical, this position did not win over the assembly. In the recorded discussion, other rabbis expressed their concern that it was not so obvious that ethical instruction could only be given with religious sanction, and in any case, it would not be good for the rabbinical group to cut itself off from the many people who thought a nonsectarian ethics possible. These rabbis felt they needed to balance their fears of Christianization against accusations of godlessness. And as Rabbi Schanfarber noted in his talk to the assembly, "Both Jews and Christian, agnostic and atheist agree that in its ultimate analysis the purpose of the public school is the formation of character and the creation of good citizenship."[20]

The place of religion in public schooling was the subject of conversation among Protestant educators as well as Catholic and Jewish. With the beginnings of professionalization among religious educators, and with the recognition of the vastly increased agenda of public education, these Protestant educators, too, had a concern that religious education was important, that it should be taught by trained religious educators, and that the best location for such education was in religious institutions, not in public schools (but in cooperation with them).[21] This position was detailed in a Declaration of Principles adopted by the Religious Education Association in 1916.[22]

Given this wide agreement on the centrality of moral instruction in the education of children, Jewish leaders developed positions regarding its place in both public and religious education. In the case of public schooling, they fought against the presence of religion in the schools, particularly as manifested in Bible reading and school prayer. They also contributed to the quest for the most effective content and methods of a *secular* moral education, increasingly referred to as character education: a curriculum that was not dependent on the Bible, prayer, or other explicitly religious—and in effect Christian—practices. Increasingly, Jewish voices came to agree that explicitly religious (sectarian) instruction was to be divorced from public schooling, even while disagreeing on what this category included. "Religious" education was to be segregated in separate institutions in a complementary role to the public school, with the latter the central educational provider for children. Indeed, the public school curriculum expanded to cover all other aspects of students' lives, no longer confined to academic preparation but also including vocational guidance, health and hygiene, manners, games, and anything else considered part of life, including a truly nonsectarian character education.[23] "Religion" was compartmentalized, set off from life, and was to be taught in Sunday schools or other such settings. The irony is, however, that character education, developed as a secularized moral instruction for public schools, was then carried over into the religious school setting as well, where Jewish educators, as well as Christian, labored to reshape religious instruction to the goals of character education. We will see later the deep impact of this effort on the retelling of Bible stories for children.

What form did character education take in public schools? Bible reading—sanctioned as "nonsectarian" despite Catholic and Jewish objections—continued in the schools for decades, but the demands for a secularized ethical instruction brought about a widened expanse of moral education, well beyond the confines of the Bible.[24] Given the prominent task of bringing social and cultural conformity to the heterogeneous immigrant groups of the period, it's not surprising that this sort of direct instruction in middle-class "Anglo-Saxon" mores—instruction that necessarily came from outside the home environment—thrived above and beyond the reading of the Bible. New books of ethical instruction for use in schools proliferated. They took two forms. First were those organized by a list of virtues to be inculcated. Common themes in these lists were honesty, responsibility, obedience, gratitude, courtesy, fair play, clean living, economy, patriotism, and self-control, though instructions could extend to something as specific as the correct way to turn pages in a book.[25] These texts served well for the "direct" method of instruction, promoted by some authors and educators, which emphasized explicit preaching and instruction, with slogans and direct moral pronouncements. C. C. Everett's discussion of "Obedience," for example, in his *Ethics for Young People*, includes the following direct advice: "The boy sometimes feels that it is childish to obey the rules of the home or the school. He feels that to set them at defiance is manly. On the contrary, *it is obedience that is manly and disobedience that is childish.*"[26] The other main genre of ethical writing for children took the form of story collections, where each story, usually centered on a particular individual, often famous, could lead to a discussion of a moral issue. These books tended to be more in keeping with the "indirect" method, advocated by some educators as a more Deweyian method of learning by doing.[27] This was ethical storytelling, where the moral message might be stated directly or left implicit. Some books combined the "character trait" and "storytelling" approaches, for example, Ella Lyman Cabot's *Ethics for Children*.[28] Cabot was a proponent of the indirect method, insisting that explicit moral statements were a wasted effort. While her book is organized by moral trait, she provides several stories to be used in teaching each trait; through discussion of the stories the appropriate virtues could be inculcated.[29] She considers "classic stories" to be the best, including a carefully selected group of Bible stories, but her own book contains a wide range of stories—mythic, historical, and contemporary—as well as poems and epigrammatic sentences to memorize and questions to consider. Biography has a special place in her scheme. Graphic or heroic incidents from particular lives are used as exemplars of the values being taught. The teacher is advised to prepare thoroughly and to know what lesson is to be brought out, and she suggests that dramatization may sometimes be used to make the moral impression of the stories more permanent.[30]

Sometimes the connections between "character education" and "Americanization" are obvious in these texts, such as in the collections that focus on American heroes (e.g., Edward Eggleston's *Stories of Great Americans for Little Americans*)[31] or in the attention to patriotic themes in the books of ethical instruction. But more important is the underlying connection between the two: their common goal of homogenizing the diversity of immigrant groups and "amalgamating" them into a uniform set of values, attitudes, and behaviors that were seen to be characteristic of the superior "Anglo-Saxon" culture of America. What one might think of today as distinctively "American values"—for example, liberty and equality—were not a significant part of this education, which instead focused on bourgeois values like cleanliness, obedience, courtesy, and self-reliance. As the historian Stephan Brumberg summarizes in speaking of the curriculum of the New York City public schools: "Running through subjects as disparate as reading, geography, history, civics, physical training/hygiene, and drawing/constructive work, is a concern for inculcating students with the proper moral and ethical values and shaping their outward behaviors to conform to this inner vision. The injunction to be clean, orderly, responsible, and polite would appear to be the implied creed of the New York City public schools."[32] The authority of the school was to take precedence over the authority of immigrant parents, whose "values, emotional attachments, loyalties, and 'tastes' [had been formed] in an alien environment."[33] Schooling was to be the agent of thoroughgoing assimilation, with no accommodations made to immigrant cultures. Racist anti-immigrant sentiment by educators (Cubberley and Mason, for example) was explicit; the desired end result, along with eliminating immigrant culture, was to enhance social efficiency and to reinforce existing social hierarchy, with immigrants on the bottom.[34]

Why then, one wonders, did Jewish immigrants so wholeheartedly embrace public schooling for their children rather than found parochial schools as Catholics had done? Why did Jews opt into an educational system that sought to obliterate distinctive cultural traditions and to amalgamate all children into the dominant culture? What appeal or benefits did public schooling have that could overcome the weight of such anti-immigrant attitudes as well as the Christian underlay of the schools? The reasons were both circumstantial and purposeful.[35]

When hundreds of thousands of Jews started arriving annually in the last two decades of the nineteenth century, there was no community organization, structure, or financing in place that could have led to a rapid development of schools dedicated to the education of Jewish children. This circumstance was due not only to the small size of the preexisting Jewish community, but also to the fact that the great majority of German Jews had been sending their own children to public schools since the 1850s, causing the demise of the all-day Jewish schools that had been established earlier in the century.[36] Emanuel Gamoran, writing for a general audience of religious educators about the development of Jewish education, asks them "to appreciate how difficult it was for American Jewry to provide for the education of its young," given "the fact that Jewish immigration to this country was concentrated . . . within the thirty-five years from 1880 to 1915, and that hundreds of thousands of human beings had to make a completely new adjustment in their economic and social life."[37] By the time a new infrastructure for the Jewish community had developed in the 1920s and 1930s, the pattern of public school attendance was well established, and Jewish educators, as we shall see, concentrated on the institutionalization of supplementary Jewish education.

But it was not just the absence of Jewish schools or the means to create them that pushed immigrant Jews into public schools. Such schooling also fit the purposes of the German Jewish population, which by this time was highly assimilated into American culture. Many German Jews were embarrassed by what they considered to be the "backwardness" of the newly arriving Jews; they wanted them to be Americanized quickly, and they saw the public school as the cornerstone of this transformation.[38] In the words of Julia Richman, an American-born Jew of German background who became assistant superintendent of schools on the Lower East Side as well as a leader in the Jewish community: "In this country we are not Jews first and Americans afterwards; we are American Jews, imbibing loyalty to our country in our American schools and under American influences, and drawing our Jewish sentiment from family tradition and congregational life. An exclusively Jewish training imparted by foreign-born Jews could never have made the children of these and other foreign Jews real Americans."[39] Schooling that was exclusively Jewish would prevent or retard this goal of becoming "real Americans." A similar plea for support of public schools was made by Richman's contemporary Rabbi Edward Calisch, who appealed to those who might be tempted to turn to private schools to instead "let [our children] suck knowledge from the broad bosom of the goddess of our common country."[40] The choice of public schooling was also made easy in that public schools were already in place and were open to these new pupils, with none of the legal exclusions or quota systems familiar to Jews from eastern Europe.

But eastern European Jews were not merely passive subjects, steered to public schools by condescending "Anglo-Saxon" Americans and German Jews. Public schooling fit their purposes as well, as is evident from the words of Abram Simon, writing in 1911 for a general audience of religious educators:

> There is no greater friend of the American public school system than the Jew. There is none more eager to grasp its opportunities and none more grateful for its privileges. . . . The enthusiasm of the American Jew for public education is woven of three threads. First, i[n] the fact that it *is* education, of which he has been a loyal devotee for thirty odd centuries; second, in the fact that it is free and public, preparing for training in the rights and responsibilities of citizenship; and third, in the fact that it is not sectarian in principle, method and character. Believing thoroughly in the wisdom of the fathers of the country in placing the public schools completely under the control of the State, the Jew contends that the school as a miniature republic is signally prepared to perform the great task of Americanization.[41]

Simon captures the enthusiasm for an educational system that was free, open to all, nonsectarian (at least in principle), and run by the government rather than by religious bodies. This was all a happy contrast with what had been known in the old country. Even though the notion of a fundamental remaking of immigrant aliens into "Americans" was a chauvinistic and ethnocentric stance, it was also, in its time, a liberal stance, signaling a willingness to accept "aliens" into the fold of American life. So too, the commitment to "training in the rights and responsibilities of citizenship" compared favorably with the restrictions on citizenship rights for Jews in eastern European states. Jews eagerly said yes to what was seen as an invitation into the mainstream of American society, an invitation backed up by the institutional structure of the school system. The Jewish educator Samson Benderly similarly expressed the importance of parallel rather than parochial schools for taking advantage of the social freedom available in America: "What we want in this country is not Jews who can successfully keep up their Jewishness in a few large ghettos, but men and women who have grown up in freedom and can assert themselves wherever they are. A parochial system of education among the Jews would be fatal to such hopes."[42] Jewish participation in public schooling was perhaps necessitated by the fact that schooling was compulsory, no viable alternative was in place, and no infrastructure was available to create it, but participation was, in general, very enthusiastic. This was something Jews wanted for themselves, and it was, happily, available to them.

Simon also attributes Jewish participation to the "thirty odd centuries" of Jewish devotion to education. One could challenge his logic here, since the centuries-long devotion that he refers to was a devotion to a thoroughly *religious* education, one centered almost exclusively on Jewish texts, taught by Jewish teachers. Public, secular schooling was a fundamental departure from this traditional education, not a continuation of it. And yet the transmutation of value seems, indeed, to have occurred. Given the other forces attracting Jews to public schooling, parents transferred their delight in the educational achievement of their children from the heder and yeshivah to the public school and university. A Jew successful in the arena of traditional Jewish education had in the past received much honor from family and community, but with the absence of a cohesive, self-contained and reproducing Jewish community in America, a traditional education resulted in few extrinsic rewards. In contrast, success in public schooling in America could lead to such rewards. Despite the intention of those in charge of public education to reinforce existing social hierarchies, common education in fact contributed to upward mobility and enhanced status for Jews and other immigrant groups. Education facilitated entry into the intellectual, economic, and even social spheres of the dominant culture.

Such entry was, indeed, desired. In Europe, Jews had been confronted with a choice between entry into the dominant culture (to the extent such was allowed) and isolation within the space, language, and structures of traditional Jewish culture. There were even some ways of adopting new ideas and associations while remaining largely within the Jewish community. But in America the situation was different. Jews found themselves in a totally new environment. The old ways lay across the ocean, not just across town. One's parents, too, might be thousands of miles away, but even if close by, their relative inexperience and unease in the new environment curtailed their authority. To thrive in this new place, there was a sense that one needed to learn all one could about this new world with its new realities, rather than try to hang on to or recreate the old world in the new. Concentrating on a traditional Jewish education would have had little payoff in America. And to maintain traditional languages, culture, and practices would, in this new land, require a conscious transplantation and transmission, rather than the more straightforward maintenance that was possible—even when challenged—in Europe. In this context, cultural transformation was actually easier to achieve than cultural continuity. While there were certainly some who maintained traditional Jewish ways and kept their children within the circle as well, the dominant response of immigrant Jews to the new environment was to find entry as quickly as possible. It was clear that to succeed in American society one needed to mix with others, and public school was a prime arena within which that mixing occurred, especially when students advanced to high school, going beyond the neighborhood elementary schools which, ironically, were composed almost entirely of other immigrant children. By World War I, the integration of Jewish children into the public school system was fully in effect, with nearly all of the 175,000 elementary school–aged Jewish children in New York City attending public schools. Jewish religious instruction was largely limited to supplementary education, with less than a quarter of Jewish children receiving even that.[43]

The desire to be "real Americans" and the diverse means and extent of achieving that desire are the subject of a vast body of scholarship on American Jewry; it can be seen as a central motif of Jewish life in the United States. What is most significant for us here is that while the vision of Americanization held by promoters of public schooling for immigrants was fundamentally an assimilationist one, advocating the erasure of immigrant cultures, Jewish leaders and educators did not passively accept such a vision. They shaped a different understanding of Americanization, an acculturationist one. This vision held that Jewish culture and values could be maintained at the same time that adaptations were made to American life.[44] These Jews had a profoundly optimistic view of the inherent compatibility of Judaism with American ideals and values—that one could be American without losing one's Jewishness.[45] Spurred by this perceived conjunction of Americanism and Jewish identity, Jews were prominent in the development of a theory of democracy and American identity that allowed for the maintenance of cultural diversity rather than its erasure. Prominently voiced during the interwar years but not politically dominant

until much more recently, the development of an ideology of cultural pluralism reinforced Jewish participation in the public school system as well
as influencing the content and direction of Jewish education itself.

Cultural Pluralism

While melting pot ideology remained dominant through the interwar
period, a pluralist Americanism, a position that endorsed the nurturing of
a variety of "hyphenated" cultures, competed with it. Both ideologies had
an impact on the shaping of Jewish education. The institutional structure
of Jewish education in America was especially influenced by the demands
of assimilation, while the content of the education was shaped not only by
assimilative forces but also by an acculturative commitment to maintaining a core of Jewish identity.

Theories of cultural pluralism developed in the same nativist, fervently
democratic, World War I context as did the assimilationist drive for Americanization. The war was fought, Americans were told, to "make the world
safe for democracy," yet the war also heightened an uneasiness about the
security of democracy at home. Immigration, which had previously been
welcomed as a boon to the economy, was now, in the context of war, seen
as a eugenic menace. The highly restrictive Immigration Act of 1924
marked the victory of this viewpoint. Yet in that same year Horace Kallen
coined a term that identifies a diverse population as a *strength* of democratic society—"cultural pluralism."[46]

Kallen was an immigrant Jew who became a prominent figure in the
American intellectual scene. Kallen's theory of cultural pluralism has its
roots in John Dewey's notion of democracy. He and Kallen were colleagues as teachers of philosophy in New York,[47] and Dewey, in his position at Teachers College (Columbia University) was the teacher of the
major figures in Jewish education, all of whom undertook training there.
Dewey's work on democracy and on the role of education in democracy, is
visible throughout the writings of Jewish intellectuals and educators of the
whole interwar period, when he was a dominant figure on the American
intellectual scene generally. Dewey thus had direct influence on Jewish
education as well as the indirect influence he exerted as the leading intellectual of his time.[48] Immigration, public schooling, and the Great War
supplied the social and political contexts within which Jewish education
developed in America; Dewey's vision of democracy established the intellectual context.

Dewey had an astonishingly long career; he was active in intellectual
and political debates from the 1890s until his death in 1952.[49] His think-

ing on democracy and its relationship to education, the aspect of his work most important to us here, was in place before World War I. Dewey was an advocate of democracy not simply as a political structure, but as a way of life. Political forms were just one means through which this way of life could be promoted. Dewey wanted to see a democratic character—a common democratic culture—suffusing the institutions of society, including educational institutions. Central to this democratic culture were the familiar ideals of liberty, equality, and fraternity, which, according to Dewey, could only be achieved when all individuals were free to participate in all aspects of political, social, and cultural life. The goal of democratic life was to provide the conditions for the self-realization of all individuals in a society, making equality of opportunity central to his vision. A democratic community was thus the culmination of the contributions of diverse individuals, who through association with each other learned from their diverse experience, but together made a harmonious unity. "Community" and "individuality" were both key terms to Dewey, and they were values that reinforced each other rather than stood in conflict.

Just as the diverse individuals within a society should be given the opportunity to develop in a variety of ways, so too should the diversity of cultures within American democracy be developed. Dewey wrote in 1917, in the midst of xenophobic war fever, that "the theory of the Melting Pot always gave me rather a pang. To maintain that all the constituent elements, geographical, racial and cultural in the United States should be put in the same pot and turned into a uniform and unchanging product is distasteful."[50] Dewey saw unity as a social goal, but not uniformity. No one cultural component of a society (i.e., the "Anglo-Saxon") should be marked out as providing the pattern to which other components should conform: "Our unity cannot be a homogeneous thing like that of the separate states of Europe from which our population is drawn; it must be a unity created by drawing out and composing into a harmonious whole the best, the most characteristic which each contributing race and people has to offer."[51]

From his earliest work, Dewey saw the school as the central locus in which democracy was to be learned. Schools should be teaching the special national character of America, which was its internationalism. Schools should "enlighten all as to the great past contributions of every strain in our composite make-up," to demonstrate that "hyphenism" is not something that separates but that connects.[52] The task was to be accomplished by making education democratic, utilizing a method of teaching that would build on the diverse experiences of individual students. The school was itself to be organized as a democratic community.[53]

Dewey's ideal of democracy was closely linked to the character of science, which had enormous prestige in intellectual circles and the larger culture at this time. For Dewey and other liberal thinkers, certain habits of mind linked democracy and science: free inquiry, free discussion, free expression, and toleration of diverse opinion. A scientific approach to inquiry was essential to effective freedom, and hence to democratic society; science and democracy were both opposed to the uncritical, passive acceptance of any "higher authority." This vision was a fundamentally secular one, complete with ideals and the capacity for moral judgment.[54] Dewey's scientific naturalism supported a relativist approach to truth that was in opposition to an absolutist stance also current in this period; his relativism provided an intellectual link to the social diversity that he saw as essential to the make-up of community.

In this conflict between relativists and absolutists, between scientific naturalists advancing the cause of objectivity and philosophical rationalists who maintained that human reason could discover immutable metaphysical principles, Jewish intellectuals lined up on the side of science, empiricism, and relativism.[55] Combining their own experience as immigrants with the theoretical base of Dewey, Jews like Horace Kallen and Isaac Berkson formulated a social model of cultural pluralism that was then institutionalized in Jewish schools and community centers.

Horace Kallen was born in Germany in 1882 and was brought to Boston five years later. His father, a rabbi, continued his son's traditional Jewish schooling as long as he could keep him from truant officers. By the time Kallen went to Harvard, however, he was disaffected by the religious practices of his family and had distanced himself from Judaism. At Harvard he came to a new understanding of Judaism, embracing Jewish "culture" rather than "religion," and in 1906, when a graduate student there, he was one of the founders of the Menorah Society.[56] Little of Kallen's subsequent writings in philosophy and social theory centered on Jews, but his own experience and his thinking about the role of Jews in America is clear in his writing on issues of democracy, freedom, and, in the term he coined, "cultural pluralism"; he was also a participant in various organizations connected to Jewish education.[57]

Kallen's basic notion of the interrelationship of diverse groups in American society was laid out in a 1915 essay in the *Nation*, "Democracy Versus the Melting Pot," written in response to a vehemently nativist book by the University of Wisconsin sociologist Edward A. Ross, *The Old World in the New*.[58] While he doesn't use the term "cultural pluralism" in this essay, Kallen clearly opposes a notion of Americanization that would have all people fuse into "beings similar in background, tradition, outlook, and spirit to the descendants of the British colonists, the Anglo-Saxon stock."[59] Kallen stresses the vitality of the immigrant cultures that have been sustained in the United States: the Irish, Germans, Scandinavians, and Jews.[60] He maintains, as had Ross, that equality is a key value in American culture, but he criticizes Ross's view of equality as necessitating sameness, noting that it is *difference,* not inequality, that troubles Ross "and so many other Anglo-Saxon Americans."[61] Difference, or diversity, was to Kallen (as to Dewey) the heart of American democracy. Kallen invokes the rich potential of unity-in-diversity through two musical metaphors, a chorus and an orchestra. He argues against singing in unison—all sounding the same notes, the same theme—in favor of singing in harmony, where one theme may perhaps be dominant but is just one among many.[62] Echoing Dewey, Kallen sees as central to democracy the realization of selfhood for individuals in all their variety. But these individuals, including the diverse palette of immigrants, "cannot change their grandfathers." Self-realization has, thus, an "ancestral endowment" that must be respected and built upon. He concludes the essay with the analogy of an orchestra, a model of how such diversity can be consolidated into a unified society.

> As in an orchestra, every type of instrument has its specific timbre and tonality, founded in its substance and form, as every type has its appropriate theme and melody in the whole symphony, so in society each ethnic group is the natural instrument, its spirit and culture are its theme and melody, and the harmony and dissonances and discords of them all make the symphony of civilization, with this difference: a musical symphony is written before it is played; in the symphony of civilization the playing is the writing, so that there is nothing so fixed and inevitable about its progressions as in music, so that within the limits set by nature they may vary at will, and the range and variety of the harmonies may become wider and richer and more beautiful.[63]

Isaac Berkson, writing a few years later, draws directly on Kallen in his book *Theories of Americanization* (1920), further developing a "community" theory of Americanization.[64] Berkson is important as someone not only steeped in the arguments over democratic culture but also deeply involved in the formation of Jewish educational institutions, not just on the edges, like Kallen. In this book, we can see his hope that a theory of cultural pluralism, and its embodiment in educational institutions, could resolve the contradictory desires of American Jews: to become Americans while also remaining Jews.

For Berkson, like Dewey and Kallen, the "quintessence of democracy" is "a pluralistic conception of value, truth, [and] reality."[65] This pluralism extends to the level of the individual, with respect for the person—for the personality—of the individual being a "supreme belief," the "first and fundamental criterion of democracy."[66] Berkson sees the goal of democratic culture, then, to be the maintenance of diverse cultural identities as embodied in individuals. Unlike Kallen, who suggests that these diverse cultures are inherited and so fairly easily transmitted ("one cannot change one's grandfather"), Berkson stresses that culture is acquired through an educational process, in which schooling is central.

While the goal of Berkson's book is to make a general case about Americanization, the main test case is that of the Jews. Berkson insists on characterizing Jews as a "cultural" group—arguing against an identity by race, ethnicity, or religion.[67] As in Kallen's work, Jews are thus on an equal plane with other immigrant groups, and the possible significance of religious identity is minimized.[68]

Berkson goes beyond theory to discuss how it would be possible to maintain diverse cultures within a unified American society. Here he provides a link between theories of cultural pluralism and Jewish education, as his program entails an array of schools supplementary to the public school. Berkson insists that the mission of the Jewish supplementary school is a double one: to retain and cultivate Jewish consciousness while also helping Jews adjust to the American environment. His book concludes with a detailed description of the Central Jewish Institute, founded to accomplish these tasks, and of which he served as first director beginning in 1917. The CJI was a community institution, not connected with a particular synagogue or religious faction. But for all Berkson's emphasis on the small role of religion in Jewish culture, the central activity of the Institute was its extensive offering of supplementary classes covering the same topics that one would see in contemporary synagogue and Talmud Torah education: prayer book, Hebrew, Bible, history, customs and ceremonies, singing. Even here at the CJI the Jewish education provided was essentially a religious education.[69]

Berkson's work embodies conflicts that run through Jewish education and that influenced the development of new approaches to studying the Bible within Jewish schools. The conflicting forces are, on the one hand, the national call for assimilation through Americanization, preached in all vehicles of popular culture, and most particularly in and through the public schools; and, on the other hand, the desire on the part of many immigrant groups, including Jews, to maintain a distinctive sense of group identity, at the same time that they find ways of being at home in America. The theory of cultural pluralism, in whose development Jews played a prominent role, claimed to reconcile these forces by saying that true democracy—which is of course what one would want to have in America—is by nature a system that incorporates many diverse groups, uniting them even while it respects and fosters their differences. This is a theory of *cultural* pluralism, with "cultural" or "ethnic" emphasized and religious identity left to the side. The theoretical emphasis on culture rather than religion came from various sources: the increasing prevalence of a secularist vision generally, a desire to create intellectual terms that would reduce or avoid Christian bias or dominance, and a desire on the part of Jewish theorists to identify Jews as one among a variety of ethnic groups in America, along with Poles, Germans, Irish, and even "Anglo-Saxons," rather than to be cast as a religious minority, which would land Jews in the same category as Catholics, a group that suffered greatly from prejudice in the United States and with whom Jews did not want to identify.

Yet even while accepting this theoretical framework of cultural pluralism, the actual institutional energy spent in maintaining Jewish distinctiveness went into the construction of a system of supplementary education for Jewish children, something without parallel among the other "ethnic" groups in America. And that education was thoroughly religious in nature, with a curriculum of Hebrew, prayer, Bible, history, customs, and ceremonies. As we look more closely at the development of these educational institutions and their curricula, we'll see that Jewish education responded to the potential conflict between being American and being Jewish with a two-pronged approach: first, it proclaimed that cultural pluralism is key to American democracy (it's OK to be different), and second, it stressed that Judaism fits right in with the dominant culture (Jews aren't so different after all). Although these are opposing assertions, the same people expressed both, usually without recognizing the opposition. A key link between the two positions was democracy, understood not only as an American value but as a value they found embedded in Jewish tradition as well. The new Jewish education was to be democratic in both pedagogic method and curricular content, connected to the Jewish past as well as to the American present and future.

In part because of this commitment to democratic values, Jewish educators saw themselves as building a supplementary system of education that contrasted with the parochial system developed by American Catholics. The Catholic system was considered antidemocratic because of its commitment to separatism, which, along with the hierarchical authority structure of the Church, reinforced a perception of the Catholic Church as inconsistent with democratic institutions.[70] An inclination to avoid association with a religious minority that was subject to severe prejudice in this period was another possible reason for avoiding a Catholic model. In contrast, Jewish educators looked upon Protestant religious education as a source of ideas and models for their newly developing institutions and curricula. This use of a Protestant model confirms the specifically religious identity of Jewish education, despite the theoretical claims of "cultural" identity. A brief examination of the nature and development of Protestant religious education will complete our survey of key factors in the social, political, intellectual, and religious landscape within which Jewish education developed.

Protestant Religious Education in America

Protestant religious education was an influential context for Jewish education, not only because it long predated Jewish developments of the early twentieth century, but also because a modernization of Protestant education occurred just before and contemporaneous with Jewish developments, providing a resource and reinforcement for Jewish educators. The structure of Protestant Sunday schools, the Bible-based curriculum, the women teachers, and a turn to character education and progressive educational theory all had an impact on the form and content of Jewish education.

The earliest Sunday schools in the United States date from the late eighteenth century and were founded on English models. The purpose of the English Sunday school was to provide free elementary education for poor urban children, on the one day of the week when they were free from factory work. The basics of reading, writing, and arithmetic were taught, as well as religion and morality. The schools were the result of a lay philanthropic effort, and were usually established outside church institutions. When transplanted to the United States, the schools developed a more evangelical purpose, targeted to religious teaching, with reading and writing a means rather than an end in itself. Sunday school was to serve the ultimate purpose of the salvation of souls, for which the reading of the Bible was central.[71] Evangelical schools spread rapidly after 1810, culminating in the foundation in 1824 of the nondenominational American Sunday School Union (ASSU), which had a missionizing goal of spreading religious and moral knowledge.[72] The earliest schools were set up for the urban poor (as in England) or were part of a missionizing effort to extend Christianity into rural and frontier areas, which otherwise might remain devoid of religious institutions. Soon the children of congregational members were added as another target population. With the development in the 1820s and 1830s of common schools providing free urban schooling, however, Sunday schools redefined their mission as complementing such schools rather than competing with them. As we have already seen, the curriculum of nineteenth-century publicly supported schools was heavily infused with Protestant precepts and assumptions as well as Bible reading, and its offering of "moral education" provided a kind of lowest-common-denominator Protestantism acceptable to a wide range of Protestant sects. The task of the Sunday school thus became a more specifically targeted religious education, which contributed to the move of Sunday schools to congregational rather than stand-alone settings, a move well underway by the 1850s; by the 1870s it was hard to imagine a church without a school.[73]

What was taught in these schools? Catechisms and question books were used, and in addition to religious subject matter the schools promoted discipline, order, and stability. But at the heart of the Sunday school curriculum was the Bible. The importance of the Bible, and of a common knowledge of specific parts of the Bible, was evident in the adoption in 1872 by the ASSU of a uniform lesson plan, replacing the practice of memorization of disparate passages of Scripture; this plan lasted for half a century. The lessons were arranged so that all pupils of all ages in all places would, every Sunday, be studying the same biblical passages. After three decades of use, the plan was modified so that the lessons were graded according to age, with specific aims and material selected for each age group.[74]

Sunday schools, structured as complementary to public schools and based on a biblically oriented curriculum, served as a model for Jewish education in the second half of the nineteenth century, and policies and methods employed in Jewish Sunday schools often copied the example of local Protestant schools.[75] The model is also clear in the formation in 1886 of the educational arm of the new Union of American Hebrew Congregations: the Hebrew Sabbath School Union of America.[76] Like its Protestant model, the American Sabbath School Union, the HSSUA aimed at providing a uniform system for all Hebrew Sabbath schools, to which end it published a variety of leaflets and books for use in the classroom. These publications centered on recounting biblical history, moral and ethical conduct, and Jewish festivals and holidays, and they included a series of guides for teachers and school organizers.[77]

In the late nineteenth and early twentieth centuries, religious educators were influenced by the same intellectual and social movements that concerned public school educators. They took an increasing interest in professionalizing themselves and in promoting the principles of progressive education. A marker of the advance of these movements was the founding of the Religious Education Association (REA) in 1903. As for other fields such as law, medicine, and the ministry, education too was now to be provided not by unevenly trained laypeople but by systematically and highly trained professionals, who would be educated in research as well as service in their field. In education this meant the development of training for educational administrators as well as teachers. A national system of Sunday school teacher education was established, with training programs for religious education initiated in college and seminary settings. At Teachers College of Columbia University, the premier institution for educational research and training, a model Sunday school was established in 1901, and faculty members specializing in religious education were on staff, including George Albert Coe, one of the leaders in the REA. John Dewey himself was a charter member of the REA.[78]

The REA was committed to a partnership between religious education and secular public education, a partnership supported by a common commitment to principles of progressive education. The commitment to scientific educational research and its application in the classroom—a hallmark of progressive education—permeates the pages of the association's journal, *Religious Education*. Religion was to be taught through means that were "thoughtfully educative" rather than simply "evangelistic."[79]

Thus, when Jewish education began its own professionalization and institutionalization in the first decades of the twentieth century, it was able to draw on a generation or more of the previous development within Protestantism of a modernized religious education. The conjunction of concerns is demonstrated by the participation of Jewish authors in *Religious Education*. After about 1915, most volumes included one or two summaries or reports on Jewish education written by Jewish authors for a Christian audience.[80] By the early 1930s, after a decade or two of expansive developments in Jewish education, more essays by Jews appeared, and the nature of the essays expanded beyond reports on Jewish education to substantive discussions of issues in religion and religious education.[81] Jewish educators had become colleagues rather than followers or token reporters on the Jewish scene. Such is evident from the recommendation to the members of the CCAR that congregations subsidize subscriptions to the REA journal for all religious school teachers.[82] By the 1940s, the REA self-consciously styled itself "an interfaith fellowship," where Catholics, Protestants, and Jews were engaging in a "significant experiment in intergroup cooperation." These words are found in a declaration prominently placed on the inside front cover of the 1945 volume of the journal, over the name of Leo L. Honor, a leading Jewish educator.[83]

With the leadership of the REA, the curriculum and pedagogy of religious education was transformed, in keeping with the progressive tenor of the times. Uniform lesson plans designed "to stimulate conversion and church membership"[84] were abandoned, and a new stress was made on development of character traits, in keeping with the similar stress we have seen in public education. The Bible would continue to be taught, but it needed to be taught in relationship to students' experiences in the modern world, not as a separate thing to be known on its own.[85] This changed purpose for Bible study, which was evident in Jewish education as well as

Protestant and is crucial to understanding the development of Bible story collections for Jewish children, will be discussed in the next chapter.

To sum up, a modernized Jewish education developed in the United States through a complex of interconnected factors—the "present exigencies" that, as we shall see, also caused the Bible to be translated from an elaborate set of laconic narratives (and other material) in Hebrew into a set of simple tales for young children. The *existence of free public schooling*, truly open to all, impelled the development of Jewish education that was separate and supplementary. The *prominence of the Bible in public education* (and in American life generally), contributed to a focus on the Bible in Jewish schooling as well. The *limitation of Jewish education to the small number of scattered hours* available after public school hours necessitated the teaching of the Bible in English, and in an abbreviated form. The *emphasis in public schooling on character education* contributed to the highly moralized adaptations of biblical text into Bible story. And the *development of Protestant institutions and methods of religious education* provided a ready model for Jewish imitation, including the development of congregational schools and a commitment to progressive education. Let us now turn to the new American Jewish education that developed in this context.

The New American Jewish Education

Although the wave of Jewish immigration that stimulated new efforts at Jewish education began in the 1880s, the systematic planning for and institutionalization of new structures to educate Jewish children did not begin for another generation. The new immigrants were poor. The efforts of the first generation were spent largely in establishing an economic foothold in this country, not in building educational institutions. Some efforts were made by "native" American Jews on behalf of the education of the new population. But substantial, sustained effort was not begun until the end of the first decade of the twentieth century, once there was a generation of Jews of eastern European background who had spent formative years in the United States. Then new institutions were founded to further the coordination, improvement, and advancement of Jewish education, especially in the period 1910–30: many cities organized boards of Jewish education, institutions for teacher training were established, and more and more congregations set up religious schools. These organizations in turn sponsored new publications: journals in which teachers and educators could discuss the issues of the day and textbooks for the students. Sample markers of these rapidly developing institutions are:

1903: The newly created Department of Synagog and School Extension

(DSSE) of the Union of American Hebrew Congregations (UAHC, the organizing body for Reform Judaism in the United States) took over the work of the Hebrew Sabbath School Union of America.[86] This body would eventually take the leading role in the development of curricula and educational materials for Jewish religious schools. This is the same year as the founding of the Protestant Religious Education Association.

1909: The Jewish Theological Seminary (JTS, the rabbinical school for Conservative Judaism) established the Teachers Institute, appointing Mordecai Kaplan principal (later, dean). This institution, and Kaplan personally, soon came to have a fundamental, shaping influence on American Jewish education; it trained an energetic cohort of men (and some women) dedicated to the establishment of a modern Jewish education in America. Other than Gratz College, founded in Philadelphia in 1895, the Teachers Institute was the first in a wave of institutions founded for the purpose of training Jewish educators.[87]

1909: The New York Kehillah (a recently established Jewish communal agency) approved a survey of Jewish education in New York to be undertaken by Mordecai Kaplan. This first systematic study found that three-quarters of school-age children in New York received no religious instruction. Of the quarter that did receive instruction, 27 percent were in hadarim (supplementary to public school, with bad conditions and immigrant teachers); 19 percent were in congregational schools, and the rest were instructed by private tutors or within Jewish settlement houses, children's homes, or Talmud Torah schools.[88]

1910: As a result of the above survey, the New York Kehillah established the Bureau of Jewish Education of New York, with Samson Benderly as its first director. The BJE of New York, which was to provide direction and service to a wide variety of schools, served as a model for other such communal agencies. Between 1920 and 1940 boards of Jewish education were founded in Baltimore, Boston, Buffalo, Chicago, Cincinnati, Cleveland, Essex County (New Jersey), Los Angeles, Omaha, San Francisco, Philadelphia, Portland (Oregon), and Toledo.

1911: The Union of American Hebrew Congregations established a Board of Editors to work in cooperation with the Department of Synagog and School Extension in the publication of educational materials for Sunday schools; the Board of Editors was renamed the Commission on Jewish Education in 1923.

1917: The Central Jewish Institute was founded in New York, with Isaac Berkson as first director. The CJI was created by Congregation Kehilath Jeshurun, where Mordecai Kaplan was the rabbi.

1923: The CCAR and the UAHC established a joint Commission on Jewish Education and hired Emanuel Gamoran as educational director. The commission developed out of earlier joint efforts focused specifically on religious educational literature, and the solicitation and publication of such material remained a central task of the group and its director. One of Gamoran's first duties was to secure writers for a complete series of textbooks and to oversee its production.[89]

1929: The National Council of Jewish Education, founded in 1926, began publishing its quarterly journal, *Jewish Education.*

1932: The DSSE of the UAHC began publication of the journal the *Jewish Teacher*, also a quarterly.[90]

As this list indicates, the major institutions of educational training and delivery were in place by the end of the 1920s. The structures put in place during this period lasted for many years, well into the 1950s, aided by a continuity of leadership. Benderly remained in his position with the BJE of New York for thirty years, retiring when it merged with the Jewish Education Committee of New York in 1941. Gamoran remained with the Commission on Jewish Education of the UAHC until 1958, and Kaplan remained dean of the Teachers Institute of the JTS until 1945. The model curriculum proposed by Gamoran in 1923 was not changed until 1958, with the new model continuing much of the old.[91] Let us look in more detail at the new educational structures that were put in place, the educational principles that were developed, and at the curriculum that was to achieve these goals. We will then be in a position to understand the new place of the Bible in Jewish education and the interpretive mode developed to make it suitable for this setting and purpose.

New Structures

The work of reshaping Jewish educational principles and institutions was undertaken by the second generation, transitional between old world and new. The aims of this generation were twofold: to professionalize and modernize Jewish educators and to develop new schools and curricula.[92]

The Training of Professional Educators   In a professionalized Jewish education system, children would no longer be taught a traditional curriculum by whatever semieducated males might be available as melamdim. Rather, a new curriculum would be launched, one thought out by educators who were up-to-date in current educational theory and committed to adapting Jewish education to its new American setting. The central figures were mostly men of eastern European background, usually with some traditional Jewish education, but in America from an early enough age to identify as and be considered "American."[93]

Three institutions in New York forged the direction of Jewish education in America: the Teachers Institute of the Jewish Theological Seminary, headed by Mordecai Kaplan, whose personal influence on a whole generation of educators was vast;[94] Teachers College of Columbia University, where many of Kaplan's students did doctoral work; and the Bureau of Jewish Education of the New York Kehillah, headed by Samson Benderly, where many of these same individuals went on to work.[95] The link between the Jewish Theological Seminary and Teachers College was established in order that JTS students study the new progressive educational theory of John Dewey and his colleagues William Kilpatrick and Edward Thorndike, for the purpose of applying new methods to the study of Jewish religion and culture, subjects they were taught at JTS.[96] Benderly, the person who employed many of the newly trained educators in New York (the demographic center of the Jewish population), expected such joint training of his teachers; eighteen people were on the staff of the Board of Education of the Kehillah and simultaneously doing graduate work at Teachers College in the years 1911–18.[97] Five of these people were so closely associated with Benderly and so influential in directing Jewish education that they became known as a group as the "Benderly Boys": Isaac Berkson, Samuel Dinin, Alexander Dushkin, Emanuel Gamoran, and Leo Honor.[98]

Two Cincinnati-based institutions of the UAHC were also crucial: the Commission on Jewish Education and the Department of Synagog and School Extension (which functioned as part of the CJE); here Emanuel Gamoran was the key player.[99] These UAHC bodies were responsible for the direction of Reform Jewish education in the 1920s and beyond. The broad range of religious school textbooks they developed were also utilized extensively in Conservative and Orthodox congregations.[100]

The Schools   As we have already seen, the schools that were encouraged and established in this professionalized setting were predominantly supplementary schools rather than day schools. It was understood that religious school was voluntary, and that it should complement public schooling, which was compulsory, rather than compete with it. The priority given to public schooling also restricted the hours available for religious schooling to late afternoon and weekends. The result was a "double school system," as modeled and disseminated by Samson Benderly in New York.[101]

The new Jewish religious schools were congregational rather than communally sponsored schools, following the lead of Protestant religious schools, which had moved in this direction in the nineteenth century. This trend was not universal or ironclad. Day schools, full-time religious schools that undertook the tasks of secular education as well as religious, were also founded; a range of older types of institutions founded by eastern European immigrants in the early years (e.g., after-school hadarim, community-based Talmud Torah schools) continued to exist; and other new types of schools were established (e.g., Yiddish schools that stressed secular Jewish learning, founded by the Workmen's Circle, and others that stressed modern Hebrew).[102] The new citywide bureaus of Jewish education attempted to coordinate efforts among these various types of schools.[103] But congregational schools proliferated in the decade following the founding of the New York Bureau of Jewish Education in 1910, and by the mid- to late 1920s they had supplanted the hadarim and Talmud Torah schools as the dominant form of Jewish education in the United States.[104]

New Purposes

The city bureaus of Jewish education, staffed by graduates of the new professional training programs, provided systematic planning, research, and oversight for a panoply of schools, both old and new. Their goal was to provide an Americanized Jewish education, a Jewish education adapted to and consonant with its new American environment. Educators of this generation were as committed to making Jews at home in America as they were to insuring the continuity of Judaism among the young. They were committed to doing their best with the small amount of time available to them. Jonathan Sarna has described these schools as being "a primary setting . . . where American Jews confront the most fundamental question of American Jewish life: how to live in two worlds at once, how to be both American and Jews, part of the larger American society and apart from it."[105] Walter Ackerman, looking back over the attempts to provide a Jewish education that supplemented public schooling and concentrated on elementary school education rather than on the advanced learning of the yeshivah, concluded that it was impossible to keep public schooling and Jewish education as equal goals; Jewish education had to be subordinate.[106] Ackerman clearly judged that American Jews would have been better off if day schools had been the dominant trend rather than supplementary schools. Perhaps he was correct, but within the social, intellectual, and religious context of interwar America the impulse to supplementary schooling was powerful. Furthermore, Benderly, Gamoran, and other educators of their generation truly saw the two worlds of America and Judaism as consonant—the view theorized in the writings on cultural pluralism of Berkson and Kallen.

The vision of American Jewish educators was both similar to and distinctive from that found in western and central Europe in the late eighteenth and nineteenth centuries. Several elements characterized modern Jewish education in Europe: use of the vernacular of the surrounding Christian culture, extensive study of secular subjects, the teaching of Judaism through textbooks designed especially for children, and a concern to take into account the emotional and intellectual development of the child in the design of educational structures. Because no long-standing Yiddish-speaking Jewish communities existed in the United States, the drive to use the vernacular of the dominant culture in Jewish education was even stronger than in Europe. Secular study was also emphasized in the United States, but in public schools rather than within Jewish education. The concern for attention to child development, which included the commitment to special texts for children, was continued in the United States. In terms of overall goals, there was a slight but significant difference. In both Europe and the United States, educators wanted to teach children a Judaism faithful to old traditions while also in accord with Enlightenment principles of reason and universalism. But in Europe, a second major goal was to make Jews useful in society, a goal consonant with the state's interest in the emancipation of Jews. In the United States, where the "usefulness" of Jews had already been established, and where there was not a background of discriminatory legislation to be overcome through emancipation, a more self-assured attitude prevailed, a presumption of "fit" that was not possible in Europe. We can see this attitude in the judgment Emanuel Gamoran made of German-Jewish education being "not an adjustment [to the surrounding environment], but a self-effacement."[107] In America, such "self-effacement" was not necessary.

"Adjustment," not self-effacement, was a task of Jewish education, according to Gamoran, not only in America but in all its preceding historical contexts as well. The Jewish curriculum had always had two tendencies: the conservation of Judaism and the adjustment of Judaism to its surroundings. According to Gamoran, education is always conditioned by the environment and must be sensitive to it. Conservation and adjustment may occur in different proportions at different times, with conservation more prominent in the highly segregated situation of premodern Jewish society in Europe, but both are ever present.

Gamoran, as educational director of the Commission on Jewish Education, was charged with establishing a modern Jewish curriculum and with soliciting a full series of religious textbooks that would advance that curriculum. He wrote extensively on the twofold goals of Jewish education in America: (1) to socialize the child into the Jewish people by transmitting Jewish values and heritage, and (2) to help the child adjust to the conditions of American life and to the values of the age. The aim was "the continuous and progressive socialization of the child into the Jewish group in harmony with the conditions of the new environment."[108] Gamoran identified four key conditions and values of the American Zeitgeist, with which Judaism needed to be harmonized: a stress on universal principles (as opposed to particularism), a scientific outlook on life, functionalism (the judging of values in the context of present-day needs), and a "democratic outlook on life."[109] Such an outlook, the core value presumed by these educators, was an explicitly Deweyian vision of democracy, where the furthering of the "unique abilities of every individual" was the basis of the progress of the society as a whole.[110]

We will see that this belief in and dedication to the consonance of American values and Jewish education had a pervasive effect on the teaching of the Bible. So too did the notion that the fundamental end of Jewish education should be the formation in the child of a Jewish identity. In traditional Jewish education, one's Jewish identity was, of course, taken for granted, having been forged in the home, the synagogue, and Jewish communal life. Education was aimed at competency in—and, if one had the talent and time to persevere, mastery of—the reading of sacred texts. The learning was a goal in and of itself. But not so in America, where Jewish education was for the sake of inculcating an identity as a Jew, or further, as a Jewish American. Perhaps fortuitously, the inculcating of identity was not necessarily as demanding of time as the mastery of texts, which could never have been accomplished in the small amount of time available in supplementary schooling. Jewish educators might have preferred more time, but they felt their new goals were potentially realizable with the time they had.

One reason Jewish educators so readily accepted the supplementary nature of Jewish schooling is that they understood the new Jewish schools as fundamentally linked to the purposes and methods of the surrounding educational institutions. The links between Jewish and public schools are most evident in their shared commitment to coeducation, to a modern progressive pedagogy, and to character education.

Parallel to developments in Europe, Jewish education in the United States was provided to girls as well as boys. Public and Protestant schools, in which girls and boys were taught in mixed classes, reinforced whatever impulse to coeducation may have been already present in modernizing Judaism.[111] With the exception of pockets of the Orthodox committed to traditional forms, Jews considered coeducational religious schooling a matter of course in twentieth-century America. The gender of those providing the education changed as well, with an increasingly female teaching staff and authorship of religious school textbooks. In 1924, 73 percent of Jewish religious school teachers were women,[112] and a large majority of the most commonly recommended Bible story collections in the 1920s and 1930s were written by women. Not all sentiment toward female teachers was positive, but this did not stop the entry of women into the field.[113] Within a generation, an institution that had been an almost uniformly male society was transformed into one in which females were making a mark as authors, teachers, and students. Women were taking on more visible roles in other areas of congregational and Jewish public life as well, although their participation was largely confined to women's organizations like congregational sisterhoods and the newly formed National Council of Jewish Women; these organizations devoted substantial commitments to religious education.[114] In Jewish education (as in Protestant), however, women were scarce in the administrative ranks of schools and congregations. As Jonathan Sarna notes, "Jewish education came to mirror the gender assumptions of American society at large: men governed and maintained control and women educated the children."[115]

The second link interconnecting Jewish education and trends in public school education was the commitment to progressive education. Once again, Dewey was a key figure. Dewey held that the classroom was to be the embodiment of democratic community; pedagogical methods were also to be democratic in character. Abram Simon, writing in 1912 about "The Jewish Child and the American Public School," asserted that "our main task in our Sabbath-schools today lies in linking them with the work of the public schools so as to create a constructive unity of education," and that a key way to achieve this link is to take "advantage of the results of modern pedagogics as applicable to our work."[116] Even while these pedagogic principles were undoubtedly more pervasive in the literature of educational research than they were in actual classroom settings, they still had an important impact on the shaping of the curriculum and how it was taught. All the key figures in Jewish education of this period were taught by Dewey and his colleagues at Teachers College, so the influence was very direct, in addition to the general dominance of the progressive paradigm in the educational scene of the day.[117]

Progressive pedagogical principles reinforced the diminished role of a central, authoritative, sacred text in the classroom. Memorization, repetition, and rote learning, the central methods of traditional Jewish (as well as secular) education, were set aside in favor of more active learning methods. Teachers were to utilize the experience of their students (a leitmotif in Dewey's work) as the base of their lessons, not impose a fixed program on all students alike. The notion of a nonauthoritative educational system, building on the diverse experience of individuals within the educational community, reflects the Deweyian vision of a democratic cultural pluralism, so important to Jewish intellectuals as well as educators of the period.

In accordance with progressive educational principles, the inculcation of subject matter—previously the focal point of education—was less important than the *development of the person* being educated, in relationship to actual life situations.[118] Dewey's philosophy of education saw experience—not divinely given authoritative texts—as the source of truth and reality. This could not help but be a profound challenge to the authority of religious tradition founded on sacred texts.

This stress on experience rather than authority brings us to the third link between Jewish education and secular education—a focus on character education or ethical instruction. Knowledge of a specific text for its own sake mattered little. Rather, texts were to be vehicles for the shaping of character. The formation of character—of one's character as an American—was fundamental to the agenda of public schooling at this time. Jewish educators adopted this same goal, adjusting it to the formation of one's character as a Jew. As Rabbi Samuel Deinard writes in an article for a special symposium on "Character Building" published in the *Yearbook* of the Central Conference of American Rabbis, "If the aim of our religious school instruction is to develop character, let us bear in mind that the Jewish religious school is to cultivate *Jewish* character, that it is to make of the Jewish child not only a religious, God-fearing man or woman, not only an upright and patriotic citizen of our country, but also a loyal Jew or Jewess."[119]

The goal of character education was also stressed when addressing a larger audience of religious educators. For example, in a 1929 address given to the first annual conference of the New England section of the REA, Samuel Wolk asserted that character building pervades all that is done within Jewish education. It affects the method with which subjects are taught. History, for example, can be turned to ethical training by connecting it up with the students' present lives:

The Jewish past is taught, of course, with a view to emphasizing the reality of the Jewish present. Our aim is to present this not as so much dead weight, but rather *as actual life, as we see it and observe it today.* We recognize that it is not an easy matter to achieve our goal. The inculcating of habits which make for ethical life—honesty, social mindedness, self-reliance and the rest—is a laborious and fine task. Dramatization, project study and, above all, skillful utilization of every incident in school life are means to the end. We try to create a school atmosphere where the practice and propagation of ethical attributes will be possible and encouraging. The importance of creating such an atmosphere cannot be over-emphasized.[120]

Emanuel Gamoran, writing in *Religious Education* a few years later, also asserted that the conjunction of character education and Jewish education develops integration into the group—here, the Jewish group. Thus the emphasis in character education is on "the development of habits, attitudes and appreciation" rather than merely on "the acquisition of information."[121]

Like the formation of identity, ethical training had traditionally been part of home and communal life, not an explicit focus of education. Some blamed women for the loss of a "Jewish atmosphere" in the home, so it is somewhat ironic that women now took a new place as moral educators in the classroom.[122]

> *In the first generation of immigrants, ethical action was still embedded in activities and institutions visible in the home and local community. Face-to-face-charity, for example, was carried out at home and on the streets. My mother, born here but brought up by immigrant parents, tells of having to accompany her mother as she took around a* pushke *(collection box for charity), soliciting funds for the local Talmud Torah in Bridgeport, Connecticut. My mother, the youngest child in the family and immersed in modern American ways, found this* schnorring *(soliciting, begging) embarrassing, and she certainly didn't take* me *around (nor was there still a Jewish neighborhood for us to do this in, in any case). Indeed, I have no idea to what charitable causes she wrote checks. It was in the context of religious school that I brought in coins for the* keren ami *("fund of my people"), rather than as a charitable action based in the home and directed toward members of our own community.*

How, then, was a new curriculum to be formulated, one that would conserve Judaism while adjusting to this new educational, social, political, and intellectual context? How would the new purposes of Jewish education—the formation of Jewish identity and character—be embodied in a structured curriculum?

A New Curricular Agenda

The translation of educational theory and new purposes into a concrete curricular agenda was facilitated by the fact that Emanuel Gamoran, one of the central proponents of a modernized, Americanized Jewish education, was also in the position to map out curriculum and solicit the writing of textbooks. A large part of Gamoran's job in the Commission on Jewish Education was to seek out textbook authors and to work with them in the development of their books; prefaces written by Gamoran introduce many of the volumes published by UAHC from the 1920s to the 1940s.[123] Other individuals prominent in writing about education also authored textbooks. For example, Jacob Golub, a close associate of Benderly and his "boys," contributed extensively to *Jewish Education* (including a curriculum for primary grades) and also wrote biblical history textbooks for children.[124]

A Sabbath school curriculum had been developed in the early years of the UAHC, and a "Plan of Religious Instruction" had been adopted in 1896. The HSSUA had published a series of leaflets on biblical history and on moral and religious duties, as well as teachers guides.[125] By the first decades of the twentieth century, however, the UAHC felt an urgent need to reformulate the curriculum, revamp textbook production, and increase the number of volumes being produced. This was the task before Emanuel Gamoran when he became educational director of the CJE in 1923, a task he undertook with seemingly unbounded energy and that he carried forward for thirty-five years.

In comparing Gamoran's vision of the curriculum, as detailed in his 1924 book *Changing Conceptions of Jewish Education*,[126] with the plans put forward in the nineteenth century, we can see both continuity and divergence. The content of the curriculum remained much the same (except for dropping the catechism that had been present in the nineteenth-century plan), including study of Hebrew, the Bible, the prayer book, postbiblical history, and religious customs and holidays; the Talmud is absent from both. The significant difference is in the rationale behind the selection and timing of material. Gamoran insists on a reconstruction of the curriculum around *values* rather than *subjects*, a reconstruction that, he maintains, would eventually entail a "complete transformation" of the curriculum.[127] The 1896 curriculum lists specific biblical passages and figures or events from Jewish history that were to be covered—a content-oriented approach to the curriculum that is reminiscent of a traditional mastery-of-text approach, even though different textual material is used. Gamoran's curriculum, on the other hand, in its focus on values, is less prescriptive of particular texts and subject matter, advising instead on values to be highlighted no matter what subject is being taught.

The values that were to be taught were not "eternal" values, but rather relative to the particular conditions and culture of the times. These were "survival values" that had "to be subjected to the criteria arising from the needs of American life and the need of adjusting the curriculum to the present Zeitgeist." The curriculum was to be developed "with the present environment in mind." Thus the curriculum would necessarily change over time, as affected by new conditions; there is no special merit in reproducing an ancient curriculum, but rather the opposite. Yet Gamoran also expressed a desire for continuity, wanting to insure that "the curriculum will not lose those relatively permanent values which should be the fundamentals in any curriculum."[128]

The place of Hebrew provides a prime example of how key curricular elements persisted and yet were to be transformed. In traditional Jewish education, Hebrew was, of course, a fundamental element, the first thing a child would learn. A basic competency in reading was necessary for prayer, and then a fuller competency for reading the Bible and for entry into the Aramaic of the Talmud. Hebrew was the sacred written language—for reading, not speaking. In modern American Jewish education, the use of Hebrew took two different paths: it held a greatly diminished place in the curriculum, and it changed from sacred, written language to a living, spoken language.

Many schools reduced the teaching of Hebrew to the minimum needed to sound out the words of prayers. This reduction was largely pragmatic, but it could be justified on principle. Pragmatically, the limited hours available were simply not enough to teach language competency. Gamoran estimated that one needed seven to eight hours weekly for several years in order to gain real reading and speaking ability in Hebrew. If that much time was not available (the case for most schools), then it was better to change the goal to participation in synagogue services, a much more easily attainable end.[129] But a de-emphasis on Hebrew was also a central leaning in Reform Judaism. The use of Hebrew—even in religious services—was something that set Jews apart from others, like Sabbath observance and kashrut. Reformers also emphasized the importance of understanding the meaning of prayers, something that many synagogue-goers, competent as they might be in speaking the prayers, could not claim. Thus, reformed congregations introduced the use of English more or less extensively into the service, rendering unnecessary extensive schooling in Hebrew. The reduction of Hebrew and other changes in religious ritual was connected to the reformers' stress on the centrality of a few core religious principles in Judaism, rather than on the details of practice; the prayers needed to be fully understood for these principles to be absorbed, and for this, praying in the vernacular was necessary. Similarly, it was important to study the Bible in English, rather than Hebrew, so that the content of the Bible, with its potential for conveying "the humane ideals of Biblical teachings" could be emphasized.[130]

But many educators promoted a new, entirely different, purpose for the learning of Hebrew—one in which Jewish identity was to be forged through learning Hebrew as a "living language." This Zionist-oriented approach was a continuation of the language emphasis of the heder metukan. Samson Benderly, who had spent his early years in Palestine, was much in favor of this approach, and Gamoran wrote one of the early textbooks for the new *ivrit be-ivrit* (Hebrew in Hebrew) method, teaching Hebrew in a "natural" way, with an emphasis on speaking, as opposed to the traditional method of word-by-word translation of sacred texts.[131] While popular in many communities, such a Hebrew program was difficult to sustain, given the number of classroom hours needed and the difficulty of finding qualified teachers; the movement collapsed in the 1970s.[132]

The Bible took on a central role in Jewish education in America. As in Europe, where Enlightenment ideals and Reform Judaism had turned new attention to the Bible, the Talmud was almost entirely abandoned, not only because of inadequate time in which to acquire the skills needed to learn it, but, more importantly, because of the perceived disjunction between the Talmud and modern values of universalism and reason. There were no "junior" versions of the Talmud developed by the UAHC, and beyond the occasional suggested book of rabbinic stories, the Talmud was absent from the Reform educational scene.[133] In premodern Judaism, the Talmud had been the shared text, recognized as the center of authority in a text-centered religion, the text that bound the Jewish community together. In America, the Bible took the place of the Talmud as such a "binding text," the text that would be called on continually for justification of not only religious principles but political and social ideals. The Bible had a special place in America generally, where it was considered the generating text of American freedom and democracy. From the early years of the colonization of North America and on through the revolutionary and early republican periods, the Bible was viewed as the cultural and political touchstone of the new commonwealth.[134] Add to this the centrality of the Bible to the Protestant beliefs and practices dominant in America, and we can well understand the prominence of the Bible in the public school. The Bible was held to be an American text par excellence, making it an enormously attractive centerpiece for American Jewish education. The Bible's importance to American Jews was reinforced both from within and without: it bound Jews together, maintaining connection with the Jewish past, while also linking Jews up with the American present and their Protestant neighbors. It was the perfect bridge between tradition and modernity, between continuity and adaptation. How better to fulfill the aims of Jewish education in America?

Yet this old text needed new methods of teaching, to adapt it to the new purposes of religious education. This brings us to the core of our study: the reshaping of the biblical text to the new goals of Jewish education in America.

4

Teaching the Bible to Children

Modern intellectual concerns and American social, cultural, and political values insured that the Bible would be central in the education of Jewish children in the United States. But in what form would the Bible be taught, and what methods would be used to teach it? The Bible was now to be taught in English rather than Hebrew. Gone would be the centuries-old method of word-by-word translation.[1] Teaching the text in English enhanced the focus on the *content* of the text, the human ideals present in the Bible, rather than on the learning of language.[2] But even in English the Bible presented problems. Christian versions were available but deemed unsuitable because of Christological interpretations embedded in the translations and the inserted section headings; a suitable Jewish translation of the Bible was not available until 1917, when the Jewish Publication Society issued its modern translation.[3] Yet this translation did not solve the problem, since educators thought the biblical text itself needed to be fundamentally reshaped. The Bible had "suffered from being a holy book,"[4] a sacred text to be memorized or recited on ritual occasions; it needed to be more of a teaching resource for the inculcation of morality and Jewish identity. To suit these new purposes, material in the Bible needed to be selected and adapted, rewritten as a new text designed especially for children.

American Jews were not, of course, the first to adapt the Bible for children. This had been done by Protestants for centuries, and Jewish educators and children's authors were well aware of these texts. But even more explicitly than translations of the full Bible, Protestant Bible stories were run through with Christian interpretation. In the absence of Jewish texts, early Jewish educators had sometimes made use of Christian Sunday School versions. Rosa Mordecai describes her experience of using such texts in Rebecca Gratz's Hebrew Sunday School: "The Scripture lessons were taught from a little illustrated work published by the Christian Sunday School Union. Many a long summer's day have I spent, pasting pieces of paper over answers unsuitable for Jewish children, and many were the fruitless efforts of those children to read through, over, or under the hidden lines."[5]

The solution was to write new books for Jewish children. Jewish educators in Europe, who harbored similar concerns about teaching the Bible to children, had produced Bible story collections designed for children. But the discussion of how to proceed in America took place with little reference to these precursors.[6] The ignoring of European models may have been due in part to insularity, but the American situation was also distinctive enough to make fresh discussion necessary. That discussion was a self-consciously American one, pitched to the situation of Jews in the particular sort of democratic society that America was, or aspired to be.

Pedagogical Issues

Discussion of the role of the Bible in American Jewish education can be found throughout the professional periodical literature of Jewish educators and of the Reform rabbinate. My analysis of this discussion relies most heavily on articles and reports in *Jewish Education, The Jewish Teacher,* the *Yearbook* of the Central Conference of American Rabbis, and the *Proceedings* of the Union of American Hebrew Congregations, as well as on book-length publications by educators. Four individuals were particularly prominent in the discussion. Two we have already met: Emanuel Gamoran, the first educational director of the Department of Synagog and School Extension (DSSE) of the Commission on Jewish Education (CJE) of the Union of American Hebrew Congregations (UAHC), a body largely responsible for the direction of Reform Jewish education in the 1920s and beyond; and Mordecai Kaplan, dean of the Teachers Institute at the Jewish Theological Seminary (JTS) from 1909, the institution where the leading Jewish educators were trained. The two other figures were Solomon Fineberg and Zvi Scharfstein. Fineberg was trained as a rabbi but also did a doctoral dissertation on Jewish education at Teachers College (a contemporary there of Gamoran's), and he was a member of the

Commission on Jewish Education. Scharfstein was a professor at the Teachers Institute of JTS. All four are of the same generation, born within fifteen years of each other in the late nineteenth century, three of them in eastern Europe. The writings of these men relating to the use of the Bible in Jewish education span the decade between 1924 and 1934, although refinements of Kaplan's position were published later, in 1948. As we have seen, the 1920s and 1930s were the formative period for the Jewish supplementary school, and these men were writing with an eye to the direct application of their ideas. While Fineberg's career eventually moved away from education,[7] Gamoran, Kaplan, and Scharfstein continued to be central figures in the world of Jewish education through the 1950s, strongly influencing the development of curriculum as well as teacher training.

These educators' discussion of the role of the Bible in American Jewish education turned on several overlapping questions: How does teaching the Bible relate to the general goals of Jewish education? What approach is best taken in the teaching of the Bible, and are different approaches needed for children of different ages? What problems are presented by the teaching of the Bible? What solutions are there for these problems?

According to Gamoran and Kaplan, the Bible has a role to play in the attainment of the two general goals of Jewish education: building identification with Judaism and harmonizing Jews with their modern American context.[8] The first goal might seem straightforward. Since the Bible has served as a unifying force in Judaism over the centuries through its role as central sacred text, knowledge of the Bible would surely help establish or reinforce identification with Judaism. But such identification was no longer assured in the modern world, since a modern person encountering the Bible might well be put off, or even repelled, by what is found in the text, due to "problems" that will be detailed below. The dissonance in this modern experience of the Bible might also seem to preclude accomplishing the second goal: harmonization with the contemporary context. Yet these educators insisted that when taught correctly, this second goal could also be achieved through the study of the Bible. Indeed, they felt that despite the problems experienced in teaching the Bible in a modern setting, one could still, through proper teaching methods, instill deep loyalty to Jewish life, a strong Jewish consciousness, and insight into human values and ideals that could guide one's life in the present moment and context.

These four educators were all committed to a "scientific" approach to the Bible, the norm in Reform circles.[9] That is, they accepted the basic historicist findings established by the "higher criticism" of the previous century. Like their Protestant peers, they accepted nineteenth-century findings about the differential authorship and age of various parts of the

Bible.[10] Given significant change over time, different parts of the text had to be understood in their own contexts. As progressive educators, they also accepted scientific premises about the workings of the natural world that called into question biblical accounts of divine intervention in natural and human events. The impact of such a scientific perspective on perceptions of the Bible is indicated as early as 1885 in the declaration of principles formulated by American Reform rabbis at an important rabbinical conference. They wrote: "We hold that the modern discoveries of scientific researches in the domains of nature and history are not antagonistic to the doctrines of Judaism, the Bible reflecting the primitive ideas of its own age, and at times clothing its conception of Divine Providence and justice . . . in miraculous narratives."[11]

In 1902 one rabbi had such confidence in the harmony of a scientific approach with the doctrines of Judaism that he declared that higher criticism would "only result in bringing out into greater prominence the imperishable worth of the Bible as a help toward 'the perfect ideal of religion.' "[12] While likewise committed to scientific understanding, Jewish educators also recognized that a critical approach to the Bible resulted in problems. One problem was the strong presence of a *supernatural element* in the text, which, when read in the light of science, produced apparently false accounts of natural events, including such occurrences as the six-day creation, God appearing in the burning bush, and the Red Sea parting for the Israelites. The second fundamental problem was what I will call *moral dissonance*: the disjunction between moral standards presented in the Bible and those of modern America.[13] Of concern here were practices like concubinage and animal sacrifice, but also the questionable morality of human actions such as Abraham's sending away of Hagar and Ishmael, Abraham's willingness to sacrifice Isaac, or Jacob's deception of his father over the blessing of the firstborn. While the concern was usually expressed with reference to human actions related in the text, educators sometimes expressed discomfort with the nature of God's actions as well. Gamoran, for example, refers to "the representation of God in unworthy aspects."[14] How could the Bible be put forward to children as a repository of moral values when it contained actions discordant with modern values?

Adults were expected to understand how the scientific approach did not damage the standing of the Bible. Supernatural forces were simply viewed as the expression of a "primitive" understanding of the world, and the "repulsive" moral practices were to be understood in their historical context as a reflection of an ancient culture.[15] But according to modern theories of childhood, children were not capable of such critical understanding. Their natural inclination was a credulous one, easily believing the miracles and other supernatural phenomena in the Bible. Sometime after age eight, and certainly by age twelve, this credulity was replaced by a materialist literalness, encouraged by the scientific Zeitgeist, a new attitude that called supernatural phenomena into question. The educators divided on how to deal with teaching the Bible to this changing audience. Three possible strategies were advocated.

The first was to go along with the credulous attitude of young children while teaching them the Bible. Since they won't see any problems in the text, why point them out? When they get older, teach them the Bible again from a modern, critical perspective. This was the method generally practiced at the time. Of the four educators we are discussing, however, only Scharfstein advocated it.[16] The others were deeply concerned about the likelihood—or as they saw it, the certainty—of skepticism that such a shift in teaching perspectives would bring about. Wouldn't children be deeply disillusioned when the lack of "truth" of the Bible became clear to them in middle childhood? And wouldn't children then distrust their teachers, who, after all, were teaching what they themselves didn't believe? Kaplan went so far as to assert that the confusion "between fact and fiction, between outlived and permanent values" caused most children to "remain mentally maladjusted for the rest of their lives."[17]

Christian educators were also concerned to not undermine the future of a child's relationship to the Bible by switching approaches as the child matures. What should a teacher do, for example, if a child asks a direct question about the reliability of Bible stories? Muriel Streibert, whose book *Youth and the Bible* was often referred to by Jewish as well as Christian educators, recommends being straightforward but brief in explaining the "poetic truth" rather than facticity of biblical stories: "An honest answer is inevitable, a negative answer is above all to be avoided, and a full answer is unnecessary. [The child] can readily be made to see that a full explanation would involve more detail than he would be interested in, until he is older."[18] The importance of being truthful to the child from the start was also voiced firmly by William Kilpatrick, Dewey's colleague and teacher of many Jewish educators at Teachers College:

We should deal fairly with our children as to the authority of the Bible. Some seem to think they may with impunity teach outworn theories to the young in the hope that they will safely outgrow them. To do so is to risk the confidence of our children in us and in our essential rectitude. We cannot afford such risk. The inherent psychology of the Bible is extraordinarily true, but much of its history and most of its science is not true. We must be truthful to our children. Similarly with the miracles of the Bible, it would seem much better to tell our children from the first that people used to believe such things but we now do not.[19]

For those who agreed with this concern and so advised against a switch in teaching method from younger to older children, other strategies were devised.

The second strategy was to avoid teaching the Bible to children until they were old enough to learn it from a scientific perspective. Although this option had its supporters,[20] it was generally considered unwise. Given the centrality of the Bible in Jewish life and ritual, not dealing with it would be difficult; moreover, such avoidance would be inadvisable, because some children leave religious school before reaching the later age at which it would be taught.

The third strategy was to teach the Bible to young children, but with modified biblical texts adapted specifically for them, texts that incorporated a scientific approach as much as possible.[21] A more developed critical approach would be taught at a later age, perhaps adding in as well an appreciation of the Bible as a great work of literature, another modern approach.

This last strategy, teaching modified texts to young children, became the dominant one. Indeed, the project of creating collections of modified Bible stories in English for Jewish American children was already well underway when these educators were writing, with two early collections issued in 1915 and 1916, followed by the first UAHC-sponsored volume of The Bible Story in the Bible Words series in 1924, and others in the 1930s.[22] During the same period, from 1910 to 1930, a new approach to the use of biblical material was being promoted by Protestant educators, an approach that recommended careful selection of particular passages "vital to the needs, capacities, and interests of the learner," rather than an "indiscriminate" study of the Bible.[23] So Jewish educators were both setting out principles as well as responding to work going on around them. Gamoran, in his position as educational director of the UAHC, was sponsoring further work. What solutions, then, did the educators propose to the problems posed by the Bible?

Rewriting the Text

Different strategies had to be applied to the two problematic elements: the supernatural and the morally objectionable. Deletion could certainly be recommended for both, and was. For example, Rabbi Ephraim Frisch, in an address published in the *Yearbook* of the Central Conference of American Rabbis in 1914, called for a Sabbath School Bible written specifically for children, one that left out the passages that "have long outworn their usefulness," a Bible that was "free from the incubus of obsolete mate-

rial and of the grosser miracles and superstitions and ethical improprieties."[24] Lenore Cohen's *Bible Tales for Very Young Children*, a two-volume
collection published in 1934–36 and used widely for decades in Jewish
religious schools, addressed this problem by beginning her collection
with the story of Abraham, leaving out entirely the "supernatural" events
of Genesis 1–11.[25] But there are limits on how far one can go with deletion
of this category of event, since actions of God (including divine speaking)
are part of the supernatural. Other than avoiding the Bible entirely, and
perhaps using rabbinic material instead (a strategy advocated in a lone
voice by Leo Honor, another prominent educator of this generation),[26]
some supernatural material had to remain. Within the deletion strategy,
however, one could cut out the "grosser" incidents, minimize attention
given to the supernatural, and be careful not to base any desirable concepts or religious truths on episodes including supernatural elements.[27]
Even Solomon Fineberg, however, who devoted his *Biblical Myth and Legend in Jewish Education* to this problem and who went extremely far in
deleting such elements from his own proposed stories, was not willing to
leave out entirely such problematic elements—after all, they are embedded in narratives with which Jewish children were expected to be familiar.[28] The burden was then to find *interpretive* strategies that would explain
to children the inclusion of these odd events.

A primary strategy, one recommended by all the authors who discussed
the problem at any length, was to present stories with supernatural elements as "legends." The teacher is to explain that such legends embody
the ancients' conception of the past—a prescientific or "primitive" conception, as opposed to the historical conception of modern people. This
strategy is fully consonant with the recommendations of contemporary
Christian educators.[29] Scharfstein further suggested that at least some of
these legends can be explained as embellishments that were told about
natural events that did occur, embellishments that embody the ancients'
view that disasters were punishment for wickedness. For example, the
destruction of Sodom and Gomorrah, which was "actually" due to an
earthquake, became attributed to the evildoings of the people there. Legends for which such natural causes can be identified might be replaced
with a naturalistic account, a strategy that borders on deletion. For example, Fineberg suggested retelling the story of Saul's consultation of the
witch of Endor so that Saul hears the witch imitating Samuel's voice,
rather than seeing and hearing an apparition of Samuel himself.[30] But this
substitution strategy, Fineberg warned, has to be used sparingly, since
children could be confused by different substitutive accounts found in different Bible story collections.

Problematic as the supernatural elements were to teaching the Bible, of equal and perhaps greater concern were the elements causing moral dissonance. In keeping with the larger educational concerns of the day, Jewish educators were concerned that religious school provide *moral education* for Jewish children. The concern for ethical training and character building that was so prevalent in the discussion of public schooling, permeated as well the discourse of religious educators in this period, both Protestant (as seen in the pages of *Religious Education*) and Jewish (as seen in both rabbinical and Jewish educator publications). Just as stories were used in public education to inculcate virtues, so too, in Jewish education, stories drawn from the Bible were used to teach Jewish virtues and values. Given the prominence of the Bible as a value in American life generally, using the Bible as a moral teaching tool also contributed to the goal of building a positive identification of Judaism and Jews with America. This dual desire—to make Bible stories central to early Jewish education, and to make those stories consonant with modern sensibilities and experience—resulted in a stream of books that adapted, often with extensive emendation, a selection of biblical stories for a specifically young, modern, American, Jewish audience. The move to such collections of moralized Bible stories for Jewish children repeated a process that we have already seen in nineteenth-century Europe. In the United States, too, educators responded to the contextual influences of scientism, new ideas about child development, and a concern for moral education. Two other factors in America reinforced the change to a new presentation of the Bible for Jewish children: a close association between people working in religious education and in public education, and a commitment to the role of education in the Americanization of immigrants.

To adapt the Bible to the purpose of moral education, two operations were required: reshaping the *form* of the text into "stories" and bringing the *substance* of the text into consonance with modern moral sensibilities—both of which tasks Christian educators dealt with as well. The issue of form was to craft a story as a moral vehicle. Wayne Booth writes that stories are, after all, "our major moral teachers," and it is through listening to and reckoning with stories that humans have long constructed their own moral character.[31] Just as much else regarding ethical training moved from the home to the school in the nineteenth and early twentieth centuries, so too the practice of storytelling. No longer embedded in the setting of home and family, storytelling needed to be learned, and a plethora of instructional how-to books on storytelling were published in these years.[32]

How does one make the Bible into a storybook? Even within the first five books of the Bible (the focus of traditional education during a child's early years), large portions are legal injunctions rather than story material. Traditionally, the child's first lesson in the Bible was the opening of Leviticus, a section about the laws of sacrifice. Such topics were no longer seen as an appropriate subject for modern children, and virtually all legal material was deleted in Bible story collections, which focus entirely on biblical narratives. Given the view of Reform Judaism that the prophetic books of the Bible are those most in keeping with modern values, one might have expected an emphasis on them in Bible story books for children. But stories drawn from Prophets form only a minor part of the collections; too much of the prophetic books are nonnarrative and not easily adaptable to the story format.

Even with these large deletions, there is ample narrative material in the Bible upon which to draw. But the original stories were not in a form considered suitable to the modern pedagogy of moral education. Biblical narratives are sometimes too short for a fully played out story, sometimes too long and complicated and not easily condensed into a simple tale, sometimes beginning in medias res, interrupted, or discontinuous. Whether short or long, biblical narrative has a characteristic style that does not lend itself to simple, direct moral lessons: a style that is laconic and ambiguous, with little direct explanation that would take us explicitly and unequivocally into the motivations of characters or into an authorial perspective of moral consequences.[33] There is little in the Bible comparable to the parables of the New Testament, for example, which are short, self-enclosed stories that draw an explicit lesson.

Following long-established Protestant models, writers for Jewish children applied several strategies to make the biblical narrative into Bible stories or tales. They broke the narrative into discrete stories, announced in a table of contents.[34] They shaped each story to center on one or two particular people, whose names were often used in the chapter titles as the identifying feature of the tales. The foreword to one early set of Bible stories, divided into weekly "graded lessons," makes this focus explicit. The author tells the students: "Every week you will receive at school a folder containing an interesting story about some Bible hero or heroine."[35]

The illustrations in the story collections also reinforce the potential for moral lesson or uplift, almost invariably showing particular characters in situations of ethical dilemma or of heroic action. All the collections are illustrated, usually with one picture per story. While some collections utilize preexisting illustrations, others have line drawings created specifically for them; these are especially helpful for our discernment of themes or issues highlighted through pictures. Illustrations in Lenore Cohen's *Bible Tales for Very Young Children* deserve our close study, since the book's wide usage from the 1930s on insures that many children saw them; Cohen's use of illustrations is also typical of that in other collections.[36]

Cohen's collection opens with the legend of Abraham breaking the idols in his father's workshop. This is the only nonbiblical story that Cohen includes in her collection, and is identified as such in her opening line: "Our first story is not found in the Bible, but it is a famous story that Jewish people have been telling to their children for thousands of years."[37] The illustration helps us understand why she may have made this exception. The picture features a sweet-faced young Abraham, confronted by his angry father who exclaims in the caption, "Wicked boy, see what you have done." The idols, both whole and broken, provide a backdrop for the scene, which invites the young reader to identify with the child Abraham, a good, if mischievous, boy, who is about to instruct his idol-worshipping father in the fundamentals of monotheism: "There is no idol, but a great God, whom we cannot see. I have heard His voice and in my dreams He has told me of a land more beautiful than this, where we shall live some day" (1:4). The story gives us background on Abraham, a figure abruptly introduced as a mature man in the Bible.[38] Cohen explains that she includes it because "it helps us to understand the life of our first hero, Abraham" (1:1). While it is true that filling out character and motivations is the purpose of many of the additions in our adapted Bible stories, to go so far as to insert a completely nonbiblical story indicates that some additional force is at work. Cohen must have been searching for an opening story that would immediately engage her child audience. Beginning with God's call to old Abraham to leave Haran would not serve this purpose. The story of Abraham as a child draws in the young reader and carries the additional exhortatory example of a child taking morally righteous action. The caption on the illustration emphasizes the drama of the falsely accused child—his father reprimands him as a "wicked boy" while the accompanying story gives an account of the child's superior religious understanding. As we will see in the next chapter, our authors make significant use of biblical stories with child characters, undoubtedly to the purpose of providing channels of identification for the modern child reader. How better, then, to open this collection, even if it means importing a story from outside the Bible?

The illustrations in Cohen fall into three main categories: some illustrate an ethical dilemma, some illustrate moral behavior (usually good), and some show a heroic figure in action (a subcategory of positive moral behavior). Examples from the ethical dilemma category include Abraham walking beside Isaac on their way to Mount Moriah, with the caption "How can we make a sacrifice without a lamb?" and Esau approaching his brother Jacob for food, after which he will sell his birthright in exchange for the pottage, with the caption "What have you got there, Jacob?" More common are the illustrations of an action rather than its prelude, for

"Wicked boy, see what you have done."

"Wicked boy, see what you have done," from Lenore Cohen, *Bible Tales for Very Young Children* (New York, 1934), 1:3. Used by permission of the UAHC Press.

example, an illustration of kind Rebekah at the well, welcoming Isaac's messenger Eliezer with the caption "My lord, I pray you drink." On the negative side, we see an illustration of Jacob, disguised as Esau, deceiving his father into giving him his blessing; the complicitous Rebekah looks on in the background from behind a curtain and the caption delivers Isaac's voice: "Are you really my son, Esau?" Illustrations of heroic action become frequent with the figure of Moses, and continue through Cohen's two volumes with other figures such as Joshua, Deborah, David, and Esther. In a chapter titled "The Sun Stood Still," we see an illustration of Joshua standing tall against the horizon, his arms uplifted, the sun setting on his left and moon rising on his right. The caption reads, "Suddenly the voice of Joshua rang out," words that brought the sun to a standstill. Deborah is shown seated under her palm tree, exhorting Barak to action: "I have heard of your courage, Barak."[39]

For the majority of stories, the illustration is closely linked to the title of the story, illustration and title combining to focus on a moral issue. For example, the chapter "Abraham Is Kind to Strangers" is illustrated by a picture of the three strangers looking toward a tent before which Abraham stands. In the chapter "Joseph Is Sold into Slavery" we have a picture of the boy Joseph being led away by a trader, with his brothers in the background and the caption "Joseph looked back at his cruel brothers" (1:14–17, 66–70). Teachers could easily use the pictures to focus a class discussion of what was going on, what decisions had been or were about to be made, and what the consequences would be.

The breaking of the biblical text into concrete tales differs not only from the original presentation in the Bible but also from the pace of textual study in traditional education, where only the first section of the weekly Torah portion would be covered in class.[40] For the purpose of moral training, a selected and shortened story, told from beginning to end, was a better vehicle than the first segment of the weekly Torah portion. This is as significant a change as the use of English instead of Hebrew. Such unified, compact stories, centered on actions relating individuals to one another and to God, could then serve as vehicles for the moral lessons that were now a central concern of educators. The focus on individual characters also connected to what educators saw as children's interest in the Bible: persons, rather than history, law, prophecy, or poetry.[41] Moral training could be joined with another purpose articulated by Gamoran: to "arouse [children's] interest and to develop pleasurable associations with biblical events and characters." Even a very cursory familiarity with Bible stories could fulfill these goals: "If, after a year or two in the early grades, children have attained little more than that they have formed pleasant associations with Bible stories and perhaps remembered a few outstanding names, we shall be satisfied. The stories told may also be used as a means of teaching ideals."[42]

Just as the overall form of the story was changed, so too was the style of language and narration. Language was, of course, simplified for the child audience, in accord with modern ideas that children needed educational material specifically engineered for them, a stark contrast to premodern Jewish children sitting down with the original text. But the writers also needed to alter the laconic and ambiguous narrative style of the biblical text, so they actually *added* material to the stories, elaborating on motivation and moral to insure that the audience would receive the appropriate ethical message.

The use of Bible stories as moral scenarios is also evident in the interest in dramatization of Bible stories. In the acting out of a story, students would take on the values embodied in the "good" characters in the story and experience the disapproval of the behavior of the "bad" characters, thus effectively reinforcing the moral messages of the story texts.[43] The reenactment of a story encourages the student to identify with the story, and in the process can create an emotive bond that also serves as a powerful memory aid.

One Friday evening, the Hillel Club students at Knox College were leading services at the local Reform congregation. I had encouraged the students to prepare a little d'var torah *(word of Torah) of some kind, to no avail. But as one student read aloud the English translation of Pikudei, the portion of the week (Exod. 38:21–40:38), a second student seated on the bimah could barely restrain his enthusiasm, and he sprang up after the reading to give an impromptu talk. This portion, which describes in elaborate detail the building of the tabernacle and its tent, was the one that his family had been responsible for acting out some years before. This was the practice at his congregation: each week a family was assigned the task of acting out in front of the congregation some aspect of the portion of the week. Such a practice meant that this student had an emotional identification with even a passage such as this, centered on building materials and dimensions. The student's response to hearing this text—his eagerness to speak of it, the affection with which he spoke of the practice of acting it out—was exactly what the educators of the 1920s and 1930s were looking for—an untroubled, positive identification with the Bible, here attained through family involvement and the use of dramatization.*[44]

In traditional Jewish education, too, the student was plunged into identification with the biblical material. In large part this had been accomplished through bodily union with the text, which, through memorization and chant, was incorporated into the body and was readily available on the lips. A modern defender of the traditional approach explains that the absence of a historical approach also encouraged identification, a direct connection between the self and the material studied. The protagonists of the Bible

> were brought in such a close and intimate relationship with the children that the "past," in so far as there could have emerged such an orienta-tion, turned into a present, or a conflation of the two. . . . Since there was no subject such as history in the curriculum, there was no Medieval period to stand between the original Biblical-Talmudic drama and the present. . . . As a result the dramatic events, and all details and implica-tions of the Jewish story, have become internalized, merging with the developing person within the child.[45]

Striking evidence of this is provided by Shmuel, an elderly Jew first edu-cated in a heder, interviewed many years later by the anthropologist Bar-bara Myerhoff: "We would talk about Jacob, what went wrong with him? We would compare him to our own fathers. You see, children, when you let them be like this, together, warm with those beautiful stories, the les-sons in them ring out, very sturdy, very sweet. Those Bible stories taught us how to live."[46]

In contrast to such conflation of past and present, the modern histori-cal approach presumed a distinction between past and present, and this distinction could undermine the identification with the Jewish past that educators sought. Working against the modern predilection toward a his-torical approach, strategies had to be pursued in the writing of Bible sto-ries for children that would accomplish the goals of identification and moral education, goals that could most easily be achieved through a sense of direct connection with the material being studied. These goals took precedence over the more intellectualized goal of historical perspective and interpretation.

In a traditional setting, this sense of connection was fostered by the bodily incorporation of the text. With that mode of familiarity unavail-able, connection was now to be built through moral engagement in story. But for biblical stories to be used for purposes of identification and moral teaching, extensive changes had to be made to their content. This brings us to the second task involved in adaptation: adjusting the substance of the biblical text as well as its form. Which biblical characters were appro-priate for children to identify with? Which actions in the Bible delivered appropriate moral messages? Just as the form and style of the original text was considered unsuitable for children, so too the content of the material was problematic. As one Protestant educator remarked, if literature is to serve for moral guidance, it "must be selected in the light of its purpose."[47] Gamoran insisted on a "functional" approach to the text, emphasizing "those Biblical ideals which can function in our life today."[48] Of the mass of material available in the biblical text, those story elements were selected that could best serve the purposes of ethical training in a modern, American setting.

We saw above that the unease caused by supernatural elements in the Bible could be assuaged only in part by deletion, since some such elements needed to be retained in the text. Elements causing moral dissonance, on the other hand, could almost always be dealt with by deletion, as there was a ready supply of biblical material viewed as morally suitable. The main strategy recommended for dealing with "ethical improprieties," then, was one of selection. But which episodes should be selected for inclusion and which deleted?

Children's Bible story collections are not the only place in which troubling passages from the Bible might be deleted. In my Reform congregation, the weekly Torah portion is read in English, with the length always cut substantially. For many years, one person was in charge of selecting the passages that would be read, a man of Orthodox upbringing and identity who in the late 1940s was one of the founders of this congregation, a combination of Orthodox and Reform families. When Mitch lost his eyesight, I took over the task. As I went through week by week, I could see by his pencil markings which passages Mitch had marked out to be read. It became clear that he had taken care to choose passages closest to modern sensibilities and to avoid others. Detailed accounts of laws were avoided, as were matters of sacrifice, sexuality, and human bodily functions. For example, in the Torah portion Kedoshim, the pages were marked so that the reader would read Leviticus 19:1–18, which includes moral instruction such as "You shall each revere your mother and your father and keep my sabbaths," and "You shall not defraud your fellow." But verses 19–31, which include mention of carnal relations with female slaves, making one's daughter a harlot, and turning to ghosts, was marked to be skipped, with the reading picking up in verses 32–34 about deference to the aged and care for the stranger. Verses 35–36, warning against falsification of measures was omitted. The verse marked to end the reading was "I the Lord am your God who freed you from the land of Egypt. You shall faithfully observe all My laws and all My rules: I am the Lord." There was also evidence of Mitch's discomfort with an image of God as harsh. For example, within the portion Ki Tavo, Moses tells the Israelites what blessings will come upon them if they observe God's commandments as well as what curses will befall them if they don't. The blessings get eleven

verses while the curses get fifty-three (Deut. 28:1–69). Mitch's marked read-
ing reduced the number of verses listing curses to just a few.[49]

When I first started choosing the selections in Mitch's stead, I took some
pleasure in selecting for reading just those sorts of passages Mitch had
avoided, in keeping with my historian's inclination to examine cultural dis-
sonance. I persisted in this until the week I chose a passage detailing the rit-
ual test to which a woman accused of adultery was to be put and the curse
that would befall her if found guilty (Num. 5:11–31). There were a number
of young children in the congregation that evening, and the parents
expressed their concern about the reading. Since then, I've followed a more
moderate path.

Since the Bible stories were now intended to be part of the ethical training of children, the stories needed to be selected with an eye to the idea
or ideal that could be stressed in each one. But what ideals were to be
emphasized? With a key goal of modern Jewish education being adaptation to general cultural values as well as Jewish ones, educators tended to
stress those values or messages that were "universal" and thus relevant to
contemporary issues and in accord with modern values; we will look at
specific examples in the next chapter. In addition to selecting for the
appropriate moral messages, educators were concerned about the textual
presence of characters with negative traits. Here the principle of deletion
could again be applied. Authors should omit anything "in the least . . .
repugnant to the moral character of the pupil."[50] Gamoran, who wrote
most extensively on this issue, emphasized that examples of negative
character traits—whether in humans or in God—were to be dropped, and
positive character traits were to be selected for.

Yet some authors recognized there was a limit to this approach, given
that all central figures in the Bible are shown in morally disturbing situations. Can one cut out Abraham's willingness to sacrifice his son, or
Jacob's deception of his father, for example?[51] Some educators suggested
interpretive strategies for such episodes. One possibility was to recognize
the wrongdoing as wrong and not to try to excuse it, but rather to explain
the historical existence of different moral systems (concubinage, for
example). Such a historical approach is in line with the interpretive strategy that contextualized miracles in terms of an older cultural system. Or,
for behavior that could not be excused even with reference to a different
moral system, one could explain that the Bible shows people as they are,
with flaws as well as positive characteristics.[52]

It is striking, however, that neither Gamoran nor Kaplan, the two educators who wrote the most on the problem of moral dissonance, suggest a
historicist tack, even though it would be in keeping with their general rec-

ommendation of a scientific/critical approach to the Bible. Gamoran focused entirely on a strategy of selecting the positive and deleting the negative. One result was that the number of stories left to be told was quite limited. In his introduction to the second volume of Lenore Cohen's *Bible Tales*, Gamoran claims that "these two books contain, to the best of our knowledge, a complete collection of all the Bible stories which can be told to little children" (2:viii). Kaplan, on the other hand, stressed another kind of interpretive strategy, that of discovering "implied values and meanings in the Bible" that are responsive to our contemporary context, developing an entirely new version of the Bible comparable to the body of midrash developed in the post-biblical period.[53] While Kaplan had adults more in mind here than children, a possible example of applying his strategy to a child audience is found in other authors: when telling the story of the *akedah* (binding of Isaac), for example, one can stress how it shows opposition to human sacrifice rather than endorsement of it.[54]

Running throughout much of this writing is a persistent inconsistency between principle and practice. On the one hand, educators endorsed in principle a critical, scientific, historical approach to the Bible, an approach that was at the base of their critique of current teaching methods in religious schools, which they saw as promoting an attitude of uncritical acceptance. On the other hand, educators recommended a strategy of deletion rather than interpretation. That is, while professing commitment to a scientific approach to the Bible, they recommended avoiding problematic material rather than confronting it. Fineberg is perhaps the most striking case; he is unrelenting in his criticism of story collections that include any supernatural elements. Gamoran, too, calls for a historical approach, and yet he insists on the deletion of all "incidental" material that relates only to the age in which the Bible was written, along with the expunging of all negative character traits, rather than recommending a thoroughly historical approach that would contextualize these moral problems.[55]

This inconsistency is understandable given the contradictory attitudes embodied in scientific and religious stances, a conflict unacknowledged by religious educators of the time. A 1928 article in *Religious Education*, "What Religious Attitude Is Compatible with the Scientific Attitude?" highlights for us the difficulty of such rapprochement. The author includes the following characterizations in his description of the scientific attitude:

> For the scientifically minded person conclusions, judgments, principles, and theories are formulated and accredited on the basis of the critical analysis of all the relevant facts obtainable. There is no authority higher

than [t]his method for discovering, testing, and verifying knowledge. . . . The scientific mind not only is expectant of change but deliberately dedicates itself to the task of discovery, invention, and creativity. . . . Open-mindedness, freedom from bias, fearlessness in facing facts, the suspended judgment, a naturalistic view of relationships and sequences—these are cardinal qualities of the scientific attitude. Nothing in the universe, be it idea, institution, custom, doctrine, hypothesis, or experience, is entitled to exemption from the analysis, description, and, if attainable, the understanding of the scientist. There are no "*verboten*" signs on the landscape which the scientist surveys.[56]

Despite the optimistic proclamation of compatibility, there are, indeed, "verboten" signs on the landscape of religious instruction, and full open-mindedness and freedom from bias can hardly be attained when, indeed, a special relationship with particular texts, customs, and beliefs were to be fostered. The attitude Jewish educators wished to inculcate in children toward the Bible was contrary to a critical approach, which would presume that the Bible is just a historical document like other documents (or a great work of literature like other great works of literature). Rather, the educators wanted to instill in children love and reverence for this special text and to fight skepticism in the young.[57]

Mordecai Kaplan is the only one of the four who faced head-on the deep conflict between the biblical worldview and modern values, but it is significant that the thoroughgoing interpretive process he suggests for the Bible is really meant for adults, not children.[58] Kaplan taught other educators, not children. Those who undertook the education of children, while heavily influenced by Kaplan, necessarily had to find a simpler approach more appropriate for the young.

It may also be that the historical approach accepted in principle by Jewish educators was avoided in practice because of the way in which Christian educators and interpreters used it to disparage Judaism, as represented by the Old Testament. When Jewish educators consulted Muriel Streibert and other Christian educators about teaching the Bible to children, they encountered the view that a historical approach could resolve many problematic aspects of biblical texts by arranging the parts of the Bible in chronological order. The earlier (Old Testament) parts were then understood as coming from an age that was "crude," "childlike," "rude," "dark," or "primitive,"[59] whereas the New Testament, coming later, was considered the culmination of all the best elements from before. According to John Prince, for example, in an essay recommended to Jewish educators by Gamoran, the historical order of the books of the Bible corresponds to "a gradual development and unfolding of moral and religious ideals, attitudes, and practices among the Hebrew people covering more than a thousand years and flowering in the exalted spiritual insight of Jesus and the faith of his early followers."[60] Similarly, the liberal Protestant writer Harry Fosdick saw biblical ideas reaching their "climax" in the teaching of Jesus: "Plainly we are dealing with ideas that enlarge their scope, deepen their meaning, are played upon by changing circumstance and maturing thought, so that from its lowliest beginning in the earliest writings of the Hebrews any religious or ethical idea of the Bible can now be traced, traveling an often uneven but ascending roadway to its climax in the teaching of Jesus."[61]

While Christians had long held that the New Testament superseded the Old Testament, that view was now strongly reinforced by the findings of higher criticism: "our fathers never possessed such concrete and detailed illustration of that idea as we have now." Armed with this new historical understanding, Christians were relieved of "the necessity of apologizing for immature stages in the development of the Biblical revelation."[62] The Old Testament is not to be discarded, as there are important truths to be culled.[63] The task of the educator was to pull out of the Old Testament the "enduring" or "universal" principles or truths, those that can be applied directly to modern experience.[64] As explained by William Clayton Bower, a professor of religious education at the Divinity School of the University of Chicago, the goal was to "abstract the enduring values of the Bible from their datable historic context, as gold is smelted from its crude ore, thus releasing them for use in contemporary situations."[65] And how was one to distinguish the gold from the crude ore of the Old Testament? One simply used the measure of Jesus' teachings, which were seen to be in perfect consonance with modern life.[66] According to John Prince, head of the Department of Religious Education at the Garrett Biblical Institute, historical study allows us to test "religious significance by the standards of Jesus."[67] Jesus himself set the model of discriminating among varying religious levels of the Old Testament, as seen in his formula "You have heard it said, . . . but I say unto you."[68] Repeatedly, Christian educators stress that the "deep" and "abiding" elements of the biblical text are to be drawn out, to be applied to *present* experience. The emphasis on teaching to "experience" is familiar to us as a progressive refrain. William Clayton Bower well summarizes how it applies to teaching the Bible: "The Bible can be meaningful and effective as the Living Word only as it is brought into functional relation to the experience of members of the continuing Christian community under the conditions of contemporary life, by releasing its enduring insights, attitudes, and values from the concrete historical context of the past and making them available for use in the changed historical situations of the evolving present."[69]

As can be seen from these Christian interpreters, a historical interpretation of the Bible in the early twentieth century corresponds to what Herbert Butterfield has characterized as the "Whig interpretation of history"—an interpretation that sees history as a linear process of moral development.[70] For Christians, as applied to the Bible, this progress reached its goal in the person of Jesus, with whom Christians can enter into a direct relationship. The principles Jesus espoused can be directly applied to modern life, and his personality can be held up as the model for children to emulate. What about a historical perspective on the New Testament itself? Wouldn't this make untenable the use of the New Testament as an unproblematic guide? It's true that some Christian authors were less assiduous in applying a historical approach to the New Testament than they were to the Old.[71] But even for authors like Muriel Streibert, who confidently applied a historical approach to the New Testament as well, problems were limited to the realm of the supernatural, not the moral. Streibert advises at length, for example, about how to explain away miracles in the New Testament, giving the same advice as she offers for the Old Testament. She also accepts the historicist chronology that differentiates between the four gospels and uses it to explain the presence of miracle stories, which she sees as proliferating the further one gets from the time of the actual events.[72] But she sees the moral sphere of the New Testament—in stark contrast to that of the Old Testament—as entirely unproblematic.[73] Indeed, its moral exemplarity is heightened through contrast with the "crude" standards—both human and divine—of the Old Testament.

Jewish interpreters, too, saw the Bible as "reflecting the primitive ideas of its own age," the characterization adopted in the official prose of the 1885 Pittsburgh Platform. Jewish educators were well aware of the approaches of their Christian colleagues, and they shared their Whiggish interpretation of history. But for Jews, it was the "Old Testament" itself that was seen as the source of enduring values. Educators were thus more comfortable with deletion than with historicization as a pedagogical strategy for the Bible. Jewish interpreters did like to emphasize the superiority of the Prophets, which are later texts than the Pentateuch and so in accord with a "moral progress" historical approach; they also had the comfort of knowing that Christians viewed the Prophets with approbation, deeming this part of the Old Testament closest in time and spirit to the New Testament.[74] But the prophetic books were not as amenable to story narratives as earlier books of the Bible.[75] Jewish interpreters needed the Pentateuch as the core text with which Jewish children were to identify; the person and principles of Jesus were not an option. Moral exemplars would have to be found—or constructed—in the Hebrew Bible. We shall see in the next chapter how this was done.

There is evidence of extensive communication between professional educators and the writers of Bible story collections, at least those who wrote for the UAHC under Gamoran's editorial eye. But because of haphazard record keeping, resulting in huge gaps in documentation, it is impossible to know to what extent educators advised the writers, or how self-consciously storytellers applied strategies recommended by educators.[76] Still, by comparing the stories with the writings of educators, we can gauge the extent to which there were concerns common to theory and practice. To educators, the most problematic elements in the Bible were those involving the supernatural and moral dissonance. Writers of children's stories shared these concerns. But they had additional ones, too. The story writers were committed to remaking the language and narrative style of the Bible into stories specifically for young children. Two universal strategies in this adaptation, long employed by Christian authors, have already been discussed: simplification of language and parceling of biblical narrative, that is, breaking it into short, cohesive tales usually focused on one character and one moral issue. Beyond these strategies, modern narrators were concerned to provide additional elaboration and explanation within each story, which they felt would enhance the child's understanding of the setting of the story and of its moral meaning. Thus, while the educators advised a primary strategy of selection and deletion, the narrators also practiced a strategy of extensive addition, sometimes verging on outright alteration—strategies not discussed by educators.[77] As one author states explicitly in her preface: "In a few instances I have taken the author's privilege to emphasize the ethical value at a slight expense of accuracy."[78] In adding to the text, modern narrators were engaging in a task similar to the centuries-old rabbinic genre of midrash, and they sometimes even utilized traditional midrash in their additions. Yet these modern retellings also differ fundamentally from rabbinic purposes. They were intended to replace the text rather than to coexist in active dialogue with the original.[79]

The task of remaking text had been urgent in the ancient world—how to make the Temple- and sacrifice-centered religion of the Tanakh relevant to life after the destruction of the Second Temple, to life in exile? Now modern rabbis, intellectuals, and educators took up the task anew—how to translate biblical culture into the values of yet another cultural setting. Various modern interpretive strategies were suitable for adults: the historical approach of the higher criticism or the critical approach of the

Bible as literature. But despite the educators' intellectual acceptance of these approaches, neither were considered appropriate for children, for whom the educational goals of ethical training through the text and personal identification with the text took priority.

What then, did the Bible look like when adapted for Jewish children in America? An examination of key issues in the retellings of specific stories will demonstrate the lengths to which storytellers went to keep the Bible alive for modern Jewish children. Once familiar with the strategies employed, we will compare these stories to other interpretive locations in both Jewish and Christian practice.

5

Bible Stories Retold:
Theory into Practice

The Texts: A Children's Discourse

The demand for new presentations of the Bible designed specifically for American children was answered by the production of more than two dozen Bible story collections between 1915 and 1936.[1] It was in 1934 that the Union of American Hebrew Congregations published Lenore Cohen's *Bible Tales for Very Young Children*. This collection became the uniformly recommended text in Reform religious schools; its success stopped the flow of competing books for over twenty years.[2] All of these texts are styled as collections of "stories" or "tales" centered on biblical characters. All are written in what we can call a children's discourse: they employ a highly simplified language, they avoid inappropriate subjects through omission or circumlocution, and they add explanatory material to enhance a child's comprehension.

As I analyze the style and content of these Bible stories written for Jewish children, my eye is always on the relationship of the stories to the various contextual elements we have considered: the legacy of emancipation and the Enlightenment, the changing Jewish environment, and the specifics of the American educational scene. My attention centers on how changes in the conditions of Jewish life are played out in the pages of children's Bible story books. We need also keep in mind, however, that, fitting as these stories are to Jewish needs (or so I hope to convince you), their form and content bear many resemblances to a long tradition of similar books written for Christian children. As Ruth Bottigheimer demonstrates in her book on this subject, Christian Bible story books had long focused on narrative portions of the Bible, had deleted with abandon material considered inappropriate for children, and had inserted commentary to fit the story to the perceived needs of the child audience, all features essential to the texts we are about to examine.[3] One is tempted to say there is thus little to explain in the Jewish texts: now that Jews are open to influence from Christian models, they simply adopt them. Surely that is a significant part of the story. And yet, had these models been inconsistent with the new Jewish context, Jewish educators and writers would not have adopted them; moreover, these educators and writers, while certainly familiar with Christian Bible story collections (as we can see by citations in the educational literature), were self-consciously creating Jewish texts, written at least in part to avoid the resort to Christian books. My analysis of these texts, then, centers on the fit between American Jewish concerns with the Bible stories adapted for children during the years 1910–40. A comparison to contemporary Protestant versions is given in the next chapter.

Within the universe of Jewish children's Bibles, I focus on the books most often recommended for school use. (They are listed in appendix 1.) To appreciate the innovations of the twentieth-century texts, we'll begin with a comparison to a late-nineteenth-century version, written before the educational developments of the Progressive era; the binding of Isaac will serve as the sample story. First, the original story from the Tanakh, here in the 1917 translation issued by the Jewish Publication Society:[4]

> And it came to pass after these things, that God did prove Abraham, and said unto him: "Abraham"; and he said: "Here am I." And He said: "Take now thy son, thine only son, whom thou lovest, even Isaac, and get thee into the land of Moriah; and offer him there for a burnt-offering upon one of the mountains which I will tell thee of." (Gen. 22:1–2)[5]

Beginning in the late nineteenth century, the Hebrew Sabbath School Union of America published *Leaflets on Biblical History,* which grew into a series of fifty-eight pamphlets.[6] We find God's instructions to Abraham in a leaflet titled *Abraham's Faith.* After two epigrams from the Tanakh (Mic. 6:8) and midrash that reinforce this message of faith, the story—or rather the lesson—begins:

> In this lesson, my dear children we are going to hear a story which will show how great was Abraham's faith in his God. In one place we are told that "Abraham believed in God, and this was counted to him for right-

eousness." This is one of the great sentences in our Bible. It is right to believe in God; He does everything for the best; He loves us and takes care of us. In this way Abraham believed and trusted in God. But his faith was tried very greatly. You can imagine how much Abraham loved the boy Isaac, the only child in his house. He loved him more than words can tell, as your fathers and mothers love you too.[7]

The narrator/teacher continues with two more paragraphs of direct explication, addressed to the child audience. Then the biblical account of the story, from Isaac's asking about the whereabouts of the lamb for the offering to the scene of the binding and the provision of a ram in the bushes, is given in one paragraph; this section is in direct (translated) biblical language. Five shorter paragraphs in the preaching mode follow, including a direct explication of the lessons of the story: the great faith of Abraham and God's demonstration that the Israelites were not to sacrifice children as other peoples did.

Certain features of this text are congruent with the concerns of twentieth-century educators: the choice of simplified language for children, the use of stories for moral education, and the bringing of the child into direct relationship with the text, here by invoking the parents' love of their children ("as your fathers and mothers love you too"). But in this turn-of-the-century children's rendition, the story material is fully subordinated to the moral lesson, rather than ethical issues arising implicitly or naturally from the story—the recommended progressive method. The story is tucked within a sermon rather than being itself a vehicle for identification and moral thought.

In books from the second decade of the twentieth century, one finds a change in appearance as well as style. Addie Richman Altman's 1915 book, *The Jewish Child's Bible Stories, Told in Simple Language* is a hard-cover book, not a set of pamphlets, set in large print and containing illustrations throughout (even on the cover)—it is clearly an object intended for children's hands.[8] A new attitude toward the child reader contributes to a stylistic change. The story is a much larger element of the text, even while it retains a moralizing frame. In Altman's book, for example, the story "The Ram on the Mountain: Isaac" begins with an explanation of an unfamiliar detail (the ram) and a brief review of Abraham's moral character:

Do you know what a ram is? It is a very large sheep with strong, curved horns. But before I tell you anything more about that, we must go back to the tents of Abraham, to see what he and little Isaac have been doing. Abraham was a very old man now, but he was just as good to every one as he always had been, and everybody loved and trusted him. (Altman, 34)

After the explanation of another contextual detail (the term "patriarch"), the story is launched, this time retold in children's discourse rather than in biblical language:

> One day, when he was there by the tent door, he heard a Voice calling: "Abraham!" and he answered: "Here am I."
> "Go up to the land of Moriah," said the Voice again. "Take the boy, Isaac, with you. Go up into the mountain, and offer the boy as a sacrifice." (Altman, 34–35)

Then Altman breaks into the narrative to set up the moral challenge central to the story, using a direct statement by the narrator to the child audience:

> Don't you think Abraham must have felt very unhappy to think that he had to take his little boy for a sacrifice? Abraham loved God and had always obeyed Him, so he knew he would obey now, even though he felt very sorry to do so. (Altman, 35)

Then the narrative picks up again and continues for two more pages, with no other direct address from the narrator to the reader, and just a little moralizing at the end about Isaac's obedience and his efforts to please his mother and father. Altman maintains a moral/explanatory frame, but reduces it in favor of a focus on the narrative events of the story. Silber's 1916 collection, *The Scripture Stories Retold for Young Israel*, uses a very similar approach.

An abrupt change of style and method from moral-frame-plus-story was introduced in 1909 in a collection put out by the Bloch Publishing Company: *The Junior Bible for the Jewish School and Home.*[9] This book was innovative in that the stories, while highly selective, were told in a language as close as possible to the biblical original; indeed, the authors worked directly from the Hebrew text to produce this children's version. Although the book had little success,[10] another in the same mode, published in 1924, was widely used and remained in print for years. This was one of the first UAHC textbooks produced after Emanuel Gamoran took over the direction of the Commission on Jewish Education: Adele Bildersee's *The Story of Genesis*, the first in The Bible Story in the Bible Words series.[11] Here the biblical narrative is divided into discrete stories, selected with an eye to those especially suited to children. The language is simplified slightly and the text is abridged. But the stories that are included stay as close as possible to the 1917 Jewish translation published by the Jewish Publication Society, and there is no added narrator voice-over, no added moralizing. Here, our sample story is called "The Trial of Abraham," and it begins:

And it came to pass after these things, that God did prove Abraham, and said to him, "Abraham"; and he said, "Here am I." And God said, "Take now thy son, thine only son, whom thou lovest, even Isaac, and get thee into the land of Moriah; and offer him there for a burnt offering upon one of the mountains which I will tell thee of." (Bildersee 1, 44)

This is unchanged from the JPS text, except for the clarification of "God" in place of a masculine pronoun. In both its selectivity of stories and its closeness to the original, without narrator intervention, Bildersee's version comes close to what some educators recommended. Moses Buttenwieser, for example, a professor at Hebrew Union College, noted the absence of "moral reflections or discourses" from the original biblical narratives, and he stresses that it is "precisely this feature which gives them their superior pedagogical worth."[12] He recognizes that "circumlocutions or omissions . . . must sometimes be made" in children's versions, but he argues strongly against emphasis on "the moral of the story" and against "constant reference" to "the practical application of the story to the child's sphere of interest." Rather, in reading biblical stories, "right feeling on moral questions [will be] nourished unconsciously."[13] While the goal was to use the stories as ethical resources for the children's own lives, the recommended educational strategy was to accomplish this unobtrusively, not through extensive, explicit moralizing.

Bildersee's text is, indeed, so close to the original that one might wonder why it was desirable or necessary to bother with a children's version. Other features make this a children's book in both form and content: the book was designed with large print and illustrations, and the stories included were carefully selected. For example, Bildersee includes Abram's leaving of Haran (Gen. 12:1–9), but she skips over the sojourn in Egypt when he passed his wife Sarai off as his sister (Gen. 12:10–13:1), picking up again with the story of the division of the land between Abram and Lot. As we will see below, this story element (Sarai as sister) would be troublesome because it shows Abram in a questionable action, as well as because of its implications of sexuality. Bildersee also intervenes in an important way beyond the manipulation of the text through omission, though outside the covers of the book. She wrote a teachers' manual to accompany each of her volumes. Each story has a chapter in the manual in which the pedagogical aim is spelled out, centering on the moral lessons to be taught. A verse is picked out for the children to memorize, and then a script is provided for the teacher to use to lead into the reading of the story itself, after which further script is provided to bring home the lesson. For example, after reading "The Trial of Abraham," the teacher is to say:

Our story to-day is spoken of as the trial of Abraham, and indeed we have seen Abraham's perfect faith in this terrible trial. But in this story is Abraham the only one who is tried? . . . Does Isaac cry out, or doubt his father's wisdom and love? . . . Is there any one who does not have some test in his life—big or little? . . . Do you know any fathers and mothers who, in the Great War, sent their sons to fight for their country? . . . Do you know any parents who encourage their boys to be doctors, so that they may bring healing to sick people even though they may have to go in danger of their lives to do it? . . . They have the faith of Abraham.[14]

So much for the Bible speaking for itself, despite Gamoran's introduction to Bildersee's manual, in which he speaks against the habit of attaching "a distinct and separate moral to every story in the Bible"; he also rails against "constant moralizing," which "defeats its own purpose, for it makes conscience callous and rarely influences conduct. As a method of Bible teaching, it is naive and ineffective."[15] One can only think that Gamoran was looking at *The Story of Genesis* itself when writing this introduction, not the teacher's manual, in which his exhortation appears.[16]

While the Bildersee book (and the other volumes in The Bible Story in the Bible Words series) were used for many years in religious school programs, publishers continued to put out Bible story collections in the mold of Altman and Silber, in which stories are significantly altered in their retelling for children. Examples of such collections are those of Elma Ehrlich Levinger, Edith Calisch, Ethel Fox, and Hyman E. Goldin, all published between 1925 and 1930.[17] With the publication of the two volumes of Lenore Cohen's *Bible Tales for Very Young Children* in 1934–1936, Bildersee was fully displaced in the lower grades. In Cohen we get a text that combines the story-only model (Bildersee) and the moral-frame model (Altman and others). Cohen tells a story from the beginning to the end of each chapter (no moral frame), but with elements added here and there that more subtly bring the moral lessons of the story to the surface. Here is the opening of the chapter called "In Place of Isaac":

Dawn had just come up over the hills. The moon was still peeping from behind the clouds, and the birds were chirping a very sleepy song. In the plain stood Abraham's blue and white tent.

"Get up, Isaac," Abraham called. "Get up, Isaac, another day is here."
"Why must I get up so early?" asked the boy. "The moon is still out and even the sheep are half asleep. Can't I sleep a little longer?"
"We are going on a journey. See, the boys are here with the donkeys. We are all ready to start."

Isaac rubbed his eyes and dressed himself slowly. Abraham watched the boy tenderly. In his old age God had given him this beautiful boy. How tall and strong he was! How young and happy he seemed! Last night Abraham had heard a voice calling. It was the voice of God, who said, "Abraham!"

"Here I am," answered Abraham.

"Take your only son, Isaac," God said, "and go into the land of Moriah. There I will show you a high mountain, where you must make a sacrifice of your son, Isaac." (Cohen, 1:22–23)

Gone are the moral frame and the direct moral address of narrator to reader. Instead Cohen begins with what we might call a character frame, introducing the protagonists in the story and their physical, social, and personal characteristics. This is a typical opening for her stories, designed to draw the readers into the characters and their life and to enhance a child's identification with the biblical figures. Moral messages are made explicit, but they come not from a narrator/teacher but from within the story itself. In this case they are spoken by God. As Abraham readies Isaac on the altar, he hears the voice of God calling from Heaven:

"Abraham, Abraham!"

"Here I am," answered Abraham.

"Do not lay your hand on your son! Do not hurt him! Now I know how much you love God. You have not even kept your son from me; but I do not want child sacrifice." (Cohen, 1:25)

In comparison, the JPS translation reads:

And the angel of the Lord called unto him out of heaven, and said: "Abraham, Abraham." And he said: "Here am I." And he said: "Lay not thy hand upon the lad, neither do thou any thing unto him; for now I know that thou art a God-fearing man, seeing thou hast not withheld thy son, thine only son, from Me." (Gen. 22:11–12)

Cohen has stayed close to the original here, substituting address by God rather than by an angel. She also changes God's test of Abraham from *fear* of God to *love*, and she adds in an explicit message against child sacrifice that is not in the original.[18] With the moral carefully embedded within the story, the tale concludes with a final "character frame." After God's blessing we are told:

Abraham was so happy; he kissed Isaac again and again.

Then Abraham and Isaac climbed down the mountain. They found the boys waiting for them. Together they returned home. (Cohen, 1:26)

Abraham's joyful kissing of Isaac is Cohen's creation. The final line of the story is actually close to the original: "So Abraham returned unto his young men, and they rose up and went together to Beersheba; and Abraham dwelt at Beersheba" (Gen. 22:19). But while the original obscures the presence of Isaac in the return journey, Cohen specifically includes it, while also adding the destination of an emotive "home" rather than a neutral place-name. We are being reassured that all is well.

Gamoran wrote an introduction to Cohen's book, as he had for Bildersee's. While he makes no direct comparison between the two books, both published under his direction at UAHC, by praising Cohen he suggests what was lacking in Bildersee. Contrary to what is thought by many writers of juvenile stories, he says, children do not need an abbreviated story but the opposite, "a story that goes into detail, that is vivid and concrete." While recognizing that not all biblical stories "are suited to the needs of little children" and that even those stories that are chosen should not necessarily "be told in their entirety," it is also the case that in some stories additional details need to be inserted.[19] Whereas Bildersee's book had been simply an abbreviation, Cohen's provides the additional "vivid and concrete" details that "little children" especially need. But she does this without the heavy-handed addition of moral material, working instead to interweave moral messages into the fabric of the story. Ten years after the publication of Bildersee's book, Gamoran has decided that Cohen's procedure is best, as he explains in his introduction: "A Bible story should be told in such a way that the underlying idea is inherent in the telling of it without attaching the main thought at the end, as the proverbial 'moral to the tale.' "[20]

Cohen's volume was a great success. It eliminated the intrusive moralizing of the nineteenth-century Leaflets on Biblical History series and of the early-twentieth-century collections like Altman's (or like Bildersee's teachers' manual). It made each chapter a narratively homogeneous *story*, as had Bildersee's collection, but it added details of character and place that would further entice and capture the interest of the child reader, while finding ways to subtly integrate moral messages into the text, readily available to teacher and student. It was in this form that generations of young Jewish children in the United States learned the Bible.

Omissions

The purpose of this form of lightly moralized, character-enhanced story was to encourage the identification of Jewish children with the Bible, to develop in them "a love of our great book."[21] To this end, authors were attentive to educators' advice to omit problematic material. As we move into discussion of various subject areas of the stories, we will see many examples of what was considered inappropriate for children. But we can look first at four general categories that commonly gave the authors pause and led either to outright omission or to some kind of circumlocution or rationalization: strange customs, laws, sexuality, and the supernatural.

Strange Customs

Certain customs accepted as normal in the Tanakh but dissonant with modern practices were eliminated or glossed over. Concubinage and polygamy, for example, were, when at all possible, eliminated from children's texts. Sometimes this was relatively easy to do by removing an entire episode. In other cases, elements of a story could be elided, without unduly disturbing the narrative. Mention of David's multiple wives, for example, could be avoided. Cohen gives a relatively full narration of various stories about David (she includes eighteen stories, from his first being brought to Saul to soothe him with song to David's death), and still manages to avoid mention of him having more than one wife at a time.[22] In other places, omission of a problematic element is more complicated. Many collections include the story of Abraham's dismissal of Hagar and Ishmael, for example. But how to explain Hagar's relationship to Abraham without mentioning concubinage? In addition, authors were reluctant to be explicit about Sarah's barrenness, infertility being a variant of procreation, and so connected with matters of sexuality, which, as we'll see, was a prime subject for omission. Apparently having more than one wife was considered more "reasonable" than concubinage, with most of our authors opting for this substitution. Altman encapsulates the whole situation (Sarah's infertility plus Hagar's concubinage) in the statement "Abraham had two wives, Sarah and Hagar, and, later, two little boys, Ishmael and Isaac" (Altman, 31). Cohen also waits to introduce Hagar until after the birth of Isaac: "Now Abraham had another wife, whose name was Hagar. Hagar was an Egyptian woman and she was also Sarah's servant. Hagar had a son, too. His name was Ishmael" (Cohen, 1:18).[23] Most surprisingly, Bildersee, whose treatment is both the fullest and the closest to the original, includes the episode of Hagar and Ishmael's dismissal, but she excludes *any* prior mention of Hagar's relationship with Abraham, thus making the episode difficult to understand (Bildersee 1, 41).

Another custom—this one pervasive throughout the Tanakh—is virtually absent in the children's books: the practice of sacrifice. Sacrifices of any kind are totally out of keeping with modern notions of worship, so references to this practice were almost always cut from the narrative, and the long legal sections of the Tanakh that detail the rules of sacrifice are, of course, deleted. Occasionally, sacrifice is so crucial to a story that it must be mentioned. This is the case for the story of Cain and Abel, which turns on the issue of the different sacrifices by the two brothers. Altman, clearly uncomfortable with having to mention the practice of sacrifice, atypically breaks into the story with a historical explanation of how "those times" were different from ours: "In those times, there were no temples, or churches, where people prayed to God, and really the people did not know how to pray. But way down in their hearts, they felt they must show in some way that they loved God—so listen to what they did" (Altman, 16).[24]

Altman goes on to explain the making of the altar from a large stone, the bringing of fruit, grain, or animals, and the setting of the fire. A similar interjection of historical explanation can be found in another collection, Calisch's *Bible Tales for the Very Young*, on the problematic matter of Abraham having two wives: "Now, all of this happened many hundreds and hundreds of years ago, and in those days things were very different than they are now. Sometimes a man had more than one wife" (Calisch, 1:36). What is noteworthy is the rarity of such historical explanations of ancient customs. Since the late nineteenth century, modernizing Jews had accepted a historical-critical approach to the Tanakh, as demonstrated in the Pittsburgh Platform's 1885 declaration that the Bible reflects "the primitive ideas of its own age," and such an approach to the Bible was consistently recommended by Jewish educators. But historical explanations emphasize differences between the present and biblical times. The story-tellers had another goal, shared with educators: that of making biblical stories consonant with the values of modern life, of carrying direct ethical messages to American Jewish children. Better for this purpose that biblical time be just like our time, and that biblical characters be just like us. To achieve this goal, omission or circumlocution was more appropriate than historicism. The concern for a direct relationship with the material in the text overrode the inclination authors might have had to treat the text in a critical, historical manner, which would have meant a distancing of biblical characters and culture from modern Jews.

Laws

After Genesis and the first half of Exodus, much of the Pentateuch is taken up with recitation of large bodies of laws, covering a wide range of human activities, from eating, sexual relations, and family and community relations to the right relationship of humans to God. Not surprisingly, given the modernizing rejection of the "particularism" of Jewish law, this body of material is excised virtually in its entirety from Bible stories for Jewish children. Not even the Ten Commandments appear in all of the books.[25] The most extensive treatment of legal material, as we might expect, is in the six-volume Bible Story in the Bible Words series, but even here, the abbreviation is stark. Bildersee's *Out of the House of Bondage* covers Exodus, Leviticus, Numbers, and Deuteronomy. The Ten Commandments are given in one chapter, with the next chapter covering other laws under the title "Some of the Laws Which God Gave Israel." This chapter is very brief—just two pages of text—and all the laws included are of a "universal" type that are applicable not just to Jews. We find here laws against oppressing a stranger, wronging a widow, lending at interest, and uttering false reports, for example, but nothing of dietary laws or the laws of sacrifice (Bildersee 2, 66–68). Selections from the whole of Leviticus take up only three chapters in the book, versus sixteen for Exodus. The first chapter, "Thou Shalt Love Thy Neighbor as Thyself," is a further listing of universalistic laws, the second chapter covers various Jewish holidays, and the third chapter gives an account of the sabbatical and jubilee years. The material from Numbers (seven chapters) is entirely narrative, with no legal material. The final two chapters, from Deuteronomy, give a repetition of the Ten Commandments along with a few other "acceptable" laws (153–54). The only other author who goes beyond the Ten Commandments is Silber. He tells the reader that Moses gave the Israelites "ever so many other laws" and then gives a sample of "just a few," again all laws— here highly simplified—that were acceptable because of their universalist cast, such as: "We must try not to be selfish. . . . We must be just to all people. . . . We must do all we can to save the lives of other people when they are in danger" (Silber, 1:185). These laws confirm that God's law has a universalist nature, which Silber explains to the reader with regard to the Ten Commandments: "all the laws of the world are taken" from them (146).[26] The severe reduction of legal material and the focus on its universality could not provide a starker contrast with the traditional initiation of a Jewish child's study of the Bible, which began with the levitical laws of sacrifice.

Sexuality

Sexuality, procreation, and other bodily matters were eliminated from the new texts as much as possible.[27] These omissions had little to do with a sense of embarrassment over customs specific to the Bible, but were rather a matter of being consistent with the sexual sanitation prevalent in children's literature of the time, both religious and secular. To take one example from early in the Tanakh, consider the arrival of Cain and Abel into the world. The Tanakh refers to human sexual activity as well as to the help of God: "And the man knew Eve his wife; and she conceived and bore Cain, and said: 'I have gotten a man with the help of the Lord' " (Gen. 4:1). Modern children's versions eliminate even this discrete reference to procreation, and most eliminate God as well. Bildersee, who stays closest to the original, simply begins the story after their birth: "And Abel was a keeper of sheep" (Bildersee 1, 10). Altman offers this version of their arrival: "One day, a little baby boy came to Adam and Eve. . . . Another little fellow came along later" (Altman, 13). Calisch begins: "After Adam and Eve went out into the world, God sent them two sons" (Calisch, 1:12).[28] Silber comes the closest to mentioning procreation in writing that "children were born to" Adam and Eve (Silber, 1:14).[29]

The Supernatural

The educators who theorized and advised about how to teach the Tanakh to children did not mention in any detail the omission of odd customs, laws, or sexual practices, referring instead in general terms to omitting elements unsuitable to children. But another category of problematic material received extended treatment by educators: What was one to do about the pervasive presence of the supernatural in the text?[30] As discussed in the previous chapter, educators recommended a historicist strategy, one of presenting stories with supernatural elements as "legends." The teacher was to explain that such legends come from a "prescientific" or "primitive" culture, different from our own. Omission of such elements, or the substitution of an alternative account, was another recommended strategy.

As we would expect from their treatment of "outmoded" customs, our Bible story authors rarely invoke the historicist approach of explaining stories with supernatural elements as legends, as this would distance the child from the content of the stories rather than build a direct relationship. The collections commonly have the word "story" or "tale" in their titles, but not "legend," a term that was used instead for midrash, rabbinic stories about the Tanakh.[31] The Bible story authors shared the educators' concern for the unsuitability of the supernatural for modern children, but they dealt with it most commonly by omission or circumlocution rather than by substitution or explanation. The problems begin at the beginning of the text, and indeed, the whole of the first eleven chapters of Genesis (creation through the tower of Babel) were so problematic that they were simply dropped entirely from Lenore Cohen's collection; the elimination of these difficult stories did not impede the popularity of this collection, and perhaps even enhanced it.[32] Other authors kept some or most of the early stories, but did their best to minimize supernatural or miraculous elements. The opening account of creation will serve as a sample. First, the JPS translation of the Tanakh:

> In the beginning God created the heaven and the earth. Now the earth was unformed and void, and darkness was upon the face of the deep; and the spirit of God hovered over the face of the waters. And God said: "Let there be light." And there was light. (Gen. 1:1–3)

In contrast, Altman's version:

> Once upon a time, many, many years ago, there was a beautiful garden, in a land very far away from here. All the nicest plants you can think of, and trees, and bushes, and grass, grew in this garden, which was just like a big park. (Altman, 7)

After further description of the vegetation and landscape of the garden, the narrator interjects:

> Don't you think that was the loveliest garden you every heard about? And there were other things there too. Birds were singing in the trees and some animals were lying on the ground. Some of the animals were running or walking around, and a man and a woman were there. The man's name was Adam, and the woman's name was Eve.
> Do you know, or can you guess who made this lovely garden; and all the things in it? It was the dear, good God, who takes care of us all—our Father in Heaven. (Altman, 8)

We are already used to the enormous difference in tone and to the narrator's direct address to the child audience, inviting participation. But notice also the avoidance of a narration of the six days of creation. Yes, after a description of the lovely garden, its making is attributed to God, but the delay in mention of the divine source, and the diminution of God's role, alleviate a modern discomfort with the "unscientific," miraculous account of creation of the universe in six days. In Altman, the focus of the first chapter is not on the creation but on the story of Adam and Eve, which is more amenable to the moral concerns of the educators and narrators. The chapter bundles the two accounts in a single narrative titled "The Garden; Adam and Eve"; here a circumlocution ("The Garden") avoids mention of creation.

Bildersee's version is very close to the original, as we would expect:

> In the beginning God made the heaven and the earth. Now the earth was without form and darkness was upon the face of the deep; and the spirit of God was upon the face of the waters.
> And God said, "Let there be light." And there was light. (Bildersee 1, 1)

This passage includes just one small change from the JPS translation—"God *made* the heaven and the earth," rather than "created." This change could be just for the sake of simplifying vocabulary, but given that other children's authors also use the verb "to make" for God's action, it seems, rather, a purposeful diminishment of the extraordinary nature of God's action, even while Bildersee goes on with a full account of the six days.[33] Bildersee's teachers' manual once again conveys a different tone and approach than the text in her *Story of Genesis*. In an effort to bring the text in relationship with the child's own experience, the teacher's script begins: "Did any child in the room look at the sky this morning? . . . Was it beautiful? . . . I have often heard little children . . . ask, 'Mother, who made the grass?' Of course, *you* know. . . . Yes, God made the grass."[34]

Calisch handles her uneasiness with creation by inserting an introductory analogy that attempts to explain at a child's level how something so new and complicated might be made:

> Once there was a little boy who had a sand pile in which he loved to play. But one night a great storm came, with wind and rain, and in the morning when the little boy awoke, he found the sand all tossed about and filled with sticks and stones and bits of leaves and grass. For a while he looked at the ugly heap, and then he set to work to make it clean and beautiful again. (Calisch, 1:1)

Another paragraph describes the boy's work on his sand pile: "For a long time he worked, and at last his sand pile spread before him like a pleasant bit of a tiny world." Then the point of this opening is made clear:

> Just so it was before God made the beautiful land we live in. The earth and the stars and the sun and moon were mixed up together. Trees and lakes, mountains and rivers, air and land and water were all stirred up in a great mass. There were no people, no birds or beasts or fish or insects.

There was not even any light, but just the sort of grey dusk we have on a rainy afternoon.

But God looked at this mass of earth and air and water, and knew that He could make something beautiful of it. (Calisch, 1:2)

Again, God's work is not that much different from human activity. But what about the more specifically miraculous occurrences in the Tanakh, things for which no human counterparts are feasible? Let's look, for example, at two of the miraculous events from Exodus: the turning of Moses' staff into a serpent and the parting of the waters of the Red Sea.

The staff-into-serpent episode occurs in the context of God's appearing to Moses in a burning bush. God tells Moses that he is sending him to Pharaoh, to bring the children of Israel out of Egypt. Moses is reluctant to take on the task, and God puts forward a number of arguments to convince him. When Moses worries that people will not listen to him, will not believe he comes with a message from God, God gives him these proofs: that his staff will turn into a serpent when cast onto the ground, that his hand will turn leprous when put into his bosom, and that water will turn into blood when poured on the dry land (Exod. 4:1–9). These are small examples of the "wonders" that God will do on behalf of the Israelites in Egypt (Exod. 3:20). The episode of the dividing of the Red Sea offers an example of a kind of collaborative miracle-working on the part of God and Moses.[35] In the Tanakh, the Israelites become afraid when they see Pharaoh's army chasing them, and they cry out to Moses that they would have been better off staying in Egypt. Moses assures the Israelites that God will come to their aid. God then speaks to Moses and tells him to "lift thou up thy rod, and stretch out thy hand over the sea, and divide it; and the children of Israel shall go into the midst of the sea on dry ground" (Exod. 14:16). The parting is then accomplished in tandem by Moses and God, Moses stretching out his hand, and God bringing a wind to push back the sea (Exod. 14:21). Just as God could make Moses' rod change into a serpent, here the same rod effects another transformation—the divided sea.[36]

Looking first at Bildersee, since her text stays closest to the original, we find that she includes a chapter on "The Burning Bush" but limits Moses' expressed concern to his slowness of speech, which is answered with the provision of his brother Aaron as spokesman. No mention of the transformations of staff, hand, or water, and indeed no mention of the possibility of wonders at all (Bildersee 2, 9–13). God is, however, maintained as the cause of the parting of the Red Sea, along with Moses. Following precisely the wording in the JPS translation, Bildersee writes: "And Moses stretched out his hand over the sea; and the Lord caused the sea to go back by a strong east wind all the night, and made the sea dry land, and the waters were divided" (42).

Altman, too, eliminates all mention of wonders in the burning bush scene, but she includes God in the parting of the waters: "God made a very strong east wind to blow over the sea" (Altman, 79).[37] The elimination of Moses' outstretched arm has the effect of naturalizing the event—the water parts because of a strong wind, a wind brought by God, yet a natural force, not miraculous like the outstretched arm. Calisch includes the wonders, she but treats them as a kind of skill that God teaches to Moses: "Then God showed Moses how to do certain wonderful things so that the people would know that God Himself had spoken to Moses. Among other things, God taught Moses how to turn the staff he carried into a serpent" (Calisch, 1:100–102). God's role is also present but somewhat diminished in the parting of the waters. After Moses' reassurance, "Fear not, but wait and see what the Lord will do," the text reports the effect of the wind without mentioning God directly as the causative force, and with no mention of Moses' outstretched arm: "Then a great wind began to blow, and the waters of the Red Sea rolled back so that there was a straight dry path through the waves" (112–13). Cohen, too, includes one of the wonders (the rod/serpent) but downplays God's role at the sea. In her version, Moses reassures the Israelites that the Lord will take care of them. Then the voice of God says to Moses:

> "Moses, wave your rod over the sea and divide it. Then you and the children of Israel will cross over on dry land."
> Moses waved his rod and the Red Sea divided in two. The Hebrews crossed to the other side safely. (Cohen, 1:136–37)

Silber goes the furthest in lessening God's miraculous power, not only omitting the wonders at the bush but also describing the passage through the Red Sea as essentially a natural phenomenon. Following the Israelites' complaints,

> "Fear not," said Moses, "the Lord will help you." And just as he said that, the tribe of Levi jumped into the sea and started to make for the opposite shore. The other tribes followed them, and they all came across safely. You see, then, God did help them, just as Moses had said He would. It was *as though* the waters of the sea had parted and formed a wall on either side of them so that they could pass in safety. (Silber, 1:132; emphasis added)

While God's help is identified as a factor, the scene elicited is one of the Israelites jumping in to swim, and then easily proceeding. Similarly, when it comes to the drowning of the Egyptians, this is described as an act not of God but of an "angry sea." The Egyptians too plunge into the water,

> just as the Israelites had done. But as they got into the sea [which has not actually divided in this account]—men, horses and chariots—the waves seemed to rise mountain high and it was impossible for them to make any headway. Realizing their danger they now wanted to turn back, but that, too, was impossible. The angry sea closed them in and, with force and fury, carried them to the bottom. (Silber, 1:133)

From this review we can see that no author leaves the miraculous untouched. The wonders at the burning bush are either eliminated (five of the six accounts) or reduced in number (Cohen). The passing through the Red Sea is too central a story to eliminate entirely, so it appears in all versions, but only Bildersee stays close to the coordinated miracle by God and Moses. Most eliminate Moses' stretching out his arm or rod and instead have the waters part solely because of the wind, which comes more or less explicitly from the help of God. Only Cohen includes Moses as instrumental in the parting of the sea, and it is only Cohen who includes the rod/serpent transformation at the burning bush. The authors are thus more comfortable with a miracle that can be elided with a naturalistic cause (the strong wind) than with a more "supernatural" miracle like the rod turning into a serpent, or the outstretched rod effecting the parting of the waters.

None of our authors omit God entirely, yet the diminishment of God's role contributes to a transformation of the nature of God in these modern American versions of the Bible. Connected with the circumscription of His role is an emphasis on certain aspects of the nature of God and the avoidance of others. We will explore these issues through a detailed analysis of a few scenes from one text, Lenore Cohen's *Bible Tales*.[38]

The Nature of God

Both the reduced presence and the changed nature of God are visible in the story of Abraham leaving Haran. In the Tanakh, God's command to Abram to leave is followed by immediate and unquestioning obedience:

> Now the LORD said unto Abram: "Get thee out of thy country, and from thy kindred, and from thy father's house, unto the land that I will show thee. And I will make of thee a great nation, and I will bless thee, and make thy name great; and be thou a blessing. And I will bless them that

bless thee, and him that curseth thee will I curse; and in thee shall all the families of the earth be blessed." So Abram went, as the LORD had spoken unto him; and Lot went with him; and Abram was seventy and five years old when he departed out of Haran. And Abram took Sarai his wife, and Lot his brother's son, and all their substance that they had gathered, and the souls that they had gotten in Haran; and they went forth to go into the land of Canaan; and into the land of Canaan they came. (Gen. 12:1–5)

The whole episode of command and departure is brief and direct. But not in Cohen's version. First comes her usual opening frame of establishing place and character.

Abraham Goes to the Promised Land

"We are the shepherds who tend the sheep,
Under the stars we eat and sleep;
Ever we wander, ever we roam,
The plain and the desert is our home."

Abraham stood in front of his tent. He was a tall man, sunburned and strong. All these hundreds of sheep were his. All the shepherds who were watering the sheep were his servants.
Sarah, his wife, came out of the tent and stood beside him.
"What are you thinking about, Abraham?" she asked. (Cohen, 1:5)

We are given details that help us see the biblical characters as ordinary folks, whom we can relate to directly. Abraham's physical environment is described in the opening verse and in the following paragraph: he is a nomadic shepherd, seen standing in front of his tent surrounded by his sheep. His physical features are described: he is "a tall man, sunburned, and strong." His human relationships are filled out as we see him in interaction with his wife Sarah. Typical of Cohen's approach, much dialogue is brought into the story. This technique adds to the reader's engagement with the characters while also making the stories easy to use for dramatization, a favored pedagogical technique. As Abraham's conversation with Sarah continues, we find a fundamental transformation of the text. The Tanakh has God speaking directly to Abram, telling him to leave his country and go to a new land that God will show him. But auditions of God are supernatural events, to be altered if possible. Cohen does this by eliminating the direct speech of God to Abram, substituting a dream, reported to Sarah, in which Abraham hears the voice of God.[39]

"I am thinking of a dream I had last night," he replied. "I seemed to stand alone in a field. Suddenly I heard the voice of God saying, 'Abraham, leave your father's house. Go to the west. There is a land of green pastures and silver streams. I will bless you, Abraham. You will be the father of a great nation.' "

"Is there really such a land?" asked Sarah.

"Yes," answered Abraham. "Look! What do you see, far in the distance?"

"Mountain tops, which look like huge, black points against the setting sun."

"There is the land I dreamed about. Tomorrow we shall rise with the dawn and start to travel there."

Abraham blew a shrill whistle. All the shepherds came running. At their head came Lot, Abraham's nephew.

"Herd all the sheep and cattle together. Pack up the tents and all our household goods. We leave this place at dawn."

"Where are we going, Abraham?" asked Lot.

"To the mountains. To a new country! A country where I can worship the one Almighty God in peace." (Cohen, 1:5–6)

While the role of God is reduced to a voice in a dream, the roles of the human characters are magnified, with Sarah and Abraham discussing the meaning of the dream and Abraham elaborating to Sarah and then to Lot why it makes sense to leave Haran and go to a new country, which, in this version, they can even see off in the distance. It is central to the biblical version that God commands Abram with no justification for the move, and the magnitude of what is being asked is emphasized through the threefold explanation of what is being left behind—his country, his kindred, his father's house. But for Cohen, if the story is to make sense to children, and provide them with some kind of model of behavior, the reasons and motivations for actions needed to be made explicit. This new land is a better land. It has "green pastures and silver streams." It's not such a big trip, as they can see the mountaintops off in the distance. And to make the new home that much more appealing to an American audience, two details are added that liken Abraham's journey to American journeys: God tells Abraham that he should "Go to the west" (just like American pioneers), and when Abraham describes to Lot where they all are going, he exclaims, "To a new country! A country where I can worship the one Almighty God in peace," conveniently foreshadowing the pilgrims' voyage to America.[40]

The remainder of the move is narrated in a similar fashion, bringing us into the midst of the entourage of people and herds, giving another evocation of the attractiveness of the land as "green and inviting," and concluding with Abraham's command to his household at the conclusion of the trip.

> What a hustle and bustle there was. At dawn everything was ready. Abraham, tall and brave, rode at the head of his household on a camel. Sarah rode beside him, while the shepherds and their wives and children followed behind. They moved slowly, for the sheep and goats had to be kept together. In this manner they traveled for many days.
>
> At last they came to the mountains. How green and inviting they seemed!
>
> "Let us stop here," said Abraham. (Cohen, 1:6–7)

God's role is reduced and human agency is enhanced. Other examples of human agency replacing God's can be found throughout the stories. Cohen includes a chapter, for example, on the building of the tabernacle. In the Tanakh, we are told of God's close connection to this work. God has given Moses elaborate instructions regarding the building (Exod. 25–28), and has also chosen the men to do the work:

> The LORD spoke unto Moses saying: "See, I have called by name Bezalel the son of Uri, the son of Hur, of the tribe of Judah; and I have filled him with the spirit of God, in wisdom, and in understanding, and in knowledge, and in all manner of workmanship. . . . And I . . . have appointed with him Oholiab . . . ; and in the hearts of all that are wisehearted I have put wisdom, that they may make all that I have commanded thee: the tent of meeting, and the ark of the testimony, and the ark-cover that is thereupon, and all the furniture of the Tent . . . [the text continues with a long list of additional things]; according to all that I have commanded thee shall they do." (Exod. 31:1–11)

In Cohen's version, God is entirely absent. The tabernacle is Moses' idea, and Bezalel is the skilled craftsman who has responsibility for the building: "When the tabernacle was finished, all the people marveled at the beautiful piece of work. They thanked Bezalel, for he had showed them how to build it" (Cohen, 1:154).

Human agency is also enhanced and God's role diminished in the military sphere. For example, the Israelites' defeat of their final enemy before entering Canaan is, in the Tanakh, clearly attributed to God:

> And [the Israelites] turned and went up by the way of Bashan; and Og the king of Bashan went out against them. . . . And the LORD said unto

Moses: "Fear him not; *for I have delivered him into thy hand, and all his people, and his land.*" (Num. 21:33–34; emphasis added)

In Cohen's version, God disappears:

Og, King of Bashan, was the last king for the Israelites to conquer before they entered the promised land. It is true that he ruled over sixty cities which were surrounded by high walls, in which were gates with bars, but there was no reason to fear him. In spite of his tremendous size, Og was weak. He had gained his power through the silly stories which had grown up about him. (Cohen, 1:177)

Rather than God reassuring Moses, in Cohen's version Moses reassures the Israelites, who express their fears to him. Moses then leads them into battle, where the big, fat Og runs away from them, and all his sixty cities are conquered. Innumerable other examples can be found where action accomplished or instigated by God is, in Cohen, described in terms of human action only. The avoidance of God accomplishes two things: it diminishes the intrusion of the supernatural realm and it focuses the story at the human level, where moral action can be modeled.

Cohen does not leave out God entirely, of course. She retains the presence of God in some of the stories related to Moses, for example, as we have seen in the accounts of the burning bush and of the Exodus from Egypt. But she is more comfortable with a God who watches over the welfare of His people than with one who intervenes in human action. It is not just the causative action of God that is bothersome, but how he behaves—the "unworthy aspects" of God that concerned Gamoran and other educators. Thus, in addition to the diminishment of God's sphere of action, our children's authors also alter the manner in which His behavior is portrayed. The modern audience was uncomfortable with behaviors of God that seemed harsh, arbitrary, or cruel. This discomfort at God's problematic behavior was assuaged by deletion, transformation, or explanation.[41] William Kilpatrick, the professor of many Jewish educators at Teachers College, warned of the "very great risk if we teach a God whose moral standards are lower than those now commonly accepted among men."[42] If God's morality was out of step with modern standards, it needed to be changed.

For example, what to do with the divinely ordained slaughter in the Israelite camp after Moses' discovery of the golden calf? In the biblical account, Moses reports God's instructions to the Israelites to slay all who do not come over to the Lord's side:

And [Moses] said unto them: "Thus saith the LORD, the God of Israel: Put ye every man his sword upon his thigh, and go to and fro from gate to gate throughout the camp, and slay every man his brother, and every man his companion, and every man his neighbour." And the sons of Levi did according to the word of Moses; and there fell of the people that day about three thousand men. And Moses said: "Consecrate yourselves to-day to the Lord, for every man hath been against his son and against his brother; that He may also bestow upon you a blessing this day." (Exod. 32:27–29)

Cohen, in contrast, eliminates the slaughter and suggests a forgiving rather than a punishing God:

Then Moses raised his hands high, and cried, "O wicked people, are there none among you who are on the side of the Lord?"

All the men of the tribe of Levi came and stood beside him.

Moses prayed to God, "The people have sinned a great sin. Wilt Thou forgive them?"

The Lord answered, "Lead My people out of this place. I will send an Angel to guide you." (Cohen, 1:150)

Another example further illustrates the preference for a less punitive divine figure. God told Moses to speak to a rock in order to get water for the thirsty Israelites. When Moses struck the rock instead, God punished him by denying him entry to the land of Canaan (Num. 20:1–13). To a modern reader this punishment seems disproportionately harsh. Cohen amends the story by making Moses do something worse than just striking the rock, which serves to better justify God's harsh punishment. The additional fault is poor leadership—Moses struck the rock out of undue anger with the Israelites. Cohen has God explain: "'I have forgiven these people all during the years of hardship. I warned you to be kind to them. In anger, you disobeyed my words.'" Therefore, Moses will not enter the promised land (Cohen, 1:172).[43]

Finally, going back to our earlier story of Abram leaving Haran, we see that Cohen was bothered by the autocratic image of God in the Tanakh, a God who commands the aged Abram to leave all that is most precious to him and to go to some unknown place, and whose command is obeyed without question. One can almost hear Kaplan and Gamoran whispering in Cohen's ear: "Not very democratic! We need to put the Bible in accord with contemporary values." This is what Cohen does, with God reduced to a voice in a dream, and the decision worked out rationally by Abram, in discussion with his wife, in contrast to the silent, immediate acquiescence to God's command that is crucial to the story in the Tanakh. In the democratic American context, such a command and compliance is uncomfortably autocratic. Throughout Cohen's text the nature and behavior of God is selected and altered in order to create an image of a distant, protecting figure rather than an intervening, authoritarian one, and such alteration is in accord with concerns and suggestions by educators regarding the nature of God to be emphasized in a democratic, American context.[44] In keeping with Dewey and the dominant intellectual currents of the time, democracy and science were seen as sharing an opposition to the uncritical, passive acceptance of any "higher authority," which in this case is extended even to God. The link between the Bible and democracy was so fundamental to the religious educators' vision of the text that a 1946 story collection, *Pathways through the Bible*, though much closer to the original biblical text than Cohen's, could have a frontispiece that proclaims: "This Bible is for the government of the people, by the people, and for the people."[45]

Discomfort with authoritarianism and punishment from God in the Bible can be found today as well. A few years ago, I visited a Reconstructionist synagogue for Shabbat services. The local minhag *(custom) is for one of the members to prepare the Torah reading for the week along with a brief d'var Torah, or word of Torah, to be followed by discussion among the congregants. On this week, the lay readers were a man and his twelve-year-old daughter, and the parshah—the weekly portion—to be discussed was Korach, which centers on challenges to the authority of Moses and Aaron.[46] This questioning of authority is answered with graphic, horrendous punishments sent by God, after close consultation with Moses. First the earth opens up to swallow the challengers and their families, then fire consumes hundreds more, and finally plague strikes the thousands of Israelites who objected to these deaths. As the text was read and as the father and daughter struggled with its possible meaning in their d'var Torah, the feeling of tension in the room mounted. What kind of leaders are these who answer questions to their undivided authority with threats of violence rather than discussion? What kind of God is this who administers such punishments? The discomfort with the text was augmented by the participation of a twelve-year-old in its interpretation—there was a sense of embarrassment that a child had to undertake a confrontation with this text, perceived as deeply contrary to modern sensibilities.*

The discomfort and embarrassment centered on what was perceived as the "undemocratic" nature of the story—the authoritarian roles of Moses as leader, Aaron as priest, and God as a punishing force and a maintainer of human authoritarianism. What struck me in the ensuing discussion was the

Frontispiece illustration by Arthur Szyk, in *Pathways through the Bible*, by Mortimer J. Cohen, copyright © 1946, by the Jewish Publication Society. Used by permission.

certainty of these congregants that the text was disconsonant with their own
modern values, and their feeling of helplessness when faced with a holy text
that seemed to them repulsive. Because Cohen and others felt empowered to
change the text, they had more flexibility in dealing with problem areas of the
Bible than we do when reading the full original.[47]

Human Characters/Moral Exemplars

One way of describing what happens to the portrayal of God in these children's versions is that God's character is evened out, made uniform or
consistent. Rather than the complicated image of God in the Tanakh—
both just and merciful, angry and forgiving—the simpler children's version stresses just one side of God, that of protection, mercy, and forgiveness. The same process is repeated in the portrayal of human characters,
who are represented as morally consistent figures. The moral ambiguity
and complexity so crucial to biblical characterization is unacceptable; the
characters are shown instead as consistently moral, in order to better
serve as moral exemplars for the child reader. In the Tanakh, no human
character is unwaveringly good; each of the great patriarchs, for example,
performs actions of questionable righteousness. These inconsistencies,
contradictions, or ambiguities may be crucial to the complexity of the
Tanakh, and to its persistence as a text calling forth religious and scholarly
commentary, but they were seen by educators as confusing to children,
who needed to be provided with simple, clear, moral lessons for young
children. The good guys had to be consistently good, and the bad guys
bad. Take Abraham, for example. All the storytellers work to show Abraham as a paragon of virtue. We've already seen how this influenced omissions from the story, such as his passing off his wife as his sister. Our
authors also delete Abraham's laughter at God's prediction that Sarah will
bear a son (Gen. 17:17), presumably as behavior unworthy of Abraham's
exemplary faith in God. Other episodes are made suitable through additions, rather than deletions. Abraham's sending away of Hagar and Ishmael, for example, seems inconsistent with the image of Abraham as a
good, kind man. Cohen accounts for the dismissal by attributing negative
characteristics to Ishmael and Hagar, which then justify the way Abraham
treats them: Ishmael "was a bad boy. He was always getting into mischief.
He tormented the goats and the sheep, and he shouted at the top of his
voice. He was older and larger than Isaac. He was always hurting Isaac and
making him unhappy" (Cohen, 1:18).[48] Hagar's failing is that she did not
tell Ishmael he was doing wrong, even when asked to do so by Sarah
(18–19). In these modern retellings, people who are punished must have

done things the audience can accept as wrong, and people who are good should not, if at all possible, be seen as doing anything bad.

Two Bible story collections published by major Jewish publishing houses in 1955 and 1972 leave out the episode of the dismissal of Hagar and Ishmael.[49] Indeed, they leave out Hagar and Ishmael entirely, thus conveniently avoiding the accompanying problems of strange customs (concubinage) and Abraham's imperfect behavior (sending away Hagar and Ishmael). Yet six of our eight sample texts from 1915 to 1936 included this story.[50] The inclusion makes sense when we see this episode in the context of other stories in which characters are figured as children. Such characters are attractive to our authors as direct models for the child reader/listener. A strong message is being directly conveyed to children in these representations of Ishmael: behave yourself around your siblings, or you're likely to be thrown out of the house!

When we look at the images presented and the messages conveyed in these texts, we see two related sorts of cultural work being done. On the one hand, the stories provide *reflections* of the norms, values, assumptions, and practices of the surrounding culture.[51] On the other, the stories also do the active work of *promotion* of particular social, cultural, and religious goals, and so may sometimes run counter to the general culture rather than reflect it. As we have seen in our earlier discussion of both secular and religious education of this period, education is a tool of enculturation, a task accomplished in part through the selection of content by designated authorities. In previous chapters we have discussed the cultural meaning of the modern shift to the Bible as the central Jewish text and the significance of the decision to teach the Bible in special children's versions. Now let us examine the texts further to identify the contemporary concerns they illustrate through the subjects they emphasize. Just as varying translations of the Tanakh convey the varying concerns of the translators,[52] so too these adaptations of the Tanakh for children convey authorial concerns, as the authors worked to make the Tanakh consonant with modern sensibilities and the American context. The educators were self-conscious, after all, about the importance of such adaptation. Gamoran, following Dewey's functionalism, held that the curriculum should focus on those Jewish values that would be functional within the specifically American context: "A value is valuable because it performs a specific function. It is valuable as it serves a certain purpose. The point of reference is to be found in human life."[53] As we examine these story collections, we will be looking out for those values judged to be functional "in Jewish life and in the life of the larger community."[54] To sample the values put forward to Jewish children in the United States between the two World Wars, we will look at three, sometimes overlapping, categories of characters: children, women, and heroes.

The Figuring of Children

If we return to Ishmael as a model of the bad child, we can see the behaviors and qualities that children are admonished to avoid: Ishmael is "wild," "mischievous," "careless" (Cohen, 1:18; Altman, 31). In some of the stories, Isaac is figured as having the opposing good traits: a "good little fellow" who listens well and obeys his parents (Altman, 31). We can see these child vices and virtues replicated in other characters as well. We'll examine here the stories of Cain and Abel, the binding of Isaac, and Jacob and Esau. All these stories figure children, and all are stories that could be potentially disturbing to children: one is about fratricide, another about the near killing of a son by his father, and the last about the usurpation of one brother's place in the family by his sibling through manipulation and deception. They are thus excellent locations for observing messages being conveyed to children.[55]

The story of the first children mentioned in the Tanakh—Cain and Abel—appears in the collections of four of the six authors who include pre-Abrahamic stories.[56] The narrative in the Tanakh is extremely laconic:

> And the man knew Eve his wife; and she conceived and bore Cain, and said: "I have gotten a man with the help of the Lord." And again she bore his brother Abel. And Abel was a keeper of sheep, but Cain was a tiller of the ground. And in process of time it came to pass, that Cain brought of the fruit of the ground an offering unto the Lord. And Abel, he also brought of the firstlings of his flock and of the fat thereof. And the Lord had respect unto Abel and to his offering; but unto Cain and to his offering He had not respect. And Cain was very wroth, and his countenance fell. And the Lord said unto Cain: "Why art thou wroth? and why is thy countenance fallen? If thou doest well, shall it not be lifted up? and if thou doest not well, sin coucheth at the door; and unto thee is its desire, but thou mayest rule over it." And Cain spoke unto Abel his brother. And it came to pass, when they were in the field, that Cain rose up against Abel his brother, and slew him.
>
> And the Lord said unto Cain: "Where is Abel thy brother?" And he said: "I know not; am I my brother's keeper?" And He said: "What hast thou done? the voice of thy brother's blood crieth unto Me from the ground. And now cursed art thou from the ground, which hath opened

her mouth to receive thy brother's blood from thy hand. When thou tillest the ground, it shall not henceforth yield unto thee her strength; a fugitive and a wanderer shalt thou be in the earth." And Cain said unto the Lord: "My punishment is greater than I can bear. Behold, Thou hast driven me out this day from the face of the land; and from Thy face shall I be hid; and I shall be a fugitive and a wanderer in the earth; and it will come to pass, that whosoever findeth me will slay me." And the Lord said unto him: "Therefore whosoever slayeth Cain, vengeance shall be taken on him sevenfold." And the Lord set a sign for Cain, lest any finding him should smite him.

And Cain went out from the presence of the Lord, and dwelt in the land of Nod, on the east of Eden. And Cain knew his wife; and she conceived, and bore Enoch; and he builded a city, and called the name of the city after the name of his son Enoch. (Gen. 4:1–17)

The entire story is told in just seventeen verses, with crucial parts of the story left unexplained. This is typical of biblical narrative, but unsuitable for a modern children's version in which ethical education was a main goal. For this purpose, character and motivations must be spelled out. Modern children's authors were not by any means the first writers to add material to fill gaps and explain puzzling details in the biblical text. Ancient and medieval authors created midrash to accomplish these same goals. Our modern authors had ready access to traditional midrash in Louis Ginzberg's *The Legends of the Jews*,[57] and in the next chapter we will compare the purposes and methods of midrash with our children's stories. Here we will focus on the substantive emendations made by our modern authors.

To understand these changes, we need to ask what problems are posed by the story of Cain and Abel. What questions does the original story not answer satisfactorily? What answers do the modern retellings provide? The most serious difficulties cluster around three major questions: Why was Abel's offering acceptable to God and Cain's not? Why did Cain kill Abel? Why did God protect Cain as well as punish him? These questions raise ethical questions about the nature of God and the extent of human responsibility. Given their concern to show God's actions as guided by reason and justice, rather than being arbitrary or unfathomable, our authors alter the story significantly or set out explanations to incorporate such an understanding of God. They are also concerned to show that human action is not random or unpredictable, as it might seem in the original, but rather is consistent and comprehensible. These conclusions in turn are directed toward the ultimate moral lesson that humans are responsible for their own actions and that bad deeds will be punished. Reward for good deeds is harder to draw out of the story, since Abel, the good sacrificer, is murdered, but some authors manage to bring in even this message. Calisch does it by adding an exchange in which Cain seeks forgiveness and God rewards his repentance, showing the "good" of repentance rewarded. Silber has Cain so sorry for his deed, and so contrite about his lie to God, that he himself decides "to go far, far away from home"—conveniently lessening God's role as punisher and at the same time teaching a lesson about the importance of taking responsibility for one's own wrongdoing, something not explicit in the original. The moral lesson is further reinforced in these versions by emphasizing an analogy between the behavior of Cain and Abel before God and that of children before their parents, with the stress on obedience and eagerness to do good.

Let's go back to the first problem with the story and survey authors' solutions. Why was Abel's sacrifice accepted and not Cain's? Our authors want God's choice to be rational, to *make sense* and not appear arbitrary. For this it helps to supply a reason why the two sons have different vocations in the first place. Altman draws on an early legend that had Adam assigning different occupations to Cain and Abel,[58] but she goes further and has this assignment based on previously established characters of the two boys: Abel is not very strong, so he gets the shepherding job, while Cain, the burly one, gets the responsibility in the fields (Altman, 15). But more serious than differences in physical strength are differences of character, which then help explain the rejection or acceptance of their sacrifices. "From the time they were both little children, they were very different in everything they did. Cain always looked cross, and angry, and miserable, and Abel was cheerful, and sweet, and happy" (13–14). This difference in temperament shows up in how the two boys respond to their parents:

> When Eve would call Cain, and tell him to bring some wood, or clean up the yard, or go somewhere for her, Cain would say in a cross voice: "Oh, dear! I don't want to work. I don't like to do things," and when she made him do it he would get very angry. Whenever she called Abel, he would come running and say in a cheerful way: "Yes, mother, dear, I will help you," and he would go quickly and do it well. (Altman, 14)

Cain also had the habit of thinking that everyone was, in Altman's words, "down on him," but it was just his own crossness that made him think so. Altman treats this as an opportunity to involve the child audience through comparison to their own experience: "Haven't you often heard children say that? They say someone is 'down on them,' but it is not very true. It is nearly always the child's own fault" (Altman, 14). This character flaw of bad temperament and blaming others allows us to understand why Cain's sacrifice didn't go well, as the way he prepared his sacrifice was in the same ungrateful, cross manner that he did everything else. In Altman's version it wasn't a difference in *what* the two sons brought as in how they laid the fire on the altar: Abel was careful to pick straight, dry sticks, and he laid them very carefully on the altar. But Cain "was cross and angry, like he always was when he had to do anything. He picked up all kinds of sticks, long and short, and wet and crooked, and he laid them very carelessly on the stone" (16). No wonder the two fires burned differently! In case we missed the point that it was Cain's own fault, the narrator explains that not only was Cain angry when he saw how well Abel's fire burned, but he thought that "even the fire was 'down on him.' Wasn't that foolish when it was all his own fault? He had brought wet wood, and was careless in piling it up, and so he spoiled his fire himself" (17).

Calisch's solution is similar to Altman's: give Cain a fundamental character flaw, in this case not crossness but laziness and forgetfulness. Abel, in contrast, loves his work (Calisch, 12). These traits are reflected in the attitude with which they approach the act of sacrifice and in what they bring: Abel decides to sacrifice in gratitude for God's goodness to him and out of a desire to share his good fortune with God. Cain, on the other hand, makes the sacrifice as a ploy to get God to let them back into the Garden, so they won't have to work so hard anymore (13).[59] In Calisch's version, both Cain and Abel pick the best of fruits of their labor for the sacrifice, but even the best of Cain's fruits and vegetables were small and dried-up because of his lack of effort. When he saw Abel's fat lamb, Cain "knew that God would not like his basket of vegetables, for they showed how badly he had tended to his farm, and how lazy and careless he had been" (16). Neither Altman nor Calisch speak of *God's* response to the sacrifices, in contrast to the biblical version (Gen. 4:4–6). For them, there's no mystery why Cain's sacrifice was not acceptable; it was his own fault, and it's so obvious to Cain himself that we don't need God explaining the problem to him. Again, expanding the realm of human agency goes along with a diminution of God's role in the story.

Cain's character traits also help explain why he struck his brother Abel; it is a simple carryover of Cain's defective nature that he would get jealous of and angry with his brother, whose sacrifice worked out better. But Altman and Calisch both insist that Cain did not mean to kill his brother; the hitting was intentional, but the killing was an accident.[60] Calisch goes so far as to add that Cain was sorry that he hurt Abel, and even more sorry when he saw he was dead (Calisch, 16).[61] The modern authors, it seems, want to protect their students from an image of humans so nasty that one brother could intend to kill another.

How is this murder, even if accidental, to be punished? The biblical text is puzzling in that the severe curse God inflicts on Cain—unfruitful yields and the life of a fugitive and wanderer—is contradicted by God's giving him a protecting sign, and by Cain's settlement in the land of Nod, after which he has a son and builds a city; so much for being a fugitive and a wanderer. Such inconsistency in God won't do in the modern versions. Altman and Silber solve the problem by speaking only of the curse, dropping mention of the protective mark and of the settlement in Nod. Altman has God say to Cain that he will "never, never have a home again," and she adds for good measure that while Cain lived to be an old man, "he could not forget what he had done to his brother, and he was very unhappy all his life" (Altman, 19).[62] Calisch includes God's behavioral change but provides a rational explanation for it: God is rewarding the change of heart that led Cain to admit he killed Abel and to ask for forgiveness. God punishes him for the murder but protects him with the mark because Cain is sorry for what he did. Then, after God thinks Cain has been punished long enough and that his behavior has changed—for he now works hard and is kind to everyone, unlike the lazy person he was earlier—God lets him make a new home in the land of Nod and live until he's an old man (Calisch, 1:17).[63]

What, then, is the moral lesson to be derived from the Cain and Abel story? The authors have worked hard to clarify the applicability of a basic biblical ethical motif to even this laconic story: If you do bad things, God knows and will punish you, as he did Cain. And if you improve your ways (in Calisch's version), God will reward you accordingly.[64] The authors are concerned to enable students to relate directly to these biblical characters. Throughout these versions, references are made to the child's own world, to children like those the students might know, to their own readiness to obey their parents or to do their work carefully. Just as the fire on Abel's altar burned brightly because he had laid out the wood carefully, so, too, Altman assures us, "whatever we do carefully turns out well" (Altman, 17). Any distance between the children and the text is forced to disappear: biblical characters were just like us, and God's actions are all consistent, rational, and just.

In the omissions, amendments, and additions that our authors made to the text, we see their sense—shared by Jewish educators—that the Bible is a problematic text for young children. These authors sought to make the text more approachable through selection and emphasis, much as Gamoran and other educators recommended. They also added a great deal to the text, something not recommended by the educators. Even Bildersee, who presented an abridged text close to the original, made similar kinds of additions in the scripts laid out in her teachers' manuals.

Both educators and storytellers were in agreement that the stories should be used for the moral education of children, although they did so—the pre–Lenore Cohen authors, at least—through explicit moralization and the insertion of new details, rather than through class discussions designed to draw the morals out from the students themselves, as Gamoran advised.[65]

To some stories the authors did not add much. Surprisingly, the story of the akedah, or the binding of Isaac, is one such story. Though one might anticipate this to be a troubling story, with God's command to Abraham to sacrifice his son and the willingness of the father to do so, little is added to these children's versions other than some unhappiness on Abraham's part.[66] Calisch adds an extra message from God after the sacrifice of the ram, namely, that Isaac and his offspring will also be blessed, "because [Isaac], too, was willing to obey without question the commands of God and of his father" (Calisch, 1:45).[67] Obedience is also stressed in the words of God to Abraham. Whereas the JPS version says, "Lay not thy hand upon the lad, neither do thou any thing unto him; for now I know that thou are a *God-fearing* man" (Gen. 22:12; emphasis added), two of our children's versions change the language to stress obedience even more clearly: "You were obedient, even when you thought God was not just" (Altman, 37); "I only wanted to see if you would obey Me, no matter how harsh my command might seem to you" (Calisch, 1:44).[68] And to assuage a concern that God may really have wanted Abraham to sacrifice Isaac, Cohen, as we've seen above, has God say, "I do not want child sacrifice" (Cohen, 1:25). These changes are minor in comparison to what we have already seen. But then, not much has to be done to this story, because these authors, with a pervasive concern for the value of obedience, find little that is troubling or problematic in it.[69] As Bildersee recommends teachers tell children when introducing the akedah, "It is a very beautiful story."[70]

For a final view of children, let's look at another sibling pair, Jacob and Esau. As with Cain and Abel, the different life outcomes for the two brothers are pinned to differences in character, with details added to the text. Esau is portrayed as the bad son, undeserving of the responsibility and duties that go along with the birthright of an eldest son. In the Tanakh, the description of the two brothers is very brief, highlighting physical traits and the brothers' differential milieus of field and tents. The text begins with the boys' birth:

> And the first came forth ruddy, all over like a hair mantle; and they called his name Esau. And after that came forth his brother, and his hand had hold on Esau's heel; and his name was called Jacob. . . . And the boys grew; and Esau was a cunning hunter, a man of the field; and Jacob was a

quiet man, dwelling in tents. Now Isaac loved Esau, because he did eat of his venison; and Rebekah loved Jacob. (Gen. 25:25–28)

After this brief description the Tanakh moves to the story of the selling of the birthright for a bowl of pottage. Silber's approach is typical in its highlighting of moral differences between the two sons, which are only lightly suggested in the juxtaposition of Esau's "cunning" and Jacob's "quiet." Esau, we're told, was a selfish boy. He

was not the kind of boy to care for the things that went with the birthright. He did not care to say prayers, and did not want to know anything about religion, nor did he like to take care of anyone but himself. He did not even like to stay in the house. All he did care for was to go hunting. (Silber, 1:60)

Jacob, in contrast, extended himself to others. He

was just the kind of boy who should have liked the things that went with the birthright. He was very much like his grandfather, Abraham, and his father, Isaac. He liked to stay at home, helping his mother around the house and his father in the field. He also loved to think and talk about religion. (Silber, 1:60)[71]

These moral differences between the two boys are reflected in their physical appearances:

When the two boys grew up, one could tell just by looking at them what sort of fellow each was. Esau was covered with hair all over and looked rough, just like one who hunts all the time and leads a wild life. Jacob always looked neat and genteel. (Silber, 1:60–61)

Another version, by Ethel Fox, enhances the negative portrayal of Esau by putting a description of Jacob's goodness and Esau's cruelty in Esau's own voice:

"I was very jealous of Jacob. I did not love him. But everybody else loved him. Jacob was not like me. Jacob was good. He was kind to everybody. I was not. I was a mighty hunter. I killed the poor, helpless birds that flew about in the skies. I shot the animals that roamed about in the woods. I was not happy either. But Jacob was always happy. Jacob loved God. Jacob loved everybody. That is why Jacob was happy."[72]

It follows, then, that Jacob's asking Esau to sell the birthright was a *good* thing, since Esau was clearly undeserving of it, and his willingness to sell it is confirmation of what was already visible in their characters.[73]

The presentation of children and the moral messages conveyed to them demonstrate the children's authors' concern to make biblical stories consonant with the values of modern life, and so to carry appropriate ethical messages to American Jewish children. This concern overrides any inclination the authors may have had to treat the Tanakh in a critical, historical manner, which would have entailed a distancing of biblical characters and culture from modern Jews. This desire to bring biblical characters directly into the modern Jewish home is figured literally in Cohen's text, in a strange (and for Cohen unique) interpolated story that follows the Exodus from Egypt. An account is given of the celebration of the first Passover, three thousand years ago. The narrator then requests: "Let us pretend that one of Moses' little sons came to a Passover feast at the home of two modern children called Joseph and Rachel." Into their "modern Jewish home" comes Gershom, "sunburned and dark" (Cohen, 1:130). He explains the Passover ritual to them, they dance together and sing songs, and then Gershom "walked right back into the book of the Seder Service and was gone" (134). Little Gershom literally joins the ancient world of the Bible to the Jewish home of the twentieth century.

Women

Child characters are especially interesting for us, given that children are the targeted audience of these story collections. Another opportune subject is the presentation of female characters and the ethical dimensions of their portrayal, given the new role of girls and women in Jewish education of this period. The teaching staff of religious schools—in parallel to public schools—became predominantly female, and girls were now educated alongside boys. In keeping with contemporary stereotypes of women, female teachers were considered to be especially suited to the moral education that was now the focus of the religious school, even though complaints about the prevalence of female teachers sometimes also surfaced.[74]

Women were also prominent in the production of educational material. Six of the eight most commonly recommended Bible story collections were written by women, and women also authored textbooks for other areas of the curriculum.[75] Women received training at the Teachers Institute of the Jewish Theological Seminary, but the most visible leaders in the field of Jewish education—the directors of Boards of Jewish Educa-

Gershom took the hands of the children.

"Gershom took the hands of the children," from Lenore Cohen, *Bible Tales for Very Young Children* (New York, 1934), 1:132. Used by permission of the UAHC Press.

tion, authors of articles in *Jewish Education* and other periodicals, speakers at annual conferences—were all men.

In the ranks of students, females outnumbered males, though not with as large a differential as in the ranks of teachers, three-quarters of whom were female. In a 1924 survey of religious schools affiliated with the UAHC, 998 schools reported a total of 53.6 percent girls.[76] This dramatic change from the male-centeredness of traditional education was in keeping with the coeducation of public schooling in the United States, though Gamoran speculated that the nature of the religious schooling being provided was perhaps more suited to girls than boys. Parents might be satisfied, he thought, with the "lesser quantity of Jewish instruction" provided in the typical Sunday School for their female children; sons could be sent elsewhere for a more intensive Jewish education. He also reported a conjecture that "the constant moralizing and the tendency to goody-goody instruction in our schools results in bringing to the school a greater proportion of girls than boys."[77] Gamoran's dismissive attitude toward "goody-goody instruction" is in keeping with his desire to move away from the heavy-handed moralizing frames of the earlier Bible story collections, but it should not distract us from Gamoran's agreement with all educators of the time concerning the centrality of character education in the religious school setting, paralleling its presence in the public school.

In this new environment, then, where females were dominant as teachers and authors (even while underrepresented in professional education bodies and in positions of authority in schools), and well represented as pupils, what messages were highlighted in or added to biblical stories with regard to the place of girls and women? What models of moral behavior were put forward? What is the place of female characters in the moral universe mapped out in our story collections? As teachers and as textbook writers, women were responsible for the inscription of Jewish identity on both male and female children, beyond the confines of the home setting to which their influence in earlier centuries would have been limited.[78] What reflections, if any, do we see of this enhanced educational role?

Concern for a female audience can be seen in the consistent inclusion of women as major characters throughout the collections, most commonly Rebekah, Deborah, Ruth, and Esther. We'll focus here on a comparison of the treatments of Rebekah and Deborah, since in the Tanakh they provide strikingly different portrayals of female action: one of female subservience to and yet manipulation of men, and one of female leadership, including scorn of and violence toward men. What transformations, if any, were needed to make these into female ethical models for young American Jews? We will see again that the authors leave intact elements of the story that provide no dissonance with contemporary values, while they delete, alter, or add to those elements perceived as problematic. The problems they perceive and the solutions they pose illuminate their contemporary concerns.

In the children's versions of Rebekah and Deborah, some elements are left close to the original while other elements are transformed. In the story of Rebekah, the modern narrators uniformly approve of Rebekah's provision of water to Abraham's servant. They also approve of her readiness to leave her family and go with the servant as Isaac's prospective bride. But they are uniformly uncomfortable with Rebekah's later deception of her husband in the matter of the blessing of the eldest son. In the story of Deborah, all authors are comfortable with Deborah's role as judge of Israel. They are a little less comfortable with her role as military leader. And they are distinctly uncomfortable with the denouement of the story, which has another woman, Jael, kill Sisera, the Canaanite enemy, by putting a tent peg through his head. A detailed analysis of the stories will show how approved ethical behavior is highlighted and how behavior perceived as unethical is adjusted to fit the desired moral message.

Rebekah is seen in the Tanakh in two settings: as a child in her father's community and as a wife and mother in her husband's home (Gen. 24–27). In the first setting, she is portrayed as a comely, compliant maiden, both in her action at the well and in her submission to marriage plans made for her. She provides water for a stranger when he asks, offering water to his camels as well. Her father and brother agree to her marriage with Isaac without asking her permission, and she agrees to leave her home without even the delay of the few days requested by her mother and brother. The picture of Rebekah as wife and mother, however, contrasts with her previous role as daughter. Most notable is her active, manipulative role in the deception of Isaac, fooling him into giving his blessing to Jacob, her favorite, rather than to Esau, the eldest son and Isaac's favorite. Of these two Rebekahs it is the Rebekah of the well and her father's home who is considered the appropriate role model for children. One reason for a focus on this persona is the youthfulness of the early Rebekah. The story writers, ever vigilant for characters in the Tanakh who can be construed as role models for children, draw attention to Rebekah as a child. All the authors include the story of Rebekah at the well, since her conduct there conforms to the virtues they stress, particularly kindness. Kindness is the basic virtue to which children should aspire; we've seen it before in the characterization of young Jacob.[79] In Rebekah's case, too, the stress on kindness necessitates modification of the text. The Tanakh describes Rebekah's physical beauty and intactness ("And the damsel was very fair to look upon, a virgin, neither had any man known her" [Gen. 24:16]), while the children's versions subordinate her beauty to her moral character. All versions describe her as "kind," with some adding other adjectives like "sweet," "polite," "modest," and "good." One version emphasizes Rebekah's kindness by the creation of a contrasting group of girls who do not notice the thirsty man and his camels. Only Rebekah notices and walks over to help him (Altman, 38–39).

The biblical treatment of the young Rebekah, daughter in her father's house, poses only a couple of small problems, which are easily cleaned up. Our authors delete reference to her virginity, and several give her the opportunity to consent to her marriage (not just to her immediate departure as in the original).[80] The main message of this part of the original text is easily compatible with a moral message appropriate for modern American girls: be kind, sweet, and good. But the next scenes, after Rebekah's marriage, are filled with problems: Rebekah is barren (a condition of the body, like virginity, related to sexuality, and so avoided whenever possible—even, as we've seen, in the story of Sarah and Abraham); fetuses struggle in the womb (again, an immodest reference to the body); each parent prefers one child over the other; Isaac, fearful of his life, passes his wife Rebekah off as his sister; Jacob gets his brother to sell him his birthright; Jacob, instructed by his mother, cheats his brother out of the blessing due the eldest son; and finally, in the wake of Esau's threat on Jacob's life, Rebekah manipulates Isaac into sending Jacob away to Rebekah's kinfolk to get a wife. God's inaction is as problematic as the human action—Isaac, Rebekah, and Jacob are all shown deceiving or cheating others, yet none of them is punished. Some of these problems are dealt with by our authors through simple deletion (Rebekah's barrenness, the fetal struggle, the wife-as-sister episode). But the central issues relating to the moral standing of Jacob and Rebekah are not so easily handled. Deleting them would mean deleting the story entirely, which the authors (except Fox) are unwilling to do. Instead, a range of adaptive strategies are applied, the goal being to bring moral consistency to the characters and the story: if Jacob is blessed as the successor to Isaac, then he must be worthy of that blessing; and if Rebekah manipulates Isaac in order to get that blessing, she must have a better reason than favoring her younger son.[81]

As we saw, the problem of Jacob is solved by contrasting him to the undeserving Esau. Reconciling Jacob's deception of his father with a consistent moral probity poses a greater challenge. Some authors mitigate Jacob's responsibility by emphasizing that his deception of his father was done in obedience to his mother, and obedience to one's parents is, along with kindness, one of the central virtues for children proclaimed throughout these collections.[82] Silber and Altman, on the other hand, go another route: they have Jacob feel guilty for his wrongdoing and seek forgiveness from God, promising to be good if he is forgiven (Silber, 1:66–68; Altman, 47).[83] The dream of angels on a ladder sent by God to Jacob in Genesis 28 becomes, in Silber's version, the sign that God has, indeed, forgiven him, and this forgiveness returns Jacob to his moral standing.

> What a great change had come over Jacob! He was no longer the selfish person that he had been. Instead of thinking of himself, he was now thinking of God. . . . When he left home he was afraid and worried. Now he was cheerful and hopeful, for he had learned that selfishness and deceit bring bitter fruit and he knew now how one must live and act to have God's love and blessing. (Silber, 1:68)

Silber's rewriting of the story is designed to be reassuring to children, who are seen as needing clear standards of right and wrong that are unambiguously supported by the authority of parents and God. Esau lost his birthright and blessing, but he didn't deserve them; Jacob, while deceiving his father, was obeying his mother; and finally, Jacob, aware, nonetheless, of the wrong of deceiving his father, feels guilty and asks forgiveness.

The authors have an easier time exonerating Jacob than Rebekah. Perhaps they try harder with Jacob because he figures as the child in this story, and the authors are concerned to present direct moral lessons to children through the lives of child characters. Bildersee explicitly acknowledges the difficulty of teaching about Rebekah, and she suggests that teachers avoid stressing the wrongdoing of the mother.[84] Rebekah's actions are somewhat mitigated by her insight into the moral character of her sons. In Cohen's version, Rebekah, having overheard Isaac promising Esau his blessing, says to herself, " 'Why should Esau have the blessing? He only cares to hunt and eat. Jacob is a teacher of men; he will do great things' " (Cohen, 1:38). The illustration accompanying the story has Rebekah look on surreptitiously but approvingly as Jacob presents himself at Isaac's bedside in place of his older brother. Silber, anticipating Rebekah's role in the transfer of blessing, adds a scene in which Rebekah hears of the earlier sale of the birthright: "When Rebecca heard about this, she was very glad, for she had thought all along that Esau was not the kind of fellow to have the birthright and was sorry to think that he would some day have to take his father's place as the head of the family" (Silber, 1:61–62). The transfer of the birthright—here seen as a just act—can then be used to justify the motivations of both Jacob and Rebekah in the switching of the blessing, which, after all, should go to the son with the birthright.[85] In the wake of the blessing exchange, Isaac is informed about the prior birthright sale, and even he is "satisfied that he had given Jacob the blessing, although he did not like it that his son had deceived him"

"Are you really my son, Esau?"

"Are you really my son, Esau?" from Lenore Cohen, *Bible Tales for Very Young Children* (New York, 1934), 1:41. Used by permission of the UAHC Press.

(Silber, 1:64).[86] Rebekah's craftiness is also de-emphasized by the deletion of her second manipulation of Isaac, when Rebekah gets him to send Jacob away for a bride, an action she desires in order to distance Jacob from Esau's wrath (Gen. 27: 42–46). The contrast between Rebekah at the well and Rebekah in her husband's tent cannot be completely erased, but it is mitigated by toning down her manipulation of her husband.

The figure of Deborah in the Tanakh could not provide a stronger contrast to Rebekah (Judg. 4–5). Deborah acts out in the open, in her own arena of judgment and battle, not in spaces defined by father, brother, or husband, even though she is identified as a married woman. Deborah's actions are direct and initiating, not manipulative or responsive. She is a woman in charge and in control, ready to act when others disappoint her. The figure of Jael, on the other hand, bears resemblance to both Rebekah and Deborah. Like Deborah, she is a woman of decisive, even violent, action, but like Rebekah, she accomplishes her deed through manipulation, tricking Sisera into her tent with a false welcome. What aspects of these female actions are considered appropriate ethical models for modern children?

Almost all our authors include Deborah as judge and leader.[87] The modern narrators are generally comfortable with her role, although they sometimes add a short explanation or comment on her being a woman. Altman remarks, for example, that while the stories so far have been only about boys and men, "there were many good and wise women in those days, and the Bible tells some pretty stories about them, too" (Altman, 88).[88] Some authors add a few touches to soften her character slightly. One author, for example, describes Deborah as "kind"—that ever-present sign of good moral character—and characterizes her role in battle as that of "encouraging" the Israelites and Barak, the leader who, in the Tanakh, refuses to go into battle unless Deborah accompanies him.[89]

More disturbing to these authors than the model of a strong woman is that of a hesitant, cowardly man. All versions but one alter the exchange between Barak and Deborah in order to make clear that he hesitates not out of any personal failing but out of concern for the people he leads.[90] Cohen goes the furthest in this regard. Deborah, who is described as having a voice "that was soft and low," asks Barak to lead the Israelites against Sisera, and he at first responds confidently to her plan. But when she lays out the plan in detail, he replies that he will not go unless she goes with him. Deborah, surprised, replies at some length, making explicit the shame of his reluctance, only implicit in the Tanakh: "'You mean you have not the courage to go?' she cried in anger. 'Aren't you ashamed to have a woman lead the men to war? Do you want it said that women have more courage than men?'" But Cohen goes on to have Barak explain his strategy, which takes into account the cowardice of the Israelites: "In order to rouse these people, we must make them ashamed of themselves. You say we have brave men, warriors, . . . but they have forgotten everything; their courage; their country; even their God. Come with me Deborah, and show these men that even a woman has courage to face the enemy. With you at my side, what man would dare to stay behind?" (Cohen, 2:39–40). Here Cohen turns Barak into the person of greater wisdom, instructing Deborah. The exchange ends with Barak's assessment prevailing: "Deborah understood. She said, 'I will go, Barak. I see you are only thinking of Israel and not of your honor. But tell me truthfully, wouldn't you feel ashamed if the people were to say, a woman conquered Sisera?' Barak smiled, 'Let them say what they please. My only thought is to conquer Sisera' " (Cohen, 2:40).

The biblical prediction that God will deprive Barak of the spoils of victory and instead "give Sisera over into the hand of a woman" (Judg. 4: 9) no longer fits the story. Cohen deletes it, as she does the whole episode that culminates in Jael's killing of Sisera. Other authors also delete the prediction and the episode, or reduce mention of Jael to a simple statement of Sisera's death at her hands.[91] One author (Goldin) includes a longer description of Sisera and Jael, but deletes her misleading invitation to him into her tent. This version still plays down the hesitancy of Barak, and makes no prediction of Sisera being delivered to a woman. The alteration of the exchange between Deborah and Barak and the deletion of Jael diminish the "virility" of these women, and also serve to eliminate the sharp sense of male/female confrontation that pervades the original text.

The change from the heroic figures of the Tanakh to the domesticated figures of the children's versions is most striking in Calisch's collection. The chapter title "Two Brave Women" leads one to expect a chapter on Deborah and Jael. Instead, Deborah is paired with Jepthah's daughter, whose bravery consists not of fighting with or against men but of submitting to the violence of her own father (Judg. 11:29–40). Jepthah, seeking victory over the Ammonite enemies of Israel, vows that "if God would let him win from the Ammonites he would offer as a sacrifice the first thing that should come forth from his house to meet him when he returned from the war" (Calisch, 2:13). When his daughter is that first thing, Jepthah laments his vow, but his daughter insists that he should carry out his promise. This account of the vow and response is close to the Tanakh, but Calisch eliminates the regret expressed by the daughter (Judg. 11:37), and instead adds an assertion of the daughter's willing compliance: "Willingly and gladly did the noble maid give up her life on God's altar, so that her father might fulfill his vow" (Calisch, 2:15). Calisch's portrayal of Jepthah's daughter, though extreme, confirms the female ethical models put forward in these stories.[92] Rebekah and Deborah, different as they are in the Tanakh, here present converging models: girls (and boys, too) should be kind, helpful, and obey their parents (like Rebekah). Women, in addition to being kind and helpful, may also be wise and brave (like Deborah). Behavior that complicates this picture with sexuality, deceit, violence, or confrontation between men and women is, wherever possible, deleted, diminished, or altered.

The prominence of women in the religious school setting—as teachers and students as well as authors—is perhaps reflected in the inclusion of at least a few stories centered on women in each collection. This is not surprising, given the prominence of these stories in Jewish tradition, and with the books of Ruth and Esther read aloud on major Jewish holidays (Shavuot and Purim). Reinforcing the presence of women in children's books is the use of female figures in the illustrations, where even minor female characters can be highlighted. The resulting combination of text and picture provides children with a view of female presence beyond what the text alone could provide. Major female characters like Rebekah, Deborah, Ruth, and Esther are the focus of the full-page illustration that usually accompanies each story. Indeed, the figure of Rebekah is interpolated into the scene of Jacob at Isaac's bedside as illustrated in Cohen (see preceding figure); Rebekah had overheard Isaac's earlier instructions to Esau and had given instructions to Jacob on how to deceive his father, but she is not present at the scene of the blessing. Other full-page illustrations incorporate female characters that figure in the stories, even if they are not major figures. In Cohen's book, for example, the dramatic story of Elisha curing the leprosy of Naaman is illustrated with a minor scene involving two females, in which a servant girl tells the wife of Naaman of the prophet Elisha (2:192). In another instance, Cohen gives a full chapter to a minor story in the Tanakh, the account of Moses' distribution of land to the daughters of Zelophehad; the story carries an illustration of the daughters before Moses (1:184).[93] The small illustrations used as fillers at the ends of chapters are another place where minor characters can be included. Cohen includes, for example: Sarah standing in the tent door (1:17, after a passage describing her happiness on hearing that she will have a son), a figure of Jochebed in a deserted landscape (1:109, under text describing her as looking off into the wilderness for her son Moses), a woman kneeling beside two jars, at the end of the story of Elijah's cure of the woman's child (2:183).

The message to children is twofold: women are important—hence their inclusion in text and illustrations—but the virtues emphasized for them are consistent with bourgeois, "Anglo-Saxon" norms of the time, norms written into collections by both male and female authors.[94] Given the overall goal of using the Bible to reinforce the ways in which Jews fit into their modern American environment (in addition to reinforcing a sense of Jewish identity), it is not surprising that the images of girls and women in the collections would fit well within the mainstream cultural views of women.

Male Models of Virtue and Vice

The moral models put forward in these stories are consistent across the characters of women and children: boys, girls, and women should be kind, obedient, and non-confrontational. What happens, however, to the presentation of leading male figures in the Tanakh, characters whose lives are beset with moral ambiguity, the necessity of military confrontation, and the problems of leadership over the quarrelsome and unappreciative Israelites? We will explore the figuring of male models of virtue and vice through children's versions of the stories of Saul and David, which together form a narrative of epic length and complexity within the Tanakh.

We can expect that the portrayal of male characters—like that of other characters, including God—will be homogenized, portraying them as either good or bad. This drive to create moral lessons for children by simplifying the contrast between good and bad meets a special challenge in the figures of Saul and David, as the drama of their narrative depends on the mixture of good and bad impulses in each of them, even while David can be seen as more meritorious and Saul more reprehensible. The length of the original narrative, which spans the whole of the books of First and Second Samuel and the first two chapters of First Kings, necessitates heavy cuts; by looking at what is usually left out and what is usually included, we can see how the authors accomplish the creation of Saul as a villain and David as a model of virtue. We will then examine the vision of kingly leadership put forward, looking for any influence of the contemporary context of democratic America.

In the Tanakh, Saul is portrayed as a good man and an effective leader of the Israelites. A man who stood out from his peers, he was selected by God to be the first king of the Israelites: Saul was "young and goodly, and there was not among the children of Israel a goodlier person than he: from his shoulders and upward he was higher than any of the people." As king, Saul provides effective military leadership of the Israelites, fighting "against all his enemies on every side"—the people of Moab, Ammon, and Edom, the kings of Zobah, the Philistines, and the Amalekites (1 Sam. 9:2, 14:47–48). But Saul's reign is destroyed by his disobedience to a specific command from God, and his subsequent jealousy of young David completes his personal and political ruin. The two sources of trouble (disobedience to God and jealousy of David) are linked in the Tanakh, in that Saul's disobedience results in the loss of God's support, which leads to the anointing of David and the introduction of David into the household of Saul.

The story of Saul and David is included in all seven of our collections that go beyond the death of Moses. As in the stories of Cain and Abel, Isaac and Ishmael, and Jacob and Esau, the storytellers take advantage of a paired character set where the bad traits of one can be played off against the good traits of the other. The task, then, is to select and highlight the parts of the story that will emphasize the flaws of Saul and the virtues of David. For Saul, this is accomplished in a variety of ways. The early accomplishments of his reign can be omitted (Levinger), or the choice of Saul can be denounced as bad from the start. Altman, for example, writes that Saul was chosen collectively by the men of Israel (rather than by God acting through Samuel) and that Samuel was disappointed with their choice: "He knew there was many a man in Israel who would be a better king than Saul, but he did not say what he thought" (Altman, 103). Even though the authors emphasize Saul's failings, all but one exclude the serious misdeed that causes God to retract Saul's kingship. This omission would be odd, except for the nature of the command that Saul disobeyed, the kind of command our modern authors were eager to avoid as an example of the "unworthy aspects" of God. As given to Saul in the Tanakh, God's command was this: "Now go and smite Amalek, and utterly destroy all that they have, and spare them not; but slay both man and woman, infant and suckling, ox and sheep, camel and ass" (1 Sam., 15:3). Saul's disobedience is that he keeps alive the captured king of the Amalekites, and he also keeps the best of their sheep, oxen, and lambs. Even the one Bible story collection that includes this story cannot face Saul's being punished for sparing the life of a human being, so it mentions only the animals and not the king.[95] All other children's versions eliminate this episode entirely, preserving the kindly nature of God but hence obscuring the reason for Saul's downfall.

Having left out this central flaw of disobedience to a specific command of God, how do our authors account for Saul's failure as king? Cohen is the most creative, making up a list of weaknesses and inattentions that prove Saul's unworthiness:

> Even though it was necessary to spend most of his time at war defending his country from the Philistines, he was nothing more than a good soldier. He did not build cities, or try to carry on trade or commerce with

other nations. He did nothing to improve the land. When not at war, he stayed within his palace a sad and moody king; always afraid he was not receiving all the honours due him as king. (Cohen, 2:91)

Other authors stay with what is readily available in the text. The common solution is to put the whole burden on Saul's jealousy of David. The authors ignore that before David ever joined Saul's household, he had already been anointed as successor by Samuel because of Saul's disobedience. The anointing of David is still included in some versions—another chance for a story about young children, with Samuel inspecting all the sons of Jesse in turn until he gets to David—but it is related without making any connection to the prior sin of Saul. The omission of the actual source of Saul's downfall changes significantly our understanding of Saul and passes up an opportunity to stress the virtue of obedience. It is obedience to human authorities such as parents (rather than God) that is more likely to be highlighted in these stories. Here the substitution of a stress on jealousy is appropriate to moralization for a child reader, who might easily relate to the feeling of jealousy of another's success.

Saul, mired in jealousy, provides a strong contrast to the portrayal of David in these collections. Of the multitude of episodes available in the Tanakh, those chosen for the story collections emphasize David's young innocence (the anointing of the humble shepherd boy, selected from all the sons of Jesse), his confidence and bravery (fighting Goliath), his gentleness (playing the harp for Saul), and his caring relations with people (his friendship with Jonathan, his desire to be reconciled to Saul, the sparing of Saul's life when he had the opportunity to kill him). These are the episodes that appear time and again in the collections, even those that condense the whole narrative of Saul and David into only two chapters.[96] The story of David and Goliath is played out at length in all the collections—a perfect story for a child audience, for in it one reads about the young David bravely facing the giant when older and more experienced warriors held back.

The adult David is a more problematic character for our authors, as we would expect. The complex story of his betrothal and then marriage to one and then another of Saul's daughters is omitted, as is any indication of David's multiple wives, not to speak of his concubines. More importantly, David's adultery with Bathsheba is either omitted or obscured, as is God's punishment of the adultery and of David's ordering the murder of Uriah, Bathsheba's husband. Two strong repulsions are working here: the authors' reluctance to mention sexual matters makes adultery off limits, and the authors' desire to set David up as a fundamentally good man to be emulated makes any significant failing of David's problematic. Further, the desire to present God as a merciful rather than punishing force militates against inclusion of God's decree against David. But if David's misdeed and its punishment are not mentioned, how then can the authors account for the divisiveness in David's house and kingdom? The answer: by not mentioning it, or by attributing it to the bad character of others. Before giving some examples from the children's versions, let's first review what is problematic in David's character as portrayed in the Tanakh.

In the original narrative, it is clear that David not only sees Bathsheba bathing but that he inquires after her, sends messengers to have her brought to him, lies with her (it even being noted that she was available for intercourse, having been "purified from her uncleanness"), and that she becomes pregnant. David then sends for Uriah, Bathsheba's husband, unsuccessfully tries twice to get him to go home—presumably to sleep with his wife—and then sends a letter to his general, Joab, telling him to send Uriah into battle in such a way that he will be killed (2 Sam. 11:1–17). God's displeasure is explicit (2 Sam. 11:17), and Nathan delivers news of God's threefold punishment to David. There will be violent division in his household ("the sword shall never depart from thy house"; "I will raise up evil against thee out of thine own house"), his wives will be given to his neighbor, and the child that will be born to him will die (2 Sam. 12:10–14). The divisiveness within David's house is developed at great length in the subsequent narrative, most importantly through the story of the rape of Tamar, sister of Absalom (son of David by Maacah) by Amnon (son of David by Ahinoam). David hears of the rape, is angry, but does nothing. Absalom, enraged by the rape of his sister by his stepbrother—and perhaps also by his father's inaction—arranges the murder of Amnon and then flees. He eventually achieves a rocky reconciliation with David but later sets himself up as a rival to his father and engages in open rebellion. His own death follows, at the hands of Joab and his men, a death deeply mourned by David despite the treason of the son. Later in David's reign, another son, Adonijah, seeks to usurp the kingship, and he is joined in this treason even by David's previously loyal general, Joab.

The only pieces of the above narrative that sometimes appear in the children's stories are the killing of Uriah and the rebellion of Absalom. The prior adultery with Bathsheba, the prediction of punishment, the rape of Tamar, the killing of Amnon, and the difficult reconciliation between David and Absalom—all are deleted.[97] These deletions are ruinous to the original narrative and its complex presentation of interconnected crimes and punishments, but useful for a simple and unproblematic moral lesson for children. Here are some examples of how it's done.

Altman's account is the shortest, most simplified, most distorted, and most clear. As mentioned above, Saul is presented as a mistake right from the start. The entire Bathsheba/Uriah sequence is omitted, making it easy to present David as a totally good person. Absalom is presented as a bad person who deserved his death:

> Absalom deserved the punishment because he did very wrong. First, he disobeyed his father's wishes, for he knew that his father wished Solomon to be king. Then he called all his friends to help him fight against his father. (Altman, 113–14)[98]

The bad people (Saul and Absalom) are punished, and David has a long reign as king, unproblematic except for the rebellion of the bad Absalom. David's wish to build "a great temple in Jerusalem" is mentioned, but the reason given for the temple not being built is that "he did not live long enough," rather than his being held back by God (Altman, 112).[99]

The most nuanced account is Schwarz's version, which, true to the approach taken in The Bible Story in the Bible Words series, is a much fuller account, including more complexity of presentation than any of the other children's versions. But even here, David's adultery with Bathsheba is omitted, with Bathsheba coming to David only after the death of Uriah. Schwarz also omits the forecast of David's punishment, as well as the rape of Tamar. The story of Absalom appears in a chapter called "A Rebellious Son," so here too, the focus is on Absalom's flaws rather than on the consequences of David's weaknesses. Cohen's presentation of the Bathsheba episode is similar—postponing contact between David and Bathsheba until after Uriah's death—but Cohen goes further in trying to present David in a sympathetic light, even in his desire for Bathsheba. The chapter on "David and Bathsheba" begins with a kind of prologue of more than a page that sets the scene as the fall of the year, with David "tired of war and bloodshed," longing for peace and reflecting on the beauty of the countryside. A chill wind sends him to his room, where he writes down his thoughts. He eats his evening meal, "lost in thought." In this dreamy, reflective state he catches sight of Bathsheba, in a romantic scene:

> That night, he again sought the roof-top. The sky was bright with the light of moon and stars. The moon cast its glow over the entire city. As David filled his eyes with the beauty of the night, he suddenly saw the figure of a woman on the rooftop of one of the houses. (Cohen, 2:150)

Cohen does inform the reader that "David was guilty of a great sin" in sending Uriah to his death, but our sympathy for him has been engaged. Silber takes another tack to reconcile David's sin with his basic goodness: he explains at length that "no human being is perfect, and even a man like David might do some wrong" (Silber 2:139). David comes out as a good man in the end, even with "a very terrible mistake," because, unlike a "bad man who has done something that is wrong [and] will not listen to anyone and will not try at all to do better," David—after he's reminded of his wrong-doing—feels "very, very sorry." Repentance, then, overturns the sin. "No man was ever more sorry or more ashamed of himself than David was as he stood there before the prophet, and he prayed to God to forgive him" (140, 141). In contrast, Absalom is introduced as "a very wicked man, worse really than you can imagine" (142). So the economy of good and bad is maintained, and God, once again, is not called upon to punish anyone harshly.

The premium on the goodness of David may contribute to another aspect of the children's version, perhaps surprising given the context of American democracy: there is no critique of kingship in the story collections. We've seen some touches of a democratic context in Cohen's book, such as the deletion of God's autocratic actions and a stress on freedom. But even though the Tanakh provides various opportunities for criticism of kingship, these are played down or dropped in our children's versions. The retellings include the information that the Israelites want a king in imitation of their neighbors, but this is not usually commented upon as a failing in itself. While some versions retain Samuel's warnings to the Israelites that the rule of a king will be more oppressive than what they are used to, none of these versions include God's own anger at the Israelites' desire for a king, God's ire at their rejection of God himself as king, or the Israelites' later recognition that the request was evil (1 Sam., 8:7, 10:19, 12:19). The failure of Saul's reign is attributed entirely to the personal failings of Saul, without the suggestion of the Tanakh that kingship in itself was problematic, and the difficulties of David's reign are entirely avoided. While a number of the texts include the treasonous action of one or the other of David's sons, Absalom and Adonijah, they exclude the larger struggle of David's establishment of his reign—not just the personal rivalries of his sons, but the opposition of larger Israelite groups that kept him at war throughout the early years of his reign.[100]

Why would our authors avoid an opportunity to promote democracy by highlighting the demonstrated weaknesses of kingship available in the Tanakh, especially given the emotional promotion of democratic virtues in the United States in the wake of World War I and the rise of fascism? After all, educators and intellectuals considered the Bible as fully in keeping with modern, democratic values. Perhaps it is just that. If we join the conviction that the Bible is in accord with modern values with the practice of using individual characters as moral exemplars, we can see why kingship itself cannot be criticized. In our children's narratives, David is the good person to be emulated (with his one admitted weakness in regard to the killing of Uriah). David is good, and David is a king; thus kingship in itself cannot be subject to criticism, even while an individual king, like Saul, may be. Furthermore, the institution as a whole cannot be treated like concubinage or sacrifice—strange customs that can either be omitted or quickly put aside as a custom "of those days"—because it is too central to the narrative of the later books of the Bible. Better to keep it in and remove criticism rather than to open the possibility that this central feature of Israelite life is a problematic or outmoded institution.

Bible Stories or Bible History?

A commitment to conflate the biblical world with our world is ever present in these texts, most notably in the exhortation to children to understand biblical characters as facing similar situations to their own. Biblical time is our time in these children's stories, and children then were just like children now. This is a hallmark of the Bible story collections, integral to their intended goal of serving the purposes of moral education. This commitment to ethical instruction, accomplished by direct application of biblical examples to modern life, is in disjunction with the critical, historical approach to the Bible advocated in principle by Jewish educators and rabbis of the period. Jewish textbooks—if not educators—were still in accord with a resolution made by Reform Jews in Leipzig in 1869: "Religious instruction in the school must avoid the critical method; the idealistic outlook of the young should not be blurred by the suggestion of doubts."[101] Yet a commitment to the historical approach, while avoided in the form and content of Bible story collections, was visible in two other ways. The first was simply to call the teaching of Bible stories "Bible history." The second and more substantive way took the form of a move, occurring around 1930, to separate Bible stories from biblical history, with the teaching of stories left to the early grades and biblical history—now a part of "Jewish history"—placed in later years.

Until the late 1920s and early 1930s, the term "Bible history" was used to refer to simplified Biblical stories for children, and some early collections of stories from the Bible were referred to as "biblical history," notably the late-nineteenth-century Leaflets on Biblical History series published by the Hebrew Sabbath School Union, mentioned earlier. "Biblical history" was, it seems, a way of distinguishing material adapted for children from the reading of the actual text of the Bible, which would be "Bible reading."[102] The HSSUA pamphlets were heavily moralized Bible stories, with no historical treatment of the material or critical perspective applied to authorship. They are "history" only in the sense of being accounts of past time as found in the Bible.

Another early and very popular text of "Bible history" was Maurice H.

Harris, *The People of the Book: A Bible History for School and Home*, first published in 1890 and continually reprinted through 1935.[103] Despite the title, in its table of contents the book is indistinguishable from the story collections that soon would take over the market. Chapter titles are "The Creation of the World," "The Two Offerings" (Cain and Abel), "The Trial of Abraham," "The Birthright," "Joseph Tries His Brothers," and so forth. The primary moral purpose of Harris's story versions is made clear in several ways. Some of the chapter titles state at the outset the character virtue or flaw to be illustrated: "Hospitality," "How Kindness Won a Husband," "Jealousy," "Temptation," "Kindness to Animals."[104] Each chapter begins with a Bible quotation from another section of the Bible, introducing the appropriate ethical message. Heading up the story of Noah and the ark, for example, is a quotation from Psalm 1: "The Lord regardeth the way of the righteous; but the way of the wicked shall perish" (Harris, 1:27). Children are encouraged to apply these lessons directly to their own lives, as we see in the conclusion to the story of Rebecca's winning Isaac as husband through her kindness to Eliezer at the well:

> Little deeds of helpfulness are never lost, and if they do not always win a husband, they will surely give you a happy disposition, and will win the love of all who know you. Do not keep your kindness only for your friends; give it freely to all. Be courteous not only to the rich and powerful, . . . but also to the poor, the stranger and the servants of your household. (Harris, 1:59)

There are touches of a historicist mode in Harris's book, elements that will become more central in the new kind of "Bible history" books written in the 1930s. More often than in the Bible story collections we have been considering, for example, one encounters the insertion of a brief historical explanation of some custom that is disjunctive with modern experience—not only practices as central as sacrifice (explained as the practice of people who "had not yet learned to pray" [Harris, 1:23]), but even a small detail such as Eliezer taking camels on his trip to look for a wife for Isaac: "How strange it would look to see people traveling on camels here! But it is the usual thing in the East" (56). The "Notes for Teachers and Advanced Pupils" at the end of each chapter lists topics or questions to pursue, most of them moral in nature, but some of them historical, such as "Why are camels used in the East instead of horses?" (60). Sometimes a historical question will combine with the moral message, such as this one following the story of Cain and Abel: "Give instances from general history where the greatness of men has been revealed in their youthful traits" (26). Pictorial illustrations serve a combination of purposes. The majority are full-page illustrations of story characters, much as in the Bible story collections (for example, Rebecca at the well, Isaac blessing Jacob), but some smaller illustrations of ancient material culture are provided as well (papyrus, sandals). Space is also given to a chart of the families of the patriarchs and a map of the journey of the Israelites from Egypt to Canaan (34, ii).[105] Finally, the first volume includes twenty pages (set off at the end as Part Two) on holidays and prayers along with a brief explanation of how the Bible was written by many authors over a long period of time. Such explanation, even while brief and subordinated to the story material, is foreign to the Bible story collections we have been considering. The latter were, in essence, replacements for the Bible, and while such explanations may have been provided in supplementary material for teachers, they would not have been included in the texts the children saw. Nonetheless, the general approach and style of Harris's book is fundamentally consonant with those of the Bible story collections.

Educational literature confirms that what was meant by "Bible history" in the late nineteenth and early twentieth centuries was historical narrative as told within the Bible, rather than history of the biblical period. Particularly illuminating is a 1909 article by Rabbi Joseph Kornfeld for the *Yearbook* of the Central Conference of American Rabbis.[106] Kornfeld decries the inclusion of miraculous accounts in Bible books for children. He makes a distinction between presentation of the Bible as "story" and as "history." The story form is what is needed for young children, and all the miracles and "fanciful" elements in the Bible—the "charm of the wonderful"[107]—should be included, in order to capture and hold the interest of these youngest children. But then there should be a shift to "history" for older children, in which the same narratives are retold, but with "scientific" explanations substituted for miraculous ones. He speaks approvingly, for example, of the two versions of the crossing of the Jordan by Joshua found in the Bible Study Union Lessons, a Christian series used in some Jewish schools. The first version, for fourth graders, gives the story "exactly as it is given" in the Tanakh. For fifth graders, however, the switch is made from "story" to "history," with the drying up of the Jordan explained as the probable result of a landslide:

> The place was probably near where the Jabbok enters the Jordan, nineteen miles in a straight line above Jericho. It is reported that a landslide of this kind took place there on December 8, A.D. 1267, which completely dammed up the river for several hours.[108]

"Bible history" thus means retelling the same narrative, but cutting out the "wonder" and supplying naturalistic explanations for events. Kornfeld despairs that the currently available children's Bibles, whether written by Christians or Jews, contain an indefensible mixture of the two modes, and he urges their firm separation.

The generation of professional educators that succeeded Kornfeld were also uneasy with the miraculous, "unscientific" elements in the Bible. But they wanted such elements excluded from the "story" versions told to the youngest children as well, and we have seen this concern carried out in the books of "Bible stories" and "Bible tales" through the 1930s. By around 1930, a new understanding of "Bible history" led to the creation of a new genre of books for somewhat older children. Still called "Bible history," these books were significantly different from the story-books-with-miracles-omitted type of "history" books produced in the nineteenth and early twentieth centuries. No longer is the biblical narrative (minus miracles) presented as the equivalent of historical narrative, but rather, events and circumstances in the Bible are put into a larger context of ancient Near Eastern economic, social, cultural, and religious life, of which biblical events and motifs then become examples. This genre, while still incorporating biblical story material more centrally than a fully critical approach would admit, is a dramatic change from the earlier books in which the Bible *was* history, rather than being just one component of data for the construction of a historical narrative. The change was announced clearly in the 1931 report of the Commission of Jewish Education to the Central Conference of American Rabbis. Chairman David Philipson remarks that the recently completed Bible Reader series (The Bible Story in the Bible Words) should no longer be taught as history, as originally intended, but as literature, and he introduces the new Jewish history textbooks authored by Jacob Golub and just published by the UAHC.[109] In this new vision of Jewish history, biblical history was the first phase of the history of the Jewish people, and was to be incorporated into an expanded account.

The leader in this genre was Golub's three-volume work mentioned by Philipson, published by the Department of Synagogue and School Extension of the Union of American Hebrew Congregations between 1929 and 1931. The last volume, *In the Days of the Second Temple*, was finished first, in 1929. Then came *Israel in Canaan* in 1930, followed by *In the Days of the First Temple* in 1931.[110] These volumes were intended for use by seventh graders, a significantly older audience than that of the Bible story books. All the apparatus of this series, from table of contents to index, speaks to a change in purpose from the earlier books of "Bible history." Golub's table of contents is utterly different from the list of character-centered tales of the story books, as can be seen by comparing the contents of *Israel in Canaan* with the first volume of Cohen's *Bible Tales*. While the inclusion of some biblical events (such as the Exodus) and characters (Moses, Saul,

Table of Contents

Table of contents from Lenore Cohen, *Bible Tales for Very Young Children*, vol. 1 (New York, 1934). Used by permission of the UAHC Press.

CONTENTS

Table of contents from Jacob S. Golub, *Israel in Canaan* (Cincinnati, 1930). Used by permission of the UAHC Press.

David) are visible among the subtopics in Golub's book, the work is organized along totally different principles from the Bible story collections. The
book presents the chronological development of the Jewish people, from
the early days of nomadism to the settled life of agriculture. First it sets out
the economic, social, and cultural context of a period, and then it turns to
specific aspects of Jewish life within this context. Biblical material is set
within a larger world-historical context, not retold as story but presented
through extracted examples of ancient practice or belief. In support of
this approach, the many illustrations in the book are predominantly of
material culture and geographical place. Sketches from archeological
finds are included, as are drawings of natural landmarks; maps and time-
lines are prominently featured. Illustrations of contemporary life in the
Middle East fill out the picture of ancient social and material life—for
example, "A Nomadic Encampment Today," "Treading Grapes Today,"
and a drawing of contemporary Bedouins to illustrate the "Midianites"
(Golub, *Israel in Canaan*, 11, 256, 171). Illustrations of biblical characters
are occasionally included, as in Bible story collections, but to a different
purpose. A Doré print of Isaac blessing Jacob, for example, found in a
number of Bible story books, is here placed in the midst of a sociological
analysis of clan and family structures. The story of Esau and Jacob is
referred to in one sentence in a subsection on family structure called
"Oldest Son Ranks Second," followed by an illustration of Isaac blessing
Jacob (20).[111] Similarly, a later section on the "Finer Side of Nomadic
Character—Hospitality" is followed by a mention of Abraham's hospitality
to three strangers, accompanied by an illustration of "Abraham Receiving
Strangers" (34–35). Although it may seem odd that the mention of Abraham comes after the mention of Isaac, this is entirely appropriate to the
organization of the book, which is by general period, not by biblical
chronology.

The questions at the end of each chapter are historical in nature rather
than moral, even while incorporating a level of ethical concern. For example: "Are large nations as a rule more civilized than small nations?" "Are
wars as frequent today as they were in nomadic times?" "What substitute
do we have today for nomadic hospitality or do we not have any?" (61).
The suggested additional readings at the end of each chapter are also
mostly historical works. Finally, the book closes with an index, appropriate
to a historical work but not a story book. All these elements indicate how
Golub's intent differs from that of authors of Bible stories. This is not a
collection of biblical stories retold for purposes of moral education. It is a
book of "Jewish history," with biblical material used as part of a presentation of "the gradual development of the Jewish people from small beginnings until it became a nation."[112]

Golub's method is fundamentally historical and contextual, showing how Jews in times past were "influenced by all the factors which shape social groups everywhere" (Golub, xiv). The overall frame of the narrative is from nomadic to agricultural society, explaining how the economic and material circumstances of these differing conditions shaped social, cultural, political, and religious life. Another hallmark of the text's historical approach is its attention to the differences between the ancient world and the modern, rather than the ahistorical conflation of biblical characters with the experience of the modern reader familiar to us from Bible story books. For example, after a long section on the religious beliefs and practices of nomadic peoples, including various "superstitions" such as the use of amulets and the belief that dreams could foretell the future, Golub comments on the vast difference between these ancient ways and modern ones:

> Such were some of the beliefs of our ancestors in the very beginning of our history. They appear to be so childlike that we wonder how grown persons could ever have held them. We must bear in mind, however, that the whole world began in the same way. . . . We, on our part, may look back with pride upon forefathers who, beginning so humbly, rose so far above the other peoples of their day in their idea of God that they could become the teachers of religion to the world. (Golub, 49)

The stress on difference can also be seen in the conclusion of the section on the nomadic period: "This is the background of our people from which we of today are sprung. Thousands of years separate us from our nomadic ancestors. Since their day we have climbed into the highest places of civilization" (Golub, 56).[113] Golub intends to show the "continuous and recurring growth" in the development of the Jewish people, and he contrasts his approach to one that portrays "a once-for-all bloom after which we have merely followed a fixed pattern." Golub sees his historical, developmental approach as essential "if we are to look forward to a Jewish future and . . . not merely rest upon our past" (xiv).

As these passages make clear, Golub's books, historical as they are, do not give the neutral presentation one might expect of a scientific, critical approach. The books were meant specifically for Jewish students, intended to foster a sense of identification with and pride in the long history of the Jewish people (with Jews referred to throughout as "our people," "our ancestors"), and to develop an appreciation of "Israel's genius" as evidenced in this history (Golub, xiv). Looked at from the perspective of the professional scholarship of today, this apologetic and didactic goal can certainly be criticized.[114] Yet in this approach, Golub's work is not that different from the nationalist (and hence inspirational) motivations of much of the professional writing of history in the nineteenth and early twentieth centuries, or from the American history textbooks designed for public school children to this day. That these were books meant for Jewish children immersed in Christian America—children arguably in need of some inspiration about connections to a glorious past of their own—may also give us some sympathy for the presentation of historical material in these texts.[115]

While the goal of positive identification with the Jewish past is common to Bible story book and new-style biblical history, the contrast in approach to biblical material can be seen in Golub's works, most visibly in *Israel in Canaan*, which covers the earliest period of Jewish history, the most problematic in terms of historical treatment. As we are led to expect from the table of contents and other elements of the book, the treatment of biblical material is fundamentally transformed. First of all, Golub deals explicitly with the problem of using biblical material for a historical account. He explains that no written records exist from the time of the events: "We have only stories, repeated by word of mouth from father to son over a period of hundreds of years, till they were finally written down in the Bible" (Golub, 10). Inevitable changes occurred as the stories were told and retold, he explains; hence these accounts by "our ancestors" "may not have been very accurate, because the science of exact history did not yet exist" (50).

Understandably, given his skepticism about the accuracy of biblical accounts, Golub often uses material from the Bible not as the basis for a historical narrative but as exemplary material to illustrate aspects of ancient life, in the way we saw him use Isaac's blessing of Jacob and Abraham's hospitality to strangers. Another example of Golub's use of such material is this explanation of the nature of government within the ancient Israelite social grouping of a clan: "The clan was a family government. The father was the supreme ruler, enjoying the rights which kings at that time had over their subjects. He could punish any member of his family by expelling him from the clan, as we find in the story of Abraham and Ishmael" (Golub, 18). No further elaboration is given about Ishmael, and the paragraph continues with descriptions of other aspects of the family patriarch's power, with no other biblical examples.

Elsewhere Golub recounts elements of the biblical narrative, "attempting . . . to reconstruct a picture of what really happened" (Golub, 53). In this reconstruction he strips the biblical account down to a bare skeleton and then fleshes it out with descriptions of the material and social environment. In the case of Abraham, for example, all that remains from the Bible in Golub's account is that he was the leader of a group of Hebrews who left northern Mesopotamia and traveled to Canaan, where they met opposition that led to settlement in the Negeb; they warred with neighbors but also seemed to have established some property rights. The many dramatic elements of the Abraham narrative in the Tanakh are gone; if Golub refers to them at all, it is because he takes them as evidence of social or political phenomena. The disagreements between Abraham and Lot, for example, are taken to be evidence of interclan disputes caused by the insufficiency of pasture land in the Negeb, and the flight of Jacob from Esau "may mean that wars broke out among the Hebrew tribes" (54, 55).[116] The Bible stories themselves are not retold. This is in part because the students are presumed to be familiar with the stories from their earlier years of reading Bible story books. Also, for students or teachers who want to compare Golub's analysis with biblical accounts, "Suggestions for Bible Study" are given at the end of each chapter. But the avoidance of biblical narrative in the book itself is also due to the nature of the historical narrative presented, which precludes incorporation of the stories. Golub wants his audience of older children to understand that there is a difference between the biblical account and a historical account, as he makes clear in a question posed at the end of one chapter: "Why are the stories in the Bible somewhat different from the history told in this book?" (62).

The impact of Golub's approach can be seen in a much shorter historical book aimed at somewhat younger children (fourth grade): Mordecai I. Soloff, *When the Jewish People Was Young*, published by the UAHC in 1934, a few years after Golub's series. Along with a sequel volume published two years later, *When the Jewish People Grew Up*, Soloff's series covers the same expanse of time as Golub's, but in about one-third of the space.[117] Once again, the format sets the book off from Bible story books, with a table of contents divided by time period, an index at the end, and maps and drawings illustrating the social and material conditions of life. Biblical material is used more extensively than in Golub (with biblical figures even referred to in some chapter titles, such as "How Did Moses Strengthen the Jewish People?") but such material is always used as illustrative of historical developments rather than as a moral lesson.[118] Soloff, like Golub, relates these developments to the social, economic, and political contexts, with a strong focus on reconstructed details of everyday life. Some story component is clearly considered important for the younger audience; but as the series editor, Emanuel Gamoran, explains, Soloff's book is a history book that includes some story material, and not a book of Bible stories, which are intended for younger children and "do not present history as such."[119]

By the mid-1930s, then, Jewish religious schools had two types of textbooks that drew on biblical material. The first was Bible story books like those by Silber, Calisch, and Cohen, intended for the youngest children,[120] composed of discrete stories self-consciously adapted to progressive notions of education (the importance of children relating their own experience to the text), to scientific notions (the diminution of the supernatural), to assumptions about what would speak most effectively to young children (simple text, more conversation, large print, ample illustrations), and to the fundamental ethical purpose of Bible instruction. In support of the moral goals, and with an assumption that such goals could best be reached through direct relationship between audience and character, biblical characters and content were selected for aspects most similar to the present or for those most "universalistic" in nature. The second type of textbook was a Jewish history book covering biblical times, no longer easily confusable with a Bible story book, intended for older children, divided by historical period rather than by main character, "scientific" not just in the thorough absence of the supernatural but in its presentation of historical context, less bound by restrictions of language given the older audience, still attentive to progressive education (with student projects in abundance), and used not to a moral purpose but to the goal of setting the Jewish people within the framework of world history.[121] The main aim of these books was not the teaching of the Bible employing historical method, but rather the incorporation of some biblical material in the teaching of Jewish history. As different as these genres were in form and content, they both served one common goal: the positive identification of Jewish children in twentieth-century America with the Jewish past. That past was made available to students either as embodied in a special text, the Bible, to which students could relate directly via the ethical examples at the center of each story, or as embodied in a historical account (informed by material taken from the Bible). In the latter, identification was produced not by direct relation but by pride in the distance Jews had traveled from nomadic days to the present, and in their special contribution to the development of civilization.

And what of the worry expressed by educators that children brought up on Bible stories would be disillusioned when later taught—through a historical approach—that these stories were not true? The problem was solved through a mutual accommodation between different kinds of texts as exemplified by those written in the 1930s. The Bible story books reduced the role of miracle and other supernatural elements enough to lessen the disjunction between the story narrative and the history. And the author of the teacher's guide to *Israel in Canaan* reassures us that the new history books, even while using biblical material more critically as historical source, still approached "what is traditional" in this material with "a respectful and reverent spirit." The attitude of the teacher as well as the text was to be "interpretation and supplementation of the biblical account rather than one of disruptive and unsympathetic criticism."[122]

Modern educators and storytellers were engaged in an act of cultural translation, a translation of the ideas and values of one culture into terms understandable and acceptable to a profoundly different culture. They sought to keep the Bible alive and central by transporting it from the ancient world to contemporary culture. They did this through the Bible story collections, a type of textbook that, with modifications, remains standard in the religious school curriculum today. Aware of the multiple appeals of secular American culture, Jewish educators felt the urgency of creating in children a strong identification with the heritage of Judaism, and they sought to accomplish this by interweaving Judaism and Americanism into a unified, synthetic whole. Jonathan Sarna has characterized this commitment of American Jews as a "cult of synthesis," evident in ritual, folk art, and writings, as well as in Jewish education.[123] This endeavor to hold Jewish and American values side by side was also played out in the way the Bible was taught to Jewish children. Jewish educators chose the Bible—the root text of Judaism and a text shared by Christian neighbors—as the prime vehicle through which a positive identification with Judaism was to be fostered. As had other modernizing Jews, they claimed the Bible not only as the quintessential text of Judaism, but also as deeply congruent with modern American values. And yet the extent of adaptation made in the children's texts shows the discrepancy between biblical and modern values and beliefs, despite the claim of congruence. In substituting biblical stories for the Bible, scientific and historical perspectives gave way before the principle of relating to the past through imaginative recreation of characters and events parallel to those of modern American children. A critical approach to the Bible, desired and yet avoided by these modern educators, relies on a presumption of distance between reader and text, and as such was incompatible with a goal of direct Jewish identification. In the context of 1930s America, the stories were designed, above all, to make children feel good about being Jewish.

The disjunction between scientific ideals and educative ends helps us understand the extent of moral homogenization in the children's texts. The Tanakh is not a "kids' book"; the moral ambiguity of its characters makes it a difficult text, one that invites multiple, conflicting interpretations. In contrast, Emanuel Gamoran encouraged children's versions that would promote an unambiguous and positive emotional attitude toward the Bible. Each story was to "constitute a real aesthetic experience," and the children were thus to associate "joy and beauty with Jewishness."[124] Storytellers felt they could accomplish this by transforming complex biblical narratives into simplified moral tales while incorporating—as best they could—modern values of science and historicism.

And what of the theoretical preference to identify Jews as an ethnic rather than a religious group, a preference we saw in the work of Kallen and Berkson, with which Jewish educators would have been familiar? I see no trace of such an ideology of ethnic identification or of cultural pluralism within these children's books. Practitioners, after all, do not necessarily practice what the theorists theorize. Indeed, rather than a celebration of cultural distinctiveness being played out in the pages of Bible story books—as would be predicted by the theories of Kallen and Berkson—we find instead a cultivation of similarity—that Jewish values and culture fit easily within American norms. As was the case for Kallen and Berkson, these educators and storytellers were engaged in working the borders between "American" and "Jewish" identities. But the imaginary maps they drew up had different terrains and different itineraries, even if the end destination—full incorporation of Jews into American life and of American life into Jews—was the same.[125]

Our discussion to this point has been geared toward explaining the form and content of Bible story books in terms of their context in interwar America, and we have seen how well suited they were to this setting. We turn now to a comparison of these books to reshapings of biblical narrative effected in different settings and with different goals.

6

Different Audiences, Different Texts

A story is fundamentally different from information. Information, as Walter Benjamin explains, lives only in the moment of genera-tion, while a story, never expended, is capable of regenerating meaning over and over again, at different times, to different people. A story "resembles the seeds of grain which have lain for centuries in the chambers of the pyramids shut up air-tight and have retained their germi-native power to this day."[1] The narratives of the Tanakh are such seeds of grain, sprouting many different retellings over the centuries and in differ-ent places. The Bible stories created in the United States between the world wars were tailored to the concerns of an audience of modern Amer-ican Jewish children; they reflected both the American setting and immi-grant adjustment to a new world. How do these retellings compare with other renditions of Bible stories, written for different audiences? What do they share, how are they different, and how do the differences reflect the various contexts? We'll begin with the retelling of the Bible in Jewish inter-pretive tradition, but for adults rather than children; such retellings flour-ished in the early rabbinic period. Comparing children's stories with retellings for adults within the same religious tradition will help to clarify the nature and purposes of the children's stories. We'll then consider Christian Bible story retellings for children, a genre that began in the six-teenth century and flourished from the late seventeenth century to the present day. From there we'll proceed to similar texts produced by European Jews in the nineteenth century, and then to the American Protestant texts of the first decades of the twentieth century—the closest companions of our main body of texts. An examination of post–World War II Jewish texts, issued by the same publishers as those of the interwar period, will point to new directions in an age of Jewish establishment in America, and the chapter will close with a consideration of the entirely different approach to teaching the Bible in Israeli schools, conditioned by a radically different geographical and political context. Our attention throughout will focus on the forms the retellings take and the purposes to be achieved in the new stories.

Retelling the Bible in Jewish Interpretive Tradition

The retelling of Bible stories for children involved not just the careful deletion of inappropriate material but also significant additions, and a reshaping of the text into a particular kind of narrative form. Viewed from a modern historicist perspective, the result looks like a deformation of the biblical text. It is one thing to provide commentary on the text, marked off by location on the page and a different typeface, or to simplify through abbreviation; but the addition of character development and moralization within the stories may evoke today a reaction of unease and dismissal, even laughter. Yet one can argue that these transformed stories fit readily within a long Jewish hermeneutical tradition in which the text of the Bible was broken up and reconstructed in other forms.

Sacred canonical texts like the Bible present a fundamental paradox. They have been canonized because of a desire to make them *fixed* texts—closed and unchangeable—and so they remain a sealed corpus over centuries. Yet even while they are held intact as a container of wisdom, truth, and law, the texts must yet be passed on, in forms that invite participation and identification by succeeding generations. It is part of the livelihood of a sacred text that it serves as a touchstone in a wide variety of cultural contexts. It cannot do this without sustaining change, sometimes radical change. Jewish tradition has preserved the Bible intact through specific customs of ritual use: The first five books—the Torah—continue to be handwritten on a special scroll, which is "dressed" in beautiful "garments," handled with great care, and read section by section from beginning to end during religious ritual throughout the year. The Torah in book form, relatively intact, was the base of a child's early education. But in other contexts the Bible was an open text. Even the process of translation allowed for changes and additions, for ancient and medieval translators did not place the same value on closeness to the original as modern translators do.[2] In addition, a vast body of texts developed that expanded upon the biblical text in the process of interpreting it—what is called *midrash*, a term that derives from the Hebrew verb meaning to search or to inquire. To understand the nature of children's Bible stories as an interpretive genre, we will compare them to midrash, especially the type of midrash found in classic collections such as Genesis Rabbah and Leviticus Rabbah, compiled between the first and seventh centuries C.E.[3] We will then turn to other ways through which midrashic material was disseminated: Rashi's eleventh-century biblical commentary, which was often the close companion of the biblical text in heder education; *Ts'enah U-re'enah*, a Yiddish compilation of biblical commentary and midrash first published about 1600 that was widely used in homes throughout Yiddish-speaking Europe; and sermons, which often included midrashic material relevant to the weekly portion on which sermons were usually based. All these forms present a contrast to the ritual reading of the "pure" text, in that they filter the biblical text through the concerns and perceptions of a later presenter/interpreter.

Certain features of midrash are familiar to us from the children's stories. Perhaps most important is that the generating impetus behind these two genres is the same: to manage the dissonance between the Bible and a current context—in other words, to deal with the religious tension that is produced by discontinuity. It is the nature of all traditions to generate new forms in the guise of continuity with the old.[4] The interpreter of the Bible faces something in the text that is puzzling, disturbing, or both. Disturbances in sacred texts cannot simply be ignored or put aside as irrelevant. Indeed, the production of midrash assumes that the Bible is continually relevant—a principle connected with the assumption of the special stature of the text as being of divine provenance.[5] These two assumptions were shared by modern rewriters for children, who reworked disturbing elements of the biblical text until unease was abated.

One chronic source of disturbance in the biblical text comes from its laconic nature—there are gaps in it, gaps of both motivation and event, that call out to be filled. The rabbis who created and collected midrash responded with additions. Sometimes the added material comes from elsewhere in the Bible itself, where the same biblical person, event, or law is treated in a different or fuller way. But often the material is a nonbiblical comment or story that elucidates the matter at hand. So the feature of the children's Bible stories that seems most odd to a contemporary reader—the insertion of nonbiblical material directly into the text, is a long-standing feature of Jewish exegesis, and the reason for such insertion is in keeping with a long tradition: to bring a dissonant text into harmony with a new context.

We saw that another feature of children's stories was the addition of moral lessons to a biblical narrative in which explicit moralizing is generally absent and in which the outcome of actions is often troubling. Earlier generations of rabbinic writers shared this concern, and some midrash draws moral lessons out of the text. Rashi's biblical commentary, which incorporates much midrashic material, inclines toward selection of midrash that furthers a moral understanding of the text, as does the selection in the *Ts'enah U-re'enah*.[6] The imposition of moral message is less central, however, to midrash than to the children's stories, which were tuned to the focus of modern American Jewish education on ethical training. Inclusion of an explicit moral/normative component is also a characteristic of modern children's literature in general, another influence on writers like Altman, Cohen, and others, who were self-consciously writing for a young audience.[7]

While the children's stories thus share some basic features of purpose and nature with a long-standing Jewish midrashic tradition, there are key differences. Exploring these differences will help us understand these stories as a modernizing phenomenon, in contrast to traditional forms of Jewish expression. We can see difference in three general spheres: interpretive style, conditions of production and consumption, and ultimate purpose of the text.

Interpretive Style

The differences of interpretive style are immediately visible from a casual glance at the texts, as the following sample from Genesis Rabbah will show. I've chosen the beginning of the section on Genesis 12:1, the command of God to Abram to leave Haran.[8]

1. Now the Lord said unto Abram: Get thee out of thy country, etc. (XII, 1). R. Isaac commenced his discourse with, *Hearken, O daughter, and consider, and incline thine ear; forget also thine own people, and thy father's house* (Ps. XLV, 11). Said R. Isaac: This may be compared to a man who was travelling from place to place when he saw a building in flames. Is it possible that the building lacks a person to look after it? he wondered. The owner of the building looked out and said, "I am the owner of the building." Similarly, because Abraham our father said, "Is it conceivable that the world is without a guide?" the Holy One, blessed be He, looked out and said to him, "I am the Guide, the Sovereign of the Universe." *So shall the king desire thy beauty* (*ib.* 12): i.e., to make thee glorious in the

world. *For he is thy Lord, and do homage unto him* (*ib.*): hence, THE LORD
SAID UNTO ABRAHAM: GET THEE, etc.

2. R. Berekiah commenced: *Thine ointments have a goodly fragrance* (S.S.
1, 3). Said R. Berekiah: What did Abraham resemble? A phial of myrrh
closed with a tight-fitting lid and lying in a corner, so that its fragrance
was not disseminated; as soon as it was taken up, however, its fragrance
was disseminated. Similarly, the Holy One, blessed be He, said to Abraham: "Travel from place to place, and thy name will become great in the
world": hence, GET THEE, etc.[9]

The commentary on one verse (Gen. 12:1) continues for another five
pages in this modern edition.

At the hub of the differences between midrash and a Bible story book
like Lenore Cohen's is the level at which interpretation is invoked:
midrashic interpretation characteristically proceeds at the level of the
word, phrase, or verse, while that of children's stories proceeds through
unification of a larger narrative unit.[10] Several interrelated characteristics
of midrash cluster around this central feature. First of all, midrash proceeds in "molecular"—and even sometimes "atomic"—units because the
biblical text is perceived as cryptic at this level, and so in need of elaboration and explanation. The sense that "in place of, or beyond, the apparent
meaning of the text is some hidden, esoteric message" propels the interpreter into a search for other sources, both biblical and extra-biblical, that
will aid in the elucidation of the text.[11] Modern educators and the writers
of children's stories, on the other hand, did not share this sense of the text
as cryptic. Rather, they felt that the meaning of the Bible—as opposed to
the Talmud—was generally clear, and it was this readily apparent meaning that was itself problematic (when dissonant with modern values or
practice) and that needed to be adjusted by radical deletion and careful
additions.

Deletion of a problematic element was not the path of midrash, for the
assumption of the Bible being cryptic worked in tandem with another
assumption: that the text, given its special nature as divine revelation, is
"perfect and perfectly harmonious."[12] Thus any "surface irregularity"—
any missing words or lines, any contradiction, any unusual word or odd
phrase—had to be smoothed over. James Kugel describes the process:

All of these are the sorts of irregularities which might cause the reader to
trip and stumble as he walks along the biblical path; and so over such
irregularities midrash builds a smoothing mound which both assures that
the reader will not fall and, at the same time, embellishes the path with

material taken from elsewhere and builds into it, as it were, an extra little life. Or—to use a shopworn but more appropriate image—the text's irregularity is the grain of sand which so irritates the midrashic oyster that he constructs a pearl around it.[13]

These irregularities occur word by word, phrase by phrase, verse by verse, with explorations of meaning inserted in the text, breaking the narrative into fragments, each with a universe of texts added in supplementation. A midrashic text is thus in form fundamentally similar to that of the Talmud, where the base text onto which commentary accrues is the Mishnah rather than the Bible. Midrash and Talmud share an anthological approach; they are citation literatures, full of quotations from other texts, "radical[ly] intertextual."[14]

This "anthological imagination" provides perhaps the strongest contrast with our children's Bible stories, which are fundamentally narrative in nature. Midrashic texts exist as *collections* of material, and the accumulative, additive drive of anthologizing is such a pervasive habit or reflex in midrash, that it necessitates a shading of the assertion that midrash has its origin in problems in the text, since page after page of material may be brought to bear on what one might easily claim is a not terribly problematic verse. For example, the opening phrase of Leviticus, "And the Lord called unto Moses," elicits many pages of commentary in Leviticus Rabbah.[15] There is a delight in an encyclopedic superfluity of piled up texts, in multiple possibilities and perspectives, rather than a concern for the unified vision of one consistent version of a story. In contrast, children's Bible stories use deletion as the major editing strategy, resorting to addition when necessary.[16]

The voice invoked in the textual citations is also important. In midrash, as in Talmud, the voice of "the rabbis" or "sages" is the dominant one, whether cited by name or referred to anonymously. If we think of the original motif from Bible or Mishnah as a musical phrase, the chorus of rabbinic voices responding to and improvising on the original transform and obscure—one can even say obliterate—the original, even while holding it to be foundational.[17] The result is the creation we call "rabbinic Judaism," in which the authority of the rabbis is at the center of Jewish thought and practice. The complete absence of cited rabbinical voices in our children's Bible stories—even when added material has its origin in rabbinic sources—is one of the surest signs that we are in another world, where the rabbis are obsolete; the text puts up a fiction of a direct relationship to the Bible, without the mediating authority of the rabbis. Rather than the named authorities of the rabbis and an anonymous redactor, the children's stories give us a surrogate Bible, presented in the unified voice of a modern narrator in a pose of passing on biblical stories directly.

Another aspect of the anthological character of traditional midrash, one that further clarifies the contrast with children's stories, has to do with the process through which the midrashic "bits" are linked together. One snip of text is connected to another through a mental process of association, rather than through a linear process of logic or narrative, both of which are directional (a chain of arguments or a chain of events) rather than associative.[18] Modern discourse, forged by the Enlightenment call to reason, has favored directional discourse rather than associative; our children's stories comply with this preference, as do contemporary reformulations of biblical and midrashic material intended for adult audiences. Louis Ginzberg's multivolume *Legends of the Jews*, for example, while based on extensive scholarly research, pulls midrashic elements out of their contexts, inserts material from folk traditions, and strings it all together into a continuous narrative from which the original biblical source-text is essentially eliminated.[19] James Kugel complains that Ginzberg "seems bent on submerging the exegetical function of midrash and turning it into mere tale-making, 'legends' ";[20] this is exactly the point, but it need not be stated pejoratively. When comparing the original midrash to Ginzberg or to the children's stories, one could easily label midrash as complicated or convoluted and Ginzberg and the children's stories as straightforward. Both provide the linear narrative that seems more natural to a modern audience.[21]

Also popular in the modern period have been collections of midrash and other aggadic material into anthologies organized by logical categories of subject matter ("death," "education," "marriage," etc.) rather than as a continuous narrative.[22] One of the earliest and most influential was the *Sefer Ha-Aggadah*, edited by Hayim Nahman Bialik and Yehoshua Hana Ravnitzky and published in three volumes between 1908 and 1911.[23] Relevant to the issue discussed above concerning the modern narrative impulse, Mark Kiel describes Bialik's mission in this book as "the presentation of the human, universal, ethical dimension of the aggadah, as a cohesive narrative composition, however fragmentary it may have been in the original."[24] Another early collection was Micha Joseph bin Gorion's *Mimekor Yisra'el*.[25] The same impulse can be seen in collections of other types of story material as well. Martin Buber collected Hasidic tales in a similar way, lifting them from a more complicated text in which they were embedded and lacing them together into a collection of stories.[26] Even more extreme are the anthologies popular in the twentieth century that bring together excerpted texts of various types, such as Louis I. Newman and Samuel Spitz's *Talmudic Anthology* and Nathan Ausubel's *Treasury of Jewish Folklore*, both of which gather material from a wide variety of sources.[27]

A clear sign of the divergence of modern discourse from traditional is that all of these modern collections have a table of contents by means of which a reader can readily navigate the text. In contrast, associative texts like midrash and Talmud cannot be schematized in such a way, and if a modern edition were to include an index, references to a particular subject or event would be found in many places. The Bible, too, itself a kind of anthology of a great diversity of texts, is not susceptible to a table of contents that goes beyond the level of major divisions. The works by Ginzberg and other modern collectors, however, just like our children's story books, divide the biblical narrative into discrete, titled chapters. Such an impulse to package the biblical text into story units is also evidenced in the popularity of modern movies on biblical themes.[28] The opposite tendency—a disregard for the forward linear movement and unity of a story—is evident in the tendency of midrashic collections to skip around and over parts of the text. That is, even while the collection as a whole proceeds in a forward direction through the biblical text, it continually brings into play pieces of text from elsewhere in the Bible, and it does not provide comment on each and every verse, instead choosing sections of text for commentary.[29] The same method holds true for the Talmud, which chooses pieces from the Mishnah for commentary. The result is a text (midrash collection, Talmud) that is hooked repeatedly into its source text (Bible, Mishnah), and yet ends up departing from it to an extraordinary degree, creating something vastly different in both content and style.

Conditions of Production and Consumption

The contrast between Bible story and midrash is further illuminated by looking at the conditions within which these different kinds of texts were produced and used. The children's stories are easier to locate in a production system than the ancient and medieval texts. They were written by laypeople (or sometimes by rabbis or professional educators), in the context of creating a literature specifically for Jewish children, to be read by or to children in religious schools or home settings. The origin and purpose of midrash is less clear, and one has to take into account both the original material—comments and stories by various sages—and the redaction of this material into the collections in which it has come down to us.

It is difficult to know exactly what material the redactors had before them as they worked. The interpretive material that they gathered into

midrash collections most likely originated as oral dialogue within rabbinic academies, passed on by oral tradition, but also, at some point, written down.[30] A deep familiarity with the whole text of the Bible—perhaps
even known in entirety by heart[31]—was presumed both by the originators
of the interpretations and by their redactors, as we can see by the way biblical quotations are handled in midrash. When the verse under scrutiny is
interpreted by reference to other verses of Scripture, these are rarely
given in full; sometimes even just the first section of a verse will be quoted
when the relevant part comes later; the reader is presumed to know the
whole verse. The biblical quotations are also given without citation—a
practice obscured by modern editions (like the one sampled above) that
mark out quotations in italics and identify them with parenthetical citations. The writer/redactor was assuming that the words would be recognized as scriptural, and that the verse itself would be recalled in full and
perhaps also in its original context.[32] The words of Scripture are like a language that can be called on by those who are fluent in it. The brevity and
sophistication of much of the interpretive material also assumes and indicates a learned audience.

This presumption of knowledge of the biblical original helps us understand the attitude of the writers/redactors toward the highly elaborated
text that they created. A modern reader cannot help but wonder about
the epistemological status of the interpretive material added to the biblical text. Were the rabbis self-consciously making up things to "fix" the
text? This is what it looks like to modern eyes, trained in a historical/crit-
ical approach in which a distinction between what is original and what is a
later version or commentary is crucial, with each accretion or change put
in its own historical context. But ancient and medieval exegetes had, in
general, little problem with a kind of synchrony between old and new writings. They were *always* appropriating and retelling stories, just as their
contemporaries appropriated and repeated artistic images. What was
important was to get to the truth(s) of a matter, rather than to worry
about precisely when and by whom it was said. There is thus an effacing of
distinction between "text" and "tradition," between "composition" and
"interpretation." Conjoining this attitude with the assumption that the
Bible was a perfect text coming from a divine source, we can conclude
that rather than seeing themselves as changing the biblical text, the writ-
ers/redactors of midrash understood themselves to be uncovering in the
text what was "always already" there,[33] pulling out meanings that were
extant but obscured. Also underlying this sense of seamlessness between
what we cannot help but see as "old" material and "new" was the rabbis'
belief that their comments—constituting oral Torah—were part of the
same revelatory experience as the giving of the (written) Torah.[34] At the

same time, the evidence of presumed knowledge of the biblical text demonstrates that readers knew the difference between the original and its later elaboration.

While these rabbinic texts were thus originally intended for, and probably first consumed by, a learned audience fully conversant with the Bible, their eventual audience was wider.[35] The broadest and most diverse audience was reached through the extensive use of midrashic material by rabbis who preached in synagogues, in sermons given in conjunction with the liturgical recitation of the Torah.[36] Those hearing such sermons could range from children and women to distinguished rabbinic visitors. To understand the sermon fully would require substantial linguistic knowledge of Hebrew, though preachers attempted to reach a varied audience.[37] Two other written sources provided a more sustained or systematic exposure to midrash for a wide audience: Rashi's eleventh-century commentary on the Chumash, and the *Ts'enah U-re'enah*, a compilation of biblical commentary and midrash first published around 1600.

While Rashi did not intend to write for the masses, his commentary was such a compact and convenient compendium of traditional rabbinic understandings of Torah that it soon became the most widely read Bible commentary, and came to be used even at the early stages of heder education. Midrashic material is not dominant in Rashi, as he prefers the "plain sense" (*peshat*) when possible.[38] But in other places he resorts to a midrashic explanation, while not usually identifying sources with specific rabbinic authorities.[39] Thus, even with no other exposure to midrash collections, any male advancing beyond the most elementary learning of Hebrew would hear or read some midrashic stories in association with the study of the Chumash with Rashi, and the midrash included in Rashi would be, as a result, the most widely known of this material.

The material in the *Ts'enah U-re'enah* (Go Forth and See) was even more widely disseminated, as this book, written in Yiddish, was in its original purpose intended for a wide audience, including, and perhaps especially aimed at, women. It was extremely popular, going through numerous printed editions and finding its way into many homes, where it was commonly used by women for their Sabbath reading of the weekly portion.[40] Its use of the vernacular and its incorporation of woodcuts mark the *Ts'enah U-re'enah* as a self-consciously popular text, distinct from earlier midrashic collections or from Rashi. The method through which the Bible is presented is much the same, however. A verse or part of a verse is quoted and then a compilation of commentary and midrash follows. The text proceeds in a linear way through the Bible, but far from every verse is included. Perhaps the author presumed enough familiarity with the original that the missing parts of the story would be filled in mentally by the reader. In practice, use of the text—with its combination of abridgment (the missing biblical text) and expansion (the added commentary and midrash)—resulted in a merged new text that replaced the Bible itself, especially when it was heard rather than read.[41]

The Overall Goals of the Texts

Replacement of the Bible itself—at least in childhood years—was clearly a goal of the Bible story collections that proliferated in the early part of this century. The Bible was central to Judaism—in fact, arguably more central to Reform Jews than was previously the case[42]—but it was inappropriate for children. Substitutes were thus created. The originating impulse in midrash is a different one—to *explain* the difficulties in the text, rather than to replace them (although we have seen that this distinction might become blurred in the texts' subsequent use by an unlearned audience). This explanatory function of midrash results in continual interruption of the text, leading the reader in multiple directions. Midrash is a form of learned commentary on a base text, and is generally found in an anthological form, a gathering of a variety of rabbinic dicta. The children's stories, on the other hand—along with modern collections like Ginzberg's and Bialik/Raznitsky's and biblical film epics—put the story itself first, with the relationship to story one of entry into the narrative line rather than understanding at a textual level. The goal was no longer to master the text through understanding (with a base in memorization) but rather to use the text as a vehicle to identify with Judaism and Jewish tradition. One way to make the Bible modern, then, is to make it a "good story" that draws us in. In either case—explanation or story—the surface irregularities of the text needed to be smoothed over. Thus Bible stories and the tradition of midrash both transformed the Bible in order to reach new generations, but with two different purposes: for midrash the goal was understanding; for children's stories, identification.

Christian Bible Story Collections

Christian writers, too, developed learned commentaries on the Bible in the late ancient and medieval periods. But Christian retellings of Bible stories intended specifically for children developed centuries before Jewish ones. They date to the radical religious change of the sixteenth century and to the contemporaneous increase in literacy; the genre was flourishing by the end of the seventeenth century. There had been earlier precursors of this kind of text, in particular Peter Comestor's late-twelfth-century work, *Historia Scholastica*.[43] Peter Comestor's work, though in Latin rather than in the vernacular, and intended for university students rather than small children, presents many of the features later found in Bible story collections for children, as it includes only narrative parts of the Bible and incorporates nonbiblical material into the presentation of the stories.[44] The book's translation into French in the late thirteenth century and the hundreds of extant manuscripts attest to the success and popularity of the text.

The Protestant focus on the Bible as religious authority certainly contributed to the development of the genre of Bible stories, yet despite differing attitudes at the official level of the Protestant and Catholic churches, the practice of Bible reading for children up until the twentieth century was actually similar across confessions. Both Protestants and Catholics have read the Bible, but—at least as children—they have read it in the form of vernacular story collections (as well as psalms and set quotations), rather than in the canonical text of the Bible itself.[45] The earliest of these collections, in the sixteenth and seventeenth centuries, stayed close to the plots of those Old Testament narratives selected for inclusion. By the mid-eighteenth century, however, a changed view of the nature of children and of childhood innocence led to the expurgation of "unsuitable" material, that is, sex, violence, and other behavior that would complicate perception of "good" characters. From cautionary tales, the stories were refigured as models of virtuous behavior.[46] The resulting books functioned as "the Bible" for children, far as they may have been from the original text.

The same characteristics—selectivity of stories, expurgation of material, and addition of extra-biblical material—were all implemented in the earliest Bible story collections intended for Jewish children.

The First Bible Story Books for Jewish Children

We have seen how the institutions and curriculum of Jewish education changed in Europe in the late eighteenth and nineteenth centuries in response to social, intellectual, and political developments. In this new context, Jews, too, turned to the use of collections of vernacular Bible stories, the earliest of which was written by Moses Mordecai Büdinger in 1823.[47] Like their Christian counterparts, Jewish authors departed radically from the traditional Jewish practice of introducing young children to the Bible through the full original text. They greatly reduced the text, selecting stories deemed suitable for children and excising material judged inappropriate. All was retold in the vernacular, rather than Hebrew. Although they altered the text, these authors refrained from inserting substantial additions within the stories; they reserved their moralizing enhancements for chapter titles, quotation headings, footnotes (Büdinger and Auerbach), or commentaries (Montefiore). The books have few or no illustrations, and were perhaps more useful for the adults in charge of the teaching of children—whether at school or in the home—than for the direct use of the intended child reader.

American Protestant Collections from the First Decades of the Twentieth Century

While Bible story collections authored by European Jewish writers existed as potential models for American Jewish educators, these texts go unmentioned in the literature of Jewish education in the United States. In looking for models of religious education for Jewish children, American Jewish educators were most attentive to models provided by Protestantism, the dominant cultural force in their immediate setting. Jewish educators' advice on how to teach the Bible to children, and the story collections that were produced to serve those purposes, were shaped in self-conscious reflection of Protestant practice.

Let's look at a sample of the contemporary Protestant texts that are likely to have been familiar to a Jewish audience.[48] One significant difference for Protestant audiences as compared to Jewish ones is that Protestants had ready access to mainstream trade publishers, whose books could be marketed to the general reading public as well as to religious schools. With mass market books available, there was less need for particular denominations to develop their own materials. We'll consider here five such books (listed in chronological order): *Story of the Bible Told for Young and Old,* by Rev. Jesse Lyman Hurlbut; *The Garden of Eden,* by George Hodges; *Bible Stories to Read and Tell,* by Frances Jenkins Olcott; *The Children's Bible,* by Henry A. Sherman and Charles Foster Kent; and *The Bible Story,* by Rev. James Baikie.[49]

These books embody a range of approaches successful among the mainstream Protestant audience. Hurlbut, Olcott, and Baikie are relatively hefty volumes (750, 486, and 472 pages respectively), with some illustrations but heavy on text, and in a smaller typeface than one would use for a readership of small children. The vocabulary is also pitched to more mature readers (teachers or parents), who in turn would tell the story to a younger audience. They were unlikely to be books that a religious school would buy in multiple copies to distribute to students.[50] The Sherman and

Kent book is significantly shorter (329 pages), but is still not meant for younger children to read by themselves; the authors note that they kept the language "simple enough so that it may easily be read to the younger children and by those who are older."[51] Hodges's book bears the closest resemblance to the Bible story books marketed for Jewish religious education; it is printed in two short volumes, has big print and many illustrations, and is written in language directed specifically at children.

The books also differ in the extent of moral and historical explanation added to or inserted within the stories. Hurlbut insists in his preface that he has not changed or added to the stories. The stories, he says, "are made plain, but they are not rewritten or changed"; he has not added any "imaginary scenes or incidents or conversations," and he criticizes other children's versions that make the stories "teach doctrines which may be right or may be wrong, but are not stated nor hinted in the Scripture stories." And yet Hurlbut does, in fact, add explanation to those stories he finds morally problematic. In the story of Abraham and Isaac, for example, he inserts a long explanation of how God really didn't mean for Abraham to sacrifice Isaac, but was rather testing Abraham's obedience at the same time that he was teaching Abraham and his descendants that child sacrifice is wrong. To the story of Jepthah's daughter, he adds an extensive account of how it could come to pass that Jepthah made such an unwise vow, explaining that Jepthah had been living in isolation and didn't understand that child sacrifice had been rejected by the Israelites.[52] Elsewhere Hurlbut is less intrusive, but ever ready to add a bit of explanation to make the story more palatable to his audience. For example, in the Cain and Abel story, there are no psychological portraits of the two brothers to explain their rivalry, but an explanation of the nature of sacrifice is added, and, more importantly, an explanation is attempted for why God rejected Cain's sacrifice and accepted Abel's: "For some reason God was pleased with Abel and his offering, but was not pleased with Cain and his offering. Perhaps God wished Cain to offer something that had life, as Abel offered; perhaps Cain's heart was not right when he came before God."[53] Baikie's 1923 book is similar. In his preface the author promises an untangling of events in a straightforward, easy to follow narrative, while in the text he inserts extensive explanations about characters, intentions, moral lessons, and historical settings.

Olcott and Sherman and Kent use a "plain text" approach, similar to The Bible Story in Bible Words series from the Union of American Hebrew Congregations. In both books, the language is simplified, and morally troubling material (e.g., Hagar and Ishmael, Jael, Saul's disobedience over Amalek, any story connected with Amnon) is deleted, but what is left is told without added explanation or insertions. No rationales are offered for Cain's anger toward Abel, or of Abraham's willingness to sacrifice Isaac, for example, and no explicit moral messages are added to the narrative. The only extra layer of moralization—a thin one—is the titling of the individual chapters with phrases that sometimes indicate an ethical message, such as "The First Disobedience" (or "The First Murderer"), "Abraham's Loyalty to God," and "The Testing of Joseph's Brothers."

Hodges's book has a moderate number of extra explanations, similar to Hurlbut's and Baikie's. The text accomplishes most of the moral work by heavy abridgment and deletion, but some interjections are made where explanation or counter-message seem necessary. For example, though no elaborations of Cain's and Abel's characters are given, nor any differentiation of their sacrifices, Hodges inserts an explanation of God's rejection of Cain's sacrifice: "*But God looked at their hearts*, and He was pleased with Abel's offering, but Cain's He would not take." Some actions perceived as disturbing, such as Jael's killing of Sisera or Jepthah's vow, are explained by the fact that this was "a long, long time ago."[54] This emphasis on distancing the reader from the time and behavior of events is a more readily available strategy for Christian authors than for Jewish. Jewish authors were committed to telling the stories in such a way that children could relate directly to the biblical characters. While Christian authors had a similar goal, distancing the children from the Old Testament was not problematic, and in some sense even laudable, as it was especially to the New Testament narrative that an identification was to be forged. T. Rhondda Williams, a British author whose *Old Testament Stories in Modern Light* was admired by Streibert as "one of the few books which does attempt to give children a correct understanding of the Bible stories," explains the distancing necessary from at least some of the Old Testament.[55] Williams includes a retelling of the story of the fall of Jericho, for example, but instead of giving a reference to the biblical passages, as he does in most other places, he warns against reading the Book of Joshua, as "it is not a book for children. If you come to read it even when you are grown up, there is one thing you must always remember, *viz.*, that you must not think of God as the Book of Joshua represents Him. [This book] contains . . . a great deal of cruelty and deception in it which the writer thought God approved."[56] The Book of Joshua, Williams recommends, should never be read without reading the Sermon on the Mount. Further on, after telling about Saul and the battle with the Ammonites, Williams inserts, "Well, now, how thankful we ought to be that those rude old days are over, and how determined we ought to be that all the barbarism of that time shall now be entirely a thing of the past!"[57]

While some Old Testament images and actions of God were a source of discomfort, these volumes generally keep God in the picture, retaining much of the miraculous and divine action. The prominence of miracles is, in fact, a point of criticism in the view of Angus Hector MacLean, whose *Idea of God in Protestant Religious Education* was published by Teachers College Press in 1930, just two years before the same press published Solomon Fineberg's *Biblical Myth and Legend in Jewish Education*, a book with very similar concerns.[58] While MacLean approvingly documents a stress on God's mercy and forgiveness in Protestant Bible story collections, and notes some diminishment of divine interventions (such as God speaking to humans or appearing in dreams), he is indignant that material inconsistent with a scientific approach is included at all, and he is critical of such material in the New Testament as well as the Old.[59]

The comparison of these Protestant books with their Jewish contemporaries shows that basic concerns were held in common. The Bible was to be presented as a series of connected narratives, written in language adapted for children and (in the case of some texts) adorned with illustrations. Adapting the stories to modern moral concerns was to be accomplished through significant deletions and (in some cases) through interpolations and explanations. The Jewish concern to have students identify directly with the text is attenuated for Christian authors with respect to the Old Testament, which opens more possibility for historical explanation of disturbing passages. Finally, the availability of mass market books by major trade publishers allowed a different use of the Protestant books. Many of them are large volumes, from which an adult would read to the child. Fewer pictures were necessary, and perhaps less moralization and explanation, which could be added extemporaneously by the adult reader.

A New Generation of Texts

Bible story collections written for an audience of Jewish children in the second half of the century preserved the central features forged in the first half: the language of the stories is changed to adapt to a child's level of understanding, illustrations are used to help engage a child's interest and to highlight lessons, moral difficulties and supernatural elements are often eliminated or significantly refigured, and, most importantly, the stories aim to teach moral lessons; they encourage the relationship of the child to the material through ethical deliberation. The educational agenda forged in the first third of the twentieth century remained in place through the end of the twentieth century.

While the core educational goals and general approach endured, two significant changes made the collections of the last decades of the twentieth century noticeably different. First, authors began to make self-conscious use of rabbinic material (Talmud and midrash) to explain issues in the stories. Second, the style of the story prose altered, with the dominant style shifting from a thoroughgoing retelling of the stories to a straightforward simplification. While these changes were small, they eliminated aspects of the earlier texts that were most dissonant to the contemporary ear.

The first postwar books showed little change. The first, Dorothy Zeligs's *The Story Bible*, bears a strong resemblance to its competitor, Lenore Cohen's *Bible Tales*.[60] Like Cohen's, Zeligs's book has two volumes, begins with the story of Abraham, and has a similar format and prose style: it is heavily rewritten and has added details of character and motivation. The story of Abraham's being told to leave Haran for Canaan, for example, is greatly expanded. Zeligs elaborates on Abraham's goal—spreading "his new ideas about God"—and the hardship he faced—leaving behind his familiar and comfortable life in Ur (which is substituted for Haran). Sarah's feelings are added in as well: "Sarah was a beautiful woman and she must have enjoyed the lovely things she had in Ur. But Sarah agreed to leave them all behind because she knew that Abraham was no longer happy there."[61]

In the mid-1950s, UAHC Press, publisher of Cohen's *Bible Tales*, put out a new Bible story book, not to replace Cohen, whose book remained in print for decades to come, but to supply a kind of primer for very young readers: Betty Hollender's *Bible Stories for Little Children*.[62] Its style evokes "Dick and Jane" books, with the characters changed to biblical ones but the story lines just as simplified and repetitive, with any hint of conflict or dubious behavior omitted from the text. No story of Cain and Abel, no binding of Isaac, and no rivalry or conflict between Jacob and Esau. The chapter on Jacob and Esau opens with an evocation of the delight of twin babies:

> Did you ever wish for a baby brother or sister?
> Isaac and Rebecca wanted a baby, too.
> They wanted a baby to love.
> They wanted a baby to hug and kiss.
> They wanted a baby to take care of.
> Isaac and Rebecca were very lucky.
> Two babies came to them.
> Two babies came to them at the same time.
> Isaac and Rebecca had twin boys!

And after a brief description of how the boys are different—Esau a hunter and Jacob a shepherd—the whole story of the conflict between the two is encapsulated in these reassuring four lines:

Esau and Jacob were like many brothers you know.
They wanted to love each other.
But sometimes they would fight.
Then they would forget all about the fight and they would be friends again.[63]

Both Zeligs and Hollender thus continued the practice of earlier Jewish collections of replacing the biblical text with a significantly altered child-oriented version of the stories. But Zeligs makes a departure that becomes increasingly evident over the next several decades: she makes explicit use of actual midrashic material as supplementary to the (retold) biblical text; indeed, the full title of her book signals this new addition: *The Story Bible: Together with Tales from the Midrash.* Cohen began her book with the story of Abraham and his father's idols, but it was the only such midrashic material used, and after a brief explanation that the story is not from the Bible but had been told to Jewish children for thousands of years, she goes on to tell the story in a way that renders it indistinguishable from the rest of the book. Zeligs, though, uses midrashic "tales" more extensively and purposively, as she explains in her preface: "Stories from the Midrash have been added for the purpose of enrichment. They have been carefully selected to fill in and supplement the biblical material, rounding it out but preserving its essential unity." After the first added story, she explains: "This story is not from the Bible itself. It comes from the Midrash, a wonderful collection of tales told long ago by the great rabbis and passed down through the years from parents to their children."[64] Other interpolations are identified with phrases like "The Midrash tells us . . ." or "There is an old legend about . . . ," making clear Zeligs's intention to keep what comes from midrash distinct from the Bible. But even with these markers, it seems likely that the child reader would not make much of the difference, as the midrashic stories are wrapped into the larger narrative, not distinguished in format or prose style from the biblical material.

Collections from the 1960s and 1970s take two further steps of significance: the narrative abandons the heavy retelling typical of earlier books, moving closer with each decade toward a simplified text rather than a retold one, and midrash is more clearly separated from the biblical narrative. Both changes are in accord with a more developed historical consciousness, one that respects the integrity of the biblical text (even while needing to simplify it for children) and that is self-conscious about the separateness in time and genre of midrash from Bible.[65]

The turn to a more straightforward prose style can be seen in Dona Meilach's *First Book of Bible Heroes*, published in 1963.[66] Meilach retells the biblical narrative, but with a much lighter hand than most earlier texts, adding bits of filler rather than whole stretches of elaboration. In Shirley Newman's *A Child's Introduction to Torah* (Behrman House, 1972), the retelling is lighter still, with a simple, straightforward narrative close to the biblical story. The effort to stay closer to the biblical text is joined here to a heightened self-consciousness about the distinctiveness of midrash. Newman includes four chapters of stories taken from traditional midrash, each subtitled as "A History-Legend," and she stops to explain these legends as the result of people's desire to know what happened in Abraham's life before the Bible story begins.[67] Rather than being inspired by a goal of teaching children about midrash, Newman seems impelled by an older-style desire to fill the gaps in the character and motivations of this key figure. The concern of educators since Newman, to teach about the nature of midrash itself, is clear in the current description of her book in the Behrman House catalog, which claims that the book "retains all the story-telling magic of the classic Bible tales but never confuses them with fairy tales. Children learn to distinguish between history on the one hand and poetic myth on the other, and to respect them both as sources of Jewish wisdom."[68]

The two changes of unadorned straightforward prose style with explicit use of midrash come to full fruition in Seymour Rossel's 1988 collection published by Behrman House, *A Child's Bible*. Rossel's prose style continues the trend of simplification rather than retelling. Wording is adapted to clarify meaning and message, but little is added; no authorial extrapolations or midrashic elements are inserted into the body of the narrative. In the story of Cain and Abel, for example, no lengthy background on Cain and Abel is added to explain the eventual rejection of Cain's sacrifice and the acceptance of Abel's:

> Abel became a shepherd, watching over goats and sheep. Cain became a farmer, planting and harvesting.
> One day, Cain brought a gift to God from his farm. And Abel brought God the best of his newborn sheep. God smiled on Abel and his gift, but paid no attention to Cain. Cain was upset and sad.[69]

Rossel considers his text a "translation for kids," not a set of "retellings."[70] The closeness to the biblical text is reinforced by citations of biblical verses placed at the head of each chapter. Each two- or three-page story is followed by two pages of further discussion marked off by colored background and a different double-column layout—no mistaking these for the story part. The discussion section has three parts: "What does it mean?" in which the author explains some factual matter or an issue raised in the text, with occasional use of rabbinic material; "What does it teach?" in which the author explains an ethical issue raised by the text, applying it to the child's own life, and "A lesson about the Torah," in which rabbinic material relevant to the preceding issue is summarized, beginning with "Our teachers say . . ." and concluding with a citation to the specific rabbinic source. Each chapter concludes with three pages of exercises, games, and puzzles. The formatted segmentation of each chapter makes it eminently clear that the Bible "text" is the base, and that any elaboration and explanation is separate from that. Midrash is invoked explicitly as a major help in the teaching of the text.[71]

The heightened historicism of this approach is reinforced by the author's approach to the "truth" of the biblical text, expressed in his introduction. The truth of the Bible is not in literal historicity, he explains, but in the moral lessons that can be learned from it:

> All the stories of the *Torah* are true. Yet this does not mean that the stories happened just as the *Torah* tells. When we talk about the *Torah*, we mean the stories are true in a different way.
>
> The stories in our *Torah* are true because they teach us how to tell the difference between bad and good. So it does not matter if the world began in seven days or if it really took millions of years. The *Torah* story about how God created the world is still true. It is true because it teaches us that we are made "in the image of God." And it is true because it teaches us that resting on the Sabbath is good.
>
> As you read the stories you should ask, "What truth is this story teaching me?" "What does this story say that I should do?" "How does this story say that I should behave?"[72]

Rossel's inclusion of many miraculous events, more than in earlier Jewish collections, affirms a historicist distance from the biblical world. The text is allowed to present its own world. God is back in the Bible, consonant with Rossel's covenant-based approach to Judaism and Jewish education.[73] The student's unproblematic direct relationship to the text is still central, as emphasized in the ethical issues addressed after each story. Lest the presence of miracles interfere with that relationship, Rossel takes care to explain that what "the Torah calls a miracle" is really just "something natural [that] occurs at just the right time and just the right place."[74]

Given the continuity of purposes (ethical instruction, positive identification with Judaism), the new prose style and the self-conscious, explicit use of midrash as an aid to interpreting the biblical text may seem minor changes. But they produce an enormous difference in the look and feel of the texts, a difference that means that texts like Cohen's produce discomfort when read aloud to adult audiences today, while texts like Rossel's sound "normal."[75] Why did the texts change in these ways? To seek an explanation would send us off in a contextual search as wide-ranging as that made for the production of the earlier twentieth-century texts, a task outside of the scope of this book. But I would suggest two contextual arenas of likely significance. The enhanced historicism of Rossel and others makes sense within the general intellectual environment of the postwar period, including a postmodern skepticism with regard to easy elision between past and present. This more sophisticated historicism is also visible in the abandonment of books of "biblical history," in which the early history of the Jews was narrated through the Bible, with supplemental archeological and historical material, and a turn instead to a more encompassing approach to "Jewish history," in which evidence from the Bible plays a much smaller role.[76]

While such historical attentiveness undoubtedly contributed to the concern to distinguish midrash from the actual biblical text, the increased and explicit use of rabbinic material may also be attributed to the more secure and established Jewish identity in America of the 1960s and beyond. Talmud (at least the aggadic elements) and midrash have been re-embraced as an important part of the Jewish tradition; the pressing concern during the preceding fifty to one hundred years—to identify Judaism by the "universal" text of the Bible, shared with Christians—has eased. Indeed, it is of great significance that this new generation of bible-story-with-commentary-supported-by-rabbinic-material departs not only from earlier Jewish texts but from the Christian models on which those Jewish texts were based and developed in parallel. Unlike the earlier generation, these late-twentieth-century books have been developed, not with an eye to Christian texts, but with a self-confident exploration of a particularly Jewish approach to the Bible. This willingness to consider rabbinic material as relevant to modern Judaism is also evident in the multiplication of rabbinic story collections in this same period.[77] We are a world away from the nineteenth-century Jewish teachers who made do by pasting over the interspersed Christological interpretations in the available Christian Bible story books for children.

The Bible in Israel

Some years ago, on a visit to a kibbutz in the north of Israel, I was convers-
ing with two members about the nature of bar mitzvah preparation for kib-
butz children. Unlike in the United States, where for many children the year
of preparation is taken up with learning enough Hebrew that they can read
the prayers and Torah portion, most often mechanically and without com-
prehension, in the kibbutz children know the language already, and they've
studied the Bible for years in school. In any case, the ritual is more of a secu-
lar coming-of-age ceremony, often done as a group, after some kind of year-
long project. There might be a small religious part to the preparation as
well. For example, they would be brought to see a synagogue, and would be
shown a sefer Torah — the Torah scrolls — neither of which they might ever
have seen before.

This was my introduction to the notion that in an Israeli setting it is pos-
sible to know a great deal of the Bible but very little about Judaism as a reli-
gion. My interlocutors were both transplanted Americans who had been liv-
ing on the kibbutz for many years. One of them, trained as a Conservative
rabbi, saw my unsettlement and remarked, "Yes, one could argue that
Judaism begins only after the Bible."

The role of the Bible in Israel has been deeply political rather than religious, rooted in early Zionist ideology and the subsequent formulation of
an Israeli identity. The radical agenda of late-nineteenth-century Zionism
was to reconnect the Jewish people with *eretz Yisrael*—the land of Israel—
and the claim to this land lay in the text of the Bible. Early Zionists from
eastern Europe, many of them thoroughly secularist, took up the Bible as
a central text when religious Jews around them would have paid it little
heed. This "return to the Scripture" was fundamentally a secular act of
nationalism, through which the Jewish claim to the land of Israel was legit-
imized.[78] A. D. Gordon, a prominent shaper of Zionist ideology and action
in Palestine, called the Bible a "charter" to the land of Israel, and David
Ben-Gurion, in his 1937 testimony before the Peel Commission, told the
British authorities that the Jews' right to Palestine "derives not from the
Mandate or the Balfour Declaration. It preceded them. . . . The Bible is
our Mandate."[79]

To secular Zionists, the Bible gave not only a title deed to the land but
also a justification for its conquest and settlement. The biblical account of
the Hebrews' relationship to the land of Canaan opens the Bible to be
read as a "book of the conquest and settlement of the Land, of nation
building in the Land, and of the formation of a glorious sovereign kingdom, a theocratic state."[80] In the twentieth-century struggle to take over,

resettle, and establish sovereignty in a land inhabited by Palestinians, Jews sought—and readily found—analogies in the biblical past, which contributed to a sense of reliving the ancient rise of Israel. The Bible was a "magic key" that opened the door to an independent, national life that had been in abeyance for two thousand years.[81] Land, nation, and Bible—three elements mentioned in the first paragraph of the Proclamation of the State of Israel—are thus inextricably intertwined in the early formation of Israeli identity.

While this use of the Bible originated with secular Zionists, it was later taken up by newer religious fundamentalist Zionists, most notably Gush Emunim.[82] The use of the Bible by Gush Emunim as a torch lighting the path to action in eretz Yisrael comes from its Zionist, not its religious, identification. These political uses of the Bible exist contemporaneously in Israel with traditionalist religious interpretations. The Bible is thus an ongoing part of political discourse and public life. Current political events that seem to resonate with biblical passages provoke intense negotiations and disagreements over the messages to be taken from the biblical analogue.[83]

The central place of the Bible in Israeli discourse—true most especially for the pre-state period and the first generation after 1948—has been reinforced in a number of ways. The passion for archaeology in Israel—for the discovery and reconstitution of ancient sites, especially to the extent that they confirm the biblical text—reinforces connection between ancient place and modern settlement, intensified further by the practice of place-naming that made the land a "mythical historical map" in accord with passages from the Bible.[84] The presence of the land is felt even in the teaching of natural sciences such as geography, botany, and zoology, in which the land of Israel is one focus.[85] Israelis are encouraged in a physical love for the land, to which many are introduced through the youth activity of hiking in nature. The connection between the Bible and military defense of the land is evident in the Bible that each soldier receives upon being sworn in to the army, each copy inscribed with a quote from Joshua, "Be strong and have courage."

The main vehicle, however, for the promotion of the Bible as the central Israeli text is the educational system.[86] The state school system in Israel is complex. There are separate schools for Jews, Arabs (as they are called by the government), and Christians; secular and religious streams for Jewish children; and subgroups within each section.[87] That the Bible would be taught in Jewish religious schools and in Christian schools is not surprising to an outsider. That it is taught as well in secular Jewish schools and in Arab schools can be explained by the Bible's use as a text of Israeli national culture, rather than as a religious text.[88] In state secular schools the study of the Bible is mandatory from the early grades through high school, is taught for as many as four hours per week, and is tested on the matriculation exam for university study. Its place in Jewish religious schooling is actually more limited, following the pattern established by traditional Jewish education. In some religious schools, more extended Bible lessons are part of "secular studies" rather than sacred, confirming the political purposes in the teaching of the text.[89] This, too, explains why the Bible is taught in schools for Palestinian children; such schooling furthers the state's goal of "Israelizing" the Palestinian population through the use of a Jewish national text.

Secular Jewish schools, which teach the largest portion of Israeli children, shape and sustain a new form of Jewish education that is essentially nonreligious.[90] How can the Bible, which seems to an American Jewish audience a self-evidently religious text—and therefore to be kept out of public schools rather than featured prominently within them—support this approach? Through emphasis on the land of Israel as the central feature of the text. A comparison between Rossel's *A Child's Bible* and its Israeli counterpart, *Bereshit Sheli* (My Genesis),[91] demonstrates the contrast between the ethical/religious and nationalist approaches of American and Israeli Jewish education. *Bereshit Sheli* was published with the approval of the Ministry of Education and Culture, and is widely used in the second grade when children begin the study of the Bible. *Bereshit Sheli* and *A Child's Bible* were published within a year of each other in the late 1980s, and are marked by many similarities in approach. They are very similar in appearance and size and have attractive color illustrations on the cover and throughout the text. Both keep biblical material separate from commentary and exercises. Both seek to engage the child reader in the world of the text, asking the child to imagine motivations and feelings of the characters.[92] But the differences in the books reflect their differing contexts and purposes. In contrast to the American books, *Bereshit Sheli* gives the full text of the Bible, in unaltered biblical Hebrew. Each section of the text includes vocabulary lists, which give modern Hebrew equivalents or definitions for unfamiliar terms, and many of the exercises in the workbook are designed to teach facility with biblical vocabulary and grammar. Obviously, the Israeli child's knowledge of modern Hebrew makes possible this use of the original text, but it is still significant that the text is not modernized, and that all verses are included. "Problem" passages are not censored, nor are nonnarrative passages, such as long genealogies. The goal is to establish a deep familiarity with the entirety of this holy "national" text, a competency supported by exercises (including memorization of verses and even whole chapters) and, after ten further years of biblical study, tested in the matriculation exam. Perhaps the closest parallel in American education is the required American history and civics courses in high school, covering the basic people, events, and texts of the national story.

One doesn't have to read the texts, however, to notice the most striking difference between the American and Israeli children's Bibles. While both *A Child's Bible* and *Bereshit Sheli* are attractively illustrated, the nature of the illustrations is entirely different. For the Cain and Abel story, for example, Rossel's book has a full-page drawing of Cain and Abel fighting. Cain raises a club against Abel, who defends himself with a shepherd's crook. A smaller drawing on the next page shows Abel lying dead on the ground. The chapter is titled "The Terrible Crime," and the illustrations further highlight the moral issues in the text. They are typical of Bible story illustrations in the United States (Christian as well as Jewish) in their focus on characters and ethically challenging situations.

The illustrations in *Bereshit Sheli* provide a stark contrast. The vast majority are photographs of landscapes or features of nature (e.g., flocks, fields, rocks). Here the Cain and Abel story (which, like the rest of the text, is identified only by chapter and verse, not by any imposed title) is illustrated by a photograph of wheat (bearing the caption "the fruit of the ground") and one of a flock of grazing sheep ("the firstlings of his flock"). The captions are quotations from the text describing the sacrifices of Cain and Abel. This practice of identifying the visual markers throughout the book binds the biblical text to the modern land of Israel, rather than fostering an exploration of moral questions. In the first 112 pages of *Bereshit Sheli*, fifty-nine illustrations are photographs of landscape or features of nature.[93] A half-dozen of these include people within the landscape, but only once as the focus; more often, living things in the photograph are animals, either sheep or camels.[94] Archeological photographs are also included with some frequency, usually objects illustrating some element of the story, such as a photograph of ancient jewelry along with the story of Rebekah, referring to the ring and bracelets that Abraham's servant gave to Rebekah, or a small stone statue of a woman kneading dough next to the story of Abraham's hospitality to the three strangers. One of these archeological artifacts provides the only illustration in the book of a problematic ethical action: an ancient mosaic depicts scenes from the story of the binding of Isaac. But the crude sticklike figures of the mosaic do little to bring the drama into the child's world. It is rather the realistic photographs of the living land that bring the story into connection with the child's life, there in the Land of Israel.[95]

In both Israel and the United States, then, Jews have reclaimed the Bible as a central text, one that provides models of behavior to be emulated by modern audiences. Yet the stimulus to and context for this reclamation is significantly different in the two settings. In the United States, the text's "universalism" was seen as its essential character, with the sharing of the Bible between Christians and Jews supporting this claim of commonality. The dominance of Protestantism in the United States further reinforced Jewish attention on the Bible. For Jews in early Zionist movements and then in Israel, the appeal of the Bible had less to do with universal values. Rather, its appeal was the very particular claim of a specific group—the Jews—to a specific place—the land of Israel, the land of the Bible. For Zionists/Israelis, the Bible helped to shape and reinforce a national identity; for American Jews the Bible contributed to a religious identity, one readily in accord with the Protestant context.[96] A final parallel, however, is that in both settings the Jewish relationship to the Bible has recently become more nuanced and complex, partly as the result of the enhanced historicist approach that has complicated the easy identification with the Bible earlier promoted in both the Israeli and American settings.[97]

Conclusion

The true Torah is a loose-leaf book in which each age writes
its own story of spiritual adventure.

LOUIS WITT

Having sketched out some of the many forms into which the Bible has been shaped over time and place, and the various meanings carried by these forms, we return now to the central focus of this study—the endeavor of Jewish educators and Bible story writers of the 1920s and 1930s in the United States to put the Bible in accord with modernity and with American life and values. When I first looked at these Bible story books, I was troubled by what I saw as a profound dilution of the depth and complexity of Jewish tradition, and I considered these books partially responsible for whatever weakness there may be—and there are many—in the current nature and extent of "Jewishness" among American Jews. I sympathized with commentators who criticized these educators for giving up too easily on day school, and for overemphasizing the "Americanization" side of their agenda. Such a critique is readily on hand from within the perspective of an ongoing commitment to Jewish education. If our questions come from within the scholarship of Jewish education, they are likely to be questions such as: Was this a successful educational endeavor? Did these educators succeed in their goal of sustaining Jewish identity while fashioning a Judaism and Jewish education suited to an American identity? Or, as one reader of an early draft of this book asked me, "So *is* it possible to present the Bible to children in a way that provides for Jewish continuity as well as proving acceptable to contemporary American norms?"

These are certainly legitimate questions, and I have continued to think about them. But from early on, the questions that propelled my research have gone in the direction of understanding rather than critique. My aim has been to understand the origins of and motivations for the endeavors of interwar Jewish educators—with a focus on their production of Bible story books for children—rather than to judge their success. When we view these educators from the broad perspective of their social, political, and intellectual context, we can see the anachronism of judgment. The retold Bible stories, which looked so peculiar to me when I first came across them, now make sense; a conjuncture of multiple, overlapping contexts provides ample explanation for the form and content of texts such as Lenore Cohen's *Bible Tales for Very Young Children.* The elements of the puzzle can be grouped into four large contexts: Jewish, Christian, American, and European. The boundaries between these categories should be understood as highly porous, with some elements belonging in two or more arenas. To understand the prevalence of Bible story books, we needed first to see how the Bible came to replace the Talmud as the "binding text" of Judaism and Jewish education. For this we needed the context of the European Enlightenment and the legal emancipation of the Jews, as well as the centrality of the Bible in Protestantism and in American culture. For the simplification of the biblical text for children we needed to see the changing theories of childhood and children's learning, as well as the changes in state-sponsored education that relegated Jewish education to supplementary schools. For the moralization of these abridged texts, we needed to explore the secularization of moral education in the form of "character education," and the application of such education in a religious setting. For the drive to both universalize and Americanize the Bible, we needed not just the background of the European Enlightenment but also the experience of a generation of immigrants responding to the xenophobia and ethnic/racial prejudice of "Anglo-Saxon" Americans as well as the competing theories of democracy in interwar America of the melting pot and cultural pluralism.

The permeability between Jewish practice and its Christian, European, and American contexts was itself a shaping feature of modern Jewish experience, within which these Bible story collections make sense. Judaism and Jewish practice have always been open to the influence of the surrounding culture, but within the United States in the last century, the possibilities for assimilation into that surrounding culture have been particularly strong and inviting, further enhancing the impulse to reshape Judaism to fit a new environment. Yes, the educators who set up the structures and curriculum for Jewish education in America were probably more successful in bringing an American identity to Jewish life than in fashioning a deep and complex Jewish way of life that would be sustainable in America. But given the time they lived in, the route they took is understandable. Not that there weren't other paths to take. Some Jews pursued secularism more consistently, founding, for example, the Ethical Culture Society or secular Yiddish schools.[1] Some pursued Judaism more traditionally, remaining Orthodox, establishing day schools. But it was overdetermined that the approach taken by Gamoran and his peers was the one that dominated the Jewish education scene between the wars and beyond: the experience of immigrants far from home; the influence of a highly assimilated, preexisting community of Jews in the United States; the availability of public schooling; the dominant ideology of democracy, science, and secularism; the existence of Protestant models of religious education and of children's Bible stories; the fears of ethnic/national division heightened by the First World War, and so on. This generation of Jews wanted passionately to belong to America, and they cared passionately about the Judaism they already had and about passing it on to the next generation. They believed that the old ways in which they had received their knowledge of Judaism would not work in America. So they created another way, from the ground up, and they institutionalized it in Jewish communities across the country. It is the depth of their passion on both parts of the agenda—America *and* Judaism—that distinguishes this generation. Now at the beginning of the twenty-first century, the fit of Jews in the American scene is assured—civil equality and a high degree of assimilation/acculturation have been achieved—but the continuation of a distinguishable Jewish culture is in question. It is appropriate now to turn up the passion on the Jewish side of the equation rather than the American. American Judaism was remade by earlier generations; the audacity of the task they undertook is quite astounding. But it is a task still in progress, the outcome uncertain.

In today's America, the melting pot image is on the defensive, no longer the dominant ideology, and there is a pervasive postmodern sense of uncertainty and even cynicism about "American values" that makes us shake our heads at the passion and confidence these earlier writers had about democratic America and its union with a "universalistic" Judaism. Compounding the challenge is the fact that the generation now in charge of shaping Jewish identity in the young is a generation without the direct experience of traditional Judaism and Jewish culture that was a formative experience of the generation who founded American Jewish education. Gamoran had a foot in both worlds, as did his colleagues. They passionately sought to pass on the redeemable portion of one world to be sustained in the new. But now, for those with both feet in America, with no direct experience of the old, whose Judaism *is* American Judaism, the task of remaking Judaism continues. For a half-century following World War II,

Jewish identity was reshaped in relationship to the Holocaust and to the founding of the state of Israel, entirely new challenges to those in charge of the education of the young. But the relationship to the more distant Jewish past, to ancient Jewish texts and practices, continues to be reformulated. Can we teach a postmodern historicism and skepticism to the young? If we did, would it foster love of and identification with Judaism? It will be for another generation to tell the story.

Appendix 1

Popular Bible Story Collections, 1915–1936

The books in this list were selected on the basis of surveys of textbooks used in religious schools and of books most often recommended for classroom use or library purchase; see appendix 2 for a list of these sources. The collections are listed here in the order of publication.

Altman, Addie Richman. *The Jewish Child's Bible Stories, Told in Simple Language.* New York: Bloch Publishing, 1915.

Silber, Mendel. *The Scripture Stories Retold for Young Israel.* Rev. ed. 2 vols. New York: Behrman's Jewish Book House, 1918; originally published 1916.

The Bible Story in the Bible Words series. All published in Cincinnati by the Department of Synagog and School Extension of the Union of American Hebrew Congregations.

Book One: Adele Bildersee. *The Story of Genesis.* 1924.

Book Two: Adele Bildersee. *Out of the House of Bondage.* 1925.

Book Three: Jacob D. Schwarz. *Into the Promised Land.* 1927.

Book Four: Jacob D. Schwarz. *In the Land of Kings and Prophets.* 1928.

Book Five: Mamie G. Gamoran. *The Voice of the Prophets.* 1930.

Book Six: Mamie G. Gamoran. *With Singer and Sage.* 1930.

Levinger, Elma Ehrlich. *Bible Stories for Very Little People.* New York: Behrman's Jewish Book Shop, 1925.

Calisch, Edith L. *Bible Tales for the Very Young.* Vol. 1, *From the Beginning to the Death of*

Moses. New York: Behrman's Book Shop, 1930. Vol. 2, *Bible Tales for Young People*. New York: Behrman's Book Shop, 1934.

Fox, Ethel. *Bible Primer for Tiny Tots*. New York: Bloch Publishing, 1930.

Goldin, Hyman E. *Illustrated Bible Stories*. New York: Hebrew Publishing, 1930.

Cohen, Lenore. *Bible Tales for Very Young Children*. 2 vols. Cincinnati: Union of American Hebrew Congregations, 1934–36.

Appendix 2

Sources Used to Assess the Popularity of Bible Story Collections

The following surveys, listed in chronological order, were used to determine which Bible Story collections were recommended or adopted most frequently.

Gamoran, Emanuel. "Jewish Education in the United States." In *Studies in Religious Education*, ed. Philip Henry Lotz and L. W. Crawford, 490–514. Nashville: Cokesbury Press, 1931.

——. "Reaching the Pre-School Child." *Jewish Teacher* 4, no. 4 (1936): 1–4.

"A Suggested List of Books for Use in a Temple Library." *Jewish Teacher* 5, no. 2 (1936/37): 13–14.

"Books for Children and Young People." *Jewish Teacher* 7, no. 1 (1938/39): 35–37.

Korey, Harold. "The History of Jewish Education in Chicago." Master's Thesis, Department of Education, University of Chicago, 1942.

Jaffe, Philip, and Sylvia Goldman. "Survey of Thirty-Six Reform Religious Schools in New York City." *Jewish Teacher* 11, no. 4 (1942/43): 1–12.

Board of Jewish Education (Chicago). *Course of Study Outline for the Jewish Sunday School.* 1944.

Golub, Jacob. *Children's Library List.* New York: Jewish Education Committee of New York, 1949.

Religious School Textbook Analyses, 2d ed. New York: American Council for Judaism, 1952.

Hertz, Rabbi Richard C. *The Education of the Jewish Child: A Study of 200 Reform Jewish Religious Schools.* New York: Union of American Hebrew Congregations, 1953.

Madison, Charles A. *Jewish Publishing in America: The Impact of Jewish Writing on American Culture.* New York: Sanhedrin Press, 1976.

Notes

A full bibliography is available at http://faculty.knox.edu/pgold/.

Organizations and works frequently cited have been identified by the following abbreviations:

BJE   Bureau of Jewish Education
CCAR   Central Conference of American Rabbis
CCARY   *Central Conference of American Rabbis Yearbook*
DSSE   Department of Synagog and School Extension
PUAHC   *Proceedings of the Union of American Hebrew Congregations*
UAHC   Union of American Hebrew Congregations

Preface

1. It was some comfort to read of a similar experience that Jonathan Kirsch had while reading the story of Noah's sons finding their father drunk and naked (*The Harlot by the Side of the Road: Forbidden Tales of the Bible* [New York: Ballantine, 1997], 2–4).

2. See especially chapter 1 in *The Vulnerable Observer: Anthropology That Breaks Your Heart* (Boston: Beacon Press, 1996). Behar's book is a good starting place for those interested in the growing use of autobiography in scholarly work. Anthropologists, whose lives are unavoidably intertwined with those of their subjects, have reflected the most on this issue, but for a recent consideration by a historian, see Robert F. Berkhofer Jr., "Partiality as Voice and Viewpoint," chap. 6 in *Beyond the Great Story: History as Text and Discourse* (Cambridge: Belknap Press of Harvard University Press, 1997).

3. For a retrospective analysis of how being Jewish probably influenced my earlier choice of medieval history as a research field, see Penny S. Gold, "A Jewish Feminist Studies Christian Monasticism: Motivations and Goals," in *Looking Back: A Celebration of Sources*, Proceedings of the Tenth Annual Great Lakes College Association Women's Studies Conference, November 9–11, 1984 (Ann Arbor: Great Lakes College Association, 1985), 54–60.

Introduction

1. For a full account, see Ruth B. Bottigheimer, *The Bible for Children from the Age of Gutenberg to the Present* (New Haven: Yale University Press, 1996).

2. Ruth B. Bottigheimer, "Moses Mordechai Büdinger's *Kleine Bibel* and Vernacular Jewish Children's Bibles," *Jewish Social Studies* 2 (1995): 83–98.

3. For institution building by second-generation American Jews, see Deborah Dash Moore, *At Home in America: Second Generation New York Jews* (New York: Columbia University Press, 1981). For the development of educational institutions in particular, see Eduardo L. Rauch, "Jewish Education in the United States, 1840–1920" (Ed.D. thesis, Harvard University, 1978); and Kerry M. Olitzky, "A History of Reform Jewish Education during Emanuel Gamoran's Tenure as Educational Director of the Commission on Jewish Education of the Union of American Hebrew Congregations, 1923–1958" (D.H.L. diss., Hebrew Union College–Jewish Institute of Religion, Cincinnati 1984).

4. Translation from *The Holy Scriptures* (Philadelphia: Jewish Publication Society of America, 1917).

5. Edith Lindeman Calisch, *Bible Tales for the Very Young* (New York: Behrman's Jewish Book Shop, 1930), 1:12–13; the story continues for another two pages before arriving at God's rejection of Cain's sacrifice.

6. From *The Holy Scriptures* (JPS, 1917).

7. Lenore Cohen, *Bible Tales for Very Young Children*, 2 vols. (New York: Union of American Hebrew Congregations, 1934–36), 1:5–7.

8. Regina M. Schwartz, *The Curse of Cain: The Violent Legacy of Monotheism* (Chicago: University of Chicago Press, 1977), 157.

9. I am using the term "cultural translation" in the sense put forward in many of the essays in *The Translatability of Cultures: Figurations of the Space Between*, ed. Sanford Budick and Wolfgang Iser (Stanford: Stanford University Press, 1996).

10. For these varieties of cultural translation, see Wolfgang Iser, "Coda to the Discussion," 295; Jan Assmann, "Translating Gods: Religion as a Factor of Cultural (Un)Translatability," 34; Karlheinz Stierle, "Translatio Studii and Renaissance: From Vertical to Horizontal Translation," 65; all in Budick and Iser, *The Translatability of Cultures*.

11. Iser, "Coda to the Discussion," 295–96.

12. Alan Silverstein, *Alternatives to Assimilation: The Response of Reform Judaism to American Culture, 1840–1930* (Hanover, N.H.: University Press of New England, for Brandeis University Press, 1995), 2. Naomi Patz and Philip Miller explain that there was little impetus to develop a significant program of children's book publication in English in the Orthodox or Conservative movements before 1950: "Jewish Religious Children's Literature in America: An Analytical Survey," *Phaedrus* 7, no. 1 (1980): 24.

13. The end date is the publication of Cohen, *Bible Tales*. This collection quickly became the uniformly recommended text in Reform religious schools, which stopped the flow of texts for a generation and more.

1. The Bible in Traditional Jewish Culture

1. Samuel M. Cohen, *The Progressive Jewish School: An Integrated Activity Curriculum* (New York: United Synagogue of America, 1932), 119–20.

2. *The Code of Jewish Law, Kitzur Shulhan Arukh*, translated by Hyman E. Goldin (New York: Hebrew Publishing, 1963), 1:28.5.

3. In Sephardi tradition, the Torah scroll is housed in a special wooden container rather than in a cloth covering. Many of the customary practices regarding the special handling of and posture toward the Torah scroll during worship are detailed in the *Code of Jewish Law*, 1:23.1–8; 1:28.

4. For an excellent analysis of the liturgical role of the Torah and its development, see Ruth Langer, "From Study of Scripture to a Reenactment of Sinai: The Emergence of the

Synagogue Torah Service," *Worship* 72, no. 1 (1998): 43–67. Langer emphasizes the symbolic role of the Torah as "the embodiment of the Sinai revelation, the sacred myth on which all Judaism stands" (51). See also Ismar Elbogen, *Jewish Liturgy: A Comprehensive History* (Philadelphia: Jewish Publication Society, 1993), 129–42.

5. The Torah is read on Mondays and Thursdays as well as on the Sabbath.

6. Moshe Halbertal, *People of the Book: Canon, Meaning, and Authority* (Cambridge: Harvard University Press, 1997), 12.

7. Harvey E. Goldberg, "Torah and Children: Symbolic Aspects of the Reproduction of Jews and Judaism," in *Judaism Viewed from Within and from Without*, ed. Harvey E. Goldberg (Albany: State University of New York Press, 1987), 116, 123.

8. Cohen, *Progressive Jewish School*, 102; Hermann Gollancz, *Pedagogics of the Talmud and That of Modern Times: A Comparative Study* (London: Oxford University Press, 1924), 62. The use of the Aramaic translation—also common practice as part of the synagogue reading—dates from a time in which Aramaic was the currently spoken language, and its usage signified the importance of understanding at least the literal content of the text as it was read. But the persistence of Aramaic in a period when it was no longer widely understood, and the absence of a current vernacular, underscores the role of the text as assimilated ritual object rather than as comprehended content.

9. For a modern English translation, see *Tz'enah Ur'enah*, trans. Miriam Stark Zakon (Brooklyn: Mesorah Publications, 1983); this text is treated further in chapter 6. For an example of this women's practice see the selection from the memorial book of Horodets in *From a Ruined Garden: The Memorial Books of Polish Jewry*, ed. and trans. Jack Kugelmass and Jonathan Boyarin, 2d expanded ed. (Bloomington: Indiana University Press, 1998), 70–71.

10. Shaul Stampfer, "Gender Differentiation and Education of the Jewish Woman in Nineteenth-Century Eastern Europe," *Polin* 7 (1992): 70–71.

11. We will come back to this process in chapter 6.

12. See chapter 2 for a more detailed comparison of the content and rhetoric of Talmud and Bible.

13. Halbertal, *People of the Book*, 6–10.

14. Jacob Katz, *Tradition and Crisis: Jewish Society at the End of the Middle Ages*, trans. Bernard Dov Cooperman (New York: New York University Press, 1993), 158.

15. In the discussion that follows, I have emphasized evidence dating from the late nineteenth and early twentieth century, the period that serves as the most immediate backdrop for Jewish immigrants to America. A useful overview of heder education may be found in Diane K. Roskies, "Alphabet Instruction in the East European Heder," *YIVO Annual of Jewish Social Science* 17 (1978): 21–53. Other helpful studies include Yekhiel Shtern, "A Kheyder in Tyszowce (Tishevits)," in *East European Jews in Two Worlds: Studies from the YIVO Annual*, ed. Deborah Dash Moore (Evanston: Northwestern University Press, 1990), 51–70 (based on Shtern's own experience and on conversations with other inhabitants of his town, in which there were two *hadarim*); Louis Ginzberg, "The Jewish Primary School," in *Students, Scholars, and Saints* (Philadelphia: Jewish Publication Society of America, 1928); Mark Zborowski, "The Place of Book-Learning in Traditional Jewish Culture," *Harvard Educational Review* 19, no. 2 (1949): 87–109; Mark Zborowski and Elizabeth Herzog, *Life Is with People: The Culture of the Shtetl* (New York: Schocken Books, 1962), 88–96; Isidore Fishman, *The History of Jewish Education in Central Europe, from the End of the Sixteenth to the End of the Eighteenth Century* (London: Edward Goldston, 1944); Shaul Stampfer, "*Heder* Study, Knowledge of Torah, and the Maintenance of Social Stratification in Traditional East European Jewish Society," *Studies in Jewish Education* 3 (1988): 271–89; Simon Greenberg, "Jewish Educational Institutions," in *The Jews: Their History, Culture, and Religion*, ed. Louis Finkelstein, 4 vols., 3d edition (New York: Harper and Row, 1960), 2:1254–87; Joshua Trachtenberg, "Jewish Education in Eastern Europe at the Beginning of the Seventeenth Century," *Jewish Education* 11, no. 2 (1939/40): 121–37; John Cooper, *The Child in Jewish History* (Northvale, N.J.: Jason Aronson, 1996); Yaffa Eliach, *There Once Was a World: A 900-Year Chronicle of the Shtetl of Eishyshok* (Boston: Little, Brown, 1998), 146–74. See also the bibliography provided by Diane Roskies: *Heder: Primary Education among East European Jews—A Selected and Annotated Bibliography of*

Published Sources (New York: YIVO Institute for Jewish Research, 1977). One study focused on the medieval period, yet illuminating for later practice, is Ivan G. Marcus, *Rituals of Childhood: Jewish Acculturation in Medieval Europe* (New Haven: Yale University Press, 1996).

16. Shtern describes at length the children's games ("Kheyder in Tyszowce," 51–54, 63–67), which are also described in Cooper (*The Child in Jewish History*, 270–73). Other authors make little mention of time for play, creating a more oppressive image of the heder.

17. This is younger than the ages recommended within the tradition itself, but the prestige of learning Talmud was so great that many teachers moved students from the Pentateuch to Talmud at eight, nine, or even earlier (Trachtenberg, "Jewish Education," 128, 131).

18. For girls in heder, see Cooper, *The Child in Jewish History*, 266–67; Shtern, "Kheyder in Tyszowce," 57; *From a Ruined Garden*, 70–72; Theo Richmond, *Konin: A Quest* (New York: Vintage Books, 1995), 45–47; Stampfer, "Gender Differentiation," 63–87.

19. Katz, *Tradition and Crisis*, 158–59, 162.

20. One of the most popular such translations was by Rabbi Moses b. Issachar Halevi Saertels, first published in Prague in 1604–5.

21. "Above all, the students are trained to be attentive to the words of the *melamed* and ready to repeat the reading or the translation of a word the moment he indicates it with the pointer" (Zborowski, "Place of Book-Learning," 95). For the fundamentally oral, social, and collective practice of "reading" the Bible in Jewish culture, see Daniel Boyarin, "Placing Reading: Ancient Israel and Medieval Europe," in *The Ethnography of Reading*, ed. Jonathan Boyarin (Berkeley: University of California Press, 1993), 11–37. A similar method was used at the early stage of Talmud learning (Stampfer, "*Heder* Study," 280).

22. Halbertal, *People of the Book*, 14.

23. Richmond, *Konin*, 38.

24. Stampfer, "*Heder* Study," 279.

25. Halbertal, *People of the Book*, 15.

26. One can hear a sample of this chant in the film *Hester Street*.

27. Roskies, "Alphabet Instruction," 39; this article includes extensive consideration of the various mnemonic devices used for alphabet instruction.

28. This ceremony is the main subject of Marcus's book, *Rituals of Childhood;* a detailed description of the ceremony can be found on pages 25–33. See also Ginzberg, "Primary School," 19–21, and Cooper, *The Child in Jewish History*, 169–77.

29. The analogy of Torah and honey goes back to the Bible: Ezekiel, commanded to eat a scroll, does so and finds that "it tasted as sweet as honey to me" (Ezek. 3:1–3). This is one of the verses on the cake eaten in the second part of the ritual.

30. Roskies, "Alphabet Instruction," 26.

31. Shtern, "Kheyder in Tyszowce," 57–60.

32. Ibid., 68. See also Zborowski, "Place of Book-Learning," 95; Emanuel Gamoran, *Changing Conceptions in Jewish Education, in Two Books*, Bk. 1, *Jewish Education in Russia and Poland* (New York: Macmillan, 1924), 92; Richmond, *Konin*, 35–38; Shmarya Levin, *Forward from Exile: The Autobiography of Shmarya Levin*, trans. Maurice Samuel (Philadelphia: Jewish Publication Society, 1967), 51–53; Eliach, *There Once Was a World*, 166–67. Ginzberg plays down the role of corporal punishment, attributing accounts of such to "the morbid imagination of certain *Maskilim*, whose animus against the Heder is probably to be sought in a hatred of the deeply Jewish atmosphere that prevailed there" (Ginzberg, "Primary School," 26). But accounts of physical punishment are so widespread, and its use so fully consistent with contemporary educational practice outside of Jewish schools, that I see no reason to doubt these accounts.

33. Marcus, *Rituals of Childhood*, 94–97; Ginzberg, "Primary School," 23; Fishman, *History of Jewish Education*, 94–95.

34. Trachtenberg, "Jewish Education," 129. Other parts of the Bible were sometimes taught as well but were not emphasized in the curriculum or studied systematically. The Five Scrolls would be studied at the appropriate ritual time of the year (e.g., Esther with Purim, Lamentations with Tisha b'Av); Prophets and Psalms might also be studied (130).

35. There were, however, some critics of this system, even as early as the seventeenth century (Katz, *Tradition and Crisis*, 162).

2. The Challenge of Modernity

1. For extensive treatment of these issues, see the wide-ranging work of Michael A. Meyer, especially *Response to Modernity: A History of the Reform Movement in Judaism* (New York: Oxford University Press, 1988) and *The Origins of the Modern Jew: Jewish Identity and European Culture in Germany, 1749–1824* (Detroit: Wayne State University Press, 1967).

2. For the notion of "present exigencies," see Wolfgang Iser, "Coda to the Discussion," in *The Translatability of Cultures: Figurations of the Space Between*, ed. Sanford Budick and Wolfgang Iser (Stanford: Stanford University Press, 1996), 295–96.

3. Jacob Katz, "Introduction," in *Toward Modernity: The European Jewish Model*, ed. Jacob Katz (New Brunswick, N.J.: Transaction Books, 1987), 9.

4. Meyer, *Response*, 17, 64–65.

5. A vivid example of this expectation may be found in the questions put to an assembly of Jewish notables called by Napoleon in 1806 (W. Gunther Plaut, *The Rise of Reform Judaism: A Sourcebook of Its European Origins* [New York: World Union for Progressive Judaism, 1963], 71–72).

6. Michael Meyer, "Modernity as a Crisis for the Jews," *Modern Judaism* 9 (1989): 156.

7. For the intolerant implications of the Enlightenment principle of universalism, see Beryl Lang, "Genocide and Kant's Enlightenment," chap. 7 in *Act and Idea in the Nazi Genocide* (Chicago: University of Chicago Press, 1990).

8. For the separation—and interactions—between Jews and Christians in premodern Europe, see Jacob Katz, *Tradition and Crisis: Jewish Society at the End of the Middle Ages*, trans. Bernard Dov Cooperman (New York: Schocken Books, 1993), especially 3–37. Benjamin Harshav gives an excellent, brief characterization of the "Jewish religious polysystem"—the network of interlocking systems that structured traditional Jewish life—and its replacement with a new "Jewish secular polysystem" in *Language in Time of Revolution* (Berkeley: University of California Press, 1993), 33–39.

9. There were, of course, Jews who wished to maintain the status quo and were opposed to emancipation, but their persistent *no* to modernization in any form is another story—parallel to, but not intersecting with our concern here.

10. Meyer, *Response*, 205–8; Robert S. Schine, *Jewish Thought Adrift: Max Wiener (1882–1950)* (Atlanta: Scholars Press, 1992), 34 and passim. The titles of some of these authors' works are indicative of the rational, universalistic project: *Religion of Reason out of the Sources of Judaism* (Cohen), *The Essence of Judaism* (Baeck). For an American statement of the universalist ethics of Judaism, beginning with the Bible, see Kaufman Kohler, "The Ethical Basis of Judaism," an Address delivered before the Young Men's Hebrew Association, December 20, 1886 (New York: Young Men's Hebrew Association, 1887), especially 8–9.

11. The first of these pamphlets was published in 1908, with a few dozen others following in the next thirty or so years. Other early titles reflective of universalistic concerns include "The Universal Lord" and "Humanitarianism of the Laws of Israel."

12. Rev. Joseph Krauskopf and Rev. Henry Berkowitz, *Bible Ethics: A Manual of Instruction in the History and Principles of Judaism according to the Hebrew Scriptures* (Cincinnati: Bloch, 1884), v.

13. Jakob J. Petuchowski, "Manuals and Catechisms of the Jewish Religion in the Early Period of the Emancipation," in *Studies in Nineteenth Century Jewish Intellectual History*, ed. Alexander Altmann (Cambridge: Harvard University Press, 1964): 47–64.

14. Michael A. Meyer, "Abraham Geiger's Historical Judaism," in *New Perspectives on Abraham Geiger: An HUC-JIR Symposium*, ed. Jakob J. Petuchowski (Cincinnati: Hebrew Union College Press, 1975), 4.

15. Emancipatory legislation did not persist in all places, and the social integration that had been an anticipated outcome of legal emancipation rarely occurred.

16. Karl Marx is an interesting example of a nineteenth-century (and in some ways Jewish) thinker who laid out a profoundly historical understanding of society, at the same time that he was deeply committed to a universalist vision of an egalitarian society. Of course, other Jewish responses to the failure of emancipation and the emergence of European nationalism were also undertaken, most notably the Zionist movement of the late nineteenth and twentieth centuries.

17. This movement began in the first half of the nineteenth century, with key journals beginning publication in the 1820s and 1830s; for example, the *Zeitschrift für die Wissenschaft des Judenthums* (1822) and the *Wissenschaftliche Zeitschrift für jüdische Theologie* (1835). For the early foundations and development of the historicist approach in Judaism, see Meyer, *Response*, 62–99.

18. Ismar Schorsch, *From Text to Context: The Turn to History in Modern Judaism* (Hanover, N.H.: University Press of New England, for Brandeis University Press, 1994), 164. Not all modernist Jewish thinkers adopted a historical approach, most notably Franz Rosenzweig (156). For the different course of Jewish scholarship in France, see Jay Berkovitz, "Jewish Scholarship and Identity in Nineteenth-Century France," *Modern Judaism* 18 (1998): 1–33.

19. Leopold Zunz, *Zur Geschichte und Literatur* (Berlin, 1845), 21, as quoted by Schorsch, *From Text to Context*, 164.

20. Schorsch, *From Text to Context*, 1. See also Yosef Hayim Yerushalmi, *Zakhor: Jewish History and Jewish Memory* (New York: Schocken Books, 1989), 85. Yerushalmi's book is a key study of the historical approach characteristic of modern Judaism and how it differs from earlier modes of thought within Judaism.

21. Jon D. Levenson, *The Hebrew Bible, the Old Testament, and Historical Criticism: Jews and Christians in Biblical Studies* (Louisville, Ky.: Westminster/John Knox Press, 1993), 75.

22. On Jewish responses to higher criticism, see S. David Sperling, "Judaism and Modern Biblical Research," in *Biblical Studies: Meeting Ground of Jews and Christians*, ed. Lawrence Boadt et al. (Ramsey, N.J.: Paulist Press, 1980), 19–44, and Schine, *Jewish Thought Adrift*, 15–69. Circumstances were different in Sephardic society, where the study of the Bible and other "modern" religious/cultural practices predate their appearance in central and eastern Europe by a century or two. See David Sorkin, "The Port Jew: Notes Toward a Social Type," *Journal of Jewish Studies* 50, no. 1 (1999): 87–97. Most notable in this context is Spinoza, whose late seventeenth-century *Theological-Political Tractate* adumbrates many of the approaches and findings of higher criticism; see Steven Nadler, *Spinoza: A Life* (Cambridge: Cambridge University Press, 1999), 272–80. There was also an Ashkenazi precursor in Judah ben Bezalel Loew of Prague (the MaHaRaL, 1525–1609), along with his students and followers (David Sorkin, *The Berlin Haskalah and German Religious Thought: Orphans of Knowledge* [London: Vallentine Mitchell, 2000], 39). Both the Prague school and the Sephardic model were influential on an early generation of *maskilim*, working as early as the 1720s (40–52).

23. Schorsch, *From Text to Context*, 165.

24. Schine, *Jewish Thought Adrift*, 21–27; Sperling, "Judaism and Modern Biblical Research," 22–23; Jacob B. Agus, "Bible Criticism and the Changing Image of the Jew," in *Jewish Identity in an Age of Ideologies* (New York: Frederick Ungar, 1978).

25. Schine, *Jewish Thought Adrift*, 15. There were exceptions: Zunz and Geiger, for example, both engaged in critical scholarship on the Bible. On Geiger, see Nahum M. Sarna, "Abraham Geiger and Biblical Scholarship," in *New Perspectives on Abraham Geiger*, ed. Petuchowski, 17–30; Susannah Heschel, *Abraham Geiger and the Jewish Jesus* (Chicago: University of Chicago Press, 1998). For a comparison of the extent of a *Wissenschaft* approach to the Bible by Zunz, Geiger, and Zacharias Frankel, see Michael A. Meyer, "Jewish Religious Reform and *Wissenschaft des Judentums*: The Positions of Zunz, Geiger and Frankel," *Leo Baeck Institute Yearbook* 16 (1971): 35–38. For Jewish reaction to Protestant scholarship on the Old Testament and on rabbinic Judaism, see Ismar Schorsch, *Jewish Reactions to German Anti-semitism, 1870–1914* (New York: Columbia University Press; Philadelphia: Jewish Publication Society, 1972), 169–77.

26. Michael A. Meyer, "A Centennial History," in *Hebrew Union College-Jewish Institute of*

Religion at One Hundred Years, ed. Samuel Karff (Cincinnati: Hebrew Union College Press, 1976), 44.

27. Sperling, "Judaism and Modern Biblical Research," 23. Schechter died in 1915. Schechter's address, "Higher Criticism—Higher Anti-Semitism," was delivered at a banquet in honor of Kaufmann Kohler on the occasion of his assumption of the presidency of Hebrew Union College in 1903. It was a controversial occasion on which to make this point, as Kohler was a prominent exponent of newer interpretive approaches to the Bible. The address is published in Solomon Schechter, *Seminary Addresses and Other Papers* (n.p.: Burning Bush Press, 1959), 35–39.

28. Meyer, *Response,* 188.

29. Resolution of the Leipzig Synod, in Plaut, *Rise of Reform Judaism,* 252.

30. Emphasis added; the full text of the Pittsburgh Platform (1885) is given in Meyer, *Response,* 387.

31. Rabbi S. Sale, "The Bible and Modern Thought," *Yearbook of the Central Conference of American Rabbis* (hereafter cited as *CCARY*) 12 (1902): 161–62; discussion of Sale's address follows on pp. 163–86.

32. Ibid., 165.

33. Charles R. Kniker, "New Attitudes and New Curricula: The Changing Role of the Bible in Protestant Education, 1880–1920," in *The Bible in American Education: From Source Book to Textbook,* ed. David L. Barr and Nicholas Piediscalzi (Philadelphia: Fortress Press, 1982), 121–42. For an overview of the development of biblical scholarship in America, see S. David Sperling with Baruch A. Levine and B. Barry Levy, *Students of the Covenant: A History of Jewish Biblical Scholarship in North America* (Atlanta: Scholars Press, 1992). For the anomaly of the opposition of I. M. Wise, president of Hebrew Union College and a key figure on the American scene in the late nineteenth century, see Naomi W. Cohen, "The Challenges of Darwinism and Biblical Criticism to American Judaism," *Modern Judaism* 4 (1984): 121–57.

34. Pittsburgh Platform, in Meyer, *Response,* 387–88.

35. Schorsch, *From Text to Context,* 221, 350. For discussion of a reversed situation in France (more scholarly attention to the Bible than the Talmud), see Berkovitz, "Jewish Scholarship," 18–20. Of course, Christian attacks on the Talmud are not a feature of the modern period only, but go back to the Middle Ages; see H. L. Strack and G. Stemberger, *Introduction to the Talmud and Midrash,* trans. Markus Bockmuehl (Minneapolis: Fortress Press, 1992), 241–44.

36. *Israelitische Annalen,* vol. 1 (1839), 169 f., as quoted in Plaut, *Rise of Reform Judaism,* 113.

37. Schorsch, *From Text to Context,* 349.

38. Ibid., 325.

39. "Report of the Committee on Post-Biblical and Patristic Literature," *CCARY* 6 (1895): 63. The passage of the resolution was not straightforward because of a disagreement on whether the language should be broader so as to include the Bible as well.

40. Of course, the criticism of Judaism as a religion of law rather than faith goes deep into Christian history, beginning with the letters of Paul.

41. Schorsch, *From Text to Context,* 307.

42. The following discussion of traditional Jewish versus modern discourse owes much to lectures by Benjamin Harshav in his 1994 NEH summer seminar on "The Modern Jewish Renaissance." Some of the same points are made regarding the incorporation of traditional Jewish discourse into Yiddish literature in Benjamin Harshav, *The Meaning of Yiddish* (Berkeley: University of California Press, 1990), 99–102, 111–14.

43. As excerpted in *The Golden Tradition: Jewish Life and Thought in Eastern Europe,* ed. Lucy S. Dawidowicz (Boston: Beacon Press, 1967), 123. Earlier maskilim were not as negative toward the Talmud; see Moshe Pelli, "The Attitude of the First Maskilim in Germany towards the Talmud," *Leo Baeck Institute Yearbook* 27 (1982): 243–60. But even these early maskilim questioned the sacred nature of the text, asserting its humanly authored status and the need to study it in historical/cultural context.

44. *Memoirs of Moses Mendelssohn, the Jewish Philosopher* (London, 1827), 2, as quoted by

Todd M. Endelman, *The Jews of Georgian England, 1714–1830: Tradition and Change in a Liberal Society* (Philadelphia: Jewish Publication Society, 1979), 157.

45. Leopold Stein, *Die Schrift des Lebens*, 2 vols. (Strasbourg, 1872–77), as quoted in Plaut, *Rise of Reform Judaism*, 261. The perception of the Bible as accessible to all, in contrast to later exegetical literature, is parallel to the Protestant embrace of the Bible as understandable on its own, without regard to later Christian writings; such a position goes back to Luther.

46. "Report of the Committee on Post-Biblical and Patristic Literature," 63.

47. *CCARY* 18 (1908): 248; emphasis in original.

48. Ibid., 234, 235, 237.

49. Meyer, *Response*, 18; the journal began publication in 1783.

50. The distance of Jews from a familiarity with German literature is reinforced by the fact that Mendelssohn's translation used the Hebrew alphabet to render the German words, a practice found in other German-Jewish writing as well as in other language traditions, such as Arabic, Spanish, and Persian.

51. See Edward Breuer, *The Limits of Enlightenment: Jews, Germans, and the Eighteenth-Century Study of Scripture* (Cambridge: Harvard University Center for Jewish Studies, 1996); David Sorkin, *Moses Mendelssohn and the Religious Enlightenment* (Berkeley: University of California Press, 1996), 78–87. The translation and commentary were published between 1780 and 1783, with the commentary a collaborative effort with Solomon Dubno, Naphtali Herz Wessely, Herz Homberg, and Aaron Jaroslav. For a detailed account of the undertaking of this translation and commentary, see Alexander Altmann, *Moses Mendelssohn: A Biographical Study* (University, Ala.: University of Alabama Press, 1973), 346–420. For the influence on Mendelssohn of an early critical, rationalist approach to biblical translation by the Christian Hebraist Johann Lorenz Schmidt, see Paul Spalding, "Toward a Modern Torah: Moses Mendelssohn's Use of a Banned Bible," *Modern Judaism* 19, no. 1 (1999): 67–82.

52. For an excellent overview, see Mark A. Noll, "The Bible in American Culture," in *Encyclopedia of the American Religious Experience: Studies of Traditions and Movements*, ed. Charles H. Lippy and Peter W. Williams (New York: Charles Scribner's Sons, 1988), 2:1075–87. See also Nathan O. Hatch, "Sola Scriptura and Novas Ordo Seclorum," in *The Bible in America: Essays in Cultural History*, ed. Nathan O. Hatch and Mark A. Noll (New York: Oxford University Press, 1982), 59–78; James Turner Johnson, ed., *The Bible in American Law, Politics, and Political Rhetoric* (Philadelphia: Fortress Press, 1985); George M. Marsden, "Everyone One's Own Interpreter? The Bible, Science, and Authority in Mid-nineteenth-Century America," in *Bible in America*, ed. Hatch and Noll, 79–100.

53. Introduction to *Bible in America*, ed. Hatch and Noll, 6.

54. Leeser's translation of the Pentateuch appeared in 1845, the complete Bible in 1853–54. On Leeser's translation, see Lance J. Sussman, "Another Look at Isaac Leeser and the First Jewish Translation of the Bible in the U.S.," *Modern Judaism* 51 (1985): 159–90. For an analysis of the historical context of this and later translations, see Jonathan D. Sarna and Nahum M. Sarna, "Jewish Bible Scholarship and Translations in the United States," in *The Bible and Bibles in America*, ed. Ernest S. Frerichs (Atlanta: Scholars Press, 1988), 83–116.

55. Bernard J. Bamberger, *The Bible: A Modern Jewish Approach* (New York: B'nai B'rith Hillel Foundations, 1955), 3–10.

56. This position was close to that of the ancient Jewish sect of the Karaites, who rejected the notion of Oral Torah. Some modern Jewish thinkers welcomed this association, while others were insistent on distinguishing themselves from it. For the development of a neo-Karaite view of Judaism among progressive Orthodox as well as Reform Jews in England, see Steven Singer, "Jewish Religious Thought in Early Victorian England," *AJS Review* 10 (1985): 181–210.

57. See Altmann's description of this theme in essays published in *Ha-Me'asef* in 1785, probably written by Mendelssohn (Altmann, *Moses Mendelssohn*, 88).

58. In Germany the term "citizens of the Mosaic persuasion" was popular (Robert S. Wistrich, "Zionism and Its Jewish 'Assimilationist' Critics (1897–1948)," *Jewish Social Studies* 4 (winter 1998): 70. The subtitle of the Haskalah journal *Sulamith*, originally "A Journal for the Promotion of Culture and Humanity within the Jewish Nation," was changed to end with

"among the Israelites," signaling a change in understanding of the political standing of Jews, as well as a turning from the now pejorative term "Jew" (David Sorkin, *The Transformation of German Jewry, 1780–1840* [New York: Oxford University Press, 1987], 101). The term "Jew" was also rejected as too associative with the particularism of rabbinic Judaism (Meyer, *Origins*, 81, 127).

59. David N. Myers, *Re-inventing the Jewish Past: European Jewish Intellectuals and the Zionist Return to History* (New York: Oxford University Press, 1995), 102–8.

60. Leo Baeck, *The Essence of Judaism* (1905; reprint, New York: Schocken Books, 1978), 22.

61. The Talmud also contained such elements, yet Baeck maintains that it was secondary in influence to the Bible, and that it proved to be a conservative, protective force (ibid., 23).

62. Ibid.; emphasis added.

63. Ibid., 31, 44.

64. Sarna and Sarna, "Jewish Bible Scholarship," 104. A more recent version of this position is readily visible in Sheldon Blank's essay "The Hebrew Scriptures as a Source of Moral Guidance," in *Scripture in the Jewish and Christian Traditions: Authority, Interpretation, Relevance*, ed. Frederick Greenspahn (Nashville: Abingdon Press, 1982), 169–82. Blank speaks specifically from a Reform perspective and focuses entirely on Prophets. Two essays by Harry M. Orlinsky give a superb exposition of how misleading such a universalist interpretation of a small number of quotations extracted from the prophetic writings (and also Leviticus 19:18) has been: "Nationalism-Universalism and Internationalism in Ancient Israel," and "Nationalism-Universalism in the Book of Jeremiah," in *Essays in Biblical Culture and Bible Translation* (New York: Ktav Publishing House, 1974), 78–116, 117–43. Orlinsky gives a contextual interpretation of each passage, showing its actual rootedness in an understanding of Israel's exclusive relationship with God.

65. For a discussion and listing of modern vernacular translations, see Max Margolis, *The Story of Bible Translations* (Philadelphia: Jewish Publication Society, 1917), 79–106. On the American translations, see Sarna and Sarna, "Jewish Bible Scholarship," and Jonathan Sarna, *JPS: The Americanization of Jewish Culture, 1888–1988* (Philadelphia: Jewish Publication Society, 1989), 97–116. On the Buber/Rosenzweig translation, see the introduction to Martin Buber and Franz Rosenzweig, *Scripture and Translation*, trans. Lawrence Rosenwald with Everett Fox (Bloomington: Indiana University Press, 1994). Christians were sensitive, too, to variations between sectarian translations. There were riots in Philadelphia in 1842 when the Roman Catholic bishop petitioned city officials to allow Catholic children to hear readings from the Douay (Catholic) version of the Bible instead of the King James (Protestant) version (Hatch and Noll, *Bible in America*, 9).

66. For example, the enormously popular collection by Rabbi Joseph H. Hertz, *A Book of Jewish Thoughts*, first published in Britain during World War I as *A Book of Jewish Thoughts for Jewish Sailors and Soldiers* and reissued many times since, most recently by Bloch Publishing in 1997; hundreds of thousands of copies have been sold. For the use of biblical material in anthologies of ethical materials, see Michael A. Meyer, "The Problematics of Jewish Ethics," *Journal of the Central Conference of American Rabbis (CCARJ)* 15, no. 3 (1968): 64.

67. Discussion following Rabbi Julian Morgenstern, "The Significance of the Bible for Reform Judaism in the Light of Modern Scientific Research," *CCARY* 18 (1908): 242; emphasis in the original.

68. The writings of Locke and Rousseau were fundamental to these new notions of childhood and educational method, and their work also spawned further writing focused on pedagogy that was directly influential on educational practitioners both in Europe and the United States, authors like Basedow, Campe, and Pestalozzi. For a useful brief summary of these and other "prophets" of the "new education," see Benjamin W. Winchester, *Religious Education and Democracy* (New York: Abingdon Press, 1917), 52–53.

69. (Berlin: Hinukh na'arim, 1782). Wessely (1725–1805) was a contemporary and close associate of Moses Mendelssohn. Wessely wrote the commentary on Leviticus for Mendelssohn's Bible, also published in 1782. Close in date, too, is Christian Wilhelm von Dohm's tract in favor of Jewish emancipation, written at the behest of Mendelssohn, and also

arguing for the state's involvement in the education of Jews and the importance of educational access for Jews: *Ueber die bürgerliche Verbesserung der Juden* (1781).

70. The following summary of Joseph's Edicts of Toleration is drawn from Charles L. Ozer, "Jewish Education in the Transition from Ghetto to Emancipation," *Historia Judaica* 9 (1947): 84–87.

71. A grace period of two to three years was allowed in order for Jews to learn German (ibid., 85 n. 14).

72. These regulations, dating from 1785 and 1810, remained in effect until 1848 (Michael Brenner, Stefi Jersch-Wenzel, and Michael A. Meyer, *Emancipation and Acculturation, 1780–1871*, vol. 2 of *German-Jewish History in Modern Times*, ed. Michael A. Meyer and Michael Brenner [New York: Columbia University Press, 1997], 112–13).

73. I have borrowed this simile from Mark Zborowski and Elizabeth Herzog, *Life Is with People: The Culture of the Shtetl* (New York: Schocken Books, 1962).

74. Conversion was a significant phenomenon in the nineteenth century, understandable in a context in which some but not all restrictions on Jews had been lifted. See Todd M. Endelman, ed., *Jewish Apostasy in the Modern World* (New York: Holmes and Meier, 1987); idem, *Radical Assimilation in English Jewish History, 1656–1945* (Bloomington: Indiana University Press, 1990).

75. Jay R. Berkovitz, *The Shaping of Jewish Identity in Nineteenth-Century France* (Detroit: Wayne State University Press, 1989), chap. 3. On Napoleon's convoking of an Assembly of Jewish Notables in 1806 to answer questions regarding such compatibility, and the establishment of the Paris Sanhedrin in the following year, which was to provide community sanction for the responses made by the Assembly of Jewish Notables, see pp. 42–48 and 77–84.

76. Extensive analyses of Wessely's tract may be found in Ozer, "Jewish Education" (despite its general title, this article is entirely on Wessely), and Z. E. Kurzweil, "N. H. Weisel's Place in Jewish Education," in *Modern Trends in Jewish Education* (New York: Thomas Yoseloff, 1964), 13–40.

77. As quoted by Ozer, "Jewish Education," 87. The first edition of the letter was not dated but seems to have been published early in 1782, written directly in the wake of Joseph's edict (87 n. 19).

78. Wessely, *Divrei Shalom ve-Emet*, as quoted in Kurzweil, "Weisel's Place," 26–27.

79. Wessely went so far as to quote the rabbinic saying "A carcass is preferable to a man learned in the Torah, who yet has no *deah* [knowledge, wisdom]," interpreting this saying to mean that a man learned in Torah but with no knowledge of secular matters was of no benefit to the Jewish community or to others, a statement that brought forth voluble objections from the rabbinic establishment (Kurzweil, "Weisel's Place," 26).

80. While the Bible and prayers were to be translated into German, these newly created textbooks were to be written in Hebrew, at a simplified level for children (Ozer, "Jewish Education," 91).

81. Sorkin, *Transformation of German Jewry*, 126–30; Mordechai Breuer and Michael Graetz, *Tradition and Enlightenment, 1600–1780*, vol. 1 of *German-Jewish History in Modern Times*, ed. Michael A. Meyer and Michael Brenner (New York: Columbia University Press, 1996), 367. On Jewish education in France, see Zosa Szajkowski, *Jewish Education in France, 1789–1939*, ed. Tobey B. Gitelle (New York: Conference on Jewish Social Studies, 1980); Berkovitz, *Shaping of Jewish Identity*; Paula E. Hyman, *The Emancipation of the Jews of Alsace: Acculturation and Tradition in the Nineteenth Century* (New Haven: Yale University Press, 1991); and Jeffrey Haus, "Liberté Égalité, Utilité: Jewish Education and State in Nineteenth-Century France," *Modern Judaism* 22 (2002): 1–27.

82. Adolf Kober, "Emancipation's Impact on the Education and Vocational Training of German Jewry," *Jewish Social Studies* 16 (1954): 155–57, with a list of over fifty different vocational programs established in Germany between 1800 and 1860, 174–76. On vocational schools in Alsace, see Hyman, *Jews of Alsace*, 113–14.

83. Brenner, Jersch-Wenzel, and Meyer, *Emancipation and Acculturation*, 113.

84. Mordechai Breuer, *Modernity within Tradition: The Social History of Orthodox Jewry in Imperial Germany*, trans. Elizabeth Petuchowski (New York: Columbia University Press, 1992),

91–95. Breuer also discusses the inadequacy of the supplemental Jewish education provided in the state schools, and the disagreements within the Jewish community over support of such programs (96–102). For an overview of systems of state education in Europe, including the place of religious instruction, see Winchester, *Religious Education and Democracy*, 54–79, 153–66.

85. Berkovitz, *Shaping of Jewish Identity*, 181.

86. For education in Britain, see Eugene C. Black, *The Social Politics of Anglo-Jewry, 1880–1920* (Oxford: Basil Blackwell, 1988), 104–32; Suzanne Kirsch Greenberg, "Anglicization and the Education of Jewish Immigrant Children in the East End of London," in *Jewish History: Essays in Honour of Chimen Abramsky*, ed. Ada Rapoport-Albert and Steven J. Zipperstein (London: Peter Halban, 1988), 111–26; and for the earlier period, Endelman, *Jews of Georgian England*, 227–47. The development of the Board schools was a fortuitous help to the Jewish education system, which would have been hard pressed to meet the needs of the large number of immigrant children after 1880 had it not been for these additional schools. In 1905, of the 30,000 Jewish pupils in London, 22,000 attended government schools while only 8,000 attended Jewish institutions (Black, *Anglo-Jewry*, 128).

87. Brenner, Jersch-Wenzel, and Meyer, *Emancipation and Acculturation*, 114.

88. Emanuel Gamoran, *Changing Conceptions in Jewish Education, in Two Books*, bk. 1, *Jewish Education in Russia and Poland* (New York: Macmillan, 1924), 45–46.

89. As quoted in Hyman, *Jews of Alsace*, 108. For further details on the large numbers of hours spent learning French and the small number of hours on Hebrew, see Szajkowski, *Jewish Education in France*, 20, 34.

90. See Petuchowski, "Manuals and Catechisms," 47–64. Catechisms were produced in the United States as well, with an early, influential one by Isaac Leeser: *Catechism for Jewish Children Designed as a Religious Manual for House and School* (1839); see Lance J. Sussman, *Isaac Leeser and the Making of American Judaism* (Detroit: Wayne State University Press, 1995), 100–101.

91. Petuchowski, "Manuals and Catechisms," 55–56.

92. L.-A. Sauphar, *Gan Raveh: Manuel d'instruction religieuse et morale* (Paris, 1850, vii); translation mine. A similar stress on moral education, accompanied by discomfort with rabbinic texts, was evident in England as well. When the Ashkenazi Talmud Torah in London was reorganized in 1788, secular learning was added, the time devoted to Hebrew reduced, and the study of Talmud made optional. While the boy receiving the annual prize in Hebrew studies traditionally delivered a talmudic discourse on a halakhic theme, after 1812 the speech was to be a moral explication of a scriptural verse or sentiment. This move to moral education was connected in England with a mission of the Jewish elite to reform the Jewish poor (Endelman, *Jews of Georgian England*, 229–30, 238–39).

93. Stuttgart: bey dem Herausgeber und in commission bey Franz Christian Löflund. On Büdinger and his influence, see Ruth B. Bottigheimer, "Moses Mordechai Büdinger's *Kleine Bibel* (1923) and Vernacular Jewish Children's Bibles," *Jewish Social Studies* 2 (1995): 83–98. For an earlier children's version of the Bible written by a German author, but in Hebrew—Aron Wolfsohn's *Abtalion* [1790]—see Ran HaCohen, "Die Bibel kehrt heim: 'Biblische Geschichte' für jüdische Kinder," *Kinder- und Jugendliteraturforschung*, 1996/7, 9–21.

94. Bottigheimer, "Büdinger's *Kleine Bibel*," 95, 90.

95. Ibid., 91; after the first edition the book was retitled *Biblische Erzählungen für die israelitische Jugend* ("Bible Stories for the Israelite Young"). To see these German children's Bibles in the context of other German-Jewish literature aimed at children, see Zohar Shavit and Hans-Heino Ewers, *Deutsch-jüdische Kinder- und Jugendliteratur von der Haskala bis 1945: Die deutsch- und hebräischsprachigen Schriften des deutschsprachigen Raums. Ein bibliographisches Handbuch*, 2 vols. (Stuttgart: Verlag J. B. Metzler, 1996).

96. Büdinger's book was initially directed specifically at girls and women, but by 1846 was addressed to "boys and girls" (Bottigheimer, "Büdinger's *Kleine Bibel*," 83–84). For an example of a 1908 German school curriculum, widely adopted by Jewish schools, that included the use of Auerbach's collection, see Solomon Colodner, *Jewish Education in Germany under the Nazis* (Jewish Education Committee Press, 1964), 104–8.

97. For analysis of the stories of Jael, Dinah, and David and Bathsheba as retold in Büdinger, see Bottigheimer, "Büdinger's *Kleine Bibel.*"

98. J. Ennery, *Le Sentier d'Israël ou Bible des jeunes Israélites, renfermant l'abrégé du Pentateuque, des prophètes et des hagiographes. Première Partie, contenant les cinq livres de Moïse, Josué, les juges et Ruth* (Paris: Bureau des Archives Israélites, 1843), 15, 17; the quotations are my English rendering of the French version given by Ennery. Ennery's book was approved by Jewish and state authorities for use in Jewish schools. It followed an earlier Bible abridgment that also focused on stories stressing morality: Michel Berr, *Abrégé de la Bible et choix de morceaux de piété et de morale à l'usage des israélites de France* (Paris, 1819); this text had earlier been adopted in many Jewish schools (Berkovitz, *Shaping of Jewish Identity*, 174–75).

99. Ennery, *Le Sentier d'Israël*, 2.

100. Ibid., 2–3.

101. Claude G. Montefiore, *The Bible for Home Reading: With Comments and Reflections for the Use of Jewish Parents and Children* (London: Macmillan, 1896). The book went through seven additional printings before the First World War.

102. Ibid., vi. He comments that the difficulty of the commentary varies, some of it understandable to a child of nine or ten, some of it only by a child of thirteen or fourteen. The second volume, however, which covers the history of the Jews from Nehemiah to the Maccabees, he holds to be suitable only for children over sixteen and their parents (vii).

103. Ibid., ii; italics in original. Page numbers are hereafter given in the text.

104. Gamoran, *Changing Conceptions*, 1:201–2.

105. Salo W. Baron, *The Russian Jew under Tsars and Soviets* (New York: Macmillan, 1964), 41–46. Odessa, in the Russian Pale of Settlement, was unusual in its early and successful establishment of a modern Jewish school with a secular curriculum, founded in 1826 and lasting twenty-six years, until its incorporation into the government school system; see Steven J. Zipperstein, *The Jews of Odessa: A Cultural History, 1794–1881* (Stanford: Stanford University Press, 1985), 43–55.

106. I have focused my account on developments in Poland and Russia. For educational developments in eastern Europe, see Elias Schulman, *A History of Jewish Education in the Soviet Union* (New York: Ktav Publishing House, 1971); Zvi Halevy, *Jewish Schools under Czarism and Communism: A Struggle for Cultural Identity* (New York: Springer Publishing, 1976); Steven J. Zipperstein, "Transforming the Heder: Maskilic Politics in Imperial Russia," in *Jewish History*, ed. Rapoport-Albert and Zipperstein, 87–109; Miriam Eisenstein, *Jewish Schools in Poland, 1913–39: Their Philosophy and Development* (New York: King's Crown Press, Columbia University, 1950); Gamoran, *Changing Conceptions*. Yaffa Eliach gives both a general overview of Jewish education in Poland and a detailed portrait of the educational landscape in one particular shtetl: *There Once Was a World: A 900-Year Chronicle of the Shtetl of Eishyshok* (Boston: Little, Brown, 1998), 451–81. For a country-by-country survey that includes information on education, see Ezra Mendelsohn, *Jews of East Central Europe between the World Wars* (Bloomington: Indiana University Press, 1983).

107. Eisenstein, *Jewish Schools in Poland*, 1–3. The Polish government was much less active, however, in establishing schools for Jews than it was for other minorities. The variety of schools set up by Jews themselves filled the gap (Eliach, *There Once Was a World*, 468).

108. There was some variation from place to place; in Odessa in the second half of the nineteenth century a significant number of Jewish students attended the city's non-Jewish schools (Zipperstein, *Jews of Odessa*, 108).

109. For statistics on enrollment in Russian hadarim, see Schulman, *Jewish Education in the Soviet Union*, 3. In 1921 a major campaign was directed against the heder, and melamdim were arrested, tried, and punished with forced labor (Halevy, *Jewish Schools under Czarism and Communism*, 162). Again, Odessa diverged, with a much earlier decline of hadarim and an earlier and larger attendance at Russian schools (Zipperstein, *Jews of Odessa*, 129–30).

110. In Russia in the 1860s, as in western Europe, a Haskalah-inspired movement proposed to change the language of schooling to Russian, but it was short-lived and largely ineffective; by the mid-1870s the goal had changed to the introduction of some measure of secular study into traditional heder education (Zipperstein, "Transforming the Heder").

111. Eisenstein, *Jewish Schools in Poland*, 30.

112. The Yiddish schools in Poland shared an Enlightenment concern for the educational psychology of the child. Influences included Alfred Binet, Comenius, Pestalozzi, Rousseau, G. Stanley Hall, and John Dewey (some of whose works were translated into Yiddish) (ibid., 22–23).

113. Yiddish schools for Jews were seen as parallel to the existence of schools in the other national languages of minority groups, such as German, Georgian, Ukrainian, Belorussian, Aremenian, Kazakh, Kirgiz, etc. (Halevy, *Jewish Schools under Czarism and Communism*, 128, 181).

114. The governing slogan was "nationalist in form" (that is, taught in the folk language) but "socialist in content" (Schulman, *Jewish Education in the Soviet Union*, 120).

115. Halevy, *Jewish Schools under Czarism and Communism*, 74 ff.; 169–80. Elias Schulman visited the Soviet Union in 1936 and gives a firsthand report of the nature of Yiddish schools and Yiddish culture generally. The Yiddish schools were wiped out by Stalin in the late 1930s as part of a general program of total and forced assimilation of the Jewish population. All Jewish organizations and institutions (political groups, newspapers, theaters) were eventually shut down (Schulman, *Jewish Education in the Soviet Union*, 120–21, 159–64). See also Nora Levin, *The Jews in the Soviet Union since 1917: Paradox of Survival* (New York: New York University Press, 1988), 1:168–92, where the development of Yiddish schools is discussed in the context of other institutions of Yiddish culture (soviets, courts, and scholarship).

116. Steven M. Lowenstein et al., *Integration in Dispute, 1871–1918*, vol. 3 of *German-Jewish History in Modern Times*, ed. Michael A. Meyer and Michael Brenner (New York: Columbia University Press, 1997), 123. The German model had more influence in Hungary than it did in Poland or Russia.

117. The question as to whether Yiddish or Hebrew was the true national language of the Jews was the source of extended and bitter debate among Haskalah-influenced Jews from the late nineteenth century through the early decades of the twentieth century; see Naomi Seidman, *A Marriage Made in Heaven: The Sexual Politics of Hebrew and Yiddish* (Berkeley: University of California Press, 1997).

118. The first such school was founded in Cracow in 1917 by Sarah Schenirer. On Bais Ya'akov schools, see Deborah Weissman, "Bais Ya'akov as an Innovation in Jewish Women's Education: A Contribution to the Study of Education and Social Change," *Studies in Jewish Education* 7 (1995): 278–99. Girls were included in the new Jewish schools in central and western Europe as well, including Orthodox schools.

119. For the Chorev and Yavneh schools, see Eisenstein, *Jewish Schools in Poland*, 81–95.

120. Eisenstein, *Jewish Schools in Poland*, 96; by 1936–37, almost 50 percent of Jewish children in Poland attended government or municipal schools (ibid., 96 n. 3).

3. The American Scene

1. The Jewish population of the United States in 1880 was about 250,000. Another four million Jews entered the country between 1880 and 1927.

2. Max Newman, "Basic Principles of American Reform Judaism and Their Reflection in the Movement's Program of Religious Education from 1848 to the Present" (Ph.D. diss., Hebrew Union College–Jewish Institute of Religion, 1963), 17. For a brief but cogent overview of Jewish education in America from its beginnings to today, see Jonathan D. Sarna, "American Jewish Education in Historical Perspective," *Journal of Jewish Education* 64, no. 1/2 (1998): 8–21; another overview may be found in the essays collected in *A History of Jewish Education in America*, ed. Judah Pilch (New York: National Curriculum Research Institute of the American Association for Jewish Education, 1969). For the history of Jewish education in mid-nineteenth- through early-twentieth-century America, see Eduardo L. Rauch, "Jewish Education in the United States, 1840–1920" (Ed.D. thesis, Harvard University, 1978); Julius H. Greenstone, "Jewish Education in the United States," *American Jewish Year Book* 16 (1914–15): 90–127; Julia Richman, "The Jewish Sunday School Movement in the United

States," *Jewish Quarterly Review* 12 (July 1900): 563–601; Dianne Ashton, *Rebecca Gratz: Women and Judaism in Antebellum America* (Detroit: Wayne State University Press, 1997), chaps. 4 and 5 (on the Hebrew Sunday School founded by Gratz).

3. Lloyd P. Gartner, "Temples of Liberty Unpolluted: American Jews and Public Schooling, 1840–1875," in *A Bicentennial Festschrift for Jacob Rader Marcus*, ed. Bertram W. Korn (New York: Ktav, 1976), 157–89.

4. For the progress of compulsory schooling legislation, see Lawrence Cremin, *American Education: The Metropolitan Experience, 1876–1980* (New York: Harper and Row, 1988), 644–45. Laws proceeded state by state, beginning with Massachusetts in 1852. New York, where many of the immigrants settled, passed such a law in 1874; it included the requirement of instruction in English, which would exclude a traditional heder education from fulfilling the requirement (Stephan F. Brumberg, *Going to America, Going to School: The Jewish Immigrant Public School Encounter in Turn-of-Century New York City* [New York: Praeger, 1986], 68). By 1920, over 90 percent of elementary school–aged children were enrolled in school (Cremin, *American Education: Metropolitan Experience*, 644–45).

5. Ellwood Cubberley, *Changing Conceptions of Education* (Boston: Houghton Mifflin, 1909), 15–16. Cubberley was professor of education at Stanford University; the building housing the Education Department there bears his name.

6. Ibid., 20.

7. Clarence Karier, ed., *Shaping the American Educational State: 1900 to the Present* (New York: Free Press, 1975), 255.

8. Thomas C. Hunt, "Public Schools and Moral Education: An American Dilemma," *Religious Education* 74 (1979): 355–56.

9. Edward George Hartmann, *The Movement to Americanize the Immigrant* (New York: Columbia University Press, 1948), 64–68. For an overview of the long-term development of Americanization, see Robert A. Carlson, *The Americanization Syndrome: A Quest for Conformity* (New York: St. Martin's Press, 1987). While the same sense of nativist superiority fueled both efforts—Americanization and restrictive legislation—these movements were also seen in opposition to each other. "Americanizers" had a more positive attitude toward immigrants and were committed to making them Americans, while those in favor of legislation restricting immigration were more negative toward immigrants and wanted the undesirable ones to be excluded entirely (98). Within the Americanization movement, one can distinguish between "conformist" Americanizers (who aimed for full assimilation of the immigrant into the dominant culture) and "pluralist" Americanizers (who had more respect for the culture the immigrants brought with them). Seth Korelitz makes this distinction when discussing the Americanization work of the National Council of Jewish Women, counting their work as "pluralist" ("'A Magnificent Piece of Work': The Americanization Work of the National Council of Jewish Women," *American Jewish History* 83 [1995]: 184 ff.).

For a full treatment of nativism in the prewar and war years, see John Higham, *Strangers in the Land: Patterns of American Nativism, 1860–1925* (New Brunswick: Rutgers University Press, 1955), chaps. 7–9. Robert Wiebe discusses three key terms that developed by about 1910: "hyphenate Americans," "assimilation," and "Americanization" (*Self-Rule: A Cultural History of American Democracy* [Chicago: University of Chicago Press, 1995], 178).

10. Gregory Mason, "An Account of What the Public Schools of Rochester Are Doing to Make Americans of Foreigners," *The Outlook* (February 12, 1916), in Karier, *American Educational State*, 267–68.

11. Edward R. Bartlett, "The Character Education Movement in the Public Schools," in *Studies in Religious Education: A Source and Textbook for Colleges, Universities, Seminaries, and Discussion Groups for Leaders and Workers in the Field of Religious Education*, ed. Philip Henry Lotz and L. W. Crawford (Nashville: Cokesbury Press, 1931), 450–71. The common school education of the nineteenth century was to be a moral education, making the population "more docile, more tractable, less given to social discord, disruption and disobedience" (David Nasaw, *Schooled to Order: A Social History of Public Schooling in The United States* [New York: Oxford University Press, 1979], 40). For an overview of character education, see Bartlett, "Character Education Movement"; Hunt, "Public Schools and Moral Education"; and

William I. Thomas and Dorothy Swaine Thomas, "Character Education in the Schools," chap. 6 in *The Child in America: Behavior Problems and Programs* (New York: Alfred A. Knopf, 1928).

12. Jonathan D. Sarna and David G. Dalin, *Religion and State in the American Jewish Experience* (Notre Dame, Ind.: University of Notre Dame Press, 1997), 182. For an excellent survey of the relationship between religious education and public schooling up through the second decade of the twentieth century, see Benjamin S. Winchester, *Religious Education and Democracy* (New York: Abingdon Press, 1917). The earliest institutions of public education, both in Germany and then in the United States, had the explicit purpose of enabling children to read Scripture (80–84).

13. A Massachusetts law of 1827 prohibited the use of school textbooks that favored "any particular sect or tenet" (Anne M. Boylan, *Sunday School: The Formation of an American Institution, 1790–1880* [New Haven: Yale University Press, 1988], 54).

14. For an overview of the use of the Bible in public schools, the Catholic challenge to use of Protestant Bibles, and the subsequent decline of use of the Bible in schools, see Paul Gutjahr, *An American Bible: A History of the Good Book in the United States, 1777–1880* (Stanford: Stanford University Press, 1999), 113–42.

15. This presumption of the Bible as nonsectarian is starkly demonstrated in two resolutions passed at the 1869 meeting of the National Teachers Association. The first resolved that "the Bible should not only be studied, venerated, and honored as a classic for all ages, people, and languages . . . but devotionally read, and its precepts inculcated in all the common schools of the land." The second held "that the teaching of partisan or sectarian principles in our public schools, or the appropriation of public funds for the support of sectarian schools is a violation of the fundamental principles of our American system of education" (as quoted in David Tyack and Elisabeth Hansot, *Managers of Virtue: Public School Leadership in America, 1820–1980* [New York: Basic Books, 1982], 74–75). The teachers apparently saw no contradiction between these two resolutions.

16. Ella Lyman Cabot, *Ethics for Children: A Guide for Teachers and Parents* (Boston: Houghton Mifflin, 1910), xviii.

17. For the riots in Philadelphia in 1844, see Gutjahr, *American Bible*, 113–18. For a useful overview of issues involved in the founding of Catholic parochial schools, see Robert D. Cross, "The Origins of Parochial Schools in America," *American Benedictine Review* 16 (1965): 194–209; for a more detailed account, see Thomas C. Hunt and Norlene M. Kunkel, "Catholic Schools: The Nation's Largest Alternative School System," in *Religious Schooling in America*, ed. James C. Carper and Thomas C. Hunt (Birmingham, Ala.: Religious Education Press, 1984), 1–34.

18. The annual reports of this committee can be found in the *Yearbook* of the CCAR (hereafter cited as *CCARY*). Both the CCAR and the UAHC (Union of American Hebrew Congregations) discussed the issue of Bible reading in schools, and kept track of legislation and practice. See, for example, the 1910 report of the Committee on Church and State on court decisions in the *CCARY* 21 (1911): 80–84, and the report of the National Advisory Board of the UAHC on practice in sixty-five cities across the country in the UAHC *Annual Report* 42 (1916): 7930–31.

19. "Report of Special Committee on Recommendations Contained in Rabbi Schanfarber's Paper," *CCARY* 21 (1911): 108. For a similar discussion five years later, see Rabbi Samuel Schulman, "Ethical and Religious Education in Public Schools," *CCARY* 26 (1916): 440–57.

20. Rabbi Tobias Schanfarber, "The Problem of Ethical Instruction in the Public Schools," *CCARY* 21 (1911): 249.

21. Winchester's book, *Religious Education and Democracy,* gives a detailed account of various plans of this sort. Opposition to religious education in public schools also came from antireligious and nonreligious elements (Carl Zollmann, "The Relation of Church and State," in *Studies in Religious Education*, ed. Lotz and Crawford, 419). Zollmann's essay details the increased concern for the exclusion of religion from public education in the 1870s and beyond (418–26).

22. The REA had been founded in 1903 and included some Catholic and Jewish educa-

tors. The Declaration of Principles can be found in Walter Scott Athearn, *Religious Education and American Democracy* (Boston: Pilgrim Press, 1917), 132–33. Published in the same year as Winchester's book, Athearn's work provides much detail on the various ways in which different cities and regions were providing religious education supplementary to public schooling; he also details the variety of approaches then current with regard to teaching the Bible within public education.

23. Brumberg, *Going to America*, 92.

24. Between 1900 and 1927 eleven states passed legislation mandating the compulsory reading of the Bible; twenty-eight others permitted Bible reading, and nine forbade it to some extent (Bartlett, "Character Education Movement," 464). For a CCAR report on the situation with regard to Bible reading in public schools across the country, see *CCARY* 25 (1915): 120–26. This report notes an organized movement to promote Bible reading in school, with discussion of how to oppose such efforts. Despite the virtual unanimity of rabbinical opposition to Bible reading in schools, voices were somewhat muted by the fear of being perceived as "antimorality." Such opposition was, in any case, not effectual. It was only in 1963 that devotional reading of the Bible, as well as recitation of the Lord's Prayer, was outlawed in public schools *(Abington Township School District v. Shempp)*. In addition to this concern about the use of explicitly religious texts in public schools, the rabbis were also concerned with the possibility that "ethical instruction" was being used as a cover for Christian instruction *(CCARY* 26 [1916]: 78–82).

25. See, for example, Jane Brownlee, *A Plan for Child Training* (Springfield, Mass.: G. W. Holden, 1905), which details the virtues to be discussed month by month through the school year. Such programs continue today, in a new context decrying the inadequate training of the child at home and the need for character building at school. The values emphasized in the spring of 2000 in my son's junior high, for example were: Respect, Honesty, Caring, and Responsibility. Signs were posted prominently around the school, just as Brownlee recommends.

26. C. C. Everett, *Ethics for Young People* (Boston: Ginn, 1891), 92; emphasis in the original. This direct method is also well illustrated in excerpts from character education manuals included in Thomas and Thomas, *Child in America*, 273–94.

27. The difference in method was also characterized as "taught" (direct pronouncements) versus "caught" (embedded in all instruction). Each had their advocates, and this discussion reflects a more general educational debate over pedagogical method; see Harold S. Tuttle, "Character Education," *Religious Education* 26 (1931): 631–36. For further examples of the literature discussing moral education, see Henry F. Cope, "A Selected List of Books on Moral Training and Instruction in the Public Schools," *Religious Education* 5 (1910/11): 718–32.

28. Ella Lyman Cabot, *Ethics for Children: A Guide for Teachers and Parents* (Boston: Houghton Mifflin, 1910).

29. Cabot laid out a sequence of seventy-two values to be taught one by one in each month of schooling from the first September of the first year through May of the eighth grade. Another book combining the two approaches is Julia M. Dewey, *Stories for Home and School* (Boston: Educational Publishing, 1891). Cabot defends storytelling as a method of ethical instruction against "several easy and useless ways of teaching ethics," such as giving lists of virtues or making pronouncements about the virtue of a particular person or action. Rather, the values must be drawn out of the children's response to the carefully selected stories (xxiii). A very similar approach, argued in the context of Jewish education, can be found in Rabbi Julius Rappaport, "Character Building and Jewish History," *CCARY* 25 (1915): 300–306.

30. Cabot, *Ethics for Children*, xx–xxi.

31. Edward Eggleston, *Stories of Great Americans for Little Americans* (New York: American Book Company, 1895).

32. Brumberg, *Going to America*, 74.

33. Ibid., 82.

34. Ibid., 185.

35. For an excellent treatment of the relationship of Jews to public schooling in this period, see Deborah Dash Moore, "Ethnic Identity and the Neighborhood School," chap. 4 in *At Home in America: Second Generation New York Jews* (New York: Columbia University Press, 1981), 88–121.

36. Leo Honor also suggests the possibility of influence from the early Sephardic settlers in America, since secular education was taken for granted among Sephardic Jews ("The Impact of the American Environment and American Ideas on Jewish Elementary Education in the United States," *Jewish Quarterly Review* 45 [1955]: 454–55).

37. Emanuel Gamoran, "Jewish Education in the United States," in *Studies in Religious Education*, ed. Lotz and Crawford, 499.

38. It was to German Jews that the New York Board of Education turned when looking for Jewish input into the shaping of the public schooling for immigrants, rather than to indigenous leaders of the Jewish immigrant community (Brumberg, *Going to America*, 86). For an overview of German Jewish attitudes toward Eastern European immigrants and their efforts to Americanize them, see Rauch, "Jewish Education," 199–223. For the Americanization efforts of the largely German Jewish women of the National Council of Jewish Women, see Korelitz, "'A Magnificent Piece of Work,'" 177–203.

39. Richman, "The Jewish Sunday School Movement," 571. Richman's attitude toward the defects of immigrant life generated some antipathy among Lower East Side Jews; see Selma Berrol, "When Uptown Met Downtown: Julia Richman's Work in the Jewish Community of New York, 1880–1912," *American Jewish History* 70 (1980/81): 35.

40. Rabbi Edward N. Calisch, "Judaism and the Public School System of America," *CCARY* 3 (1892): 130. This antipathy to Jewish organizations that might work against American democratic ideals extended beyond schools. In his 1909 report as director of the Department of Synagog and School Extension of the UAHC, Alfred Godshaw notes that on his travels to various communities promoting religious education, he found in some towns Hebrew Political Clubs, which he opposes as "un-American and un-Jewish." Where possible, he helped to end such associations (*Proceedings of the UAHC* 35 [1909]: 6079); hereafter cited as *PUAHC*.

41. Abram Simon, "The Jewish Child and the American Public School," *Religious Education* 6 (1911/12): 527–28; emphasis in original.

42. Samson Benderly, "Jewish Education in America," *The Jewish Exponent*, January 17, 1908, as cited in Nathan H. Winter, *Jewish Education in a Pluralist Society: Samson Benderly and Jewish Education in the United States* (New York: New York University Press, 1966), 48.

43. Brumberg, *Going to America*, 70.

44. There were certainly also Jews who supported an assimilationist position, most notably the many German Jews who actively encouraged the assimilation of eastern European Jews. For a vehement critique of the Educational Alliance in New York—a Jewish social settlement agency dominated by "old" immigrant Jews devoted to the "de-orientalization of the Russian Jew," see Isaac B. Berkson, *Theories of Americanization: A Critical Study, with Special Reference to the Jewish Group*, Contributions to Education, no. 109 (1920; reprint, New York: AMS Press, 1972), 56–58. Berkson, as we will see below, was one of the architects of the ideology of cultural pluralism.

45. See Eli Lederhandler, "America: A Vision in a Jewish Mirror," in *Jewish Responses to Modernity: New Voices in America and Eastern Europe* (New York: New York University Press, 1994), 104–39; Jonathan D. Sarna, "The Cult of Synthesis in American Jewish Culture," *Jewish Social Studies* 5 (1998/99): 52–79. The desire to combine American and Jewish identities is also persistently demonstrated in Moore, *At Home in America*.

46. Much of the writing of this period on cultural pluralism bears a strong resemblance to more recent writing on multiculturalism. For a discussion of this similarity, and the commonality of a response to new waves of immigration (for the later period, following revision of immigration policy in 1965), see David A. Hollinger, "Jewish Intellectuals and the De-Christianization of American Public Culture in the Twentieth Century," in *Science, Jews, and Secular Culture: Studies in Mid-Twentieth-Century American Intellectual History* (Princeton: Princeton University Press, 1996), 22.

47. Dewey was one of the founders of the New School for Social Research in 1919, where Kallen taught from 1919 to 1952 and remained as a research professor until 1965.

48. For the influence of Dewey on Jewish education, see Samuel M. Blumenfield, "John Dewey and Jewish Education," in *Judaism and the Jewish School: Selected Essays on the Direction and Purpose of Jewish Education*, ed. Judah Pilch and Meir Ben-Horin (New York: Bloch Publishing, 1966), 144–55; Meir Ben-Horin, "John Dewey and Jewish Education," *Religious Education* 55 (1960): 201–2; Samuel Dinin, "The Influence of John Dewey on Some Pioneer Jewish Educators," *Jewish Education* 48 (spring 1980): 6–11, 18; Ronald Kronish, "John Dewey's Influence on Jewish Education in America: The Gap between Theory and Practice," *Studies in Jewish Education* 1 (1983): 168–91; idem, "The Influence of John Dewey upon Jewish Education in America," *Studies in Jewish Education* 2 (1984): 104–21; Michael Rosenak, "'From Strength to Strength': Dewey and Religious Jewish Education," *Courtyard* 1, no. 1 (1999/2000): 66–80. For the influence of the notion of cultural pluralism on Jewish educators, see Kronish, "Influence of John Dewey," 109–11. Dewey's work is referenced throughout the writings of Jewish educators, both Reform and Conservative.

49. The literature on John Dewey is enormous. The discussion here relies largely on Robert B. Westbrook, *John Dewey and American Democracy* (Ithaca, N.Y.: Cornell University Press, 1991).

50. John Dewey, "The Principle of Nationality," *The Menorah Journal* 3 (October 1917): 206. See note 56 below for a description of this journal, founded by Jewish students at Harvard University.

51. John Dewey, "Nationalizing Education" (1916), *Middle Works*, 10:204, as cited in Robert B. Westbrook, "On the Private Life of a Public Philosopher: John Dewey in Love," *Teachers College Record* 96 (1994): 197. Westbrook discusses how Dewey saw this ideal of harmony among divergent cultures potentially embodied in his passionate relationship with the Jewish novelist Anzia Yezierska.

52. Dewey, "Nationalizing Education," 205.

53. Dewey's writings on this subject include *The School and Society* (1900), *The Child and the Curriculum* (1902), and *Democracy and Education* (1916); the first two were particularly influential among educators of the day. The influence of wartime on the salience of the term "democracy" is evident in the titling of the 1916 book, the working title of which was "Philosophy of Education," still visible on the running head of the page proofs of the book. The change to "Democracy and Education" must have come between the printing and the binding of the book (from Philip Jackson, professor of education at the University of Chicago, in a talk to the Midwest Faculty Seminar on Dewey, February 1998).

54. Westbrook, *John Dewey*, 169–70, 418, 436. For more on the linkage between science, democracy, and secularism in this period, see Hollinger, *Science, Jews, and Secular Culture*. Despite this intellectual position, and despite his own break with institutional religion in the 1890s, Dewey was supportive of religious education, not only in his work with Jewish educators but also as a charter member of the Religious Education Association, founded in 1903. For a full study of the place of religion in Dewey's life and thought, see Steven C. Rockefeller, *John Dewey: Religious Faith and Democratic Humanism* (New York: Columbia University Press, 1991); also of interest is the assessment of religion in Dewey's philosophy by George A. Coe, "The Definitive Dewey," *Religious Education* 35 (1940): 45–50, and by Alan Ryan, *John Dewey and the High Tide of American Liberalism* (New York: W. W. Norton, 1995), 265–76. Samuel Dinin, a Jewish educator who himself studied with Dewey, has an interesting, brief description of the interchange between the non-believing Dewey and his Jewish students ("Influence of John Dewey," 11).

55. Their most notable contributions were in the developing fields of sociology and anthropology. Robert K. Merton (born Meyer Schkolnick) and Franz Boas are examples of prominent Jewish contributors to these fields. For a superb analysis of the intellectual contest between relativist and absolutist approaches to truth, see Edward A. Purcell Jr., *The Crisis of Democratic Theory: Scientific Naturalism and the Problem of Value* (Lexington: University Press of Kentucky, 1972).

56. Susanne Klingenstein, *Jews in the American Academy, 1900–1940: The Dynamics of Intel-*

lectual Assimilation (New Haven: Yale University Press, 1991), 41. The Menorah Society was founded in 1906, and its periodical, the *Menorah Journal*, in 1915. The goal of the journal was to "(re-)create in its pages a Jewish secular culture that could match in dignity and interest the culture of America, if not of Europe" (42). The *Menorah Journal* had contributors, both Jewish and non-Jewish, from across America's intellectual elite, and its readership and influence went far beyond the members of the Menorah societies that sprang up on college campuses. The Menorah movement was crucial in shaping a secular Jewish identity that would have meaning for college-educated American Jews; see Lauren B. Strauss, "Staying Afloat in the Melting Pot: Constructing an American Jewish Identity in the *Menorah Journal* of the 1920s," *American Jewish History* 84 (1996): 315–32. For an overview of Kallen's life and work, see Milton R. Konvitz, "Horace Meyer Kallen, 1882–1974: Philosopher of the Hebraic-American Idea," *American Jewish Yearbook* 75 (1974–75): 55–80; Moses Rischin, "The Jews and Pluralism: Toward an American Freedom Symphony," in *Jewish Life in America: Historical Perspectives*, ed. Gladys Rosen (New York: Ktav Publishing House, 1978), 69–80; and William Toll, "Horace M. Kallen: Pluralism and American Jewish Identity," *American Jewish History* 85 (1997): 57–73. A bibliography of his writings can be found in *Vision and Action: Essays in Honor of Horace M. Kallen on His 70th Birthday*, ed. Sidney Ratner (New Brunswick, N.J.: Rutgers University Press, 1953); contributors to this festschrift include John Dewey and T. S. Eliot.

57. For example, he was a member of the Commission on New Approaches to American Jewish Education (an affiliate of the Jewish Education Commmittee of New York); he gave an address at the dinner in honor of the American Association for Jewish Education (February 22, 1948), later published as "Critical Problems in Jewish Education," *Jewish Education* 19, no. 3 (1947/48): 11–16; in 1955 he participated in a symposium on "The Goals of Jewish Education" at Dropsie College.

58. Edward A. Ross, *The Old World in the New: The Significance of Past and Present Immigration to the American People* (New York: Century, 1914). The book expanded on a series of articles Ross had published in *The Century Magazine* in 1913 and 1914; he successfully popularized the Dillingham Commission's exclusionist findings on immigration.

59. Horace Kallen, "Democracy versus the Melting-Pot," *Nation* 100 (18 February 1915): 192. Kallen criticized Jews like Zangwill who supported the notion of a "melting pot" (193). (This essay continues into the February 25 issue of the *Nation*; it is reprinted in *Culture and Democracy in the United States: Studies in the Group Psychology of the American Peoples* [New York: Boni and Liveright, 1924], 67–125.)

60. He treats Jews last in the list, just as another example, though he also discusses how the experience of Jews is different in the lack of a "homeland" from which Jews came, and in the degree of their autonomy and self-consciousness "in spirit and culture" (February 25, 1915): 218.

61. Ibid., 219.

62. Ibid. Dewey's notion of the "harmonious whole" is similar to this formulation of Kallen's.

63. Ibid., 220. For Dewey's response to this essay (positive, but with concern about the degree of geographical separation of ethnic groups envisaged by Kallen), see Westbrook, *John Dewey*, 214. The musical metaphor was not original to Kallen, but was popularized by him; for an earlier example by Rabbi Judah Magnes in 1909, see Moses Rischin, "The Jews and Pluralism," 69. Another metaphor for diversity-with-unity common by the 1930s was of a "mosaic" (Cremin, *American Education: Metropolitan Experience*, 116); Randolph Bourne, another prominent voice for pluralism (and a disciple of Dewey's), speaks of a woven fabric with threads of all sizes and colors ("Trans-National America," *Atlantic Monthly* 118 [July 1916]: 96). The echoes of current discussions of multiculturalism—and the now common metaphor of a quilt—are striking. Dewey, Kallen, and Bourne are the names generally mentioned as the formulators of a pluralist democratic vision; for a brief review of Bourne's life and work, see Carl Resek, introduction to *War and the Intellectuals: Essays by Randolph S. Bourne, 1915–1919* (New York, Harper and Row, 1964), vii–xv.

64. The book is a published version of Berkson's dissertation at Teachers College. In the

acknowledgments to the book, Berkson thanks John Dewey, "whose inspiration and encouragement led me to undertake the writing" (v). Berkson is explicit about the role of his own experience as a Jew in the development of his ideas (2).

65. Berkson, *Theories*, 21–22.

66. Ibid., 24, 71. He describes the community theory of Americanization as offering "the greatest opportunity for the creation of a free, rich and lofty Personality" (118).

67. In some places, he does identify Jews and other groups as "ethnic groups" or "foreign ethnic groups." His concern is to distinguish these groups by their cultural identity—"minority *communities* bound by common tradition" rather than by a biological (racial) identity (148; emphasis in original). He sees himself as differing from Kallen by defining the group in terms of culture rather than race (79 ff.).

68. Although Berkson does also factor in a significant religious component when discussing the range of Jewish identification of Jews in America (ibid., 113–16). It is possible that contributing to this stress on culture or ethnicity rather than religion is the desire to distinguish Jews from Catholics, who were at the time the other currently prominent and problematic religious minority in America. Catholics had responded to American demands for conformity with public education by establishing a system of parochial education. Berkson was fundamentally opposed to such a separatist approach.

69. For the curriculum, see ibid., 196–97; it is, in fact, called the "Talmud Torah curriculum." Some activities at the CJI related more directly to Americanization, for example, clubs and holiday celebrations, and a few of the activities were centered on specifically American themes. Yet most of these clubs and celebrations related to Jewish themes. For a discussion of the divergence of Berkson's practice from theory at the CJI, see Kronish, "John Dewey's Influence," 178–83.

70. On this concern to protect the Jewish community from accusations of separatism or disloyalty, see Walter Ackerman, "The Americanization of Jewish Education," *Judaism* 24 (1975): 423. For a summary of Berkson's view on parochial education as antidemocratic, see Arthur Goren, *New York Jews and the Quest for Community, the Kehillah Experiment, 1908–1922* (New York: Columbia University Press, 1970), 122–23. Berkson attacked Kallen's call for "a federation of nationalities" as ethnic autonomy, which Berkson feared would lead to ethnic segregation.

71. Boylan, *Sunday School*, 9–10. On early Sunday Schools, see also Jack L. Seymour, *From Sunday School to Church School: Continuities in Protestant Church Education in the United States, 1860–1929* (Lanham, Md.: University Press of America, 1982). The Bible had a special place in the home as well, both as material object and as read text; see Colleen McDannell, "The Bible in the Victorian Home," in *Material Christianity: Religion and Popular Culture in America* (New Haven: Yale University Press, 1995).

72. The work of the ASSU is covered extensively in Boylan, *Sunday School*. The Union not only established Sunday schools throughout the country, but also undertook the provision of teaching materials; it was a major publisher of children's literature throughout the nineteenth century. The organization eventually became the International Sunday School Council of Religious Education, later shortened to the International Council of Religious Education.

73. Seymour, *From Sunday School to Church School*, 158.

74. Karl R. Stolz, "Historical Development of Religious Education in America," in *Studies in Religious Education*, ed. Lotz and Crawford, 34. For a thorough consideration of the changing use of the Bible over the course of the nineteenth century, see William L. Sachs, "Stabilizing a Changing Culture: The Bible and the Sunday School in the Late Nineteenth Century," in *The Bible in American Education: From Source Book to Textbook*, ed. David L. Barr and Nicholas Piediscalzi (Philadelphia: Fortress Press, 1982), 77–96.

75. Rauch, "Jewish Education," 61.

76. The UAHC was itself founded in 1873. One of the resolutions from its first meeting was a call for a report on the improvement and unification of Sabbath schools (Newman, "Basic Principles," 47). The work of the HSSUA was taken over in 1903 by the Department of Synagog and School Extensions. An example of conscious modeling on Protestant practice

can be seen in the establishment in 1896 of a religious magazine for Jewish children, *Helpful Thoughts*. One of the magazines editors, Julia Richman, describes the motivation in starting the magazine as recognition of "how far behind our Christian friends we Jews are in providing proper ethical reading for children of our own faith," so she and others determined to provide a paper "on lines similar to those adopted in all Protestant Sunday schools" (Richman, "The Jewish Sunday School Movement," 574–75). Richman was active in the National Council of Jewish Women, founded in 1893, one of whose three general committees was established for religious school work.

77. For a list of its publications, see Newman, "Basic Principles," 77–78. Jewish Sabbath schools date back to the 1830s, with the first founded by Rebecca Gratz in 1838. A scattering of other such schools were established in succeeding years, paralleling Protestant schools of similar nature, but for both groups there was a change and expansion in the latter decades of the nineteenth century, following the thoroughgoing establishment of universal public schooling.

78. Orville L. Davis, "A History of the Religious Education Association," *Religious Education* 44 (1949): 41.

79. Laird T. Hites, "The Religious Education Association," in *Studies in Religious Education*, ed. Lotz and Crawford, 391. The association was committed to inspiring "the educational forces of our country with the religious ideal" as well as "the religious forces of our country with the educational ideal"; in conjunction with this goal, REA members led in the movement for character education in public schools (393, 396).

80. The earliest such report was written by Rabbi Louis Grossman, "Jewish Religious Education: The Training of Jewish Teachers of Religion," *Religious Education* 6 (1911/12): 278–81. Though Jewish authors were few in these years, their presence at all is significant; there were even fewer articles on Catholic education than on Jewish.

81. For example: Solomon Freehof, "Let There Be Faith," *Religious Education* 31 (1936): 83–84; Abba Hillel Silver, "The Decline of the Individual," *Religious Education* 32 (1937): 211–16; Baruch Braunstein, "The Cult of Disillusion," *Religious Education* 32 (1937): 241–44.

82. Louis L. Mann, "Report of Committee on Religious Education," *CCARY* 40 (1930): 113. Jewish/Christian collegiality is also evident in the inclusion of a chapter on Jewish education (and another on Catholic education) in a major guide and textbook of religious education published in the early 1930s: Lotz and Crawford, *Studies in Religious Education*. The dialogue between Christian and Jewish educators was not limited to the Reform movement, as educators in the Conservative movement were also encouraged to consult Christian writers on religious education as well as *Religious Education* (Rabbi Alter F. Landesman, *A Curriculum for Jewish Religious Schools* [New York: United Synagogue of America, 1922], 26 and passim).

83. Inside the front cover of number 4 of the 1945 volume.

84. Cremin, *American Education: Metropolitan Experience*, 90.

85. William Clayton Bower, "A Critical Re-evaluation of the Biblical Outlook of Progressive Religious Education," *Religious Education* 38 (1943): 3–9. Bower sums up the views of progressive educators on teaching the Bible from George Coe's *Social Theory of Religious Education* (1917) to his own day.

86. "Synagog" changed to "Synagogue" in 1928.

87. Other institutions included the Teachers Institute of the Mizrachi, subsequently Yeshiva University (1919); Hebrew Teachers College of Boston (1921); the Teachers School of the Hebrew Institute of Pittsburgh (1923); the College of Jewish Studies of Chicago (1924). On the history of the Teachers Institute at JTS, see Mel Scult, "Mordecai Kaplan, the Teachers Institute, and the Foundations of Jewish Education in America," *American Jewish Archives* 38 (1986): 57–84; and David Kaufman, "Jewish Education as a Civilization: A History of the Teachers Institute," in *Tradition Renewed: A History of the Jewish Theological Seminary of America*, ed. Jack Wertheimer (New York: Jewish Theological Seminary, 1997), 566–629.

88. Goren, *New York Jews*, 88–90.

89. For a review of the relationship of these efforts to those of a generation or more earlier by the Hebrew Sabbath School Union, see George Zepin, "Director's Report on Synagog and School Extension," *PUAHC* 52 (1926): 10008–9. For a list of the more than sixty books

edited by Gamoran between 1924 and 1962, see Kerry M. Olitzky, "A History of Reform Jewish Education during Emanuel Gamoran's Tenure as Educational Director of the Commission on Jewish Education of the Union of American Hebrew Congregations, 1923–1958" (Ph.D. diss., Hebrew Union College–Jewish Institute of Religion, 1984), 233–38.

90. An earlier quarterly with this same name was published by the Jewish Teachers Association of New York beginning in 1916, but it seems not to have lasted beyond the mid-1920s.

91. Olitzky, "History of Reform Jewish Education," 152.

92. For background on institution building by second-generation American Jews, see Moore, *At Home in America.* For the development of educational institutions in particular, see Rauch, "Jewish Education," and Olitzky, "History of Reform Jewish Education."

93. Emanuel Gamoran, for example, was born in Belz, Russia, in 1895 and emigrated to the United States in 1907, where he continued his traditional Jewish studies until high school; Mordecai Kaplan was born in 1881 in Svencionys, Lithuania, and emigrated at the age of nine; Samuel Dinin was born in Russia in 1902; Alexander Dushkin was born in Poland in 1890 and came to the United States in 1901; Leo Honor was born in Russia in 1894; Israel Chipkin was born in Vilna in 1891 and emigrated to the United States in 1892. Exceptions to this pattern among the key figures of this generation were Samson Benderly, who was born in Safed (Palestine) in 1876 (his family was of eastern European origin) and came to the United States in his early twenties (having first gone to Beirut for a number of years for university and medical education), and Isaac Berkson, who was born in New York in 1891.

94. William Cutter, "Kaplan and Jewish Education: Reflections on His Influence," in *The American Judaism of Mordecai M. Kaplan,* ed. Emanuel S. Goldsmith, Mel Scult, and Robert M. Seltzer (New York: New York University Press, 1990), 371.

95. On the collaboration between Benderly and Kaplan, see Kaufman, "Jewish Education," 581–82. On the shaping influence of Benderly, see Winter, *Jewish Education in a Pluralist Society.*

96. For recollections of these arrangements between JTS and Teachers College by one of the early participants, see Alexander M. Dushkin, *Living Bridges: Memoirs of an Educator* (Jerusalem: Keter Publishing House, 1975), 9–10, 15–17.

97. Goren, *New York Jews,* 119.

98. While these five men are usually cited as the group of "Benderly Boys," there was a larger group of selected students, including a few women, who received special attention from Benderly (Kaufman, "Jewish Education," 584). Alexander Dushkin names thirteen men and three women as a core group of Benderly "disciples"; the three women were all wives of men in the group (Alexander M. Dushkin, "The Personality of Samson Benderly, His Life and Influence," *Jewish Education* 20 [1949]: 10).

99. For an excellent analysis of the early figures, institutions, and purposes of American Jewish education, see Ackerman, "Americanization of Jewish Education," 416–35. These developments are also covered in Rauch, "Jewish Education," 420–49. For personal reflections written later by two of the key players, see Dushkin, *Living Bridges;* Samuel Dinin, "These Things I Remember," *Jewish Education* 60, no. 1 (spring 1993): 6–13 (publication of an address given in 1966); and idem, "Influence of John Dewey," 6–11, 18.

100. "Annual Report of the Board of Managers of the Synagogue and School Extension," *PUAHC* 66 (1940): 41. By the early 1950s, some 350 books, plays, and teacher guides had been produced by the UAHC (Richard C. Hertz, *The Education of the Jewish Child: A Study of 200 Reform Jewish Religious Schools* [New York: Union of American Hebrew Congregations, 1953], ix). Conservative congregations were organized later than Reform; the United Synagogue of America (parallel to the UAHC) was founded with twenty-two congregations in 1913. While the Conservative movement had a goal of greater commitment to the teaching of (and in) Hebrew, the reality was that most of its congregations had two schools, one meeting three days a week, with significant instruction in Hebrew, and one meeting just on Sundays, with a curriculum similar to Reform Sunday schools. Despite Conservative goals to the contrary, most children attended only on Sundays (Honor, "Impact of the American Environment," 468–69). For the lag in development of a comprehensive educational plan in the

Conservative movement, see Moshe Davis, "The Ladder of Jewish Education: A Program for Jewish Education in Conservative Judaism," *Conservative Judaism* 4, no. 3 (1948): 1–14.

101. Winter, *Jewish Education in a Pluralist Society*, 47–50.

102. On Jewish day schools, see Eduardo Rauch, "The Jewish Day School in America: A Critical History and Contemporary Dilemmas," in *Religious Schooling in America*, ed. Carper and Hunt, 130–65; Norman Drachler, *A Bibliography of Jewish Education in the United States* (Detroit: Wayne State University Press, 1996), 176–203; Alvin Irwin Schiff, *The Jewish Day School in America* (New York: The Jewish Education Press, 1966). On the earlier schools, see Rauch, "Jewish Education," 371–75, 378–83, 392–411. On the development of Yiddish and Jewish secular schooling in the United States, see ibid., 449–56; Drachler, *Bibliography of Jewish Education*, 204–42; Honor, "Impact of the American Environment," 481–85. On the democratic modification of the Talmud Torah in America to a school for all Jewish children in a community rather than just poor children, see Honor, "Impact of the American Environment," 479–80.

103. Goren, *New York Jews*, 110–33.

104. Dushkin, *Living Bridges*, 79. For data on numbers and types of schools in 1927, see Gamoran, "Jewish Education," 497–98. The survey showed that in 871 communities there were 1,481 congregational schools, 261 noncongregational schools, and 12 parochial schools.

Another institution of Jewish education for children formulated in this same period was the Jewish summer camp. Isaac Berkson, author of *Theories of Americanization* and founder of the Central Jewish Institute, founded Camp Cejwin, the first Jewish educational camp, in 1919. Just as the new religious schooling was designed to provide knowledge and experience that was no longer available in Jewish homes, the camps were to provide a seamless Jewish life that was unavailable in school as well as home. On Jewish camping see Dushkin, *Living Bridges*, 62–72, and Drachler, *Bibliography of Jewish Education*, 417–21.

105. Sarna, "American Jewish Education," 9.

106. Ackerman, "Americanization of Jewish Education," 425, 435. Ackerman laments the shift of focus to the early years, which he sees as resulting in the "denigration of the intellectual effort and capability required for a true understanding of Judaism" (435).

107. Emanuel Gamoran, *Changing Conceptions in Jewish Education, in Two Books* (New York: Macmillan, 1924), 1:202. The first volume of Gamoran's book, *Jewish Education in Russia and Poland*, was dedicated to the memory of his father; the second, *Principles of the Jewish Curriculum in America*, was dedicated "To my teacher, Mordecai M. Kaplan, a pioneer in the revaluation of Jewish values." The book is the published form of his Teachers College dissertation.

108. Gamoran, *Changing Conceptions*, 2:68. Gamoran thought that the goals themselves needed to be context-sensitive. That is, the goals of Jewish education in Russia and Poland would necessarily be different from goals in an American context. This is a central point of Gamoran's book, and a point on which he was strongly influenced by his teacher Mordecai Kaplan. Kaplan, while stressing the socialization into Jewish life (rather than American), explicitly presupposed "a type of Jewish life which is completely integrated into a progressive and dynamic American life" (Mordecai M. Kaplan, *Judaism as a Civilization* [1934; reprint, New York: Schocken, 1967], 482). The mesh between Judaism and American life was also visible in the aims of Conservative religious education as listed by Landesman, which included: "To make the children aware that the ideals and the distinctive character of the Jewish people are compatible with and promotive of American ideals and life" (*Curriculum*, 1). As was true of the Reform movement, this goal was paired with one that focused on the primacy of Jewish identity: "To bind the children in love for Judaism and in loyalty to the Jewish people." Harmony between Jewish and American ideals continued to be stressed in subsequent decades, as is evident in this 1948 reformulation of the goals of Conservative religious education: "To give the child an awareness of the essential harmony between the ideals and traditions of American democracy and the ideals and traditions of Judaism to the end that he may be happily adjusted as a Jew, a citizen and an heir to the great American and Jewish traditions" (*The Objectives and Standards for the Congregational School*, rev. ed. [New York: United Synagogue Commission on Jewish Education, 1948], 6).

109. Gamoran, *Changing Conceptions*, 2:101.

110. Ibid., 27, with citations to Dewey.

111. For the secular context, see David Tyack and Elisabeth Hansot, *Learning Together: A History of Coeducation in American Public Schools* (New Haven: Yale University Press, 1990).

112. Emanuel Gamoran, "Preliminary Survey of Jewish Religious Schools Affiliated with the Union of American Hebrew Congregations," *CCARY* 34 (1924): 363–64. In the nineteenth century as well, Jewish Sunday Schools had female teachers; the first such school was set up by a woman, Rebecca Gratz.

113. For a passionate plea in 1896 for Jewish women to "give themselves heart and soul to reviving the religious spirit in the home" rather than "direct[ing] their attention to management of the schools," see David Philipson, "President's Address" to the Biennial Conference of the Hebrew Sabbath School Union of America, *PUAHC* 23 (1896): 3718. Thirty years later, Gamoran reports on concern at the preponderance of female teachers (Gamoran, "Preliminary Survey," 363–64). On the issue of the "feminization" of Jewish teaching, see Kaufman, "Jewish Education," 571–72, 578, 583–84. Thirty-five years after Gamoran, Judah Pilch, a historian of Jewish education, blamed what he perceived as a decline of the religious school curriculum on women who, like the children, were more interested in "play and fun" than in the "reading of books of Jewish interest" ("Changing Patterns in Jewish Education," *Jewish Social Studies* 21 [1959]: 100). For an analysis of the extent and consequences (or lack thereof) of the feminization of teaching in public schooling, see Madeleine R. Grumet, "Pedagogy for Patriarchy: The Feminization of Teaching," chap. 2 in *Bitter Milk: Women and Teaching* (Amherst: University of Massachusetts Press, 1988), 31–58.

114. Karla Goldman, *Beyond the Synagogue Gallery: Finding a Place for Women in American Judaism* (Cambridge: Harvard University Press, 2000), chap. 7. On the National Council of Jewish Women, see Faith Rogow, *Gone to Another Meeting: The National Council of Jewish Women, 1893–1993* (Tuscaloosa: University of Alabama Press, 1993).

115. Sarna, "American Jewish Education," 15.

116. Simon, "Jewish Child," 532–33.

117. Works by Dewey and Kilpatrick appear regularly on reading lists for Jewish teachers, so those who did not study at Teachers College were still expected to be familiar with the literature of progressive education. Presentations at rabbinical conferences further disseminated these ideas. See, for example, the published versions of presentations on the "project method" (central to progressive educational method) given at the 1926 annual meeting of the Central Conference of American Rabbis (Emanuel Gamoran, *The Project Method in the Jewish School: A Symposium* [Cincinnati: Department of Synagogue and School Extension of the UAHC, n.d.]).

118. For a clear statement of this change in goal in Protestant education, see William Clayton Bower, "The Nature, Content, and Form of the Curriculum," in *Studies in Religious Education*, ed. Lotz and Crawford, 177–78.

119. Rabbi Samuel N. Deinard, "Character-Building and the Study of Hebrew," *CCARY* 25 (1915): 313; emphasis in original. This is one of seven articles in this issue devoted to character building.

120. Samuel Wolk, "Character Education in the Synagogue," *Religious Education* 24 (1929): 818; emphasis added.

121. Emanuel Gamoran, "The Jewish Curriculum and Character Education," *Religious Education* 29 (1934): 138.

122. For examples of blaming women, see Rabbi David Goldberg, "Women's Part in Religious Decline," *Jewish Forum* 7 (1921), cited in Ann D. Braude, "Jewish Women in the Twentieth Century: Building a Life in America," in *Women and Religion in America*, vol. 3, *1900–1968*, ed. Rosemary Radford Ruether and Rosemary Skinner Keller (San Francisco: Harper and Row, 1981), 139; Pilch, "Changing Patterns in Jewish Education," 92. Christians, too, lamented the need to shift the teaching of moral education from the home to the religious school; see, for example, Stolz, "Historical Development of Religious Education," 51.

123. Two contributing UAHC authors were also related to Gamoran: his wife, Mamie Gamoran (author of *The Voice of the Prophets*, the fifth volume in the UAHC Bible series, and

Hillel's Happy Holidays) and his sister, Rose Lurie (author of *The Great March: Post-Biblical Jewish Stories*). Both women were also graduates of the Teachers Institute of the JTS.

124. Jacob Golub, "A Curriculum for the Primary Grades," *Jewish Education* 3, no. 1 (1931): 49–55. The three volumes of his biblical history were published by the Department of Synagog and School Extension of the UAHC: *Israel in Canaan* (1920), *In the Days of the First Temple* (1931), and *In the Days of the Second Temple* (1929). Golub was the director of the Bureau of Jewish Education in Cincinnati.

125. A summary of the 1870s curriculum can be found in the "Report of the Committee on Sabbath-Schools," *PUAHC* 1 (1873–79): 143; the 1896 curriculum in "[Report of the Committee on Plan of Religious Instruction]," *CCARY* 7 (1896): 30–43. The 1896 curriculum remained in effect until Gamoran's new curriculum of the 1920s (Newman, "Basic Principles," 60).

126. Gamoran, *Changing Conceptions*, 2:140–73.

127. Ibid., 140–41.

128. Ibid., 101, 64–65.

129. Ibid., 142–43. For the stronger emphasis on Hebrew in the religious schools of the Conservative movement, see Landesman, *Curriculum*. Landesman proposed four different curricula, varying according to how many hours per week the student was in religious school. He gives the most detail for the curriculum with the most hours (6½ to 7 hours per week), clearly the preferred model. In this curriculum, facility in reading Hebrew is fundamental, and much of the teaching is supposed to take place in Hebrew as well.

130. Gamoran, *Changing Conceptions*, 2:150.

131. Emanuel Gamoran and Abraham H. Friedland, *Gilenu: The Play Way to Hebrew* (Cincinnati: Department of Synagogue and School Extension of the Union of American Hebrew Congregations, 1932). For the development and significance of the *ivrit be-ivrit* method, see Sarna, "American Jewish Education," 16–18.

132. Sarna, "American Jewish Education," 18. See also Alan Mintz, ed., *Hebrew in America: Perspectives and Prospects* (Detroit: Wayne State University Press, 1993), especially the essays by Ackerman and Elazar.

133. The DSSE published some rabbinic story books, but they were intended as supplementary reading, rather than as a core textbook like the Bible story books. One might have expected retention of the Talmud in Conservative religious education, but here too it was largely abandoned. Landesman's curriculum for Conservative schools includes occasional mention of the Talmud, and the Pirkei Avot is recommended reading, but no place was made for systematic study of Talmud (*Curriculum for Jewish Religious Schools*). No articles on teaching the Talmud appear in either *Jewish Education* or the *Jewish Teacher*, until two articles in the former journal in 1981.

134. See *The Bible in American Law, Politics, and Political Rhetoric*, ed. James Turner Johnson (Philadelphia: Fortress Press, 1985), especially the articles by Mark A. Noll, "The Bible in Revolutionary America," 39–60, and by Mark Valerie and John F. Wilson, "Scripture and Society: From Reform in the Old World to Revival in the New," 13–38.

4. Teaching the Bible to Children

1. Here Reform education differs from Conservative, at least in principle, since the goal of Conservative religious schools was to teach the Bible in Hebrew. Yet in the Conservative curriculum, too, there were fundamental divergences from traditional goals and methods. A version of the text adapted to children was preferred, and similar concerns were raised about passages to be selected (or omitted) and moral lessons to be drawn (Rabbi Alter F. Landesman, *A Curriculum for Jewish Religious Schools* (New York: United Synagogue of America, 1922).

2. Emanuel Gamoran, *Changing Conceptions in Jewish Education, in Two Books* (New York: Macmillan, 1924), 2:149–50.

3. Isaac Leeser's 1853 translation was seen as outdated, particularly in comparison to

the popular 1885 English Revised Version prepared by the Anglican Church. For an excellent discussion of issues related to Bible translation in the United States, see Jonathan D. Sarna and Nahum M. Sarna, "Jewish Bible Scholarship and Translations in the United States," in *The Bible and Bibles in America*, ed. Ernest S. Frerichs (Atlanta: Scholars Press, 1988), 83–116.

4. Emanuel Gamoran, "Problems in the Teaching of Bible," *Jewish Education* 2, no. 1 (1930): 24.

5. "Memoir of Rebecca Gratz and the Hebrew Sunday School of Philadelphia," excerpted in Lloyd P. Gartner, *Jewish Education in the United States: A Documentary History* (New York: Teachers College Press, 1969), 56.

6. For the European texts, see pp. 51–55.

7. Fineberg joined the American Jewish Committee in 1939 as a community relations consultant.

8. Of these four educators, Gamoran and Kaplan wrote at greatest length about goals of Bible teaching. See Gamoran, "Problems"; idem, *Changing Conceptions;* Mordecai M. Kaplan, *The Future of the American Jew* (New York: Macmillan, 1948). Kaplan also taught about the Bible at JTS and twice taught a course on interpretation of the Bible at Teachers College, in 1915/16 and 1918. On Kaplan and the Bible, see Mel Scult, "Torah and Salvation: Interpreting the Bible," chap. 9 in *Judaism Faces the Twentieth Century: A Biography of Mordecai Kaplan* (Detroit: Wayne State University Press, 1993). David Kaufman describes Kaplan's course on Bible interpretation and Jewish thought as central to the Teachers Institute curriculum, and he discusses its strong influence on students at the Institute ("Jewish Education as a Civilization: A History of the Teachers Institute," in *Tradition Renewed: A History of the Jewish Theological Seminary of America*, ed. Jack Wertheimer (New York: Jewish Theological Seminary, 1997), 610–16. For an account by one of Kaplan's students, see Israel Scheffler, *Teachers of My Youth: An American Jewish Experience* (Boston: Kluwer Academic Publishers, 1995), 133–37. For an autobiographical essay by Kaplan that includes discussion of the evolution of his thinking on the Bible, see "The Way I Have Come," in *Mordecai M. Kaplan: An Evaluation*, ed. Ira Eisenstein and Eugene Kohn (New York: Jewish Reconstructionist Foundation, 1952), 283–321.

9. For example, Gamoran held that the Bible should be approached with "a scientific outlook on life" and that we should "learn to read the Bible in the light of the time it was produced" (*Changing Conceptions*, 2:148). For the wide acceptance among American rabbis of a scientific approach to the Bible, see chapter 2 above at note 31. On the other hand, the educators all attended the Teachers Institute of the Jewish Theological Seminary, a Conservative seminary in which critical approaches to the Bible were not taught, and where Kaplan, who did wholeheartedly espouse such an approach, was viewed with some hostility (Scult, *Judaism Faces the Twentieth Century*, 244).

10. For attitudes among Protestants, see Grant Wacker, "The Demise of Biblical Civilization," in *The Bible in America: Essays in Cultural History*, ed. Nathan O. Hatch and Mark A. Noll (New York: Oxford University Press, 1982), 121–38; and Charles R. Kniker, "New Attitudes and New Curricula: The Changing Role of the Bible in Protestant Education, 1880–1920," in *The Bible in American Education: From Source Book to Textbook*, ed. David L. Barr and Nicholas Piediscalzi (Philadelphia: Fortress Press, 1982), 121–42.

11. Principle 2 of the Pittsburgh Platform, in Michael A. Meyer, *Response to Modernity: A History of the Reform Movement in Judaism* (New York: Oxford University Press, 1988), 387. For the general prominence of a scientific world view in this period, see David Hollinger, *Science, Jews, and Secular Culture: Studies in Mid-Twentieth-Century American Intellectual History* (Princeton: Princeton University Press, 1996), especially 80–96, 155–74.

12. Rabbi S. Sale, "The Bible and Modern Thought," *Yearbook of the Central Conference of American Rabbis* (hereafter cited as *CCARY*) 12 (1902): 161.

13. Zvi Scharfstein characterized these two problem areas as "the sense of the real" and "the sense of the ideal" (Zvi Scharfstein, "Traditional versus Historical Approach in the Teaching of the Bible," *Jewish Education* 2, no. 1 (1930): 4.

14. Gamoran, "Problems," 19.

15. "Repulsive" and "repugnant" are both terms used by Rabbi Dr. E. Schreiber, "How to Teach Biblical History in Our Sabbath Schools," *CCARY* 1 (1890): 61.

16. Scharfstein, "Traditional versus Historical," 6–7.

17. Mordecai M. Kaplan, *Judaism as a Civilization* (1934; reprint, New York: Schocken, 1967), 501–2. For similar concern, see Solomon A. Fineberg, "A Critical Evaluation of the Reform Religious School," *CCARY* 39 (1929): 447–48; Landesman, *Curriculum*, 72. While accepting the new historical approach of biblical criticism, Landesman also warns that such study is in its infancy "and that its most prominent followers are non-Jews" (73).

18. Muriel Anne Streibert, *Youth and the Bible* (New York: Macmillan, 1924), 190–91. Streibert taught biblical history and religious education at Wellesley College; her book was warmly recommended by Solomon Fineberg, *Biblical Myth and Legend in Jewish Education* (New York: Behrman's Jewish Book House, 1932), 30–32.

19. William Kilpatrick, "Thinking in Childhood and Youth," *Religious Education* 23 (1928): 140.

20. This position was suggested by Leo Honor (one of the "Benderly Boys" along with Gamoran) in "Guiding Principles for the Teaching and Writing of Jewish History," in *Selected Writings*, ed. Abraham P. Gannes (New York: Reconstructionist Press, 1965), 278–87.

21. There were some rabbis who found no difficulties with the Bible itself; see the discussants to Rabbi Ephraim Frisch, "The Use of the Bible as a Text-Book in the Religious School" (CCARY 24 [1914]: 339–45). These rabbis were out of sync with the view of educators that children are so different from adults that they need different sorts of texts—in both style and content.

22. See appendix 1 for a list of these and other popular collections of Bible stories.

23. John W. Prince, "The Past, Present, and Future Place of the Bible in Religious Education," in *Studies in Religious Education: A Source and Textbook for Colleges, Universities, Seminaries, and Discussion Groups for Leaders and Workers in the Field of Religious Education*, ed. Philip Henry Lotz and L. W. Crawford (Nashville: Cokesbury Press, 1931), 204–5.

24. Frisch, "Use of the Bible as a Text-Book," 343.

25. Lenore Cohen, *Bible Tales for Very Young Children*, 2 vols. (Cincinnati: Union of American Hebrew Congregations, 1934–36).

26. Honor, "Guiding Principles," 284.

27. Fineberg, *Biblical Myth*, 34, 146, and passim.

28. Fineberg's book includes a detailed, severe critique of the story collections then in circulation, using the one criterion of inclusion of the supernatural. Fineberg was disgusted at the "backwardness" of virtually all the children's material in circulation in the early 1930s.

29. For example, Streibert, *Youth and the Bible*, 25–26, 30, and passim. A convenient summary of the liberal Protestant perspective can also be found in the writings of the popular preacher and writer Harry Emerson Fosdick; see Fosdick, *The Modern Use of the Bible* (New York: Macmillan, 1926), 150–58.

30. Fineberg, *Biblical Myth*, 139–40. The Bible story collections that include this episode do usually alter Samuel's apparition, for example, Edith Lindeman Calisch, *Bible Tales for the Very Young* (New York: Behrman's Jewish Book Shop, 1930–34), 2:52; and Cohen, *Bible Tales*, 2:129. The original story can be found in First Samuel 28:15–19.

31. Wayne Booth, "'Of the standard of moral taste': Literary Criticism as Moral Inquiry," in *In Face of the Facts: Moral Inquiry in American Scholarship*, ed. Richard Wightman Fox and Robert B. Westbrook (Washington, D.C.: Woodrow Wilson Center Press; Cambridge: Cambridge University Press, 1998), 149–51.

32. A subgenre of such volumes is books on how to use stories in religious education, for example: Margaret W. Eggleston, *The Use of the Story in Religious Education* (New York: George H. Doran, 1920); and Louise Seymour Houghton, *How to Tell Bible Stories* (New York: Charles Scribner's Sons, 1929; first published 1905). Other books on the subject may be found in Laird T. Hites, "A Selected Bibliography of Books in Religious Education," *Religious Education* 21 (1926): 662.

33. On these characteristics of biblical narrative, see Robert Alter, *The Art of Biblical Narrative* (New York: Basic Books, 1981).

34. This is in strong contrast to the Bible itself, which even in modern editions would have only the major divisions by book in a table of contents. Modern Jewish editions have also resisted the prevalent Christian practice of inserting subheadings within the text to indicate the flow of the subject matter; both twentieth-century Jewish Publication Society editions kept to the traditional practice of marking only the beginning of weekly Torah portions.

35. *The Junior Bible for the Jewish School and Home,* part 1, *From Abraham to Moses* (International Graded Bible Lessons for Jewish Religious Schools), prepared by Charles F. Kent and Eugene H. Lehman (New York: Bloch Publishing, 1909–10). Charles Kent was a Christian author, the Woolsey Professor of Biblical Literature at Yale University, and the coauthor of a later, popular children's version of both the Old and New Testaments: Henry A. Sherman and Charles Foster Kent, *The Children's Bible* (New York: Charles Scribner's Sons, 1922). This focus on individual character and on moral lesson is also visible in the Conservative curriculum, most strikingly in the recommendations for teaching the Bible to the youngest children in the fewer-number-of-hours-per-week models (see chapter 3, note 129). Some recommended stories center on individuals and others on "moral problems of home life." Landesman asserts that "each story should tend toward a human need, a human truth, a human experience . . ." (Landesman, *Curriculum,* 247, 133). For a discussion of the focus on "heroes" in Jewish history textbooks of the 1950s, see Joel Gereboff, "Heroes and History in American Jewish Education," in *Crisis and Reaction: The Hero in Jewish History,* ed. Menachem Mor (Omaha: Creighton University Press, 1995), 107–50.

36. According to a survey done in 1948, Cohen's collection was used in 92 of the 162 schools surveyed; no other Bible story collections were used widely enough to make it into the charted list of most frequently used textbooks (Richard C. Hertz, *The Education of the Jewish Child: A Study of 200 Reform Jewish Religious Schools* [New York: Union of American Hebrew Congregations, 1953], 83). Other collections with specially drawn illustrations include Elma Ehrlich Levinger, *Bible Stories for Very Little People* (New York: Behrman's Jewish Book Shop, 1925), and Calisch, *Bible Tales.*

37. Cohen, *Bible Tales,* 1:1. Volume and page numbers are hereafter cited in the text.

38. This is one of many midrashic stories on the early life of Abraham. For easy access to these stories, see Louis Ginzberg, *The Legends of the Jews* (Philadelphia: Jewish Publication Society of America, 1909–38), 1:185–217; for the story of Abraham breaking the idols in his father's shop, see 1:197–98.

39. The illustration of Abraham and Isaac is in Cohen, *Bible Tales,* 1:24 (compare Calisch, *Bible Tales,* 1:43; Levinger, *Bible Stories,* 13); Jacob and Esau, 1:36; Rebekah at the well, 1:30 (cf. Calisch, 1:49; Levinger, 17); Isaac, Jacob, and Rebekah, 1:41 (cf. Calisch, 1:57; Levinger, 23); Joshua, 2:31 (cf. Levinger, 69); Deborah, 2:37 (cf. Calisch, 2:9).

40. In the Conservative curriculum model for the most extensive program, a weekly focus on the portion was employed, but the teacher was to discuss its overall content and then choose a selection of appropriate verses for student translation (Landesman, *Curriculum,* 84).

41. See Arthur T. Jersild, *Child Psychology,* rev. ed. (New York: Prentice-Hall, 1940), 417 (in a chapter on children's morals and religion), citing G. E. Dawson, "Children's Interest in the Bible," *Pedagogical Seminary* 7 (1900): 151–78.

42. Gamoran, "Problems," 23.

43. See, for example, Edith L. Thomas, "Music, Drama, and Art in Religious Education," in *Studies in Religious Education,* ed. Lotz and Crawford, 231. Gamoran recommends Elizabeth E. M. Lobingier, *The Dramatization of Bible Stories, an Experiment in the Religious Education of Children* (Chicago: University of Chicago Press, 1918).

44. Thanks to Matt Wafer for this story.

45. Leibush Lehrer, "Reflections on Traditional Jewish Education," *Jewish Education* 28 (1957–58): 11.

46. Barbara Myerhoff, *Number Our Days: Culture and Community among Elderly Jews in an American Ghetto* (New York: Penguin Books, 1979), 59.

47. Harold S. Tuttle, "Character Education," *Religious Education* 26 (1931): 635.

48. Gamoran, *Changing Conceptions*, 2:150.

49. Micth wasn't the only one bothered by the laws of Kedoshim. One Friday evening in the spring of 2003, the half-dozen adults who came to services at Temple Sholom did an impromptu study of the week's Torah portion, reading the whole portion aloud. As we read through the laws of Kedoshim, comments were made about the odd mixture of laws, such as "you shall not oppress your neighbor" along with "you shall not eat sacrificed offerings on the third day" and "you shall not sow your field with two kinds of seed"; discomfort was also expressed at the harsh punishment (usually death) dictated if these laws were broken. When we came to the end of the portion, one of the participants asked, in all sincerity, "Why are we reading this still today?"

50. Schreiber, "How to Teach Biblical History," 61. This uneasiness about questionable practice by humans or God is visible in conservative educators as well; see Landesman, *Curriculum*, 83–84.

51. Actually, the binding of Isaac was deleted from two later collections: Betty R. Hollender, *Bible Stories for Little Children* (Cincinnati: Union of American Hebrew Congregations, 1955), and Shirley Newman, *A Child's Introduction to Torah* (New York: Behrman House, 1972).

52. Schreiber, "How to Teach Biblical History," 61; Scharfstein, "Traditional versus Historical," 12. For a more recent treatment of this same issue, see Howard Deitcher, "The Child's Understanding of the Biblical Personality," *Studies in Jewish Education* 5 (1990): 167–82.

53. Kaplan, *Future*, 468. See also Kaplan, "The Belief in God and How to Teach It," *Jewish Education* 12 (1940/41): 112–13.

54. Schreiber, "How to Teach Biblical History," 61. On Kaplan's position, see Scult, *Judaism Faces the Twentieth Century*, 240–53.

55. Gamoran, "Problems," 19.

56. Hedley S. Dimock, "What Religious Attitude Is Compatible with the Scientific Attitude?" *Religious Education* 23 (1928): 126. Dimock was professor of psychology and religious education at the Young Men's Christian Association College in Chicago.

57. Scharfstein, "Traditional versus Historical," 4, 15; Gamoran, "Problems," 17, 20, 23.

58. Kaplan also did not carry out this project, which would have been enormous. See Scult, "Torah and Salvation," in *Judaism Faces the Twentieth Century*, which analyzes examples of piecemeal work of this kind from Kaplan's unpublished writings.

59. Such terms are found throughout the writings of the Christian interpreters mentioned above: Streibert, *Youth and the Bible;* Prince, "Past, Present, and Future Place"; Houghton, *How to Tell Bible Stories;* and Fosdick, *Modern Use of the Bible.*

60. Prince, "Past, Present, and Future Place," 206.

61. Fosdick, *Modern Use of the Bible*, 8.

62. Ibid., 8, 27.

63. One Christian author goes so far as to query why Christian educators should teach anything besides the prophets and Jesus, given the problematic nature of the rest of the Old Testament. His pragmatic answer is that children will be learning about the Old Testament in other places, because of the "prestige" of the text, so they should learn about it first in a context where it can be taught properly. He also recognizes that since the Bible is a popular classic, reading it will give students a sense of common life and fellowship with other Christians, past and present (T. G. Soares, *Religious Education* [Chicago: University of Chicago Press, 1928], 142–44).

64. See, for example, Streibert, *Youth and the Bible*, 4–6, 8, 13, 14; Houghton, *How to Tell Bible Stories*, 2; Edwin E. Aubrey, "Teaching the Bible in an Age of Science," *Religious Education* 23 (1928): 152.

65. William Clayton Bower, "A Critical Re-evaluation of the Biblical Outlook of Progressive Religious Education," *Religious Education* 38 (1943): 7.

66. Complementing the criterion of accordance with Jesus' teaching is, according to Streibert, the strong feeling of conviction that a particular value is true. The right view is "the one we are sure of" (*Youth and the Bible*, 219). Streibert raises the troubling issue that if we,

today, find fault with the values of the Hebrews, might not others after us find fault with us? The thought is quickly, though perhaps not convincingly, dismissed (219–20).

Jewish writers also applied the measure of current norms to discern rightness. In a book written for an adult Jewish audience, *The Bible and Our Social Outlook* (New York: Union of American Hebrew Congregations, 1941), Abraham Cronbach sets out to demonstrate that many contemporary social values have their origin in Jewish values found in the Bible, with examples being old age pensions, the abolition of child labor, and minimum wage legislation. (Cronbach was promoting the Jewishness of progressive social values.) Other values found in the Bible but which are troublesome to a modern person—such as a belief in many gods, polygamy, and sanctioned acts of cruelty—he asserts to be "not Jewish" (10). The link to goals of the education of Jewish children is made clear in a brief introduction to Cronbach's book written by Emanuel Gamoran, who insists on the importance of linking contemporary social experience with Jewish teaching: "If Jewish education is to be realistic, it must envisage as part of its program, a careful study of modern social problems, and it must invoke Jewish religious sanctions for desired ethical behavior" (v).

67. Prince, "Past, Present, and Future Place," 206. See also Streibert, *Youth and the Bible*, 100; and William Clayton Bower, "The Nature, Content, and Form of the Curriculum," in *Studies in Religious Education*, ed. Lotz and Crawford, 193.

68. Bower, "Nature, Content, and Form," 193.

69. William Clayton Bower, "Critical Re-evaluation," 5. Further, the experience and stage of development of the particular audience of children needed to be considered. Laura Esther Haugh lays out tables indicating stages of development and the type of story to be used for different ages (*The Bible Story in Religious Education* [Elgin, Ill.: Elgin Press, 1925], 22–41; similarly, Katherine D. Cather, *Religious Education through Story-Telling* [New York: Abingdon Press, 1925], 74–119).

70. Herbert Butterfield, *The Whig Interpretation of History* (London: G. Bell and Sons, 1931).

71. A practice complained about by Streibert (*Youth and the Bible*, 124). Angus Hector MacLean also laments the inconsistent application of scientism across the Old and New Testaments in a wide variety of Protestant educational material for children (*The Idea of God in Protestant Religious Education* [New York: Teachers College, Columbia University, 1930], 38–39, 61).

72. Streibert, *Youth and the Bible*, 165; the subject of miracles in the New Testament is taken up in chapters 11, 12, and 13 of Streibert's book.

73. With one counterexample: Streibert explains that the episode where Jesus curses a fig tree is not worthy of him and must be a made-up story (ibid., 137).

74. E.g., Streibert, *Youth and the Bible*, 99. Kaplan objects to this preference for the Prophets and insists on the primacy of the Pentateuch for the education of children ("Belief in God," 111–12).

75. Landesman makes the point that the Prophets are "beyond the grasp of young children" in both "thought and style" (*Curriculum*, 88).

76. The Commission on Jewish Education served as the editorial board for educational materials published by the UAHC, with each manuscript usually having three readers. Correspondence between Gamoran and a prospective author, as well as subsequent readers' reports and author responses, have survived in a few isolated cases, showing us that such communication did take place. Unfortunately, the correspondence that survives includes very little on the Bible story collections published by the UAHC. Some material on Adele Bildersee's *The Story of Genesis* (1924) is on file, but readers' reports, while referred to, are missing. No material on Lenore Cohen's collection remains on file. What material does survive may be found in the Jacob Rader Marcus Center of the American Jewish Archives. One resource there is material from Emanuel Gamoran: E. Gamoran, Miscellaneous Correspondence and Other Material during Tenure as Educational Director of the Department of Synagogue and School Extension for the UAHC, March 1, 1926 to November 12, 1956. The rest is within the compiled records of the UAHC (Collection no. 72): DSSE, Board of Edi-

tors, 1918–19 (extensive correspondence), Box 43/4-6; DSSE, Minute Book of the Board of Editors, 1911–23 (including the material on Bildersee), Box 72/1; a complete collection of materials presented at the March 1925 meeting of the CJE, Reel 1662.

77. Gamoran does mention and explain the need for additions in his introduction to Lenore Cohen's *Bible Tales*, even though he does not discuss this strategy in his professional writing on the subject. One major Bible story collection specifically eschewed an additive strategy: *The Bible Story in the Bible Words*, a multivolume series published by the UAHC in the 1920s. This series was an abridgment of the new Jewish Publication Society translation of the Bible, rather than a retelling of biblical stories, though the volumes were so highly selective, both in choice of story and of elements within a story, that they could still accomplish adaptive goals (goals made explicit in the teachers' manuals that accompanied the series). Cohen's two volumes of Bible stories, also published by the UAHC, were meant to replace or supplement this series.

78. Addie Richman Altman, *The Jewish Child's Bible Stories, Told in Simple Language* (New York: Bloch Publishing, 1915), 4.

79. A comparison of these modern Bible stories to midrash will be taken up in chapter 6.

5. Bible Stories Retold

1. Story collections were identified from lists of books recommended for school libraries and from surveys of actual book usage. In the discussion that follows, I have focused my attention on eight of the collections most frequently recommended and utilized. See appendix 2 for a list of the sources used to identify these collections. For a history of the Jewish publishers who issued many of these books, see Charles A. Madison, *Jewish Publishing in America: The Impact of Jewish Writing on American Culture* (New York: Sanhedrin Press, 1976).

Page numbers of several frequently cited works are given parenthetically in the text and in the notes, preceded by the author's last name when necessary:

Altman: Addie Richman Altman, *The Jewish Child's Bible Stories, Told in Simple Language* (New York: Bloch Publishing, 1915).

Bildersee 1: Adele Bildersee, *The Story of Genesis* (Cincinnati: Department of Synagog and School Extension, Union of American Hebrew Congregations, 1924).

Bildersee 2: Adele Bildersee, *Out of the House of Bondage* (Cincinnati: Department of Synagog and School Extension, Union of American Hebrew Congregations, 1925).

Calisch: Edith Lindeman Calisch, *Bible Tales for the Very Young*, 2 vols. (New York: Behrman's Jewish Book Shop, 1930–34).

Cohen: Lenore Cohen, *Bible Tales for Very Young Children*, 2 vols. (New York: Union of American Hebrew Congregations, 1934–36)

Golub: Jacob S. Golub, *Israel in Canaan* (Cincinnati: Department of Synagog and School Extension, Union of American Hebrew Congregations, 1930).

Harris: Maurice H. Harris, *The People of the Book: A Bible History for School and Home*, 3 vols. (New York: Bloch Publishing, 1929).

Silber: Mendel Silber, *The Scripture Stories Retold for Young Israel*, rev. ed. (New York: Behrman's Jewish Book House, 1918).

2. Some twenty years after publication, the two volumes of Cohen's *Bible Tales* were the third and fourth most widely used books in the primary grades of Reform religious schools, following history and holiday books (Rabbi Richard C. Hertz, *The Education of the Jewish Child: A Study of 200 Reform Jewish Religious Schools* [New York: UAHC, 1953], 83). Betty Hollender's *Bible Stories for Little Children* (New York: UAHC, 1955–60) differs from Cohen's *Bible Tales* in being exceedingly simplified; her collection provided an alternative to Cohen's, not a replacement.

3. Ruth B. Bottigheimer, *The Bible for Children: From the Age of Gutenberg to the Present* (New Haven: Yale University Press, 1996). Bottigheimer's wide-ranging analysis is based on over

three hundred children's Bibles from the Middle Ages to the present, including a dozen or so Jewish texts. Her analysis centers on the Christian texts, with occasional comparison to Jewish examples, which include several nineteenth-century books, a couple from the 1930s, and a half-dozen or so from the 1950s to the 1980s.

4. I will refer to the Tanakh when distinguishing the full, original text from the adaptations of the Bible stories.

5. I use here the translation that would have been most familiar to all authors after 1917: *The Holy Scriptures, according to the Masoretic Text: A New Translation* (Philadelphia: Jewish Publication Society of America, 1917).

6. The leaflets were picked up by the Department of Synagog and School Extension of the UAHC and published into the early twentieth century. The leaflets themselves are undated; the Hebrew Union College catalog marks their copies as dating from 1897/98 to 1900/1901.

7. *Leaflets on Biblical History*, ser. 1, no. 9, p. 34. The emphasis on Abraham's "faith" may have been influenced by Protestant interpretation, which, in keeping with the Protestant stress on faith over law, made much of Genesis 15:6. For a discussion of Protestant versus Jewish interpretations of Abraham's "righteousness," see Jon D. Levenson, *The Hebrew Bible, the Old Testament, and Historical Criticism: Jews and Christians in Biblical Studies* (Louisville, Ky.: Westminster / John Knox Press, 1993), 56–61.

8. Twelve editions of Altman's *Jewish Child's Bible Stories* were published between 1915 and 1946. This change corresponds to one in the larger book market as well. Anne Scott MacLeod notes that a divergence of children's literature from adult literature and the professionalization of children's literature occurred by 1910, with the 1920s being "halcyon years for children's literature as a profession and as a publishing enterprise" (*American Childhood: Essays on Children's Literature of the Nineteenth and Twentieth Centuries* [Athens: University of Georgia Press, 1994], 124, 158).

9. Charles F. Kent and Eugene H. Lehman, *The Junior Bible for the Jewish School and Home*, 3 vols. (New York: Bloch Publishing, 1909–10). Lehman published a companion guide for teachers several years later: *The Jewish Teacher: An Aid in Teaching the Junior Bible for the Jewish School and Home*, 3 vols. (New York, Bloch Publishing, 1914).

10. It was not usually recommended on book lists, and there are very few extant copies; the library of Hebrew Union College has one copy of volume 3. Though this volume is bound, it looks like the original was a series of leaflets. Unlike *The Junior Bible* itself, Lehman's companion book continued to be printed into the 1930s, though as early as 1915 the title was changed to mark its usefulness as a guide to more than one book: *The Jewish Teacher: An Aid in Teaching the Bible, especially the Junior Bible for Jewish School and Home*.

11. The book includes an introduction by Emanuel Gamoran. Five subsequent volumes of this series, which presented material drawn not only from the Pentateuch but also from Prophets and Writings, were published between 1925 and 1930. Bildersee authored the first two volumes of the series, *The Story of Genesis* and *Out of the House of Bondage* (cited as Bildersee 1 and Bildersee 2). Bildersee was an assistant professor of English at Hunter College and principal of the Temple Beth-El Religious School when she began this series; she later was dean of students and director of admissions at Brooklyn College. I have also used the third and fourth volumes in the series: Jacob D. Schwarz, *Into the Promised Land* (Cincinnati: Union of American Hebrew Congregations, 1927); idem, *In the Land of Kings and Prophets* (Cincinnati: Union of American Hebrew Congregations, 1928).

12. Moses Buttenwieser, "The Presentation of Biblical Stories to Children," *Biblical World* 35 (1910): 391.

13. Ibid., 392, 394.

14. Adele Bildersee, *The Story of Genesis: Teachers' Manual* (Cincinnati: Department of Synagog and School Extension, Union of American Hebrew Congregations, 1924), 54; ellipses in the original.

15. Emanuel Gamoran, introduction to *Story of Genesis: Teachers' Manual*, by Bildersee, ix.

16. Gamoran also wrote a brief introduction to *The Story of Genesis*. There he does not speak about the place of moralizing but focuses instead on the relationship of the book to

the recent JPS translation. This children's version omits "only such phrases and passages . . . as seem to interpose a barrier between the child and the understanding and enjoyment of the narrative" (Emanuel Gamoran, introduction to *Story of Genesis*, by Bildersee, viii–ix).

17. Elma Ehrlich Levinger, *Bible Stories for Very Little People* (New York: Behrman's Jewish Book Shop, 1925); Calisch, *Bible Tales;* Ethel Fox, *Bible Primer for Tiny Tots* (New York: Bloch Publishing, 1930); Hyman E. Goldin, *Illustrated Bible Stories* (New York: Hebrew Publishing, 1930).

18. For a lucid discussion of the modern inclination to interpret the Abraham/Isaac story as a message against child sacrifice, see Carol Delaney, *Abraham on Trial: The Social Legacy of Biblical Myth* (Princeton: Princeton University Press, 1998), chaps. 3, 4.

19. Emanuel Gamoran, introduction to *Bible Tales,* by Cohen, 1:vii.

20. Ibid.

21. Ibid., viii.

22. In the story "David and Abigail," Cohen mentions that Abigail became David's wife "sometime later" (2:137). In "Solomon Is Anointed King" she describes the rivalry between David's sons Solomon and Adonijah but does not mention that they were children of different wives. She does, however, include the fact that Solomon had multiple wives. In describing how Solomon no longer kept with the simplicity of his father's household, she mentions a "harem of a thousand wives" in Solomon's palace (2:168).

23. Cohen includes the promise made by the three visitors to Abraham's tent that Sarah will have a son within a year, but there is no mention of her advanced age (indeed, there is a drawing of Sarah at this place in the text looking young and lovely), and there is no laughter from Abraham or Sarah at the notion of such a birth (1:17).

24. Silber gives a similar explanation (1:15).

25. A list of ten commandments is omitted from Cohen, who gives only three commandments (1:146), and from Ethel Fox, who has a chapter on the commandments but includes neither the text nor a paraphrase (*Bible Primer*, 97–98). A full list appears in the other six collections, with these emendations. In Levinger the commandments are paraphrased, and the seventh commandment against adultery is omitted. In Altman, this same troubling commandment is altered to a universalistic proclamation: "Thou shalt not do any wrong act" (84); a very similar wording is used by Goldin (*Illustrated Bible Stories*, 91).

Christian texts had also long focused on narrative rather than legal material, not surprising given the Christian rejection of Old Testament law.

26. The self-conscious stress on universalistic characteristics in the text can be seen in the instructions of Mortimer Joseph Cohen to Arthur Szyk, the illustrator of Cohen's *Pathways through the Bible* (Philadelphia: Jewish Publication Society of America, 1946), a text for teenaged children. He was *not* to emphasize the differences between past and present, so "the clothes on the figures in the pictures, therefore, should be of a universal character" (quoted in Jonathan Sarna, *JPS: The Americanization of Jewish Culture, 1888–1988* [Philadelphia: Jewish Publication Society, 1989], 206). For the similar reduction of Jewish law to the universal in Jewish history textbooks for children, see Walter Ackerman, " 'Let Us Now Praise Famous Men in Their Generations': History Books for Jewish Schools in America," *Dor LeDor: Studies in the History of Jewish Education* 2 (1984): 12–13.

27. For comparison to Christian texts from the sixteenth century forward, see Bottigheimer, *The Bible for Children*, 116–41. While early collections included explicit mention of sexuality, children's books were generally desexualized from the eighteenth century onward.

28. We will see later that medieval midrash often shared some of the moral concerns of modern authors. But on the matter of sexuality, midrash is not squeamish. Some medieval versions, for example, relate Cain's birth as the result of carnal intercourse with Satan (Louis Ginzberg, *The Legends of the Jews*, trans. Henrietta Szold, 7 vols. [Philadelphia: Jewish Publication Society of America, 1909–38], 1:105–6). Because the authors of modern Bible story collections had ready access to traditional midrash through this great early-twentieth-century collection of midrash (published in seven volumes from 1909 to 1938), I have cited comparisons to midrash primarily through citations to material in Ginzberg. Many of the

interpretive strategies taken by our authors were probably modeled on traditional interpretations, and seeing the range of interpretation available in midrash helps us understand the choices made by modern authors. James L. Kugel's analysis of early midrash, *The Bible as It Was* (Cambridge: Belknap Press of Harvard University Press, 1997) is also an excellent resource (though it covers a more limited range of biblical subjects), and corresponding pages will be cited in this book as another way for readers to access a comparison to midrash. For Cain as the son of Satan, see Kugel, *Bible as It Was*, 86–87.

29. Cohen, Levinger, and Goldin do not include the story at all, Cohen because her book begins with Abraham, and Levinger because she has only the stories of Eden and the flood before moving on to Abraham.

30. For comparison to Christian texts, see Bottigheimer, *The Bible for Children*, 162–79.

31. For example, Lillian S. Freehof, *The Bible Legend Book* (New York: Union of American Hebrew Congregations, 1948), which is a collection of midrashic stories to be read along with Bildersee's *Story of Genesis* or some other children's version of the Bible (Gamoran, introduction to *The Bible Legend Book*, viii). A second and third volume of Bible legends were put out by Freehof in 1952 and 1956.

32. This solution was repeated in popular collections published in the next generation of texts: Hollender, *Bible Stories*, and Shirley Newman, *A Child's Introduction to Torah* (New York: Behrman House, 1972).

33. Similarly Silber: "Well, the one who made all these things, the world and all that is in it, is God" (1:5); and Goldin: "Up above, high, high in the heavens, was the One who had made the earth and the water that covered the earth" (*Illustrated Bible Stories*, 3). Silber's and Goldin's texts are longer than Altman's and Calisch's, and both provide some account of the various things made by God; neither, however, indicates that this happened within six days. Silber, it is true, includes an explanation of the Sabbath, but the explanation is simply that the Sabbath was set by God's command, not in imitation of God's own action: "After man was created God did not make anything new, leaving it now to man to make things in the world. But He told man to work only six days in the week and to rest on the seventh" (Silber, 1:6). Note also the similitude of the "making" of things by God and man—again, a diminishment of the unusual, supernatural process of creation.

34. Bildersee, *Story of Genesis: Teachers' Manual*, 9; ellipses and emphasis in the original.

35. Bottigheimer discusses at length the treatment of the parting of the Red Sea (*The Bible for Children*, 162–74).

36. For Muriel Streibert's advice to educators on dealing with the miracle at the Red Sea, see *Youth and the Bible* (New York: Macmillan, 1924), 67–70.

37. Similarly Goldin, who omits the wonders at the burning bush, includes God at the Red Sea, and omits Moses' outstretched arm (*Illustrated Bible Stories*, 76, 85).

38. For the treatment of God in Christian texts, see Bottigheimer, *The Bible for Children*, 59–69.

39. A similar change in voice is made when God speaks to Hagar in the wilderness (Cohen, 1:21; cf. Gen. 21:17.) For a principled discussion of why lines such as "And the Lord spoke unto Moses, saying . . ." are inappropriate in an age when we no longer ascribe a "voice" to God; see Claude G. Montefiore, *Outlines of Liberal Judaism, for the Use of Parents and Teachers* (1912; London: Macmillan, 1923), 190–92. Montefiore's book is a useful resource of reform ideology on God, miracles, and the nature of biblical authorship and authority. Montefiore originally intended to write the book for children aged eight to fifteen, which makes it particularly useful for comparison to educational texts for children. But while writing it, he found that much of it was appropriate only for children over fifteen, or for adults to read in order to inform them for the teaching of their children (9). Montefiore spoke from his own experience of writing a Bible for children: *The Bible for Home Reading: With Comments and Reflections for the Use of Jewish Parents and Children* (London: Macmillan, 1896), discussed in chapter 3.

40. My thanks to Gary Chamberlain for originally pointing out the significance of these passages. Another echo of the American context is the frequency with which Cohen characterizes the Israelites as either being or striving to be a "free" people. Joseph, in prison, for example, says to his companions that "I come from a land that's free"; and Joshua, hav-

ing crossed the Jordan, declares that "From this day on we are free men" (Cohen, 1:76, 2:11).

41. Rabbinic Judaism was similarly uncomfortable with what appeared to be too harsh divine justice. The rabbis made alterations not by diminishing God's role, but by emphasizing God's love over God's justice and by interpreting divine interventions as evidence of this love (Max Kadushin, *The Rabbinic Mind*, 3d ed. [New York: Bloch Publishing, 1972], 219–20).

42. William Kilpatrick, "Thinking in Childhood and Youth," *Religious Education* 23 (1928): 140.

43. But Cohen is also uneasy with her portrayal of Moses' lapse in good leadership skills, so she gives Moses the excuse of being unhappy at the recent death of his sister Miriam, which distracted him from careful leadership. "In his grief, he lost patience with these people he had watched over so long" (1:171).

Other story collections similarly elaborate on the rationality of God's punishment of Moses. For example: "Then, instead of speaking quietly to the rock as God had commanded, Moses took his rod and struck the rock twice. . . . But God was displeased, for Moses had disobeyed Him. If Moses himself did not do as God told him, how could the other people be expected to obey Him at all times?" (Calisch, 1:145).

44. The claim of biblical support of democratic ideals was made in the English context as well. Claude Montefiore, for example, claims: "Both the Prophets and the Law may justly be called 'democratic.' There is a true sense in which their ideals—or some of their ideals— might, without inaccuracy, if anachronistically, be described in the familiar words, Liberty, Equality, Fraternity" (Montefiore, *Outlines*, 272, with further discussion at 269–71).

45. M. Cohen, *Pathways through the Bible*. Cohen tried to get this quotation removed from the frontispiece, on the grounds that it was spurious, but he was unsuccessful (Sarna, *JPS*, 336 n. 68).

46. Num. 16:1–18:32. For example, the challengers say to Moses and Aaron: "You have gone too far! For all the community are holy, all of them, and the Lord is in their midst. Why then do you raise yourselves above the Lord's congregation?" (Num. 16:3).

47. Not surprisingly, the story of Korach is omitted from most of the children's versions (Altman, Cohen, Fox, Calisch, and Levinger), though a few do include it. Silber gives a very short, highly sanitized version, in which Korach and his men wrongfully accuse Moses of selfishness. Moses feels sorry for them and tries to "talk nicely to them and to reason with them," but when they will not listen Moses just leaves "these bad men" behind. "None of them was ever seen again. They were simply lost and forgotten *as though* the earth had swallowed them" (Silber, 1:171–73; emphasis added). Bildersee includes a full version of the story (Bildersee 2, 115–22), but in the teachers' manual she advises: "This, it need hardly be said, is a story of many difficulties. If the teacher prefers, it may be omitted." Bildersee is reluctant to attribute punishment directly to God. She recommends that this story be framed as a tale told by fathers to children "long after the years in the wilderness were over." It becomes, then, a story made up by humans to explain something in the past, rather than a historical account. Bildersee explains: "The people, as they looked back upon their past, felt, as people did then—as, indeed, some do even now—that their sins were followed by direct and immediate punishments" (Bildersee, *Out of the House of Bondage: Teachers' Manual* [Cincinnati: DSSE of the UAHC, 1927], 121). Finally Goldin includes a short, one-page version of the story that includes God's punishment of the rebels, as an earthquake opens the earth and swallows them; the subsequent plague is not mentioned (*Illustrated Bible Stories*, 97).

48. A similar approach is taken by Altman (31), Bildersee (*Story of Genesis: Teachers' Manual*, 51), Goldin (*Illustrated Bible Stories*, 29–30), and Silber (1:39–42). Calisch takes a different tack by explaining the dismissal as a kind of gift rather than a punishment. In her version there is no party at which Ishmael misbehaves. Rather, God spontaneously intervenes and tells Abraham to send away Hagar and Ishmael; just as God told Abraham to leave his old home for Canaan, now it's Ishmael's time. He, too, "will become a strong man" and the father of twelve Princes (Calisch, 38). Calisch has solved the problem of Ishmael's unduly harsh punishment by eliminating it, and by changing the story so that it relates to another major theme: obedience, here Abraham's to God.

49. The two are Hollender, *Bible Stories* (1955), and Newman, *Child's Introduction to Torah* (1972); both leave out the Akedah as well.

50. Only Levinger and Fox, the two shortest, most simplified collections, leave out Hagar and Ishmael.

51. This is the approach emphasized by Bottigheimer in her study of the long-term development of Bible stories for children, where the changes in style and content of the stories can be seen to reflect larger cultural changes (Bottigheimer, *The Bible for Children*, with an overview on such factors on p. 218).

52. For examples from English translations in the United States, see Jonathan D. Sarna and Nahum M. Sarna, "Jewish Bible Scholarship and Translations in the United States," in *The Bible and Bibles in America*, ed. Ernest S. Frerichs (Atlanta: Scholars Press, 1988).

53. Emanuel Gamoran, *Changing Conceptions in Jewish Education* (New York: Macmillan, 1924), 2:102.

54. Ibid., 103.

55. For the presentation of parents and children in Christian texts, see Bottigheimer, *The Bible for Children*, 70–90; for Abraham and Isaac, 73–81. For the context of the treatment of family issues in American children's literature generally, see MacLeod, *American Childhood*, 157–72.

56. Altman, Bildersee, Calisch, and Silber.

57. This seven-volume collection was published by the Jewish Publication Society between 1909 and 1938.

58. See Ginzberg, *Legends*, 1:107.

59. Bildersee makes a small word change in the JPS translation to emphasize that Abel brought "of the best of his flock," replacing the more ambiguous "of the firstlings of his flock and of the fat thereof" (Bildersee 1, 10). In her teachers' manual, Bildersee shifts to a difference in intention in the two offerings, with Cain giving his reluctantly (*Story of Genesis: Teachers' Manual*, 21–22). Silber has Cain's character flaw as his being "not very generous" (Silber, 1:15). Authors of midrash also sought explanation for the rejection of Cain's sacrifice. According to some midrashim, Abel selected the best of his flocks, while Cain ate his meal first and just offered leftovers, "a few grains of flaxseed"; furthermore, his offering was from the ground that had been cursed by God (Ginzberg, *Legends*, 1:107–8; Kugel, *Bible as It Was*, 89–90).

60. Midrash presents a more evil image of Cain: He hates Abel not only because of the rejected sacrifice, but because he desires Abel's beautiful twin sister and wants Abel out of the way (Ginzberg, *Legends*, 1:108; Kugel, *Bible as It Was*, 88). And when Cain and Abel are fighting, Abel is stronger and is winning. Cain asks for mercy, and Abel responds by letting go; evil Cain then turns and slays him (Ginzberg, *Legends*, 1:109).

61. The midrashim included in Ginzberg's collection do not include any repentance, but rather have Cain blaming God for the deed, excusing himself (for not knowing that stones could kill anyone), feigning repentance, or, in one version, being sent down to the lowest of the seven earths and being frightened into repentance (Ginzberg, *Legends*, 1:110–17). See Kugel, *Bible as It Was*, 96, for a few versions that bring in some sense of repentance.

62. Silber has Cain's punishment self-imposed: he "decided to go far, far away from home" (1:19). But he is unable to rest or settle down (no protection granted), and for many years he "lived like an animal, wandering in the mountains, always thinking of the terrible things he had done" (1:19); he ends up being killed accidentally by a hunter who mistook him for a wild beast.

63. While Bildersee maintains the enigmatic punishment plus protective mark, she de-emphasizes the perplexing issue of the settlement by cutting the story off with this final line: "And Cain went out from the presence of the Lord, and dwelt in the land of Nod, to the east of Eden" (Bildersee 1, 11). In the teachers' manual she adds the remark that at last Cain felt how terrible his sin was (*Story of Genesis: Teachers' Manual*, 22). Explanations for God's relenting are also found in midrash; see Ginzberg, *Legends*, 1:111–14.

64. All of the versions avoid the unsettling challenge to such an ethic: if Abel was good in contrast to Cain being bad, why did Abel get killed?

65. Emanuel Gamoran, "Problems in the Teaching of the Bible," *Jewish Education* 2, no. 1 (January 1930): 20–21.

66. For example, in Altman: "Don't you think Abraham must have felt very unhappy to think that he had to take his little boy for a sacrifice? Abraham loved God and had always obeyed Him, so he knew he would obey now, even though he felt very sorry to do so" (Altman, 35). And when he answers Isaac's question about the whereabouts of the sacrifice, Abraham "turned his head away, so Isaac should not see the tears in his eyes" (36). For a comparison with midrashic treatments, see Ginzberg, *Legends*, 1:274–86, and Kugel, *Bible as It Was*, 165–78.

67. Bildersee also mentions Isaac's obedience in *Story of Genesis: Teachers' Manual*, 54.

68. Cohen changes the language to love: "Now I know how much you love God" (1:25); Bildersee retains the JPS language.

69. Given the stress on obedience in these books, I expected to see the same emphasis in the character education books designed for use in public schools. But obedience, although present, is not as prominent a value as I anticipated. For example, in Ella Lyman Cabot, *Ethics for Children: A Guide for Teachers and Parents* (Boston: Houghton Mifflin, 1910), seventy-two values are covered, one of which is obedience (under a year's theme of "work"); a theme of the second year is "home life," but this strand does not include a stress on obedience to parents. Linda Kerber suggests that obedience may have been particularly important in an immigrant context, given the special independence of children from first generation parents (private communication). For a similar point, see Julia Grant, *Raising Baby by the Book: The Education of American Mothers* (New Haven: Yale University Press, 1998), 72.

70. Bildersee, *Story of Genesis: Teachers' Manual*, 54. Sensitivities are enough changed by the 1950s that the next UAHC Bible story collection, published in 1955, eliminated the akedah entirely, as does a subsequent Behrman House collection, published in 1972.

71. In contrast to the biblical text, which implies that Rebekah's love for Jacob is connected to his dwelling in tents (a female realm), Silber adds an association of Jacob with the male line—his likeness to his grandfather, Abraham, and his father, Isaac.

72. Fox, *Bible Primer*, 33–34.

73. One sentence in the Tanakh, stating that Esau "despised his birthright," contributes to the negative view of Esau (Gen. 25:34). For comparison to midrashic treatments, which also differentiate the characters of the brothers, see Ginzberg, *Legends*, 1:311–45, and Kugel, *Bible as It Was*, 197–214.

74. On the differential appeal of moral education to women, see Gamoran, "Preliminary Survey of Jewish Religious Schools Affiliated with the Union of American Hebrew Congregations," *Central Conference of American Rabbis Yearbook* 34 [1924]: 363–64. For complaints about female teachers, see chapter 3 note 113.

75. Gamoran's wife and sister, Mamie G. Gamoran and Rose G. Lurie, were among these authors; both were graduates of the Teachers Institute, and the wedding ceremony between Mamie Goldsmith and Emanuel Gamoran was performed by Mordecai Kaplan, "teacher and master to them both" (Albert P. Schoolman, "Emanuel Gamoran—His Life and Work," *Jewish Education* 34 [1963/64]: 78). Rose Gamoran Lurie retained a strong relationship with her brother throughout her life.

76. Gamoran, "Preliminary Survey," 354.

77. Ibid.

78. Women, of course, continued to be educators in the home. Indeed, while our story collections were geared toward a school setting, a couple of the collections make specific reference to the usefulness of the story book at home as well, where the mother was to read the stories to the child (Cohen, 1:viii, 2:viii; Levinger, *Bible Stories*, preface). There was also, however, a concern about a decline in the Jewish atmosphere of the home, which some attributed to the lack of attentiveness of the "modern Jewess" (Rabbi David Goldberg, "Women's Part in Religious Decline," *The Jewish Forum* 7 [1921], cited in Ann D. Braude, "Jewish Women in the Twentieth Century: Building a Life in America," in *Women and Religion in America*, vol. 3, *1900–1968*, ed. Rosemary Radford Ruether and Rosemary Skinner Keller [San Francisco: Harper and Row, 1981], 139). The same complaint was made decades later by Judah Pilch, "Changing Patterns in Jewish Education," *Jewish Social Studies* 21 (1959):

92–93). Indeed, the focus on ethical training in the schools was seen as a replacement for the now insufficient training in the home.

79. A couple of other examples from Altman: She writes that all love Joseph because "he had always been so kind to everyone" (Altman, 60), and that all love Moses because "he was gentle and kind to everyone, and he was very good to animals" (69).

80. Cohen, Levinger, Silber, and Goldin.

81. These concerns had also been pursued in midrash, although other matters of preoccupation in midrash are entirely absent in the modern versions—for example, the struggle of the twins in the womb and the prophesy of their future given to Rebekah. Such confluence is not always the case, however, as we will see for the case of Deborah and Jael.

82. See Levinger (*Bible Stories,* 21) and Goldin (*Illustrated Bible Stories,* 42). Bildersee, as always, keeps her version of the story close to the original, but she discusses the issue of Jacob's obedience to his mother at length in the teacher's manual for *The Story of Genesis.* She claims that instruction in obedience is so strong that children are unlikely to perceive Jacob as doing anything wrong, since he's just obeying his mother (Bildersee, *Story of Genesis: Teachers' Manual,* 70).

83. Levinger has Jacob feeling "less happy with the blessing than he had been without it" but does not have him seek forgiveness (*Bible Stories,* 25). Cohen also presents Jacob as guilty, but has the guilt resolved by punishment rather than forgiveness; in her version Jacob's being sent away after the blessing is construed as punishment (Cohen, 1:45). Bildersee's *Story of Genesis: Teachers' Manual* gives a similar interpretation (70).

84. Bildersee, *Story of Genesis: Teachers' Manual,* 70.

85. Calisch uses the same justification.

86. None of the versions take advantage of the support in the Bible for Rebekah's greater knowledge of the future of her two sons. Tied to the episode of the struggle in the womb is Rebekah's inquiry to God and His prediction regarding the fate of the sons, namely that the elder is to serve the younger (Gen. 25:22–23). Since the fetal struggle is uniformly eliminated, so is this prophetic knowledge.

87. Levinger omits the story; it is beyond the scope of Fox's collection, which ends with the death of Moses.

88. See also Silber, 34.

89. Goldin, *Illustrated Bible Stories,* 118.

90. The one version that does not add excuses for Barak is Schwarz, *Promised Land,* 19–20. Midrashic versions have different concerns when adding to the biblical narrative. Lest Deborah's dealing with men be seen as an impropriety, Barak is made into her husband, and other explanation is added as well. But no changes are made in the interchange between Deborah and Barak itself, the locus of most attention in the modern versions. Jael's seductiveness is not eliminated but enhanced; the violence of her action is mitigated by her seeking signs from God before she acts (Ginzberg, *Legends,* 4:34–39).

91. Omitted in Altman, Calisch, and Cohen; brief statement in Silber. Even Schwarz, who includes the whole episode in terms close to the original, eliminates the praise of Jael in the song that closes the story (*Promised Land,* 21–22). Bottigheimer analyzes the depiction of Jael in *The Bible for Children,* 142–51.

92. Calisch is the only one of our authors to embrace the story of Jepthah's daughter with such enthusiasm. Most omit the story entirely, while Silber and Schwarz write sanitized versions, emphasizing Jepthah's role as leader of the Israelites; Silber obliquely mentions Jepthah's vow at the end of the chapter, leaving it ambiguous as to whether the daughter was actually sacrificed (Silber, 2:48–53; Schwarz, *Promised Land,* 31–34). For a striking contrast with midrash, see Ginzberg, *Legends,* 4:43–47. Here the horror of Jepthah's vow is lingered upon and alternatives to its carrying out explored. Compare Bottigheimer, *The Bible for Children,* 72.

93. Cohen's choice of this story is interesting, given its message of women's ability to inherit property in the absence of sons. Cohen even emphasizes Moses' justice on this score by writing that "Moses thought differently" from the people who "murmured among themselves, 'What can women do with land?'" (Cohen, 1:185). Such additions of even mildly feminist sentiments are rare in these children's books, whether by female or male authors.

94. Contrary to my expectations, I could find no significant difference in the treatment of female characters in collections authored by women compared with those by men. Paula Hyman notes more generally that she has not seen "in the writings of modern women who preceded contemporary feminism any themes or style that clearly distinguish their historical and theological reflections from those prevalent in the denominations with which they were affiliated" (Paula E. Hyman, *Gender and Assimilation in Modern Jewish History: The Roles and Representation of Women* [Seattle: University of Washington Press, 1995], 166–67).

95. Schwarz, *Promised Land,* 66–67. This volume is in *The Bible Story in the Bible Words* series, so we expect the fullest treatment here. As with Bildersee's volumes in this series, the text stays very close to the parts of the original that are included, so the omission of the sparing of the king is a clear indication of the discomfort of the author.

96. Altman provides the briefest account, with just two chapters (12 pages). Other brief accounts are Levinger (4 chapters), Calisch (5 chapters), and Goldin (5 chapters), with longer accounts in Silber (14 chapters), Schwarz (17 chapters), and Cohen (22 chapters; 88 pages).

97. Bottigheimer analyzes two elements of David's story: David and Bathsheba and David and Absalom (*The Bible for Children,* 127–32, 81–83).

98. According to Altman, David was very old, tired of being king, and had made clear his desire that Solomon succeed him (112).

99. Several other versions mention that David was not allowed to build the temple because he was a "man of war" or had "blood on his hands," an explanation transplanted from a later passage of the Tanakh, when Solomon is explaining his own building of the temple (1 Kings 5:16–19).

100. Calisch is the one author to make a brief reference to this: David's "faithful followers were ready to make him their ruler at once, but it was several years before *all* in Israel were willing to call him king. First, David had to show them that he was still brave and strong, wise and good. Little by little, all the tribes of Israel decided that David was indeed chosen by God to rule over them, and they gladly became his friends and loyal subjects" (Calisch, 2:54; emphasis in the original).

101. Resolution 5 of the Leipzig Synod, in W. Gunther Plaut, *The Rise of Reform Judaism: A Sourcebook of Its European Origins* (New York: World Union for Progressive Judaism, 1963), 252.

102. For example, a proposed Sabbath-school curriculum included classes in the first four years on "Biblical history," described for the first year as "oral instruction in the narratives contained in the Book of Genesis," as well as a class in "Bible reading," beginning in the fourth year, whose description details the specific biblical passages to be read and explained (M. Mielziner, "[Report on the Plan of Instruction in the Jewish Sabbath-School]," *CCARY* 6 [1895]: 26–30).

The use of the term "Bible history" for story books was consistent with European practice going back to the seventeenth century. Bottigheimer notes that the words *Geschichte* and *histoire* in German and French signify both "story" and "history," while English has the two separate words ("The Child-Reader of Children's Bibles, 1656–1753," in *Infant Tongues: The Voice of the Child in Literature,* ed. Elizabeth Goodenough, Mark A. Heberle, and Naomi Sokoloff [Detroit: Wayne State University Press, 1994], 46, 53 n. 3).

103. Originally published in New York by Philip Cowen, beginning in 1908 Harris's work was published by Bloch Publishing Company. I have used the three-volume 1929 edition by Bloch Publishing.

104. The last is in a block of ten chapters on "The Law," a larger treatment of the laws of Moses than is found in later Bible story collections. These chapters are a combination of narrative and summary of legal topics.

105. For the use of historical material in nineteenth-century Christian Bibles (not children's story books, but Bibles meant for home use), see Colleen McDannell, *Material Christianity: Religion and Popular Culture in America* (New Haven: Yale University Press, 1995), 95. Such Bibles could contain copious supplementary historical material, included not to support a critical view of the Bible but rather to demonstrate "how historical scholarship fully supported every text in the Bible."

106. Rabbi Joseph Kornfeld, "Our Biblical Histories," *CCARY* 19 (1909): 353–87. Kornfeld was following up on an 1890 article by Rabbi Dr. E. Schreiber, "How to Teach Biblical History in Our Sabbath Schools," *CCARY* 1 (1890): 59–61; for a discussion of Schreiber's article, see chapter 4 at notes 52, 54, and 56.

107. Kornfeld, "Our Biblical Histories," 384, 369.

108. Ibid., 368, quoting from the Bible Study Union Lessons.

109. David Philipson, "Report of Commission on Jewish Education," *CCARY* 41 (1931): 140.

110. *Israel in Canaan* and *In the Days of the First Temple* were later published together in one volume as *The Golden Dawn* (Cincinnati: Union of American Hebrew Congregations, 1942).

111. The illustration is mislabeled as "Jacob Blesses Issac," a mistake perhaps facilitated by the absence of the story itself in the book.

112. From Emanuel Gamoran, introduction to *Israel in Canaan*, by Golub, ix.

113. Similarly the first chapter of Mordecai Soloff, *When the Jewish People Was Young* (Cincinnati: Department of Synagogue and School Extension of the Union of American Hebrew Congregations, 1934), which asserts the difference between Jews of today and those of "long ago" and explains why we should nonetheless study the past; this book is discussed in more detail below. In many of the illustrations in Golub's book, a picture from current Arab or Bedouin life is given to stand as an example of the biblical way of life being described. Rather than conflating biblical characters with American Jewish children today, Golub conflates biblical peoples with "less civilized" peoples of today.

114. For cogent critiques of the writing of Jewish history textbooks for children from the late 1920s to the 1970s, see Walter Ackerman, " 'Let Us Now Praise Famous Men' "; Joel Gereboff, "Can the Teaching of Jewish History be Anything but the Teaching of Myth?" in *The Seductiveness of Jewish Myth: Challenge or Response?* ed. S. Daniel Breslauer (Albany: State University of New York Press, 1997), 43–69; idem, "Heroes and History in American Jewish Education," in *Crisis and Reaction: The Hero in Jewish History*, ed. Menachem Mor (Omaha: Creighton University Press, 1995), 105–50.

115. Ackerman's and Gereboff's critiques seem overly harsh to me, not sufficiently taking into account the social and educational context of the writing of these texts. Gereboff wishes that these authors of children's books would take on "the difficult task of historical reconstruction, pursued with a commitment to an open-ended interpretation" (Gereboff, "Heroes," 115); Ackerman laments that these textbooks do not present history as it should be taught, "as a continuous search for meaning which permits the student the freedom of his own conclusions" (Ackerman, " 'Let Us Now Praise Famous Men,' " 34). These criticisms do not sufficiently take into account the audience for which these books were written, which was not a professional, scholarly one. It seems unrealistic to expect that textbooks written for Jewish religious school children in 1930s America should be any more "open-ended" than, say, United States history textbooks written for public school children. Soloff states a twofold aim for *When the Jewish People Was Young*: to provide an account of the development of the Jewish people, and "to imbue the children with a justifiable pride in the past, loyalty to the present and faith in the future of Jewish life" (Mordecai Soloff, *When the Jewish People Was Young, Teacher's Book* [Cincinnati: Department of Synagogue and School Extension of the Union of American Hebrew Congregations, 1935], 1). One could substitute "American" for "Jewish" life in this sentence and thereby describe a continuing primary goal of American history teaching in our public schools.

116. Similarly the enmity between Joseph and his brothers or between the sons of Leah and the sons of Rachel are considered representations of "disputes among the tribes" (Golub, 56).

117. A third volume covering the modern period was published in 1940: *How the Jewish People Lives Today* (Cincinnati: Union of American Hebrew Congregations). Even shorter is a book very similar to Soloff's in style and content, also intended for fourth graders and published one year after his: Dorothy F. Zeligs, *A Child's History of the Hebrew People: From Nomadic Times to the Destruction of the Second Temple* (New York: Bloch Publishing, 1935). Both the Soloff and Zeligs books were popular textbooks and continued to be used into the 1950s.

118. An interesting example is Soloff's treatment of the figure of King David. The title chapter would lead us to expect a moralistic interpretation: "Why Do We Jews Love David?" But instead of rooting Jewish love for David in his character—always the tack taken in Bible story books—here it is accounted for by David's political success in defeating the enemies of the Jews, in uniting the tribes into one nation, and in making a capital in Jerusalem (*When the Jewish People Was Young*, 166–67).

119. Emanuel Gamoran, introduction to *When the Jewish People Was Young*, by Soloff, ix.

120. Cohen's book was intended for first and second graders (*Proceedings of the UAHC* 60 [1934]: 56).

121. Given the separation of these genres in the 1930s, it makes sense that Maurice Harris's old-style "Bible history" (but really story) book was reprinted for the last time in 1935, after having been in print since 1890.

122. Edward A. Nudelman, *Israel in Canaan, Teacher's Guide* (Cincinnati: Department of Synagogue and School Extension of the Union of American Hebrew Congregations, 1935), 1–2. Soloff also speaks of his effort to be true to the facts of history while still not slighting tradition. He trusts "that this book may not be considered either anti-traditional or untrue to fact" (*When the Jewish People Was Young*, xiii).

123. Jonathan D. Sarna, "The Cult of Synthesis in American Jewish Culture," *Jewish Social Studies* 5 (1998/99): 52–79. Sarna traces the history of this cult from the early nineteenth through the twentieth centuries, with a significant turn away from synthesis in the 1960s and 1970s.

124. Gamoran, introduction to *Bible Tales*, by Cohen, 2:vii–viii.

125. Some of the biblical history books of the 1930s, as opposed to the Bible story books, show some inclination to an ethnic approach in their use of the term "the Jewish people" (Soloff) or "the Hebrew people" (Zeligs) in their titles.

6. Different Audiences, Different Texts

1. Walter Benjamin, "The Storyteller," in *Illuminations*, ed. Hannah Arendt (New York: Harcourt, Brace and World, 1968), 90.

2. The two most important ancient translations (*targumim*) of the Bible were the Septuagint (into Greek) and Targum Onkelos (into Aramaic). On the close relationship between *targum* and midrash, see Geza Vermes, "Haggadah in the Onkelos Targum," *Journal of Semitic Studies* 8 (1963): 159–69; Paul V. McCracken Flesher, "The Targumim in the Context of Rabbinic Literature," in *Introduction to Rabbinic Literature*, by Jacob Neusner (New York: Doubleday, 1994), 611–29.

3. The designation of a "classical" period of midrashic collections is problematic, as the practice of anthologizing midrash continued into the Middle Ages; see Jacob Elbaum, "*Yalqut Shim'oni* and the Medieval Midrashic Anthology," *Prooftexts* 17, no. 2 (1997): 133–51. For an entry into the vast literature on midrash, see Barry W. Holtz, ed., *Back to the Sources: Reading Classical Jewish Texts* (New York: Summit Books, 1984), chap. 3; James L. Kugel, "Two Introductions to Midrash," *Prooftexts* 3 (1983): 131–56; idem, *The Bible as It Was* (Cambridge: Belknap Press of Harvard University Press, 1997); Gary G. Porton, "Defining Midrash," in *The Study of Ancient Judaism*, vol. 1, *Mishnah, Midrash, Siddur*, ed. J. Neusner (Hoboken, N.J.: Ktav Publishing House, 1981), 55–92; idem, *Understanding Rabbinic Midrash: Texts and Commentary* (Hoboken, N.J.: Ktav Publishing House, 1985); Daniel Boyarin, *Intertextuality and the Reading of Midrash* (Bloomington: Indiana University Press, 1990); H. L. Strack and G. Stemberger, *Introduction to the Talmud and Midrash*, trans. Markus Bockmuehl (Minneapolis: Fortress Press, 1992); Michael Fishbane, *The Exegetical Imagination: On Jewish Thought and Theology* (Cambridge: Harvard University Press, 1998), especially 1–21; Gerald L. Bruns, "Midrash and Allegory: The Beginnings of Scriptural Interpretation," in *The Literary Guide to the Bible*, ed. Robert Alter and Frank Kermode (Cambridge: Belknap Press of Harvard University Press, 1987), 625–46.

4. For a classic study of the functioning of tradition, see Edward Shils, *Tradition* (Chicago: University of Chicago Press, 1981).

5. Kugel includes these principles as two of the four fundamental assumptions he sees as characterizing ancient biblical interpretation. The other two assumptions are that the Bible is a fundamentally cryptic document and that it is a "perfect and perfectly harmonious" text (*The Bible as It Was*, 18–22).

6. Chaim Pearl, *Rashi* (New York: Grove Press, 1988), 45; *Tz'enah Ur'enah*, trans. Miriam Stark Zakon (Brooklyn: Mesorah Publications, 1983), 1:xii.

7. See Anne Scott MacLeod, *American Childhood: Essays on Children's Literature of the Nineteenth and Twentieth Centuries* (Athens: University of Georgia Press, 1994).

8. A modern children's version of the same passage may be found in the preceding chapter, pp. 134–36).

9. *Midrash Rabbah*, trans. H. Freedman and Maurice Simon, 3d ed. (1939; reprint, London: Soncino Press, 1983), 1:313.

10. A significant exception to this generalization is the genre of midrash referred to as "rewritten Bibles"; see notes 16 and 21 below.

11. Kugel, *The Bible as It Was*, 18.

12. Ibid., 20.

13. Kugel, "Two Introductions," 144–45.

14. Boyarin, *Intertextuality*, 16 (speaking of midrash). On midrash as a "citation literature," see Strack and Stemberger, *Talmud and Midrash*, 60. On the similarity between midrash and other rabbinic literature in this regard, see Eliezer Segal, "Anthological Dimensions of the Babylonian Talmud," *Prooftexts* 17 (1997): 33–61. For the pervasiveness of anthological forms in Jewish writing, see the three special issues on "The Anthological Imagination in Jewish Literature," *Prooftexts* 17, nos. 1 & 2 (1997) and 18, no. 1 (1999), especially the introduction by David Stern, *Prooftexts* 17, no. 1.

15. *Midrash Rabbah*, 4:1–13. Leviticus Rabbah is an example of homiletical rather than exegetical midrash (on this distinction, see Strack and Stemberger, *Talmud and Midrash*, 261–62), and its particular style is to use just the first words of a section as the jumping off point for a collection of texts on a particular theme (for this verse, the nature of Moses and his prophecy); for analysis of this first section of Leviticus Rabbah, see Porton, *Understanding*, 191–223. For a comparison to another midrashic commentary on Leviticus, see Porton's treatment of Sifra's commentary on the same opening verse (19–51).

16. This is a differentiating feature between our children's stories and ancient and medieval "rewritten Bibles"—some of which are similar in their unbroken narrative, but share with midrash the delight in additions to the biblical original.

17. Neusner, *Rabbinic Literature*, 243.

18. For a discussion of associative versus directional discourse in relationship to modern attitudes toward the Talmud and other traditional Jewish texts, and the shaping influence of the Enlightenment on such attitudes, see pp. 36–37.

19. Louis Ginzberg, *The Legends of the Jews*, 7 vols. (Philadelphia: Jewish Publication Society of America, 1909–38).

20. Kugel, *The Bible as It Was*, 151 n. 33.

21. To be sure, there are associative countercurrents in modern writing, such as stream-of-consciousness novels and the dense citation style of poetry like Ezra Pound's, but the impact of such texts rests on their working against the "normal" assumptions of linearity. On the other hand, current scholarly interest in midrashic literature is fueled by the postmodern inclination to abandon Enlightenment mental habits. The associative activity of web surfing may also come to influence thought and writing patterns in hard text as well as cyberspace.

One text problematic to place in a schema of traditional versus modern discourse is the *Sefer Ha-Yashar*, usually dated to the eleventh or twelfth century, but more likely composed at the beginning of the sixteenth century (Strack and Stemberger, *Talmud and Midrash*, 359). This text comes the closest of any of the premodern texts to the children's Bibles of the modern period, being a retelling of the Bible in a simplified form and entirely without explicit citation of rabbinic sources, even while they are used throughout. Other kinds of "rewritten Bibles" exist, and in fact are considered some of the earliest carriers of midrash, but they tend to be closer to the "text and elaboration" model that is at the heart of midrashic discourse. For a discussion of the characteristics particular to the genre of "rewritten Bible," as derived from its earliest exemplars, and including comparison to rabbinic midrash, see Philip S. Alexander, "Retelling the Old Testament," in *It Is Written: Scripture Citing Scripture; Essays in Honour of Barnabas Lindars, SSF,* ed. D. A. Carson and H.G.M. Williamson (Cambridge: Cambridge University Press, 1988), 99–121.

22. This modern transformation of story into legend and folklore is also connected with the rise of nationalistic identity. As noted by scholar David C. Jacobson:

> When the whole corpus of retold versions of traditional Jewish narratives by twentieth-century Hebrew writers is taken into account, it may be seen not only as a continuation of the midrashic tradition of the rabbinic and medieval periods, but also as a product of the revival of interest in myths, legends, and folktales that has spread throughout western culture in the past two centuries. Members of national or ethnic groups who have been undergoing a period of cultural redefinition have turned to the traditional narratives of their particular literary heritage as important sources of self-understanding (*Modern Midrash: The Retelling of Traditional Jewish Narratives by Twentieth-Century Hebrew Writers* [Albany: State University of New York Press, 1987], 4–5).

23. English translation by William Braude, *The Book of Legends, Sefer Ha-Aggadah: Legends from the Talmud and Midrash* (New York: Schocken Books, 1992). Part 1 of the collection organizes material chronologically by subject, from the beginning of the Bible through the destruction of the Second Temple. Later sections are organized topically (e.g., "Good and Evil," "A Man's Household"); there is also a large section on "The Deeds of the Sages." On *Sefer Ha-Aggadah,* its origin, influence, and relationship to nationalist and romantic trends, see Mark W. Kiel, "*Sefer ha'aggadah:* Creating a Classic Anthology for the People and by the People," *Prooftexts* 17 (1997): 177–97. Through careful selection and added explicit pointers to moral issues through section headings and story titles, Bialik and Ravnitzky, like Bible story authors, were able to shape their text to the cultural and pedagogical purposes critical to early-twentieth-century modernizing, nationalist Jews. (My thanks to Michael Fishbane for clarification on the nature and purposes of these modern collections.)

24. Kiel, "*Sefer ha'aggadah,*" 187. David Stern's introduction to Braude's translation of the *Sefer Ha-Aggadah* also provides a useful analysis of the transformation from aggadah—fragmentary, condensed, and elusive, embedded haphazardly in the commentary of biblical or Mishnaic commentary—to a thematically organized book of stories (Braude, *Book of Legends,* xvii–xxii).

25. Bin Gorion is the pseudonym of Micha Joseph Berdyczewski. This work was completed in manuscript by 1921 but published in 1938–45. It was translated into English as *Mimekor Yisrael: Classical Jewish Folktales,* 3 vols. (Bloomington: Indiana University Press, 1976). On Berdyczewski's extensive anthological program, see Zipora Kagan, "*Homo Anthologicus:* Micha Joseph Berdyczewski and the Anthological Genre," *Prooftexts* 19, no. 1 (1999): 41–57.

26. Martin Buber, *Tales of the Hasidim,* 2 vols. (New York: Schocken Books, 1947).

27. Louis I. Newman and Samuel Spitz, *The Talmudic Anthology: Tales and Teachings of the Rabbis: A Collection of Parables, Folk-tales, Fables, Aphorism, Epigrams, Sayings, Anecdotes, Proverbs and Exegetical Interpretations* (New York: Behrman House, 1945); Nathan Ausubel, *A Treasury of Jewish Folklore: Stories, Traditions, Legends, Humor, Wisdom and Folk Songs of the Jewish People* (New York: Crown Publishers, 1948).

28. See Bruce Babington and Peter William Evans, *Biblical Epics: Sacred Narrative in the Hollywood Cinema* (Manchester: Manchester University Press, 1993). Biblical epics were most popular in the 1920s and 1950s (4–6).

29. Sifre Numbers, for example, contains interpretations not on the whole of Numbers, but on chapters 5–12, 15, 18–19, 25:1–13, 26:52–31:24, and 35:9–34 (Porton, *Understanding,* 77).

30. That the midrashic collections "are structured as conversations rather than as systematic expositions" comes, too, from the relationship of rabbis to text. Modern reading practices posit a "solitary reader isolated with the scriptural text and trying to divine an intention

(or his or her own private understanding)" while the relationship of the rabbis to the text "was always social and dialogical, and even when confined to the house of study (*beit midrash*) it was never merely formalist or analytical. They saw themselves in dialogue with each other and with generations of wise men extending both backward to Koheleth and Solomon . . . and forward to the endless openings of the Scriptures upon new questions that are put to them" (Bruns, "Midrash and Allegory," 630).

31. For memorization as the primary method of learning, see Strack and Stemberger, *Talmud and Midrash*, 13.

32. Sometimes a quotation will begin with a marker like "thus scripture says," or "a scriptural tradition says," but as many or more are not (Boyarin, *Intertextuality*, 156 n. 8).

33. Michael Fishbane, introduction to *The Midrashic Imagination* (Albany: State University of New York Press, 1993), 2.

34. My thanks to Gary Porton for clarifying this point.

35. Kugel claims a lay audience for these texts, the "average Jew" (*The Bible as It Was*, 549), and Joseph Heinemann claims they are addressed to "simple folk and children" ("The Nature of the Aggadah," in *Midrash and Literature*, ed. G. Hartman and S. Budick [New Haven: Yale University Press, 1986], 49). Given the nature of the texts, though, it seems much more likely that the original audience was learned, even while the texts later were consumed by more ordinary folk.

36. When the practice of preaching in synagogues began is unclear. For a convincing case that the rabbis who originated midrash were doing so in the context of the schoolhouse, with an audience solely of other rabbis and those in training to be rabbis rather than in a synagogue (preaching) context, see Gary Porton, "Rabbinic Midrash: Public or Private," *The Review of Rabbinic Judaism* 5, no. 2 (2002): 141–69. Direct evidence of preaching in synagogues exists only from the medieval period.

37. "Indeed, the problem of the diversity of the audience, the difficulty of coping with such diversity, and the challenge of satisfying the variety of levels and tastes was reiterated so frequently [in sermons] that it became a homiletical commonplace" (Marc Saperstein, *Jewish Preaching, 1200–1800: An Anthology* [New Haven: Yale University Press, 1989], 51). For further discussion of the audience of sermons, and discussion of the language(s) used in preaching, see Robert Bonfil, "Preaching as Mediation between Elite and Popular Cultures: The Case of Judah Del Bene," in *Preachers of the Italian Ghetto*, ed. David B. Ruderman (Berkeley: University of California Press, 1992), 67–88.

38. For example, at Genesis 12:3: "There are many Agadoth concerning this but the plain sense of the text is as follows . . ." (Rashi, *Chumash with Targum Onkelos, Haphtaroth and Rashi's Commentary*, trans. Rabbi A. M. Silbermann [Jerusalem: Feldheim Publishers, 1934], 1:49). For an overview of medieval critique of midrash, see Marc Saperstein, *Decoding the Rabbis: A Thirteenth-Century Commentary on the Aggadah* (Cambridge: Harvard University Press, 1980), 1–20.

39. For example, at Genesis 11:28: "Midrash aggadah says . . ." (Rashi, *Chumash with Targum Onkelos*, 1:47).

40. Joseph P. Schultz notes 210 editions in the text's three centuries of life ("The 'Z.e'enah U-Renah': Torah for the Folk," *Judaism* 36 [1987]: 84). Another popular Yiddish book aimed at both men and women, contemporary with the *Ts'enah U-re'enah* and including midrash among its stories was the *Mayse Bukh* ("Story Book"); see Chava Weissler, *Voices of the Matriarchs: Listening to the Prayers of Early Modern Jewish Women* (Boston: Beacon Press, 1998), 37, 41–42.

41. A similar replacement could occur if Rashi was heard rather than read, since the distinction between original and commentary, already set off less markedly than in modern editions and translations, is even less apparent when the text is experienced aurally. Yaffa Eliach explains: "As the melamed read and translated the weekly portion, which the students repeated in unison after him, he also incorporated various homiletic and midrashic commentaries into his recitation. This he typically did so seamlessly that for the rest of their lives the students made no distinction between the text proper and its numerous exegeses; in their minds all these elements were part of one long, carefully wrought, continuous work"

(*There Once Was a World: A 900–Year Chronicle of the Shtetl of Eishyshok* [Boston: Little, Brown, 1998], 158). Hayim Nahman Bialik gives an amusing account of reciting Chumash and Rashi in heder (though in this case with some inkling of their separation) in his story "After-growth." The children "had to pipe up together in common chant and at the top of our voices, all kinds of words [i.e., Rashi] which the teacher ordered us to repeat at the end of each verse written in the Pentateuch. Where the teacher discovered those words, who gave them to him and what they had to do with whatever may have been written in the Pentateuch text, was something I did not know" (*Aftergrowth and Other Stories*, trans. I. M. Lask [Philadelphia: Jewish Publication Society, 1939], 78–79).

42. See chapter 2.

43. The following brief overview of the history of Christian Bible story collections is drawn from the definitive work of Ruth B. Bottigheimer: *The Bible for Children from the Age of Gutenberg to the Present* (New Haven: Yale University Press, 1996). Several of Bottigheimer's earlier essays are also useful, including "Bible Reading, 'Bibles,' and the Bible for Children in Early Modern Germany," *Past and Present* 139 (1993): 66–89; "The Child-Reader of Children's Bibles, 1656–1753," in *Infant Tongues: The Voice of the Child in Literature*, ed. Elizabeth Goodenough, Mark A. Heberle, and Naomi Sokoloff (Detroit: Wayne State University Press, 1994), 44–56; "Religion for the Young in Bible Story Collections (Kinderbibeln)," *Fabula: Zeitschrift für Erzählforschung* 32 (1991): 19–32.

44. Bottigheimer, *The Bible for Children*, 15–23.

45. Ibid., 36–39.

46. Bottigheimer, "Bible Reading," 74–75; idem, "Child-Reader," 51–52, idem, "Religion for the Young," 26–27.

47. See pp. 51–55 for a more detailed discussion of such books, including those by Büdinger and Moses Montefiore.

48. The main source used to compile a sample of Protestant Bible story collections was the bibliography in Muriel Streibert's *Youth and the Bible* (New York: Macmillan, 1924), 242–44, a book used by Jewish educators. Three of these books (Olcott, Baikie, and Sherman and Kent) were discussed in Solomon Fineberg, *Biblical Myth and Legend in Jewish Education* (New York: Behrman's Jewish Book House, 1932), confirming Jewish awareness of Protestant books; so too an analysis of six Protestant books (including Hodges) by Rabbi Joseph Kornfeld ("Our Biblical Histories," *CCARY* 19 [1909]: 358–71). Kornfeld mentions that these books were available for and sometimes used in Jewish religious schools.

49. Jesse Lyman Hurlbut, *Story of the Bible Told for Young and Old* (Philadelphia: John C. Winston, 1904). Editions of the full version of this book continued to be printed through 1977, with simplified versions appearing in more recent years, including an audiotape publication in 1996. The book continues in use today. George Hodges, *The Garden of Eden: Stories from the First Nine Books of the Old Testament* (Philadelphia: Curtis Publishing, 1908; Boston: Houghton Mifflin, 1909), reprinted in 1937. Hodges's second volume of Old Testament Stories was published as *The Castle of Zion* (Boston: Houghton Mifflin, 1912). Frances Jenkins Olcott, *Bible Stories to Read and Tell: 150 Stories from the Old Testament with References to the Old and New Testaments* (Boston: Houghton Mifflin, 1916), reprinted by Blue Ribbon Books in 1932. Henry A. Sherman and Charles Foster Kent, *The Children's Bible: Selections from the Old and New Testaments* (New York: Scribner's, 1922), with four subsequent editions published through 1936. James Baikie, *The Bible Story: A Connected Narrative Retold from Holy Scripture* (New York: Macmillan, 1923), reprinted five more times through 1930.

The text of the stories in Sherman and Kent is virtually identical to those written by Kent (with Eugene Lehman) for *The Junior Bible for the Jewish School and Home* (New York: Bloch Publishing, 1909–10), which itself relied on earlier material of Kent's. This rare cross-authorship is an important indication of the intersection between Jewish and Christian children's Bibles. Aside from minor changes of wording (e.g., from "Abraham was very, very old" to "Abraham was very old"), the main difference between the books is that "God" of the Jewish collection is "Jehovah" in the Christian. Sherman was head of the Department of Religious Literature at Scribner's; Kent was Woolsey Professor of Biblical Literature at Yale University.

50. When I asked a local minister about this, he thought it likely that teachers had for

many years been doing what he had done the previous Sunday (using Hurlbut)—reading the story aloud while the children sat and listened.

51. Sherman and Kent, *Children's Bible*, v.

52. Hurlbut, *Story of the Bible*, 11, 69, 228–31. Similarly, Elsie Egermeir, another Christian author, offers the explanation that Jepthah perhaps hadn't read about the part of the law that forbade child sacrifice (*Bible Story Book* [St. Louis: Concordia Publishing House, 1922], 188–89).

53. Hurlbut, *Story of the Bible*, 38.

54. Hodges, *Garden of Eden*, 6, 89–90, 123; emphasis added.

55. T. Rhondda Williams, *Old Testament Stories in Modern Light: A Bible Guide for the Young* (London: James Clarke; Boston: Pilgrim Press, 1911); Streibert, *Youth and the Bible*, 243.

56. Williams, *Old Testament Stories*, 54.

57. Ibid., 106.

58. The two men undoubtedly knew each other's work from the Teachers College setting, and Mrs. Solomon Fineberg is cited warmly in MacLean's acknowledgments.

59. An author who might have satisfied MacLean is Hendrik Willem Van Loon (*The Story of the Bible* [New York: Boni and Liverwright, 1923], with further editions from various publishers through 1985). Van Loon wrote extensively for children, and was the first winner of the Newbery Award in 1921 for his *Story of Mankind*. In keeping with other writings of his, Van Loon's approach to the Bible is thoroughly historical, explaining the problematic nature of both the Old and New Testaments as historical sources, emphasizing (particularly for the Old Testament) that these are stories passed down, not records of historical fact. Moral lessons are eschewed, as are direct appearances or visions of God. Van Loon was one of a number of well-known twentieth-century authors recruited to write Bible story books for a general audience; Walter de La Mare, Pearl Buck, and Norman Vincent Peale were others (Bottigheimer, *The Bible for Children*, 48).

60. Dorothy F. Zeligs, *The Story Bible: Together with Tales from the Midrash*, 2 vols. (New York: Behrman House, 1949–51).

61. Ibid., 1:21, 25.

62. Betty R. Hollender, *Bible Stories for Little Children*, 3 vols. (New York: UAHC, 1955–60). These volumes are still currently in print. Cohen, now out of print, was only recently replaced by Steven E. Steinbock's *Torah: The Growing Gift* (New York: UAHC Press, 1994). This book follows the model of Seymour Rossel's *A Child's Bible*, discussed below.

63. Hollender, *Bible Stories*, 1:21.

64. Zeligs, *The Story Bible*, 1:5, 14.

65. Bottigheimer notes a similar return to the canonical text in Protestant retellings from the 1980s (*The Bible for Children*, 207, 214–15).

66. Dona Z. Meilach, *First Book of Bible Heroes*, 2 vols. (New York: Ktav Publishing House, 1963).

67. Shirley Newman, *A Child's Introduction to Torah* (New York: Behrman House, 1972), 23.

68. Behrman House catalog, 2002–3, 40.

69. Seymour Rossel, *A Child's Bible*, 2 vols. (New York: Behrman House, 1988–89), 1:24.

70. Seymour Rossel, interview by author, July 24, 2002.

71. This format of a biblical story followed by explanation, application of midrash, and exercises/games is picked up in the 1991 republication of Dona Meilach's *First Book of Bible Heroes*, retitled *Let's Learn Bible* and entirely reformatted. The stories themselves are taken bodily from the 1963 edition, but the use of midrash is entirely new, as is the explanation of its use given in a revised introduction. Some very small but interesting changes have been made in the story texts. The text has become more gender-sensitive (eliminating the male pronoun for God, changing "man" to "human," adding in a bit more on Eve) and has introduced a bit more Hebrew (changing "Sabbath" to "Shabbat").

72. Rossel, *A Child's Bible*, 1:7.

73. Rossel, interview.

74. Rossel, *A Child's Bible*, 2:12; see also 1:154–55.

75. These developments are found in other Bible story books of this period, including Shirley Rose [Seymour Rossel], *Let's Discover the Bible* (New York: Behrman House, 1992), a series of leaflets designed for K–2 that provide a stark contrast to Hollender's earlier "primer" approach (my thanks to Seymour Rossel for informing me of his authorship of this publication); Steinbock, *Torah: The Growing Gift;* Joel Lurie Grishaver with C. J. Glass, biblical translations by Everett Fox, *Torah Toons I* (Los Angeles: Torah Aura Productions, 1998). An earlier book by Grishaver, *Being Torah: A First Book of Torah Texts* (Los Angeles: Torah Aura Productions, 1985), is unique in its inclusion of a rhetorical analysis that highlights "theme words" and "number words," which could not be done unless using language close to the Bible's. The use of Everett Fox's translation, itself attentive to maintaining Hebrew word repetition in the English, influences and supports this endeavor.

76. See, for example, *My People: Abba Eban's History of the Jews*, adapted by David Bamberger (New York, Behrman House, 1978), and Seymour Rossel, *Journey through Jewish History*, 2 vols. (New York: Behrman House, 1981–82). Rossel was also the Behrman House editor in charge of the Abba Eban book project.

77. See, for example, Lillian S. Freehof, *The Bible Legend Book* (New York: Union of American Hebrew Congregations, 1948), republished in 1987 as *Bible Legends: An Introduction to Midrash*, with introductions and commentaries by Howard Schwartz (note the addition of the term "midrash" in the title); *Lessons from Our Living Past*, ed. Jules Harlow (New York: Behrman House, 1972); Francine Prose, *Stories from Our Living Past* (New York: Behrman House, 1974); Steven M. Rosman, *Sidrah Stories: A Torah Companion* (New York: UAHC Press, 1989); Seymour Rossel, *Sefer Ha-aggadah: The Book of Legends for Young Readers*, 2 vols. (New York: UAHC Press, 1996–98). One of the few such collections done before World War II was by Edith Lindeman Calisch, who also authored a Bible story collection. Her book is notable for the title, which plays down the specifically Jewish source of the stories: *Fairy Tales from Grandfather's Big Book: Jewish Legends of Old Retold for Young People* (New York: Behrman House, 1938). The 1970s Behrman House collections *Lessons/Stories from Our Living Past* (done under the editorial guidance of Seymour Rossel) were published in the same format, color palette, and illustration style as Newman's *Child's Introduction to Torah*, one of the earliest Bible story collections to separate off midrashic material. *Lessons/Stories* put midrash into separate books, each of which begin with an explanation for parents and teachers about the nature of Jewish myth and legend. Unusually, these two books each include a few stories taken directly from the Bible (e.g., "Abraham Argues with God"), scattered among rabbinic stories such as "Akiva and the Rock," "Hillel's Great Rule," and "The Field of Brotherly Love." This treatment of material drawn directly from the Bible as "legendary" is unusual, although it is consistent with the turn to a more thoroughgoing historicism. Rossel explains that they wanted to create a "vocabulary of stories" with which Jewish children should be familiar; this key vocabulary included both rabbinic and biblical stories (Rossel, interview).

It is notable that most books presenting rabbinic sources focus on aggadic (story) elements rather than halakhic (legal), though Behrman House has published a book on Pirke Avot by Seymour Rossel (*When a Jew Seeks Wisdom: The Sayings of the Fathers*, 1975) and two books by Jacob Neusner on Mishnah and Talmud for grades 6–9 (*Learn Mishnah* and *Learn Talmud*, 1978 and 1979).

78. Gideon Aran, "Return to the Scripture in Modern Israel," *Bibliothèque de l'Ecole des Hautes Etudes, Section des Sciences Religieuses* 99 (1993): 102, 122; Uriel Simon, "The Place of the Bible in Israeli Society: From National *Midrash* to Existential *Peshat*," *Modern Judaism* 19, no. 3 (1999): 218. See also Zali Gurevitch and Gideon Aran, "The Land of Israel: Myth and Phenomenon," *Studies in Contemporary Jewry* 10 (1994): 195–210. In addition to the scholarship cited here and below, I am grateful to several Israelis for conversations about the Israeli scene: Muhammed Abu Samra, Tzvi Howard Adelman, Gideon Aran, David Fishelov, Zali Gurevitch, Benjamin Harshav. Special thanks to Tzvi Howard Adelman for his generous pursuit of relevant material in Israel, and for talking through this material with me during his stay as a visiting professor at Knox College.

79. As quoted by Simon, "Place of the Bible," 236 n. 1.

80. Aran, "Return to the Scripture," 112.

81. J. Schoneveld, *The Bible in Israeli Education: A Study of Approaches to the Hebrew Bible and Its Teaching in Israeli Educational Literature* (Assen: Van Gorcum, 1976), 32; idem, "New Meaning in Ancient Sources," *Studies in Jewish Education* 5 (1990): 49.

82. See Aran, "Return to the Scripture," 103 and passim; Ian S. Lustick, *For the Land and the Lord: Jewish Fundamentalism in Israel* (New York: Council on Foreign Relations, 1988), 102–8.

83. Aran gives examples of political problems to which biblical precedents have been applied, such as rules of behavior toward stone-throwing Palestinians and the question of whether to give sanctuary to Palestinians who have collaborated with Israeli authorities ("Return to the Scripture," 116). See also Uriel Simon's description of the "exegetical storm" in the Knesset in December 1994 over whether King David could be considered to have sinned in his affair with Bathsheba—with political implications for whether conquests across the borders of Israel (like David's) should also be considered immoral (Simon, "Place of the Bible," 239).

84. Gurevitch and Aran, "Land of Israel," 202.

85. Zvi Adar, *Jewish Education in Israel and in the United States*, trans. Barry Chazan (Jerusalem: Samuel Mendel Melton Center for Jewish Education in the Diaspora, 1977), 52; first published in Hebrew in 1970.

86. Two excellent sources for the place of the Bible in Israeli education are Schoneveld, *The Bible in Israeli Education*, which covers Israeli education from the early Zionists of the late nineteenth century through the early 1970s, and Adar, *Jewish Education*, which includes detailed analysis of all streams of Israeli education in the 1960s.

87. My discussion is limited to state-sponsored schools. There is a parallel variety in private schools in Israel as well.

88. Schoneveld reviews the various reasons for attachment to the Bible across all ideological trends in Israel (*The Bible in Israeli Education*, 249).

89. Simon, "Place of the Bible," 231.

90. Adar, *Jewish Education*, 55–56.

91. Dalia Korach-Segev and Iona Zielberman, *Bereshit Sheli* (Tel Aviv: Modan, 1987; with the approval of the Ministry of Education and Culture).

92. In *A Child's Bible* all accompanying materials are located in sections following the Bible story, as described above. In *Bereshit Sheli* some material is separated off at the bottom of the page; further questions and exercises on each chapter are in an accompanying workbook. The material at the bottom of the page includes vocabulary words and midrash-like elaborations of elements in the story. For example, in the chapter on Cain and Abel, this segment asks, "What was the quarrel about?" and it then lays out a conversation between Cain and Abel to fill the gap in the text that occurs within Genesis 4:8.

93. The last fifty pages of the book have a different balance of illustration. These pages cover the story of Joseph, with most of the illustrations taken from ancient Egyptian wall art. Joseph's being "brought down to Egypt," for example, is illustrated by a fresco showing long lines of travelers with their animals (*Bereshit Sheli*, 122–23).

94. The one illustration with a conspicuous human figure is a photograph of a young woman filling a water-skin. The photograph accompanies the story of Abraham sending out Hagar with a bottle of water (*Bereshit Sheli*, 57). The skin-bottle in this photograph is very large, half the size of the young woman herself, perhaps a way of suggesting concern and generosity on Abraham's part as he expels his concubine. (Thanks to Tzvi Howard Adelman for this interpretation.)

95. The archeological illustrations mentioned are on pages 70, 47, and 62.

96. On the general issue of Jewish identity in Israel as "national" and in the United States as "religious," see Daniel J. Elazar, "Jewish Religious, Ethnic, and National Identities: Convergences and Conflicts," in *National Variations in Jewish Identity: Implications for Jewish Education*, ed. Steven M. Cohen and Gabriel Horenczyk (Albany: State University of New York Press, 1999), 42–43.

97. For the more recent impossibility of a straightforward nationalist appropriation of the Bible in Israel, see Simon, "Place of the Bible," 234.

Conclusion

1. The Ethical Culture Society was founded by an earlier generation of German Jews, led by Felix Adler, but it was also appealing to some Jews of eastern European background.

Index

Page numbers in italics refer to illustrations.